Quest for Adventure

Quest for Adventure

REMARKABLE FEATS OF EXPLORATION AND ADVENTURE FROM 1950 TO 2000

Chris Bonington

A Seven Dials Paperback

CONTENTS

Introduction

I ORIGINALLY WROTE *Quest for Adventure* through 1979 and 1980, setting my start point at the end of the Second World War, a period that was not only within my own conscious memory and the beginning of my own personal quest, but also one which marked so many huge social, economic and political changes. Bringing my investigation up-to-date covers just over half a century, and reveals some changes in the style and nature of people's quest for adventure which are not necessarily for the best.

The what and the why of adventure is the reason for this book. I should like to go back to my own beginnings, since I suspect that it is only through one's own experience that one can analyse motives and feelings. For me it started with a picture book of the Scottish hills, picked up at the age of sixteen. The pictures were in monochrome, showing rolling hills, rocky crags and shimmering waters. I was captivated in a way that I had never been before, longed to be among them, to reach their tops, to see beyond the confines of the page.

And then came a trip to stay with my grandfather in Ireland. He lived to the south of Dublin, and from his garden I could see the Wicklow Hills. I caught a bus and set out on my first mountaineering expedition to climb one of the outlying hills but fled, frightened, when a great cloud of cumulus threatened to engulf me. I had no compass and anyway did not know how to read one.

But this was adventure. Tentatively, I was stepping into the unknown, had an awareness of danger – admittedly more imagined than real – and a love of the wild emptiness of the hills around me. The following winter a school friend and I hitch-hiked from London up to Wales. It was the long hard winter of 1951, and the whole country was clad in snow. Viewed from Capel Curig the Snowdon massif had for us all the scale and majesty of a Himalayan peak. Clad in school macs and wearing Army boots, we tried our Everest by the Crib Goch Ridge, but were avalanched off a long way from the top. My school friend had had enough and hitched home, but I stayed on and made a solitary attempt on Glyder Fach the next day. It was a brilliant blue, sparkling day with great galleons of cloud sweeping over the tops. Once again I fled, afraid of getting lost, but on the way down stopped to watch some climbers on the Milestone Buttress, just above the road. They were roped together, moving slowly up the sheer rock, one at a time, tiny coloured blobs against the grey of the rock and the white of the snow that covered every ledge. I knew then that was what I wanted to do. I can't define why or how, had never read a book about rock climbing, didn't even know that the game existed.

I found a friend of the family who did a little climbing and he took me to Harrison Rocks, a small outcrop of sandstone just south of London. It wasn't ten metres high. You climbed with the protection of a rope hitched round one of the many trees at the top of the crag. At the end of the day, I knew that I had found something I was good at and loved doing. The basic satisfaction of climbing is both physical and mental – a matter of co-ordination similar to any other athletic attachment. But in climbing there is the extra ingredient of risk. It is a hot, heady spice, a piquancy that adds an addictive flavour to the game. It is accentuated by the fascination of pitting one's ability against a personal unknown and winning through. Being master of one's destiny, with one's life literally in one's hands, is what gives climbing its fascination.

It also gives a heightened awareness of everything around. The pattern of lichen on rock, a few blades of grass, the dark, still shape of a lake below, the form of the hills and cloud mountains above might be the same view seen by the passenger on a mountain railway, but transported to his viewpoint among a crowd, he cannot see what I, the climber, can. This is not an elitist ethic, but rather the deeper sensuous involvement that the climber has with the mountains around him, a feeling heightened by the stimulus of risk.

These are the elements of adventure that I have discovered in climbing – the physical satisfaction of having complete command over one's body, a sense of risk in the process, an awareness of beauty and the exploration of the unknown. At its most satisfying this would mean one of the rapidly dwindling unknown parts of the world, but almost equally satisfying is a personal unknown, even if others have trodden that path before. The romantic adventurer has always had strong links with science and intellectual curiosity; the very act of trying the unknown, whether it be a stretch of unclimbed rock, a sheet of polar pack ice or an attempt to be the first to sail alone around the world, holds a challenge of the mind as well as the body.

But there is one more ingredient that appears in almost every adventure, as it does in everyday life – the spirit of competition, gratification of ego, call it what you will. Though today competition climbing has developed its own line of athleticism with set rules, historically and in theory climbing is a non-competitive sport. In practice, however, there is a very high level of competition. At its simplest level, a group of climbers bouldering almost inevitably start to compete, trying to outdo each other, to solve a climbing problem that has beaten the others. On bigger crags or mountains, it is reflected in the sense of urgency to be the first to complete a new route, be it on Scafell, the North Wall of the Eiger or Everest itself. In any activity competition is a spur to progress. Although there are undoubtedly exceptions, I am sure that most of us respond to the stimulus of competition and, having won, enjoy the fruits of success, be it the approval of one's peers or acclaim from a much wider field.

History has offered plenty of opportunities for the adventurously inclined to sail the seas in search of merchandise or plunder, to trek overland to distant Cathay, but adventure as we know it today is a very recent phenomenon. The concept of climbing mountains or sailing small boats just for the fun of it could only come to those with sufficient wealth and time to indulge their whims. It came on the back of the Industrial Revolution, which brought a certain amount of leisure and money, at least to a privileged minority. At the same time, the growing safety and blandness of urban life sparked the desire to escape and seek the stimulus of the unknown, the thrill of defying danger and enjoying the physical beauty of nature entirely for its own sake. During the first half of the twentieth century, adventure games remained the prerogative of a small, middle-class minority. If you were working a six-day week, with only a week's holiday each year, even if you were able to afford to buy a small boat, you would not have had time to sail it. It was cheaper to go climbing, but, without a full weekend, there was not enough time to get started. In addition, two destructive world wars consumed the energies and, in many cases, the lives of two generations.

It has only been since the Second World War that the field has been laid open to almost anyone in the developed world who craves such a release. This is the reason why people in their thousands tramp the hills, sail their boats, fly their gliders. The ordinary person has been given both the time and the money to do it. It is also why comparatively few people from the Third World play the adventure game – they have not yet reached this level of affluence or leisure. The Sherpa in Nepal is happy to be a high-altitude porter, frequently enters into the spirit of an expedition, is keen to reach the summit, but he is still doing this entirely professionally. For the Nepalese to organise their own expeditions to their high mountains is still a rare occurrence. The more successful ones could undoubtedly afford it, for they are well off, even by Western standards, but I suspect they are too busy consolidating their new-found positions. They are members of a society in a state of fast transition and it is their children or grand-children who will, perhaps, feel the restless urge towards adventure for its own sake.

In this book I want to look at a wide spectrum of adventurous activities, to see what they have in common, not so much in motive – the why of it – but rather the 'how'. In studying what took place in an adventure, be it an attempt to sail round the world, cross one of the Poles, or climb a mountain, the reasons for doing it emerge on their own. But the field of adventure is so wide I have given myself a few ground rules in deciding which ventures to study.

To me, adventure involves a journey, or a sustained endeavour, in which there are the elements of risk and of the unknown, which have to be overcome by the physical skills of the individual. Furthermore, an adventure is something that an individual chooses to do and where the risk involved is self-imposed and threatens no one but himself. It could be argued that the man who volunteers to join the Army, or becomes a mercenary or perhaps a member of the security services, is also an adventurer answering the tempting call to play the danger game. I am aware that this is what attracted me to the Army when I became a professional soldier for a few years. It is something the recruiting posters play upon, but in the end one cannot escape from the fact that the soldier's adventures and thrills are at the expense of others, and that part of the thrill of adventure can become the thrill of the hunt. This goes outside my own ground rules.

There are different levels of adventure which one can separate in the same way as the athlete distinguishes between a hundred-metre sprint or a marathon. The hundred-metre dashes of adventure are activities that are very intense but of short duration. Take the solo rock climber making a new route in North Wales or the English Lake District. His is undoubtedly the ultimate in adventure, for his life is literally in his hands and, if he makes a mistake and is a couple of hundred metres above the ground he will almost certainly die. He is faced with the challenge of the unknown and the extreme limits of muscular control. It needs an intense level of commitment, but the period involved is comparatively short. At the top of the crag the tension is over and the climber can return to a pint at the pub, home, family, friends. The same can be said of other extreme-risk sports – steep gully skiing, white water canoeing, hang gliding or dinghy sailing on a stormy day; in all there is an immense concentrated commitment.

I am fascinated by what seems at first glance to be impossible. To me, the ultimate in adventure is to convert this impossible to the feasible

The marathons of adventure are to Himalayan peaks, to the Poles and across the oceans. The biggest difference is the obvious one of scale, where the element of time is perhaps as important as size. The immediate risk and skill level might not be so concentrated, but the expedition requires both physical and mental stamina, the capacity to live with others for a long period of time or, perhaps even harder, to be alone and self-sufficient.

From my own point of view I have worked my way through the various levels of the game; first as a necky young rock climber, tackling the most difficult rock climbs in Britain, next to the middle-distance of the Alps, with climbs like the Central Pillar of Frêney and North Wall of the Eiger, and then, in more recent years, to the great peaks of the Himalaya, with all the complexities of logistics, human relations and the sheer scale of everything involved.

In this book I want to look at my fellow marathon-runners, to see what we have in common, where we are different. I am not unduly concerned by the level of mechanical aid used in the adventures I have selected, since in almost every case some kind of tool or mechanical assistance is needed. My own personal ethic in planning an expedition has always been to use the minimum force that I have felt would give the enterprise concerned a chance of success. Thus, on the South-West Face of Everest, we had a team of very nearly a hundred, using oxygen, specially designed tents that were like miniature fortresses, and the best equipment available at the time. Since five expeditions that had been similarly equipped had failed, this seemed a reasonable scale of effort at that particular time. Having achieved success, I would never want to launch a similar expedition, since the challenge is forever to reduce the size and force of each enterprise to its most fundamental simplicity. Reinhold Messner succeeded in climbing Everest from the north side on his own, without the help of oxygen. In 1988 four Czech climbers succeeded in climbing the South-West Face alpine-style, without using oxygen, but perished on the way down, exhausted after spending too long above 8000 metres. Is there perhaps a finite barrier to what human beings can achieve either in high-altitude performance or in athletics? Who can tell? Perhaps someone some day will climb the South-West Face solo and survive to tell the tale.

In my selection of adventures I have only been able to deal with a limited number of subjects in the detail that is essential to convey the story of what happened. So I have chosen the ventures which have been important, innovative 'firsts' – the first ascent of Everest, the first crossings of both Poles, the first circumnavigation of the world by balloon, the first non-stop solo voyage in a sailing boat round the world. I am uncomfortably aware that I will inevitably have left out many ventures that readers will feel are either more representative or more outstanding than those I have included; my answer can only be that the ones I have chosen are ones that especially inspired me and are examples which, I hope, will illustrate a broad spectrum of post-war adventure.

In checking out adventures over the last twenty years for this new edition I became aware of the huge increase in the numbers of people undertaking all forms of adventure, linked to a decreasing number of obvious firsts to achieve. In the climbing field the 8000-metre peaks had all been climbed by 1962, Everest was soloed by Messner in 1980 and, although there are still a huge number of smaller unclimbed peaks and even more unclimbed faces and ridges on some of the highest peaks in the world, the easily identifiable superlatives have been achieved. The same can be said of sailing, while in polar travel there has been a refinement in style rather similar to that of climbing, with a reduction of numbers and level of support, the ultimate goal being to traverse the Poles alone and unsupported. It could be argued that the last unique first, the equivalent of the first ascent of the highest point on earth, was in the air with the first complete non-stop circumnavigation of the world by balloon in the spring of 1999. The year before, Brian Milton, became the first man to fly round the world in a microlight.

While there has been an explosion in the number of people going adventuring, the way adventure is pursued has changed. We seem to have entered an era of adventure-on-a-plate, neatly packaged and sold at an appropriate price. You can join a commercial expedition to attempt Everest for prices ranging from $25,000 to $65,000, race around the world in a 18-metre yacht for around £25,000 or be conducted to one of the Poles. The terrain remains the same – Everest, the Southern Ocean or the wastes of the Polar Ice Cap are no different from when the original adventurers climbed or crossed them. The fact that they are more attainable does not render them less dangerous. However, that special quality of the unknown has vanished from this level of adventuring. The guided client need hardly think, indeed is encouraged not to take the initiative.

On Everest the tents are erected, the food is cooked, the fixed rope set up, the acclimatisation programme carefully planned until the client sets out for the summit from the South Col. It can, of course, all go terribly wrong, as it did in the spring of 1996 when nine died in an appalling storm. Guides, starved of oxygen, made faulty decisions; clients, without the experience to cope for themselves in a crisis, just sat and waited to be told what to do or, in trying to get down, lost their way. The very shallowness of the tailor-made adventure-on-a-plate proved their undoing. There has also been a change of emphasis amongst the elite. This is particularly noticeable in the field of mountaineering.

With the obvious firsts already climbed, the next step is to try to make ascents that are faster, in better style, without supplementary oxygen or the aid of Sherpas. There is the challenge of skiing or paragliding from the summits and the growing popularity of collecting summits – the seven highest peaks of each continent or, much more challenging, the fourteen peaks of more than 8000 metres, all of which are either in the Karakoram or the Himalaya. The first person to do so was Reinhold Messner, arguably the greatest innovative climber of all time, and yet in setting this trend he has changed the emphasis in climbing from exploration to peak-bagging, which ends up all too often in following the easiest possible known route to the summit.

It is very noticeable that fewer new routes are being tackled today. The ascent of new routes, which I believe is at the core of climbing adventure, has always been a minority activity. The vast majority of climbers are happy to follow in the footsteps of others, guide books clutched in their hands. But there is and always has been a small elite who have gone for new routes and unclimbed summits. There are still literally hundreds of unclimbed peaks of between 5000 and 6000 metres in Central Asia. There are unclimbed faces and ridges on many of the 7000-metre peaks. In describing the first ascent of the North Face of Changabang, climbed in 1997, I have tried to capture the magic and challenge of this style of climbing.

I am still attracted by what seems at first glance to be impossible. To me, the ultimate in adventure is to convert this impossible into the feasible, and this is what all the adventures I have chosen have in common. Together they represent a complex mosaic, the component pieces of which differ enormously in so many ways, but which contribute to a fascinating overall pattern.

CHRIS BONINGTON

ONE

1

Kon-Tiki

Thor Heyerdahl's Raft Voyage Across the Pacific, 1947

THE WORLD WAS STILL RECOVERING FROM WAR; the rubble of ruined European cities had not yet been cleared, there were food shortages and everywhere people were trying to pick up the threads of their lives where they had been left five or six years earlier. Thor Heyerdahl was one of those millions. Like so many others, his life and career had been interrupted at a crucial point; he had made the best of frustrating, uncomfortable and sometimes dangerous years through the war and now, in 1946 at the age of thirty-two, was returning to the intellectual quest that was the driving force of his life.

Heyerdahl never considered himself to be an adventurer. 'I don't think I'd call myself a real adventurer, although I suppose I've become one. I don't look for adventure for the sake of adventure. The closest I can say that I go to it is that I love nature. I love the wilderness and to be in touch with the wilderness.'

As a boy and young man this took him on long walks and ski treks in the Norwegian mountains. His clear, analytical and intensely inquisitive mind led him into science and his passion for nature channelled him to biology, which he studied at university. It was during his university course that he conceived his scheme to renounce present-day material benefits by going to live for at least a year on a Pacific island without a single product of modern technology. He even set about finding himself a mate to share this return to Paradise, and together they sailed to Tahiti in 1937 and were landed by a copra schooner on the shores of the beautiful and incredibly remote Fatu Hiva, an island in the Marquesas group. Originally, Heyerdahl had intended to deny himself all modern implements, but the South Sea Island chief who had befriended them in Tahiti persuaded him to take along a machete and a metal cooking pot. These were the only concessions they made; they took no drugs, medicines or even matches.

At first it seemed a paradise, a Garden of Eden where bananas and coconuts grew in abundance, where it was always warm and lush and beautiful; but the hand of Western man had already affected the balance of its society. Originally, the island had had a population of several thousand but they had been decimated by white man's diseases and only a handful of ragged, rather suspicious natives were left. The idyll quickly began to wear thin; the natives did their best to part them from their money and possessions; they were caught in the middle of a feud between a Catholic missionary and a native Protestant pastor whose flock had shrunk to one – his sexton. The natives became increasingly hostile, slipping poisonous centipedes and scorpions into the dried grass of their bedding; soon, they were covered in sores that would not heal; in the rainy season they were permanently soaked to the skin and began to suffer from malnutrition in this island paradise. The bananas were out of season and all the coconuts had been harvested. They ended up hiding in a remote sea cave, afraid for their lives, while they waited for the copra schooner to make its annual visit to the island and carry them away.

But there had been many idyllic moments and it was on Fatu Hiva that the seeds of an idea which was to dominate his life to the present day were sown. Sitting on the beach one moonlit evening, admiring the waves, his wife said, 'It's queer, but there are never breakers like this on the other side of the island.' They were sitting on the windward, eastern shore, and the mighty waves, driven before the prevailing trade wind, had surged all the way across nearly 7000 kilometres of empty ocean from South America. How Heyerdahl came to use this simple observation as one more link in his theory connecting the old Polynesian god, Tiki, with the legendary Peruvian sun god, Kon-Tiki, is now well known. A world war intervened, however, before he was given his chance to prove that the people with white skins and long beards who had built the monuments in the Andes before the arrival of the Incas and who were said to have fled from them across the Pacific on their balsa-wood rafts could have been the ancestors of the Polynesian islanders.

BELOW The mainsail bore the stylised head of Tiki, pre-Inca sun god of Peru, whose legendary migration west towards Polynesia inspired Thor Heyerdahl's voyage.

His research all seemed to be fitting together, but he was unable to persuade any of the academics to take it seriously. They resented the intrusion of this unknown young Norwegian whose only qualification was an honours degree in biology. The main stumbling block was the question of how the South American Indians could possibly have crossed 6500 kilometres of ocean to the nearest South Pacific island, Easter Island, with its silent guard of huge stone figures. Neither the South American Indians nor the Polynesians had discovered how to make a planked boat with a keel, but the Indians had used big sea-going rafts, driven by sails, for their coastal trade. The wood they used was balsa, very light and buoyant but it also absorbed water and the experts declared that there was no way a balsa-wood raft could stay afloat for more than a few hundred miles without becoming waterlogged and sinking. Therefore, quite obviously, there was no way that the South American Indians could possibly have crossed the Pacific Ocean.

Faced with this impasse, there seemed only one way to prove that at least the journey could have been made. In desperation Heyerdahl decided to build a balsa-wood raft and sail it from Peru to the Pacific Islands. His purpose was to prove his theory possible, but the spirit that drove him on was the same restless, adventurous curiosity that had taken him to Fatu Hiva before the war. He knew practically nothing about the sea or boats, was even frightened of water, but once he had made up his mind he plunged into the planning with a thoroughness that eventually was to ensure his success.

He met a young engineer called Herman Watzinger at the seaman's hostel in New York where he was living while he tried to win acceptance for his theory. They began talking and Watzinger, having expressed an interest in Heyerdahl's plans, was promptly invited to join him. Apart from anything else, Heyerdahl probably needed someone close at hand to confide in and share both the work and the rebuffs that inevitably accompany any expedition in its early stages. Slowly, he managed to raise the money, much of it from personal loans which somehow he would have to repay at the conclusion of an expedition which all the pundits guaranteed would fail. He also got together all the food and equipment he reckoned they would need. Here, he was faced with a fundamental decision of whether he should try to reproduce in full the experience of the pre-Incas, carrying only the food he assumed they would probably have used in ancient times. In this instance, influenced perhaps by his experience on Fatu Hiva, he decided against it, feeling that the challenge of sailing a balsa-wood raft across the Pacific was quite enough. They planned, therefore, on using Army processed rations, cooked on a kerosene stove. Initially Heyerdahl did baulk when Watzinger suggested they needed wireless communications, not so much to call for help which, anyway, would not be available in the empty reaches of the Pacific, but to send out reports on their progress and weather information which could be used for meteorological research. Eventually Heyerdahl agreed to this.

He had decided on a crew of six and therefore needed to find four more for the team. On this, his first venture, he wanted people he knew well and immediately invited three old friends. One was Erik Hesselberg, an easy-going giant of a man who had been to navigation school and had sailed several times round the world in merchant ships before settling down as an artist. He would be the only crew member with any experience of the sea. The other two were old friends of Heyerdahl's wartime days in the Norwegian Resistance, Knut Haugland and Torstein Raaby, both of whom were skilled wireless operators. The sixth place was to be filled only when they reached Peru, by Bengt Danielsson, a Swedish ethnologist who was interested in Heyerdahl's migration theory and attracted by the romance of the adventure. The team was formed, as in the case of so many ventures, through a combination of personal friendship and chance meetings, and yet it all worked out, mainly through Heyerdahl's instinctive judgement of personality. He was attracted by people with a sense of humour who were easy going and would fit into a small group, and yet who had the drive and determination to carry a venture through.

At last, in March 1947, Watzinger and Heyerdahl flew down to Lima to start building their raft. They were armed with a host of introductions to important people, ranging all the way up to the President of Peru. Heyerdahl understood the art of personal and public relations. These introductions and his confident but easy manner were to prove invaluable in getting the help he needed to get the project under way. But first he had to get the balsa logs for the raft. The Incas had cut them in the coastal jungle of Ecuador, floating them down the rivers to make up their sea-going rafts on the coast. It seemed simple enough, but Heyerdahl was quickly told that he had arrived at the wrong time of the year. They were now in the rainy season and it would be impossible to reach the jungle where the big tree trunks they would need could be found. They would have to wait another six months for the dry season. He certainly could not afford to do this and so resolved to get into the jungle from the landward side, the Ecuadorian highlands. Eventually, after several misadventures, he managed to reach the jungle and find someone who could guide him to some suitable trees. At last Heyerdahl could feel that the adventure was under way.

BELOW Each man took a two-hour turn at the great six-metre steering oar, learning prehistoric steering from scratch. Lashing a cross-piece onto the handle of the oar provided a lever to turn against the immense forces of the sea.

They cut twelve large balsa logs near the banks of the Palenque river, tied them together in a rough raft and floated down to the sea where they were loaded onto a coastal steamer and carried to Callao, the sea port of Lima. By going to the President of Peru, Heyerdahl had managed to get permission to build the raft in the Naval Base. The rest of his team had now assembled in Lima and the next few weeks were spent building their reproduction of a pre-Inca raft.

Sea-going rafts had been in use well into the nineteenth century and so there were plenty of pictures from which to copy the basic designs. Since the Incas had not discovered the use of iron, no nails or wire hawsers were used. They chose nine of the thickest logs for the raft, floating them side by side to see how they fitted naturally into each other, with the longest log of about thirteen metres in the middle and the remaining ones ranked symmetrically at either side to give the effect of a bluntly tapered bow. Deep grooves were then cut in the wood to give both protection to the ropes binding the logs together and also to stop them slipping. At various places where there were gaps between the logs, five solid fir planks were squeezed between them to protrude a metre and a half down into the water to act as a kind of centreboard or keel, to limit sideways drift. This had been a feature of the old Inca rafts. Herman Watzinger, the engineer, supervised the construction of the raft, helped by Bengt Danielsson, who was the only member of the crew who could speak fluent Spanish and thus transmit Watzinger's instructions to the Peruvian workers.

Heyerdahl put a great deal of thought not only into the seaworthiness of his craft, but also into the little details of day-to-day living on what was to be their tiny world for the months ahead:

'We gave the little deck as much variation as possible. The bamboo strips did not deck in the whole raft, but formed a floor forward of the bamboo cabin and along the starboard side of it where the wall was open. The port side of the cabin was a kind of back-yard full of boxes and gear made fast, with a narrow edge to walk along. Forward in the bows, and in the stern as far as the after wall of the cabin, the nine gigantic logs were not decked in at all. So when we moved round the bamboo cabin we stepped from yellow bamboos and wicker-work down on to the round grey logs astern, and up again on to piles of cargo on the other side. It was not many steps, but the psychological effect of the irregularity gave us variation and compensated us for our limited freedom of movement. Right up at the masthead we placed a wooden platform, not so much in order to have a look-out post when at last we came to land as to be able to clamber up while en route and look at the sea from another angle.'

They were immensely proud of their raft as it took shape in the Naval Dockyard surrounded by submarines and destroyers, the modern weapons of war. Their many visitors were less impressed, however. They were assured the balsa would absorb water and they would sink like a stone before they were half way. Or the ropes would wear through and the whole thing disintegrate. The dimensions were all wrong. The raft was so small it would founder in a big sea and yet was just long enough to be lifted on the crests of two waves at the same time. So it would break in half and that would be the end of them.

'Are your parents still living?' one well-wisher asked Heyerdahl. When he replied that they were, the man commented: 'Your mother and father will be very grieved when they hear of your death.'

No one gave them any chance of success and the amazing thing is that their morale remained so high. Knut Haugland told me that this was largely the result of the confidence which they all had in Heyerdahl's planning, judgement and attitude to risk. He did not believe in taking risks – he was convinced that the raft would carry them across the Pacific. Of the team the most seriously worried was Bengt Danielsson, partly perhaps because he had known Heyerdahl for the shortest time but also

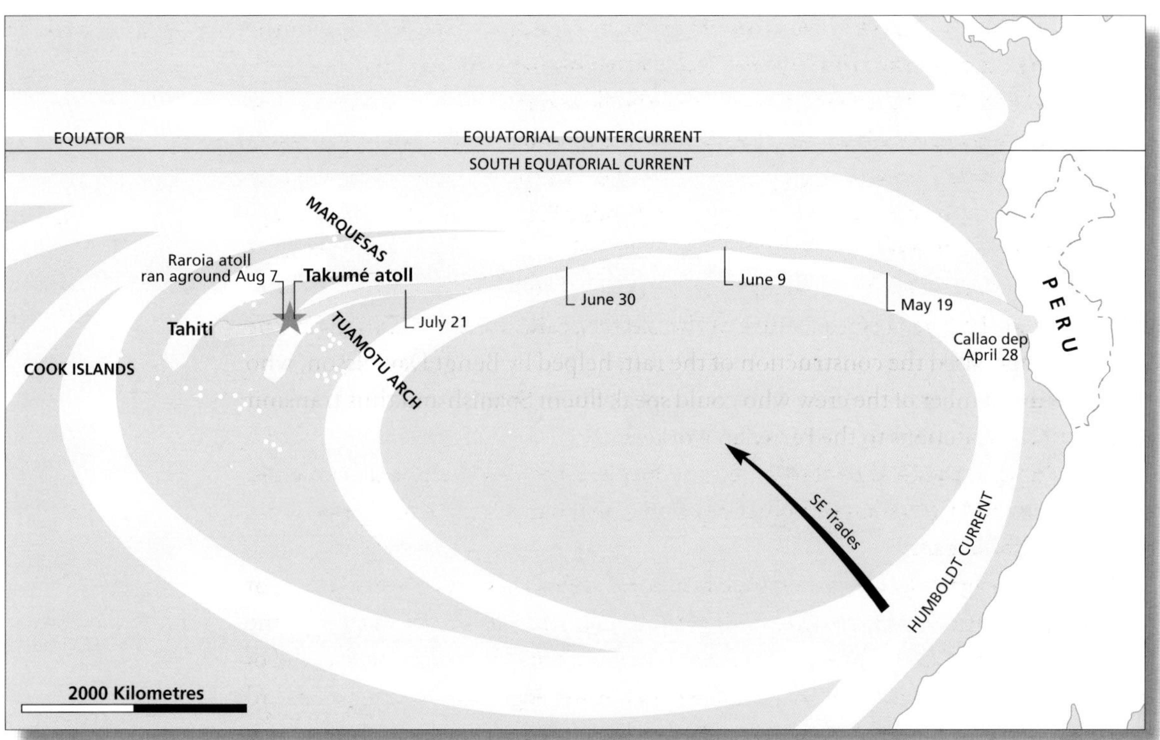

ABOVE The voyage of Kon-Tiki.

because he had lost his heart to a local girl. He was tempted to withdraw and it is a tribute to his own courage and Heyerdahl's personality that he stayed on with the expedition in spite of his doubts.

At last, on April 28th, everything was ready. A huge crowd had assembled around the harbour to watch the send-off; dignitaries from the Government and embassies had also joined the throng. The decks of *Kon-Tiki* were piled high with a chaos of bananas, fruits and sacks of fresh food, purchased at the last minute. There was a babble of excited talk, well-wishers thronging the boat, while all of the crew, with the exception of the leader who was weighed down with a sense of responsibility, had gone off for a last drink with friends and sweethearts. The noise on the quay rose to a crescendo; the tug which was going to tow them out to sea had arrived, nosing its way up to the throng of small boats crowded around *Kon-Tiki*. A motor launch carrying the tow rope sidled up to the raft as Heyerdahl, with a nightmare vision of being towed out to the Pacific without a crew, tried to explain with his few available words of Spanish they would have to wait:

'But nobody understood. The officers only smiled politely, and the knot at our bows was made fast in more than exemplary manner. I cast off the rope and flung it overboard with all manner of signs and gesticulations. The parrot utilised the opportunity afforded by all the confusion to stick its beak out of the cage and turn the knob of the door, and when I turned round it was strutting cheerfully about the bamboo deck. I tried to catch it but it shrieked rudely in Spanish and fluttered away over the banana clusters. With one eye on the sailors who were trying to cast a rope over the bows, I started a wild chase after the parrot. It fled shrieking into the bamboo cabin, where I got it in a corner and caught it by one leg as it tried to flutter over me. When I came out again and stuffed my flapping trophy into its cage, the sailors on land had cast off the raft's moorings and we were dancing helplessly in and out with the backwash of the long swell that came rolling in over the mole. In despair I seized a paddle and vainly tried to parry a violent bump as the raft was flung against the wooden piles of the quay. Then the motor-boat started, and with one jerk the *Kon-Tiki* began her long voyage. My only companion was a Spanish-speaking parrot which sat glaring sulkily in a cage. People on shore cheered and waved, and the swarthy cinema photographers in the motor-boat almost jumped into the sea in their eagerness to catch every detail of the expedition's dramatic start from Peru. Despairing and alone I stood on the raft looking out for my lost companions, but no-one came. So we came out to the *Guardian Ries*, which was lying with steam up ready to lift anchor and start. I was up the rope-ladder in a twinkling and made so much row on board that the start was postponed and a boat sent back to the quay. It was away a good while, and then it came back full of pretty *señoritas*, but without a single one of the *Kon-Tiki*'s missing men. This was all very well, but it did not solve my problems and while the raft swarmed with charming *señoritas*, the boat went back on a fresh search for *los expedicionarios noruegos*.'

Another cause for concern was that the ropes holding the raft together might be worn through by abrasion

An hour went by and the other five members of the crew trickled back to the wharf to be ferried out to *Kon-Tiki*. It was a delightfully haphazard, slightly chaotic departure that underlined the relaxed control Heyerdahl exerted on his team and the free, essentially happy, spirit of the entire enterprise.

Accompanied by a fleet of small boats, the tug towed them out into the bay. Soon they were bucking up and down in the Pacific swell, as the tug hauled them eighty kilometres out, beyond the coastal winds and currents, into the open sea. The tug cast off and the six men were left alone in the empty ocean on a vessel of a design that had last sailed off the coast of South America two hundred years before, but had only ventured out into the Humboldt Current on the morning offshore wind and had always returned to land on the evening shore winds. It was, perhaps, a thousand years since a pre-Inca fleet had carried the god-king Tiki and his tall, fair-skinned people in their desperate flight towards the setting sun across the great empty ocean. What did Tiki think he was going to find? How could he know that there was going to be land at the end of the voyage, or was he content to entrust the lives of his people to the sun god whom they were following?

The crew of the modern-day *Kon-Tiki* raised the mainsail, with its stylised picture of the head of Tiki, and waited for the wind to drive them ever westward. At first hesitantly, and then with a steadily growing strength, the South-East Trades drove them remorselessly into the empty ocean of the South Pacific. That night they saw the lights of two steamers; they signalled with their kerosene lamps but the lookouts were not alert, not expecting to see anyone, let alone a pre-Inca raft heading out into the Pacific. These were to be the last two boats they saw all the way across. They were now totally committed. There was no way they could sail against the wind; all they could do was to sail before it, relying on the constant direction of the South-East Trades to take them to their 6500-kilometre-distant destination.

That night the seas rose steadily, piled high by the growing wind; great rollers of dark water swept down, so much faster than the raft, curling above the stern, breaking over it and smashing down onto the deck. The two helmsmen, always on duty on the great six-metre steering oar, were learning from scratch how to control this prehistoric boat. They quickly discovered that the best way was to lash a cross-piece onto the handle of the oar so that they had a kind of lever to turn against the immense force of the seas but, as the waves increased, they found that they had to lash the steering oar loosely in position to prevent it being torn from their hands. When the great combers came rolling in from behind, the helmsmen had to leap up and hang on to a bamboo pole that projected from the cabin roof, while the waves surged across the deck beneath their dangling feet, before running away between the numerous gaps and chinks between the logs. Already, quite a few of the prophecies of doom had been laid low. The raft rose and fell easily between the crests and troughs of the waves with the buoyancy of a cork. They could not be swamped because the water simply flowed away through the logs and over the side. The worst that could happen was that the cabin could be swept by a breaker, particularly if they let themselves get abeam to the waves, but provided they kept the stern into the sea, the waves rarely reached the cabin before dissipating.

After three days of battering by heavy seas the wind eased and the waves became more even. The team were able to settle into a steady rhythm of living, though there were still some serious worries. Would the balsa wood become waterlogged? After a week, Heyerdahl surreptitiously broke off a small chunk of wood and dropped it into the sea; it sank like a stone. The prophets of doom might have been right after all. Then he dug his knife into the wood and found that only the outer couple of centimetres had absorbed water and most of the log was still dry. With luck, the sap further in would act as an impregnation and check the absorption.

Another cause for concern was that the ropes holding the raft together might be worn through by abrasion. There was a constant movement and flexing as the raft responded to the contours of the waves, shifting, creaking, water gurgling between the logs. Lying in the little shelter at night it was easy to imagine the constant friction and stress on the cordage, and the consequences if it started to come apart. Each day they examined the ropes, but there was no sign of wear; the balsa wood was so soft that the ropes had cut deep into it, getting their own protection and, at the same time, lubrication from the salt water in the smooth channels they had worn.

Day followed day, with blue skies, the constant wind of the South-East Trades and a blazing sun that dropped over the western horizon each evening, just as it always had done, just as it had led the original Kon-Tiki and his fleet of rafts to their unknown destination.

The modern-day sailors were already beginning to tire of their processed foods, but the sea provided plenty of alternatives. Travelling only just above the sea's surface, and little faster than the current, weed and barnacles on the undersurface of the raft gave small fish an attractive shelter and it soon became a moving home for

Above *There were no concessions to modern-day comforts and the original South American Indians who might have made this voyage were probably no more comfortable.*

fish as well as humans. The variety was incredible. It ranged from clouds of tiny, multishaped and multicoloured plankton to the huge whales which harvested the plankton. They were accompanied by shoals of sardine, dorado (dolphin), schools of porpoise, flying fish, which provided breakfast each morning, and a huge variety they had never seen or heard of before. Some of them were new discoveries. One night, Torstein Raaby, who was sleeping by the entrance of the shelter, was awakened when the lamp by his head was knocked over. He thought it was a flying fish, grabbed for it in the dark and felt something long and slimy that wriggled out of his hand and landed on Herman Watzinger's sleeping bag. Eventually, when they managed to light the lamp, they saw an extraordinary snake-like fish with dull black eyes, long snout and a fierce jaw, filled with long sharp teeth. Watzinger grabbed it and under his grip a large-eyed white fish was suddenly thrown up from the stomach out of the mouth of the snake-like fish; this was quickly followed by another. These were obviously deep-water fish and, later on, the team were to discover that they were the first people ever to see alive the *Gempylus*, a deep-water mackerel, though its skeleton had been seen in the Galapagos Islands and on the coast of South America.

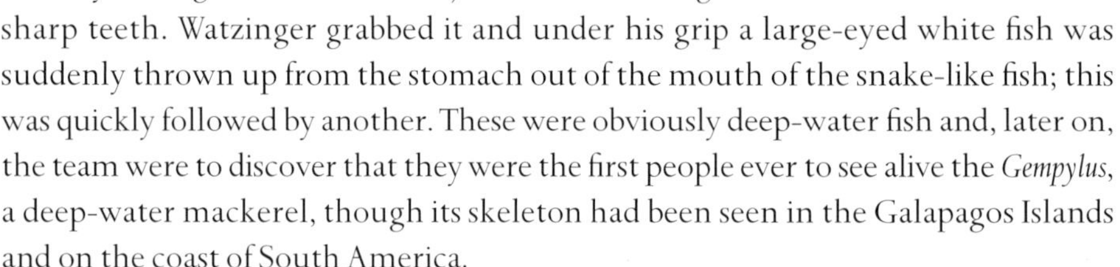

A few days later Knut Haugland saw the biggest and ugliest shark he had ever seen. At least fifteen metres long, as it swam round the raft and then started ducking underneath it, its head was near the surface on one side and the tail lashing the water on the other. The head was broad and flat, like a frog, with two small eyes at the side and jaws over a metre wide. If angered, it could undoubtedly have smashed the raft to pieces with its massive tail. It was the very rare whale shark, the biggest of the species, and it circled the craft for over an hour, the crew watching it, apprehensive yet fascinated. At last, as it cruised under the raft and came up the other side, just beneath Erik Hesselberg, he drove a harpoon into its head with all the force he could muster. The shark erupted into fury, lashed the water with its huge tail and plunged into the depths. The strong rope attached to the harpoon parted as if it were cotton and a few moments later a broken-off harpoon shaft came to the surface.

They devised games to lure sharks onto hooks baited with dorado, or they would simply allow the shark to bite through the dorado, which it could do with a single snap of its powerful jaws; as it turned to swim away one of the crew would seize the shark by the tail and heave the tail up onto the stern logs, where it would thresh around until it either managed to heave itself off and regain its freedom, or until they managed to drop a noose over the tail and so caught it until it thrashed away its life.

And the days slipped by with the routine of daily sun shots, the recording of windspeed and weather, the daily radio call, the round of fishing and the turns at the steering. Heyerdahl, as skipper, kept a gentle, unobtrusive but positive control over his little crew, his natural air of authority leavened by a rich sense of humour. They had agreed to various rules which they all enforced: that the helmsmen should always be attached by a rope to the raft and that no-one should swim away from the raft for fear of being swept away – they could not possibly sail back against the wind to pick anyone up. Losing someone overboard was a nightmare risk of the voyage and it happened on July 21st, when they were getting close to the Pacific Islands. A gust of wind caught one of the sleeping bags which were hanging out to air; Watzinger dived to catch it, toppled on the edge of the deck, was unable to regain his balance and flopped into the sea:

'We heard a faint cry for help amid the noise of the waves, and saw Herman's head and waving arm, as well as some vague green object twirling about in the water near him. He was struggling for life to get back to the raft through the high seas which had lifted him out from the port side. Torstein, who was at the steering oar aft, and I myself, up in the bows, were the first to perceive him, and we went cold with fear. We bellowed "man overboard!" at the pitch of our lungs as we rushed to the nearest life-saving gear. The others had not heard Herman's cry at all because of the noise of the sea, but in a trice there was life and bustle on deck. Herman was an excellent swimmer, and though we realised that his life was at stake, we had a fair hope that he would manage to crawl back to the edge of the raft before it was too late.

'Torstein, who was nearest, seized the bamboo drum round which was the line we used for the lifeboat, for this was within his reach. It was the only time on the whole voyage that this line got caught up. The whole thing happened in a few seconds. Herman was now level with the stern of the raft, but a few yards away, and his last hope was to crawl to the blade of the steering oar and hang on to it. As he missed the end of the logs, he reached out for the oar-blade, but it slipped away from him. And there he lay, just where experience had shown we could get nothing back. While Bengt and I launched the dinghy, Knut and Erik threw out the lifebelt. Carrying a long line, it hung ready for use on the corner of the cabin roof but today the wind was so strong that when they threw the lifebelt it was simply blown back to the raft. After a few unsuccessful throws Herman was already far astern of the steering oar, swimming desperately to keep up with the raft, while the distance increased with each gust of wind. He realised that henceforth the gap would simply go on increasing, but he set a faint hope on the dinghy, which we had now got into the water. Without the line which acted as a brake, it would perhaps have been practicable to drive the rubber raft to meet the swimming man, but whether the rubber raft would ever get back to the *Kon-Tiki* was another matter. Nevertheless, three men in a rubber dinghy had some chance, one man in the sea had none.

'Then we suddenly saw Knut take off and plunge head first into the sea. He had the lifebelt in one hand and was heaving himself along. Every time Herman's head appeared on a wave-back Knut was gone, and every time Knut came up Herman was not there. But then we saw both heads at once; they had swum to meet each other and both were hanging on to the lifebelt. Knut waved his arm, and as the rubber raft had meanwhile been hauled on board, all four of us took hold of the line of the lifebelt and hauled for dear life, with our eyes fixed on the great dark object which was visible just behind the two men. This mysterious beast in the water was pushing a big greenish-black triangle up above the wave-crests; it almost gave Knut a shock when he was on his way over to Herman. Only Herman knew then that the triangle did not belong to a shark or any other sea monster. It was an inflated corner of Torstein's water-tight sleeping bag. But the sleeping bag did not remain floating for long after we had hauled the two men safe and sound on board. Whatever dragged the sleeping bag down into the depths had just missed a better prey.'

It had been a narrow escape and everyone was badly shaken, but there was no time to reflect before another storm was upon them. They were hammered by winds and sea for another five days. At the end of it the steering oar was broken, the sail rent and the centreboards below the raft hung loose and almost useless, the ropes that held them tight having parted or lost their tension with the violent motion of the waves. The gaps between the logs were now very much wider and everyone had to be on their guard to avoid catching an ankle in between the constantly flexing logs; but the raft was still sound, the cargo dry and the crew were fit. On July 17th they had their first visit by land-based birds, two large boobies; the flying fish, also, were of a different species, similar to those that Heyerdahl could remember catching off the coast of Fatu Hiva which was now only 500 kilometres to the north.

They began to worry about their landing – probably the most dangerous part of the entire voyage. Heyerdahl had vivid memories of the huge surf smashing against the jagged cliffs of Fatu Hiva. The coral atolls to the south could be even more dangerous, with their widespread reefs like hidden minefields lying just below the surface. If caught on one of these, *Kon-Tiki* and its crew could be smashed to pieces by the breaking surf while still far out from any island haven. Swept before the wind, their ability to manoeuvre was slight; it was unlikely that they would be able to creep round an island or reef into its sheltered lee.

For a couple of days they headed towards Fatu Hiva, but then a north-easterly wind blew them down towards the Tuamotu atolls. They were now accompanied by the constant scream of sea birds, as they wheeled and dived upon the raft. Land was undoubtedly close by. At last, at dawn on July 30th, they sighted a low silhouette, little more than a faint shadow against the red-gold blaze of the rising sun, on the far horizon. They had passed it during the night; there was no chance of back-tracking against the wind; they would have to wait until they were swept onto another island. They were subdued rather than jubilant:

'No extravagant outbursts were to be heard on board. After the sail had been trimmed and the oar laid over, we all formed a silent group at the mast head or stood on deck staring towards the land which had suddenly cropped up, out in the middle of the endless all-dominating sea. At last we had visible proof that we had been moving in all these months; we had not just been lying tumbling about in the centre of the same eternal circular horizon. To us it seemed as if the island were mobile and had suddenly entered the circle of blue empty sea in the centre of which we had our permanent abode, as if the island were drifting slowly across our own domain, heading for the eastern horizon. We were all filled with a warm quiet satisfaction at having actually reached Polynesia, mingled with a faint momentary disappointment at having to submit helplessly to seeing the island lie there like a mirage while we continued our eternal drift across the sea westward.'

Later that day they sighted another island; having seen early enough this time they were able to head for it. Soon they could pick out the dense palm trees that grew down to the shore, could see the still waters of the lagoon inside the reef, but between them and the end of their voyage was the reef itself, a confusion of white, thundering spray that occasionally cleared to show the jagged brown teeth of coral. If thrown onto this their chances of survival would be slight. Edging in as close as they dared, they could actually see the separate trunks of the trees, the texture of the sand on the beach, so very close to them and yet still unattainable. As they coasted down, parallel to the reef, there was a mixed feeling of holiday excitement tinged with underlying fear. Erik Hesselberg, a big Peruvian sun-hat on his head, played the guitar and sang sentimental South Sea songs; Bengt Danielsson prepared an elaborate dinner, which they ate sitting on the bamboo deck under the cloudless blue sky. Somehow, all this emphasised the incongruous menace of the tumbling, crushing surf between them and safety.

It was beginning to get dark and they were very nearly at the end of the island when they spotted some figures among the trees; two canoes came streaking out through the surf and in a few minutes, for the first time in three months, they spoke to strangers – the descendants, perhaps, of Kon-Tiki and the original voyagers. With a mixture of sign language and the few words of Polynesian that Heyerdahl could remember, they indicated that they wanted to find a way in through the reef. The islanders replied by saying 'Brrrrrr', indicating that the white men should switch on their engine. They could not conceive that there was none and Heyerdahl had to make them feel underneath the stern to prove that this was the case.

Then they joined in trying to paddle the raft in towards land. Two more canoes came out but, as dusk fell, an offshore easterly built up, slowly pushing them away from the reef. It was now pitch dark; they gathered from the islanders that there were only the four sea-going canoes on the island, although there were plenty of men on shore who could help paddle them in, if only they could get out to the raft. Knut Haugland volunteered to take the rubber dinghy in to collect some more helpers and disappeared into the dark.

But the wind steadily increased in strength as they were blown out from the shelter of the island and they began to wonder if Haugland would ever manage to return. They paddled desperately, but were growing increasingly exhausted. At last, out of the dark came a shout. He had managed to return with some of the islanders, but now it was too late; quite obviously, they would never get to the island. The Polynesians leapt back into their canoes and paddled home into the dark toward the invisible island. It hardly seemed to matter any more, so glad were the crew to be reunited. They had become such a tight-knit little group of over the months, that this seemed the most important thing of all. After all, there were more islands for them to land on.

They sailed on, drifting ever closer to the dangerous reefs of the Takumé and Raroia atolls; then the wind veered to the north, bringing a hope of creeping round to the south of them. They were tense, worrying days, the memory of the breakers smashing down onto the coral reef all too vivid. Now so close to success, they could very easily lose their lives within easy sight of their goal. On the morning of August 7th they sighted some low-lying coral islands in their path; they were being swept inexorably towards them and soon they could see the white chain of breaking surf that barred their way to safety.

The previous days had been spent in preparation for their seemingly inevitable shipwreck, as they packed all their documents and films into waterproof bags, securing them in the cabin which they lashed with a tarpaulin. Also, with great difficulty, they pulled up the centreboards, now encrusted with seaweed and barnacles, through the gaps between the logs to reduce their draft to the minimum. As they worked they drifted ever closer to the crushing breakers. Heyerdahl kept the log almost to the last moment:

'9.45: The wind is taking us straight towards the last island but one, we can see behind the reef. We can now see the whole coral reef clearly; here it is built up like a white and red speckled wall which just sticks up out of the water in a belt in front of all the islands. All along the reef white foaming surf is flung up towards the sky. Bengt is just serving up a good hot meal, the last before the great action! It is a wreck lying in there on the reef. We are so close now that we can see right across the shining lagoon behind the reef, and see the outlines of other islands on the other side of the lagoon.

'9.50: Very close now. Drifting along the reef. Only a hundred or so yards away. Torstein is talking to the man on Rarotonga. All clear. Must pack up log now. All in good spirits; it looks bad, but *we shall make it!*'

Now very nearly among the wild upsurge of breaking waves, to give themselves a few more moments to tap out their position on the morse key of the radio, they dropped the heavy anchor, attached to their thickest length of rope. It held just long enough to swing *Kon-Tiki* round, so that the stern was facing the reef, then started dragging along the bottom as the raft was swept inexorably towards the thundering, boiling spray of the great Pacific waves smashing onto the reef.

'When we realised that the sea had got hold of us, the anchor rope was cut, and we were off. A sea rose straight up under us and we felt the *Kon-Tiki* being lifted up in the air. The great moment had come; we were riding on the wave-back at breathless speed, our ramshackle craft creaking and groaning as she quivered under us. The excitement made one's blood boil. I remember that, having no other inspiration, I waved my arm and bellowed "hurrah" at the pitch of my lungs; it afforded a certain relief and could do no harm anyway. The others certainly thought I had gone mad, but they all beamed and grinned enthusiastically. On we ran with the seas rushing in behind us; this was the *Kon-Tiki*'s baptism of fire; all must and would go well.

'But our elation was soon damped. A new sea rose high astern of us like a glittering green glass wall; as we sank down it came rolling after us, and in the same second in which I saw it high above me I felt a violent blow and was submerged under floods of water. I felt the suction through my whole body, with such great strength that I had to strain every single muscle in my frame and think of one thing only – hold on, hold on! I think that in such a desperate situation the arms will be torn off before the brain consents to let go, evident as the outcome is. Then I felt that the mountain of water

ABOVE The cabin was smashed flat and the mast broken like a matchstick, but the logs still held together in their bonds. Kon-Tiki was a wreck, but an honourable wreck.

was passing on and relaxing its devilish grip of me. When the whole mountain had rushed on, with an earsplitting roaring and crashing, I saw Knut again hanging on beside me, doubled up into a ball. Seen from behind the great sea was almost flat and grey; as it rushed on it swept just over the ridge of the cabin roof which projected from the water, and there hung the three others, pressed against the cabin roof as the water passed over them.'

The raft was still afloat, lying in the trough of the breakers just short of the reef. Another wall of water came rolling in, towered above the raft, toppled and smashed down up on it, engulfing the raft, tearing at the men, so tiny and puny, who clung to it. Another and then another wave swept across them and each time they were edged closer to the sharp jaws of the reef, then the biggest wave of all, a sheer green wall curling above them, smashed over the raft, lifting it onto the reef itself, so that the raft was now held immobile against the savage force of the sea. They clung on to their bits of rope, lungs bursting as the sea boiled around them, and then it fell away leaving a momentary lull when they could glimpse the appalling havoc. The cabin was smashed flat, the mast broken like a matchstick but, worst of all, Heyerdahl could see only one other member of his crew:

'I felt cold fear run through my whole body. What was the good of my holding on? If I had lost one single man here, in the run in, the whole thing would be ruined, and for the moment there was only one human figure to be seen after the last buffet. In that second Torstein's hunched-up form appeared outside the raft. He was hanging like a monkey in the ropes from the masthead, and managed to get onto the logs again, where he crawled upon the debris forward of the cabin. Herman too now turned his head and gave me a forced grin of encouragement, but did not move. I bellowed in the faint hope of locating the others, and heard Bengt's calm voice call out that all hands were aboard. They were lying holding onto the ropes behind the tangled barricade which the tough plating from the bamboo deck had built up.'

Wave followed wave. Each time they were pulled a little further over the reef; each time the undertow tore at them, trying to draw them back into the maelstrom of breakers. But the force of the waves began to diminish and soon were just foaming around the stranded raft. They were able to let go their holds, take stock of the damage, and found that the raft was still remarkably intact, with the cabin flattened rather than destroyed, the logs still held together by their bonds.

Exhausted but jubilant, they salvaged vital items of gear and then waded through the still waters behind the reef to a low-lying palm-covered island. Their voyage was over; they had proved that a balsa wood raft could cross the Pacific Ocean.

Heyerdahl wrote: 'I was completely overwhelmed. I sank down on my knees and thrust my fingers down into the dry warm sand.'

The voyage of *Kon-Tiki* was the first great romantic venture after the Second World War and it caught the imagination of the entire world, particularly once Heyerdahl had published his book telling the story. There was an element of lighthearted schoolboy adventure in tales of near escapes with sharks and storms, of desert islands and palm trees, combined with the fascination of Heyerdahl's determination to prove how an ancient legend could actually have been fact. This venture provided the general public with exactly the relief from the drab violence and ugliness of war that everyone wanted.

But Heyerdahl had less success with his fellow scientists, who dismissed his voyage as an adventurous stunt with little relevance to serious scientific proof or study. Part of the reason was because Heyerdahl wrote his popular account first, so that he could pay off the huge debts incurred in making the voyage. His serious study, *American Indians in the Pacific*, was not finished until 1952. But when confronted by hostile academics, he showed the same implacable but good-humoured determination that he had shown through the frustrations of preparing for and making his voyage. Slowly, he won over the academic world to his view. final victory did not come, however, until after he had mounted another expedition, this time one that was purely scientific, to Easter Island, 'the navel of the world', whose strange giants of stone had mystified all the scientists who gazed upon them.

Heyerdahl chartered a trawler and took a team of archaeologists to the island to complete the first comprehensive dig that had ever been made there. Once again he used his breadth of view and intense curiosity combined with a deep humanity to gain a completely original view of what had happened on the island. The story of his discoveries on Easter Island is, intellectually, as exciting an adventure as anything on board *Kon-Tiki*. As before, he wrote a popular book that deservedly became a huge best-seller and then followed it by a serious study, *Easter Island and the East Pacific*. The academic world was at last convinced that his theory of migration must be correct, giving him their unanimous endorsement at the Tenth Pacific Science Conference in Hawaii in 1961.

But for Heyerdahl the mystery was not completely solved. There was the intriguing similarity between the pyramids and other archaeological remains of Mexico and Peru and those of ancient Egypt and Mesopotamia. There was no evidence of any such civilisations further north on the American continent, the acknowledged route of countless migratory waves of people who had crossed the Bering Strait from Asia. Was it possible that ancient man had crossed the Atlantic from the Mediterranean? In the case of the Pacific migrationary theory, Heyerdahl had been on his own, but on the Atlantic there were two schools of thought already, the Diffusionists who believed that there must have been some kind of migration direct from Europe to Mexico, and the Isolationists who considered that this was impossible and that the Aztec and Inca civilisations had evolved on their own among the Indians who had originated from Asia. Their strongest argument was that the American Indians had not discovered the use of the ribbed and planked wooden hull which, of course, both the Phoenicians and Vikings had. On the other hand, both reed boats and balsa rafts were in use in America and had been used on the Nile and in Mesopotamia at the dawn of civilisation.

Heyerdahl was immediately fascinated by the prospect of the practical experiment, of re-creating a reed boat and sailing it across the Atlantic. Once again, it was the spirit of science and adventure. On the first attempt they were baulked just short of success, when their boat, *Ra I*, disintegrated. He returned the following year with a boat whose design they had improved in the light of experience, and this time managed to complete the crossing, reaching the island of Barbados. Also, on *Ra II*, they took only food which would have been available in ancient times – grain, dried nuts, fruit, olive oil and wine. They ate better than any of them had ever done on previous expeditions!

But still he was not content. *Ra II*, like *Kon-Tiki*, had only been able to sail before the wind. It had, therefore, been at the mercy of the wind and currents and could only have made a one-way voyage. Heyerdahl wanted to discover whether these reed boats could have manoeuvred against the wind, whether they could have sailed the high seas, through the Persian Gulf, the Indian Ocean and the Red Sea, carrying both merchandise and passengers between the ports of the ancient world. And so *Tigris* was born.

Tigris was a reed boat built on the banks of the River Tigris, using the reeds of the Marsh Arabs under the direction of a group of Bolivian Indians from Lake Titicaca, the only men who still build and sail boats made from reeds. The boat was a success; she could carry a good load, could sail the seas with and against the wind, but to Heyerdahl's eyes the real problem derived from the world around them – not from wind and sea, but from what man has done to the land and ocean. They had innumerable narrow escapes when nearly run down by giant tankers, saw hideous slicks of oil and chemicals polluting the Persian Gulf and Indian Ocean and were barred from landing anywhere on the shores of the Red Sea because of the conflicts in the area. finally, in protest against unrestricted armament delivery from industrialised nations to a corner of the world where civilisation began, Heyerdahl and his crew decided to burn *Tigris*, in a dramatic gesture of disillusionment at what man is doing to his planet.

There are so many levels to Heyerdahl's adventures, the pure, thrilling romantic adventure, the fascinating and practical work of historical detection and, on yet another level, that of social experiment, for on both *Ra* and *Tigris*, Heyerdahl sought to affirm his belief that people of different countries and backgrounds can work and live together by selecting an international crew, many of whom he did not even know personally before hand.

For a man who does not consider himself to be an adventurer, Heyerdahl has throughout his life tackled some extraordinarily challenging and potentially dangerous schemes, but has done so, not for the sake of playing a risk game, but rather because he was prepared to accept the risks and then neutralise them as far as he could to attain his end. As an outstandingly bold and innovative man of science and of action, Thor Heyerdahl emerges as one of the great adventurers of the post-war period.

TWO

2

The Man who Raced Himself

Francis Chichester's Single-Handed Circumnavigation, 1966-67

IT IS JOSHUA SLOCUM who enters the ocean-going record books as the first man to circumnavigate the world single-handed aboard his famous sloop *Spray*. He set out from Boston in 1895 and returned three years later in 1898. This leisurely seeming progress had, however, been a magnificent achievement, for Slocum had none of the self-steering equipment and strong lightweight gear and winches used by the modern yachtsman. Nor, of course, did he have GPS (Global Positioning System) to help pinpoint his position. He made plenty of stops along the way. He prudently avoided the empty, storm-ridden expanses of the Southern Ocean and got round the tip of South America by going through the Magellan Straits.

Francis Chichester had a very different approach to the adventure of solo circumnavigation and a more ambitious objective. Testing himself to the limit was not something new to Chichester. When he set sail from Plymouth on August 27th 1966, he had already established his individuality and success several times over, not just in the field of sailing but also as a pioneer of long-distance solo flying. Not only did he aim to sail round the world single-handed, he meant to go faster, with fewer stops, than anyone had ever done before.

With his great sense of history, he wanted to follow the old clipper route but, characteristically, was not content merely to follow the clippers; he sought to beat their time from England to Sydney and then back home to England round Cape Horn. His plan was to make only the one stop at Sydney, and achieve the longest continuous voyage ever attempted by any small craft, let alone one that was single-handed. By the mid-sixties only nine small boats had been round the Horn and, of these, six had been capsized or pitchpoled. No single-handed boat had ever been round. The fact that Chichester was sixty-five when he set out on his attempt made it even more remarkable.

He had always had an intensely competitive urge, combined with an adventurous, technically-minded curiosity. The son of an English parson, he had a lonely childhood with little love or understanding at home. He was sent off to prep school and then to Marlborough, a public school that has produced several outstanding venturers, including John Hunt. Like many of his fellow-adventurers', his school career was undistinguished and, at the age of eighteen, without consulting his father he decided to abandon all ideas of going to university and the career in the Indian

RIGHT Time for ablutions.

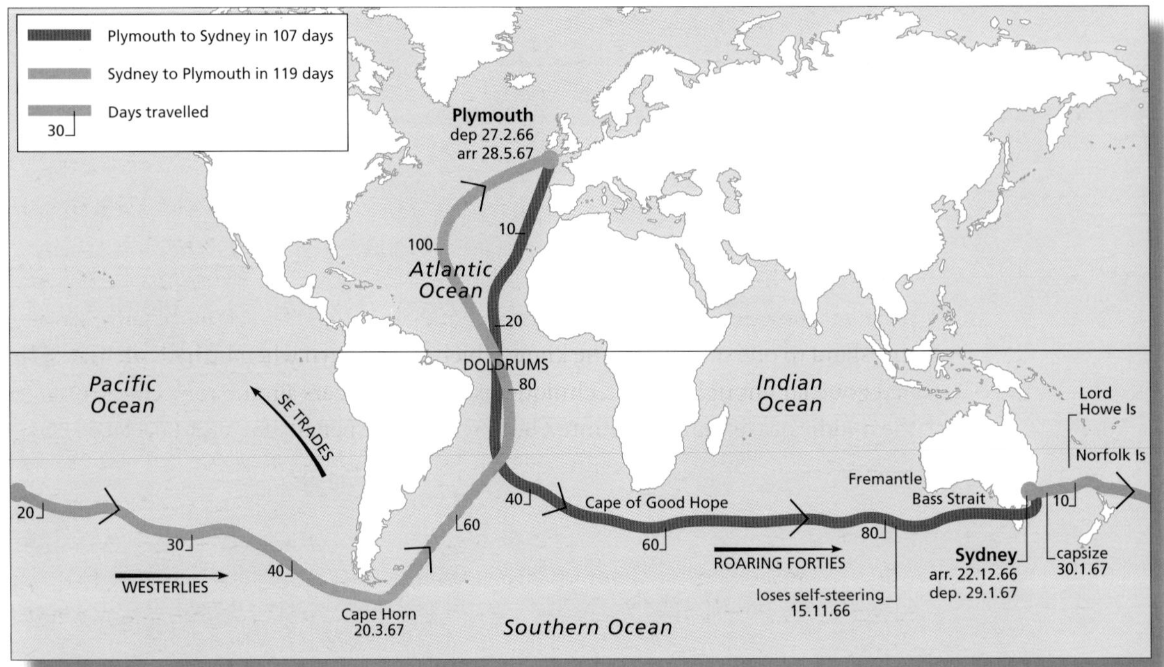

ABOVE The voyage of Francis Chichester in Gipsy Moth IV, a total of 29,630 miles in 226 days.

Civil Service which had been planned for him and, instead, emigrated to New Zealand, travelling steerage with £10 in his pocket. It sounds like the classic schoolboy adventure story, and Chichester certainly lived up to this conception. He was determined to make his fortune and took on a variety of jobs, ending up in property development. At the age of twenty-seven he was making £10,000 a year – in those days a great deal of money. He returned to England in 1929, having achieved his aim of making £20,000 before going back home.

There was nothing particularly original about a wealthy young businessman taking up flying, but now, after twenty-four flying hours of instructions, he decided to buy a 'plane and fly it to Australia, hoping to beat the time taken by Hinkler, the only other man to do it. Chichester did not get the record, but he did manage to fly his 'plane to Sydney. He also flew into the depression, which took away the greater part of the fortune he had built, but he did not let this deter him and threw most of his energy into further flying projects. In those days flying was adventurous in a way that it has long ceased to be. There were no radio beacons or flight control paths. The Gipsy Moth had an open cockpit, a range of under a thousand miles and a top speed of just over a hundred miles an hour.

No-one had ever flown across the Tasman Sea from New Zealand to Australia. Chichester now dreamt up a plan of flying all the way from New Zealand to England over the Pacific, thus circumnavigating the globe, flying solo, something that had not yet been done. For a start, though, flying the Tasman Sea offered a huge challenge. It was 1200 miles wide, two-thirds of the distance across the Atlantic, with weather which is even more unpredictable. Even if he stripped everything out of the Gipsy Moth and carried extra petrol tanks, his 'plane could not have made that distance in a single hop. Looking at a map, he noticed there were two inhabited islands on the way, Norfolk and Lord Howe, but neither had airfields. Then he got the idea of fitting floats to the aircraft so that he could land on the sea, but still he had to find the islands – Norfolk Island, 481 miles out into the featureless ocean, and Lord Howe another 561 miles on. There were no radio aids and so he would have to do it by a combination of dead reckoning and taking shots of the sun, no easy matter while flying a juddering, bucking 'plane. He only had to be a half-degree out in his reckoning and he could miss the island altogether; he would not have enough fuel to get back to New Zealand, had no radio to call for help and would have had little chance of being picked up by a ship. He hit upon the technique of aiming off – of intentionally missing the island to one side, so that he knew which way to turn when he had calculated he had gone far enough. It is a technique used by orienteers aiming for a checkpoint in the middle of a featureless country, but for them the penalty for a mistake is dropping a few places in a race; for Chichester it could well have been his life.

An Australian, Menzies, beat him to the first solo flight across the Tasman Sea, flying it in a single hop with a 'plane that had sufficient fuel capacity. This did not deter Chichester, who was fascinated by the navigational challenge of trying to make a landfall on a tiny island. He was busy learning astro-navigation, adapting a sextant to his own specialist use as a solo pilot.

Ready at last, on March 28th 1931, he took off from the far north tip of New Zealand, full of apprehension about what he was trying to do:

'At noon I flew over the edge of New Zealand; it was Spirit's Bay, where the Maoris believed there was a vast cavern through which all the spirits of the dead passed. I flew from under the cloud into the clear sky. All my miserable anxieties and worries dropped away, and I was thrilled through and through. Over my left shoulder, the last of New Zealand receded rapidly. Ahead stretched the ocean, sparkling under the eye of the sun; no sport could touch this, it was worth almost any price. I seemed to expand with vitality and power and zest.'

He was putting into practice a whole series of techniques he had developed for calculating drift and position as a solo flyer:

'I had to try a sextant shot to find out how far I was from the turn-off point, and at the same time to check my dead reckoning. I trimmed the tail as delicately as I could to balance the 'plane, but she would not stabilise and I had to use the control-stick for the whole time while adjusting the sextant... I had just got the sun and horizon together in the sextant, when terrific acceleration pressing my back made me drop the sextant. I grabbed the stick and eased the seaplane from its vertical nose dive into a normal dive and then flattened it out.'

He managed to get a sun sight, took some more shots and, at last, came to the point where, according to his dead reckoning and after working out his sun sight, he should make his right-angled turn. He was now going to put this theory into practice:

'The moment I settled on this course, nearly at right-angles to the track from New Zealand, I had a feeling of despair. After flying in one direction for hour after hour over a markless, signless sea, my instinct revolted at suddenly changing direction in mid-ocean. My navigational system seemed only a flimsy brain fancy: I had been so long on the same heading that the island must lie ahead, not to the right. I was attacked by panic. Part of me urged, for God's sake, don't make this crazy turn! My muscles wanted to bring the seaplane back onto its old course. "Steady, steady, steady," I told myself aloud. I had to trust my system, for I could not try anything else now, even if I wanted to.'

He made his landfall at both Norfolk and Lord Howe Island before disaster struck. A squall during the night sank the seaplane at its anchorage in the harbour. It seemed a complete write-off, but Chichester would not accept defeat and resolved to rebuild the 'plane and its engine, sending for what parts he needed, even though he had very little experience of the necessary practical mechanics. The wings alone had about 4000 separate wooden struts, some of them no thicker than a pencil. He had to take them to pieces, repair or remake the damaged parts and put them together again. He also had to strip and clean the engine – ironically, the only part to give serious trouble was the brand-new replacement magneto. With the help of the islanders, he took just ten weeks to do it and complete his crossing of the Tasman Sea, staking his life on makeshift repairs.

But this, of course, was only the start of his odyssey. He was determined to fly to Britain across the Pacific and might have if his journey – and very nearly his life – had not been terminated when his 'plane hit some unmarked electricity cables across the mouth of a Japanese harbour.

Back in England he met Sheila. His first marriage had been unhappy and short-lived. His marriage to Sheila, however, was to be the bedrock of all his further achievements. But these were still far away. In 1939 the war intervened, putting a stop to any ideas he, or anyone else, had of adventure. Chichester volunteered for the Royal Air Force but was told that his eyesight was not good enough and he was too old. He refused to be rejected and finally managed to find himself a niche, teaching navigation to flyers.

At the end of the war he started a map publishing business which commanded all his energies until 1953, when he became restless for adventure. He abandoned the idea of flying as being too expensive and now lacking in adventure. He liked the idea of sailing, however, particularly as it was something he could share with his wife and son, Giles. But he had not the temperament of a casual weekend yachtsman. Almost immediately he started racing, first crewing for experienced skippers, but as soon as possible entering his own boat, which he had named *Gipsy Moth II*. At first he had little success but he learnt fast, using his skill and knowledge as a navigator as well as his inventive ingenuity to improve his boat's chances. He was leading a similar life to that of many active, successful businessmen, working hard through the week, then stretching himself at weekends and holidays on the yachting circuit.

But this regime took its toll. Chichester was a worrier over business matters; while decisive, with superb split-second judgement at the controls of a 'plane or helm of his yacht, he could be indecisive when it came to decisions over money or long-term planning. I can sympathise with this seeming contradiction, being very similar in temperament. The world of the sea, air or mountain is wonderfully simple, a place of black and white, or life or death, but the world of commerce, or even everyday life, is so much more complex.

RIGHT Gipsy Moth IV. Note the comparatively fragile vane of the self-steering gear on the stern.

He became very run down and, in 1957, he faced the greatest crisis of his life. A massive cancerous growth was discovered in his lung. His chances of survival seemed slight. The surgeons wanted to operate but Sheila Chichester stood out against it, feeling that it would almost certainly kill him and sensing, perhaps, that even if it did not, it would leave him an invalid. With the help of his family he fought through the illness, going to the very brink of death before the cancerous cells became inactive and he was back on his way on the road to recovery. He commented: 'When I was a boy at home, I used to hear my father pray every Sunday, "From sudden death, good Lord deliver us." This had always puzzled me; sudden death seemed a fine way to go out. Now the meaning seemed clear, the prayer should read, "From death before we are ready to die, good Lord deliver us."'

As soon as he finished a short convalescence he started crewing for fellow yachtsmen as navigator, but during his illness he had seen a notice on the board of the Royal Ocean Racing Club, proposing a single-handed race across the Atlantic. This immediately appealed to him as having all the right ingredients, the huge scale of the challenge, the need for innovation and the fact that it was for an individual solo effort. He instinctively knew from his flying days that he functioned best working by himself. Later, in *Alone Across the Atlantic*, he wrote: 'Somehow I never seemed to enjoy so much doing things with other people. I know now I don't do a thing nearly as well when with someone. It makes me think I was cut out for solo jobs and any attempt to diverge from that lot only makes me half a person. It looks as if the only way to be happy is to do fully what you are destined for.'

Already, he had on the stocks a new boat, *Gipsy Moth III*, which was bigger and faster than his previous one, and just thirty-two months after being taken ill, only fifteen from a shaky convalescence, he was on the start line with three other boats. At the age of fifty-eight, when most other men have long before slowed up, he was about to enter the most exacting race that had ever been devised. Pushing himself and his boat to the limit, using his cunning as a navigator and his ingenuity in designing the solo sailing devices, particularly his self-steering gear, Miranda, he won the race in forty and a half days.

Most men would have been content with such a record, but not Chichester; convinced that he could improve on it, he did not want to wait for the next trans-Atlantic race and, in 1962, set out on his own to try to beat his own record, cutting it down to thirty-three days fifteen hours. He was already looking for other challenges and it was at this stage that he started thinking of circumnavigating the globe on the old clipper trail. In 1964 he entered the trans-Atlantic race once again but, although he broke his own record by coming in a few minutes short of thirty days, he was beaten by the outstanding French sailor, Eric Tabarly. *Gipsy Moth III* was now just four years old, while Tabarly's boat was very much lighter and had been specially designed for the race, but more than this, Tabarly – besides being a superb sailor – was a very much younger man and single-handed racing is a ferociously strenuous game, demanding not only skill but also tremendous stamina. After this race Chichester saw, perhaps, that he could no longer compete with a rising generation of experienced sailors in this particular field, but he was already one step in front of it with his plans to circumnavigate the globe, thus confirming not just his ability but also his position as a great innovator and pioneer.

Chichester's aim was almost unbelievably ambitious; in wanting to race the clippers round the world, he was taking on three- or four-masted boats of up to 300 feet in length with crews of over forty. A fast time for a clipper was around a hundred days. To equal this Chichester would have to sail around 137.5 miles a day, averaging six knots, day and night throughout the voyage to Sydney. To do this, he wanted an even bigger and faster boat than *Gipsy Moth III*; she would have to be robust enough to face the ferocious seas of the Southern Ocean and yet be a craft which he, now aged sixty-five, could handle on his own.

Speed in a yacht is determined by the length of the boat on the waterline, combined of course with the design of the hull and its sail area. *Gipsy Moth III* had been built while he was ill, practically without supervision, and, but for a few almost inevitable teething problems, she had proved an excellent boat of which Chichester had been very fond. His new boat, *Gipsy Moth IV*, suffered perhaps from over-supervision, with the ideas of the designer, John Illingworth, and those of Chichester at times coming into conflict.

The whole project was obviously going to cost a great deal of money – more than Chichester could afford to pay out of his own pocket. He was grateful, therefore, when his cousin, Lord Dulverton, offered to pay for the boat. There were changes and modifications throughout, and as a result it took longer to build, cost considerably more than had been planned and even when it was launched finally, in the spring of 1966, only a few months before he was due to sail, there seemed to be some serious faults. At the launch, several things went wrong; the bottle of champagne, swung by his wife Sheila, did not break on first impact, the boat stuck on the launching ramp and Chichester had to leap down to give it a push to make sure it slid down the greased way and then, when it hit the water, in Chichester's words, 'There, the hull floated high on the surface; she didn't look right. Then, two or three tiny ripples from a ferry steamer made folds in the glassy surface, and *Gipsy Moth IV* rocked fore and aft. "My God," Sheila and I said to each other, "she's a rocker!"'

They barely had time enough left to correct her tendency to rock and heel or to sort out all the other problems, some of which appeared to have been fundamental to the design of the boat. Chichester describes all these troubles at length in his book *Gipsy Moth Circles the World* and grumbled about them at the time, earning a fair amount of criticism from both friends and the press for what, at times, sounded like peevish recrimination. On the other hand, one needs to understand how he must have felt, trying to combat these faults on his own over a long period, across thousands of miles of storm-wracked ocean.

He was ready to sail from Plymouth on August 27th 1966. Sheila, his son Giles and a close friend had crewed the boat with him from London to Plymouth; they sailed with him out into the harbour and were taken off by boat. Left on his own, he tacked up and down behind the start line, competitive as always, determined to cross the line the very moment the start-gun fired, even though he was racing against no-one but himself and the voyage ahead was over 14,000 miles.

At sixty-five, despite age and his struggle against illness, he was extraordinarily fit and trim. He had become a vegetarian, mainly to combat arthritis, and regularly undertook yoga-based exercises, becoming a great believer in the benefits of standing on his head. Chichester was only around five foot nine and yet, because he was lithe and thin and wiry and through the sheer vibrant energy of his personality, he gave the impression of being a much taller man, with his strong face, firm jaw, thin lips that almost vanished when he smiled and prominent nose, framed by glasses. A laconic, dry sense of humour made him good company. I only met him once, when he took me out to lunch in 1972; he wanted to learn as much as possible about the climber's use of jumar clamps in climbing a rope. He thought he might be able to use them to climb his mast, if he had to do any work on it. He was a delightful host but it was easy to see the single-minded determination below the surface. It was that of someone who would use anyone and anything to the full to achieve his objectives and, of course, without this drive he would not have achieved a fraction of what he had done in a uniquely full life.

As he set sail from Plymouth there were no regrets and few doubts. He was used to being alone – indeed he welcomed it. Very matter-of-factly he had got down to the business of solitary sailing. The key challenge of the voyage was the empty windswept seas of the Southern Ocean and, in a way, the run down the Atlantic was a time to shake down, to sort out problems, work out systems, even to get one's sea legs. During the first few days Chichester suffered from sea-sickness. At the same time, being in the shipping lanes, he had the constant worry of being run down by an unobservant merchant ship, one of the greatest hazards of the yachtsman, particularly a solitary one. In a normal race *Gipsy Moth IV* would have had a crew of six, taking turns to sleep, change the sails, run watches, cook the meals and take care of the endless round of minor repairs and maintenance that beset any yacht being driven hard.

BELOW An intensely competitive man, Francis Chichester was sixty-five and already had a reputation as a 'thirties solo long-distance flyer, when he followed up winning the first Observer single-handed Atlantic race with the idea of racing the clipper ships round the world.

Chichester was racing himself on the longest race that anyone had ever undertaken, intensely aware of each day's progress, setting himself targets that he was determined to attain. fifty-one days out, he reached the latitude of the Roaring Forties, the great Southern Ocean where the winds, uninterrupted by land, are spun by the revolution of the earth in a westerly direction and the seas are driven up by the winds into fifty-foot waves. It is a watery wilderness of chill winds and rain, of successive depressions that carry violent storms, where there is very little let-up for a solitary yachtsman. This is where the stress to man and boat is at its most acute. With day after day of high seas everything becomes damp; there is no opportunity for drying out sleeping bags and the only way to dry out one's clothes is to go to bed wearing

ABOVE To get the best from the boat the sailor must constantly check the trim of the sails and make minor adjustments to the course, even in a steady wind.

them, still damp, and dry them by one's own body heat. On wild nights the solo sailor usually goes to bed fully clad in oilskins, to avoid the delay of getting dressed each time some emergency summons him on deck through the night. The boat itself is permanently heeled, when it isn't being tossed all over the place by squall or storm. There is little or no relaxation, rarely an uninterrupted sleep of more than a few hours, the agony of time and time again forcing oneself out of the comparative warmth of a damp sleeping bag, into the savage wind, spray and rain of a pitch-black night to adjust sails, to put the boat back on course. This means stumbling across a bucking deck in the dark, waves smashing in from all sides, struggling with ropes and winches, clearing fouled yards with numbed fingers.

Chichester wrote:

'I was fagged out and I grew worried by fits of intense depression. Often I could not stand up without hanging on to some support and I wondered if I had something wrong with my balancing nerves. I felt weak, thin and somehow wasted, and I had a sense of immense loneliness and a feeling of hopelessness, as if faced with imminent doom. On November 5th I found that I could not stand on my legs without support, just as if I had emerged from hospital after three months in bed. I was exhausted after a long struggle with the radio on the previous evening, and a long-drawn battle with the mainsail during the night finished me off. Then I thought, "Husky young men on fully-crewed yachts during an ocean race of a few days have been known to collapse from sheer exhaustion. I have been doing this single-handed for more than two months. Is it any wonder that I feel exhausted?" That cheered me up a bit, and I made two resolutions: firstly to try to relax and take some time off during the day; secondly to eat more nourishing food.'

He managed to keep going through a combination of determination and self-discipline, but the boat's gear was now beginning to fall apart. One of the most important pieces of equipment, and certainly the most fragile, is the self-steering. This is a small vane or even sail, usually at the stern, which is either linked to the rudder itself or sometimes to a small extra rudder, which reacts to any change of course the boat takes to bring it back onto its original heading in relation to the wind; it enables the solitary yachtsman to get some sleep at night, to work on maintenance jobs during the day and even to relax occasionally to read a book. It is not the complete panacea, however, and to get the best from the boat the sailor must constantly check the trim of the sails and make minor adjustments to the course, even in a steady wind. Chichester's self-steering gear was slightly damaged in the first storm to hit him in the Roaring Forties and, some days later, was completely destroyed – an experience shared by almost all single-handed circumnavigators. It was a grim moment for Chichester:

'The sight of the self-steering gear broken beyond repair acted like a catalyst. At first I turned cold inside and my feelings, my spirit, seemed to freeze and sink inside me. I had a strange feeling that my personality was split and I was watching myself drop the sails efficiently and lift out the broken gear coolly. My project was killed. Not only was my plan to race a hundred days to Sydney shattered, but to take a non-stop passage there was impossible too. Then I found that I was not really crestfallen; it was a relief. I realised that I had been waiting for this to happen for a long time.'

He altered course to head for Fremantle, Western Australia, and started to adjust his tackle to try to make the boat sail on its own without the self-steering. On November 17th his resolve returned. His habitual ingenuity had, at least partly, solved the problem. He swung the boat back on course for Sydney. He realised that now he had little hope of reaching his target of a hundred days, but he came extraordinarily close to it, pulling into Sydney harbour on December 12th to find a hero's welcome on his 107th day.

The first part of his journey was over. He had made both the longest and fastest ever non-stop, single-handed voyage. But it had taken a severe toll; he was undoubtedly weakened and tired, both physically and mentally. He was very sensitive about two pictures taken on his arrival in Sydney, one of him embracing his son, Giles, who towered over him, making him look like a frail old man in tears, and another of him seeming to be helped by a policeman off the boat. As a result of these there was a strong outcry both in the press and from close friends. Lord Dulverton, the principal owner of the *Gipsy Moth IV*, sent a telegram urging him to abandon his circumnavigation, newspaper columnists and prominent members of the yachting world foretold doom but Chichester, although needled by the constant sniping, was determined to go on. To this end he had the boat completely overhauled, altered the shape of the keel, increasing its weight and changing the stowage.

After seven weeks he set out from Sydney on January 29th with a boat that was improved. Both he and his boat were put to the test all too soon. A tropical storm was forecast in the Tasman Sea, but this had not deterred him. He was buffeted throughout the day by violent winds and mounting seas, and was feeling queasy from what, at the time, he thought was sea-sickness, though later decided was the after-effects of Australian champagne. As a result he could not bring himself to secure with a rope the net carrying his two big genoa sails, which were stowed amidships. He fled below from the bucking deck, took off his oilskins and lay down on the bunk, the only way of withstanding the violent rocking of the boat. Switching off the light he dropped off into the fitful sleep of the sailor who, rather like a wild animal, probably always has some level of consciousness to detect any change in the state of the boat. He did not hear the huge wave which must have hit the boat, but was conscious of her rolling over. It just did not stop.

'I said to myself, "Over she goes!" I was not frightened, but intensely alert and curious.'

This is the sensation shared, I think, by most people in the actual moment of disaster; I have had the same feeling in a climbing fall, with a flash of curiosity wondering what it will be like when I hit the ground. Most of us feel fear, but this is usually in anticipation of danger rather than at the time of disaster. Then, there is no time for it; there is even an excitement in getting out of the situation. Chichester describes his own response:

'Then a lot of crashing and banging started, and my head and shoulders were being bombarded by crockery and cutlery and bottles. I had an oppressive feeling of the boat being on top of me. I wondered if she would roll over completely and what the damage would be; but she came up quietly the same side that she had gone down. I reached up and put my bunk light on. It worked, giving me a curious feeling of something normal in a world of utter chaos. I have only a confused idea of what I did for the next hour or so. I had an absolutely hopeless feeling when I looked at the pile of jumbled up food and gear all along the cabin. Anything that was in my way when I wanted to move I think I put back in its right place, though feeling as I did so that it was a waste of time as she would probably go over again. The cabin was two foot deep all along with a jumbled-up pile of hundreds of tins, bottles, tools, shackles, blocks, two sextants and oddments. Every settee locker, the whole starboard bunk, and the three starboard drop lockers had all emptied out when she was upside down. Water was swishing about on the cabin sole beside the chart table, but not much. I looked into the bilge which is five feet deep, but it was not quite full, for which I thought, "Thank God."'

I am sure Chichester's approach to the shambles to which his boat had been reduced and the danger of another capsize, was as matter-of-fact as his description. On deck, most important of all, he found that his mast was still standing with the rigging undamaged, mainly because he had taken down all the sails before turning in that night. A monohull boat, when rolled over by waves or wind, will always right itself because of the weight of ballast and that of the keel; the real danger, though, is that the mast might break, particularly if there is any sail set. There is also the danger that the dog house, coach roof or hatches might be smashed, laying the boat open to the waves. Fortunately, in Chichester's case, there was no damage and his only loss was one of the genoa sails and some lengths of rope he had failed to tie down the night before.

The wind was still howling through the rigging, the seas mountainous, but he was desperately tired and realised he needed to conserve his energies. He decided, therefore, 'To Hell with everything', went down below, cleared the mess of cutlery, plates and bottles from his bunk, snuggled down into the soaking wet bedding, fully dressed in his oilskins, and fell into a deep sleep, not waking until it was broad daylight.

When he awoke the wind was still gusting at between forty and fifty-five knots but he set to, first checking the boat for serious structural damage and then starting the appalling task of clearing up the mess. Although only two days out, it never occurred to him to return to Sydney or call in at a New Zealand port. Damage to the boat was superficial and, remarkably, the self-steering gear had survived the capsize, though the socket for the vane shaft was very nearly off. He fixed this, however, without too much trouble and sailed on, north of New Zealand, heading for Cape Horn.

There were more crises, falls and minor injuries, the constant wear and tear to his own sixty-five-year-old frame and that of his boat. There were more storms, but none as dangerous as that of the Tasman Sea and when, at last, he reached the Horn – the most notorious place for storms anywhere in the world – it was almost an anticlimax. The seas were big and the wind strong, but they were nothing to some of the seas that Chichester had had to face It was also positively crowded compared to the Southern Ocean. The Royal Naval Ice Patrol ship HMS *Protector* had come there to greet him, a tiny Piper Apache chartered by the *Sunday Times* and BBC flew from Tierra del Fuego to film him from the air as his boat, under the storm jib, raced through the white-capped seas of the Horn. In some ways it was a natural focal point of the voyage, a kind of oceanic summit but, like reaching the summit of a mountain, the adventure was by no means over; having got up, you have got to get back down again. In Chichester's case he had a long haul, a good 9000 miles There were more storms, more wear and tear, but he was now heading into kinder climes.

Yet he never stopped competing with himself, never ceased trying to get the very best out of his boat, making runs of up to 188 miles a day, driven on by the winds of the North-East Trades, doing 1215 miles a week. These were records for single-handed sailing, something of which he was intensely aware.

And then, at last, towards the end of May he entered the English Channel and came in to a welcome that is certainly unique in post-war adventure – even greater, perhaps, than that for John Hunt and his party after Everest. It had been announced

BELOW Bowling along in high seas.

ABOVE The constant wear and tear to his own sixty-five-year-old frame and that of his boat.

on his arrival at Sydney that Chichester would receive a knighthood. This honour no more than reflected the huge popular acclaim he had already achieved. He was met by a fleet of boats outside Plymouth; a quarter of a million people watched him sail into the harbour and many millions more saw his arrival on television.

One man who was not there was Donald Crowhurst, a businessman and amateur sailor who had followed Chichester's voyage avidly, had been inspired, as had others, to wonder if he could perhaps cap this achievement by sailing single-handed non-stop round the world. That day Crowhurst chose to go off sailing with a friend in the Bristol Channel. They listened to the commentary of Chichester's arrival on the yacht radio and, perhaps out of envy, chose to belittle and joke about the adulation Chichester was receiving. But the yachting world joined the vast majority of the British public in recognising not just Chichester's achievement but the enormous stature of the man himself. The whole voyage of 29,630 miles had taken just nine months and one day, from Plymouth to Plymouth, of which the sailing time was 226 days.

Chichester was an innovator, one of the greatest ever in the adventure field. It is in no way belittling to the achievements of Ed Hillary and Tenzing to say they achieved what they did on Everest as part of a team, using traditional methods and following practically all the way in the steps of the Swiss team that so nearly reached the summit in 1952; (indeed, it was the Swiss team that broke some of the greatest physical and psychological barriers).

Chichester, on the other hand, brought a completely new concept to small boat sailing, both in terms of distance and speed; he set his own rules, conceived his own challenges and had done so throughout his life, from the days he set up flying records in the 'thirties until this, his crowning glory. His achievement in going round the world on his own with only one stop, faster than any small boat had done so previously, would have been an extraordinary feat for a man of any age; the fact that he was sixty-five made it all the more incredible and certainly increased its public appeal still further.

Chichester undoubtedly enjoyed both the acclaim and the money he was able to make by exploiting his achievement. Several of his friends have mentioned, sometimes wryly, that he was a good self-publicist. Perhaps he was, but I am quite sure that the real drive that spurred him on was not the need to make a name for himself. In Chichester the most important motive seems to have been his intense competitiveness, combined with an adventurous curiosity that was undoubtedly technically orientated. He was not in the least bit interested in the direct physical effort required to climb a mountain or row the Atlantic; he enjoyed working through machines that were still sufficiently simple to have a close and direct contact with the elements, firstly in the open cockpit of the Gipsy Moth and then behind the helm of his yachts.

The competitiveness and curiosity never left him; having circumnavigated the globe he sought other challenges that he, an ageing but indomitable and realistic man, felt he could meet. Once again he created the competition, wrote his own rules and then tried like hell to win. He had a new boat built, *Gipsy Moth V*, which was even bigger than *Gipsy Moth IV* and very much easier to sail. He set himself the challenge of sailing 4000 miles in twenty days, to average 200 miles a day – this in his seventieth year. He didn't quite make it, taking twenty-two and three-tenths days for the run. On the way back across the Atlantic he was hit by a storm as ferocious as any he had encountered in the Southern Ocean; his boat capsized but recovered, and he was able to sail her back to port.

But by now his health was beginning to fail; he was a sick man but, still refusing to give up, he entered for the 1972 trans-Atlantic single-handed race. His agent, George Greenfield, described how at the start he was so weak he could barely climb down a ten-foot ladder from the wharf to his boat. He set sail all the same, in considerable pain, heavily dosed with pain-killing drugs. A short way out into the Atlantic he was involved in a collision with a French weather ship that had come too close. It is not clear what their intentions had been, whether to give him help or whether just out of curiosity, but the collision broke *Gipsy Moth*'s mast and damaged the hull. There was no question of being able to continue the race. His son, Giles, and friend and editor of many of his books, John Anderson, were flown out by Royal Naval helicopter to help him and Giles, with a Royal Naval crew, sailed the boat back to Plymouth.

Chichester went straight into hospital and died shortly afterwards from cancer. His prayer – at least in part – had been answered: 'From death before we are ready to die, good Lord deliver us.'

Few people can have led such a full life.

THREE

Golden Globe

The Contest to be the First Non-Stop Round the World Single-Handed

Robin Knox-Johnston, first officer of the passenger liner *Kenya* berthed at London, watched the arrival of Francis Chichester on television and immediately began to wonder whether it would be possible to sail round the world without a single stop. He analysed his motives for me:

'In a way, it's relatively simple. One: I think there are so few things to do in this world and so many people, that it is rather nice to turn round and say you're the first to do something. Two: I was happy in the Merchant Navy but in some ways frustrated by the fact that while in South Africa I had very briefly commanded a ship and I realised that this would be my future for the next thirty-five years; I also wondered whether it offered enough. I thought I'd get terribly bored. Just looking at my peers, I could see that they were fat and getting fatter, that the job didn't require an awful lot of them and I thought that life should offer more. And thirdly, I heard that Tabarly was building a new trimaran, *Pen Duick IV*, which I thought he must be planning to use to beat Chichester's time round the world. At the time the French were being very arrogant, trying to keep us out of the Common Market, and then when Tabarly had just won the single-handed trans-Atlantic race *Paris Match* had screamed that the Anglo-Saxon ocean had been dominated by the French and that we weren't even a second-rate power – we were third-rate.

'That annoyed me intensely and I felt that if anyone was going to do it, it should be one of us because we wouldn't make the fuss that they would about it.'

And so, with a desire to make his mark and get out of a career which was not entirely satisfactory, combined with a strong, even aggressive, sense of patriotism, Knox-Johnston resolved to sail single-handed around the world.

He had always loved the sea, building his first boat, a raft made from orange boxes, at the age of seven. This sank the moment he climbed onto it. He was the eldest of a family of four boys and one girl; his father worked in a shipping office before the war and took an active part in local government, becoming mayor of Beckenham. They were a typical well-to-do suburban family, with all the boys going to public school.

Knox-Johnston, almost from the very beginning, wanted to go to sea. The Royal Navy was his first choice but he failed the physics paper in the entrance exam for Dartmouth, could not bring himself to sit again and therefore opted for the Merchant Navy, joining the British India Steam Navigation Company's cadet ship, *Chindwara* as

an officer cadet. The cadets worked the ship as seaman and, at the same time, received the theoretical and technical training they were going to need as Merchant Navy officers. It gave Knox-Johnston the basic grounding that was going to be so useful to him as a lone sailor. A vast fund of restless, exuberant energy led him into running races up Table Mountain, scuba diving and playing in a ship-board group which was very popular at all the ports of call, particularly in South Africa.

He met Sue in England and they married on completion of his cadetship before going out to Bombay where he was to be based for the next four years, running pilgrims and cargo to the Persian Gulf. He thoroughly enjoyed his work as third officer and filled his leisure time swimming and scuba diving in the clear seas of the Gulf. He even thought of building a dhow, but was dissuaded because it would have been very difficult to sell; finally he decided to go in with a fellow-officer to build an ocean-going family cruiser that they could use both as a base for skin diving and to sail back to England. They wrote off to a firm in Poole, Dorset, for a set of plans and, though the design was old-fashioned, Knox-Johnston liked the look of it; it was obviously very robust. He also had good materials to work with, for Indian teak, one of the finest boat materials known, was readily available. Rigging plans had not been included; these were an extra, so Knox-Johnston, with characteristic ingenuity, designed his own. The boat was built by Indian craftsmen using the traditional tools and methods with which the old eighteenth-century ships of the line had been built. Knox-Johnston named her *Suhaili*, the name given by Arab seamen in the Persian Gulf to the south-east wind.

LEFT Chay Blyth could not resist entering once he heard John Ridgway was competing, even though he had never sailed before, knew nothing about navigation and had to borrow a boat even less suited than Ridgway's.

LEFT John Ridgway had intended entering for the 1968 Atlantic single-handed race, but changed his mind after Francis Chichester's successful circumnavigation had thrown down the gauntlet, even though English Rose IV was not entirely suited to the longer voyage.

FAR LEFT Donald Crowhurst – winning would solve everything.

She was not a modern-looking, streamlined boat; her jib boom, broad beam and the square-cut raised cabin gave her a homely, old-fashioned but very durable appearance. She was not finished until September 1965, too late for the North-East Monsoon which would have driven her across the Indian Ocean to the coast of Africa. Knox-Johnston had to return to Britain anyway, to sit the examination for his Master's Ticket and fulfil his Royal Naval Reserve service. In addition, his personal life was a mess; his marriage had broken up and his wife had returned to Britain. It was not until the following year that he, his brother and a friend returned to Bombay and sailed *Suhaili* back, with a long stop in South Africa where they all took on jobs to replenish funds. He sailed non-stop from Cape Town to Gravesend, thus confirming *Suhaili*'s seaworthiness and also the excellence of her balance. *Suhaili* could be sailed for long periods close hauled with very little attention.

Knox-Johnston was not a yachting man, had done practically no racing and comparatively little messing about in small boats, but he was a professional seaman who, through his down-to-earth apprenticeship, knew every aspect of the job at sea in a way that he would not have had he gone to Dartmouth and risen up through the ranks of the Royal Navy. His long-distance sail from Bombay to London had also given him the kind of practical experience that he was going to need to get round the world.

Even so, having decided to try a non-stop single-handed circumnavigation, he found it difficult, as a completely unknown Merchant Navy officer, to convince potential sponsors. Ideally he wanted a new and bigger boat made from steel, but to pay for it he needed £5,000. He tried to sell *Suhaili* but there were no buyers; she was, perhaps, too old-fashioned in appearance. He wrote over fifty letters to various firms asking for sponsorship but without success. He even applied to his own company for support but, although they had a warm respect for his ability and sympathy for the project, the board refused, telling him that times were hard. Knox-Johnston would not give in, however, and resolved to attempt his circumnavigation in *Suhaili*. At least he knew all of her foibles and she had even touched the Roaring Forties around the Cape of Good Hope.

Knox-Johnston was not the only person to be inspired by Chichester's achievement. By the end of 1967 at least five sailors were planning the voyage. The most advanced in his plans was Commander Bill King, an ex-submarine skipper with plenty of good contacts in the ocean-racing world. He already had sponsorship from the *Daily* and *Sunday Express* and in close consultation with Blondie Hasler, the Daddy of the trans-Atlantic solo races and pioneer of self-steering gear, was having built a specially-designed boat with a streamlined deck surface and revolutionary junk rig. The two masts were self-supporting without any stays, with a single big square sail to each. This makes it easier to sail single-handed, but imposes a great deal of strain on the mast. At this stage King undoubtedly seemed to be one of the favourites.

But the most serious contender was Bernard Moitessier, a lean almost frail-looking man of forty-three, with the gaunt features of an ascetic which were lightened by a warm smile betraying an impish sense of humour. Born in Saigon, he had spent all his early years in the Far East, most of them at sea in small sailing boats, at first traditional cargo-carrying junks and later in boats he had built himself, wandering, a vagabond of the sea, across the Pacific and Indian Oceans. Having sailed with his wife from Tahiti to the coast of Portugal, a voyage of 14,212 miles, he already held the long distance record for small boats. He was not obsessively competitive in the way that Chichester was. Moitessier was a romantic adventurer who loved the sea with an intense, almost mystical passion. It was the thought of committing himself and his boat to this gigantic voyage of over 30,000 miles, to be alone in the oceans with the wind and the restless sea, that attracted him more than the idea of establishing a record. Publicity was a painful means of getting the money he needed for the voyage. Like Knox-Johnston, he was planning to use his own, well-tried boat, but *Joshua*, named after Joshua Slocum, was eminently better suited to the voyage than *Suhaili*; she was bigger, had a welded steel hull, which Knox-Johnston had wanted, and was built for both speed and strength.

John Ridgway had no trouble in getting sponsorship. He was still a celebrity, a name that the press could recognise, that manufacturers could use to promote their products. In 1966 he and Chay Blyth had made a name for themselves by being the first to row the Atlantic in his Cape Cod dory, *English Rose III*. Originally Ridgway had intended to enter the 1968 Atlantic single-handed race and had been promised a boat for this; with Chichester's successful circumnavigation, he changed his mind, but for a time used the single-handed race as a cover to keep his own plans secret. He did confide in Chay Blyth, however, never thinking that this one-time partner might become a competitor. Ridgway and Blyth had been a wonderful partnership on their

Atlantic row, but afterwards the publicity, the pressures of money and ego took their toll in a way that so often happens when the spotlight goes on the world of shared adventure. Team spirit had given way to rivalry. Blyth's spirit of competition was immediately kindled when he heard that Ridgway was entering the Atlantic single-handed race. He told me: 'For Christ's sake, knowing John as I did then, if he could do this thing, there was absolutely no way in the world that I could not.'

This sense of competition was probably kindled by the stress that had already entered their relationship, with Ridgway getting the lion's share of attention after their rowing the Atlantic. At this stage Blyth did not have a boat, had never sailed before and knew nothing of navigation, but with the same dogged but practical determination that he had rowed the Atlantic, he started preparing for the voyage, getting the loan of a production model thirty-foot family cruiser, *Dytiscus III*. Then, when he learned that Ridgway had changed his objective to a solo circumnavigation, he did so as well. Ridgway felt a great sense of betrayal, partly because he thought Blyth should have told him earlier, but there also seems to have been a feeling that Blyth had broken a partnership – even though Ridgway was doing this equally on his own account.

Donald Crowhurst, who had been so scathing about Chichester's reception, had also entered the lists. A keen weekend sailor with his own boat, he was certainly more experienced than Chay Blyth, but he had never exposed himself to the levels of risk and hardship that Blyth had known both on the Atlantic and in the course of his work in the Parachute Regiment. Crowhurst was thirty-five, happily married and the father of four young children. He was born in India where his father had worked on the railways, but they returned to Britain at the time of Independence, when the family went through the painful process of transition faced by so many ex-colonial families. Donald Crowhurst was doing moderately well at Loughborough College when he was forced to leave after getting his school certificate, his father having died of a heart attack and his mother being desperately hard-up. He joined the RAF and continued his studies in electrical engineering at Farnborough Technical College, eventually learning to fly and getting a commission.

The story could have been the same as that of Ridgway – or, for that matter, myself – but in Crowhurst there was always a need to be the centre of attention, to seem to be the daring leader of practical jokes, of wild pranks, racing round in souped-up cars (he owned a Lagonda for a time, until he smashed it). The adventure was superficial, of the bar-room variety. One of Crowhurst's pranks led to him being asked to leave the RAF, so he went into the Army, was commissioned, but continued to lead the same sort of life. He lost his licence for a variety of driving offences and was finally caught trying to borrow someone's car without their permission. This led to the resignation of his commission.

Shortly after this he met Clare, an attractive dark-haired Irish girl who was captivated by his whirlwind courtship and mercurial personality. They got married and, after a number of unsatisfactory jobs in electronics, settled in Bridgwater, Somerset, where he set up in business manufacturing electronic aids for yachts on the South Devon coast. He had excellent ideas, but was less adept at putting them

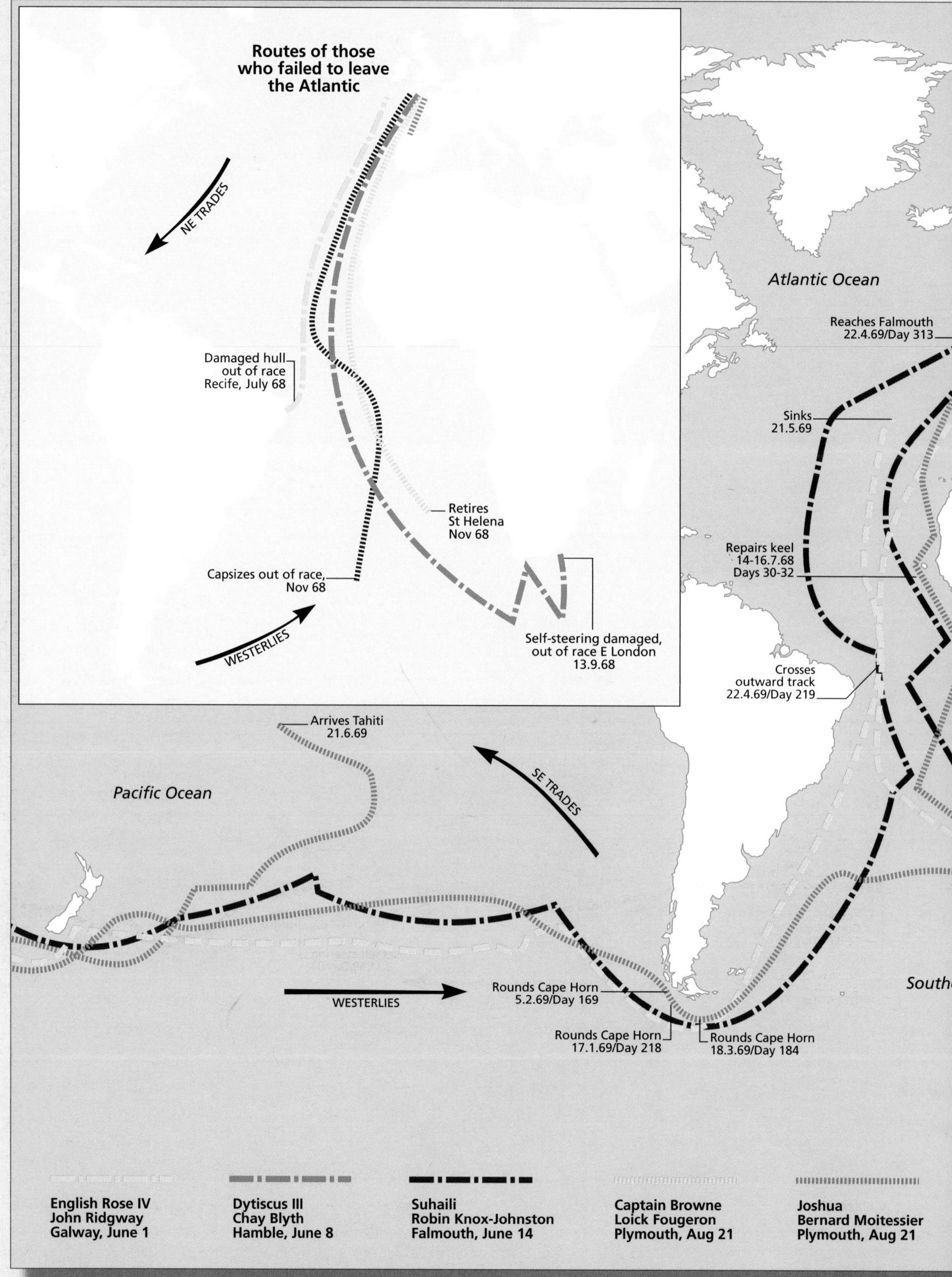
Routes of those who failed to leave the Atlantic
NE TRADES
Damaged hull out of race Recife, July 68
Retires St Helena Nov 68
Capsizes out of race, Nov 68
WESTERLIES
Self-steering damaged, out of race E London 13.9.68
Atlantic Ocean
Reaches Falmouth 22.4.69/Day 313
Sinks 21.5.69
Repairs keel 14-16.7.68 Days 30-32
Crosses outward track 22.4.69/Day 219
Arrives Tahiti 21.6.69
Pacific Ocean
SE TRADES
WESTERLIES
Rounds Cape Horn 5.2.69/Day 169
Rounds Cape Horn 17.1.69/Day 218
Rounds Cape Horn 18.3.69/Day 184
Southe
English Rose IV
John Ridgway
Galway, June 1
Dytiscus III
Chay Blyth
Hamble, June 8
Suhaili
Robin Knox-Johnston
Falmouth, June 14
Captain Browne
Loick Fougeron
Plymouth, Aug 21
Joshua
Bernard Moitessier
Plymouth, Aug 21

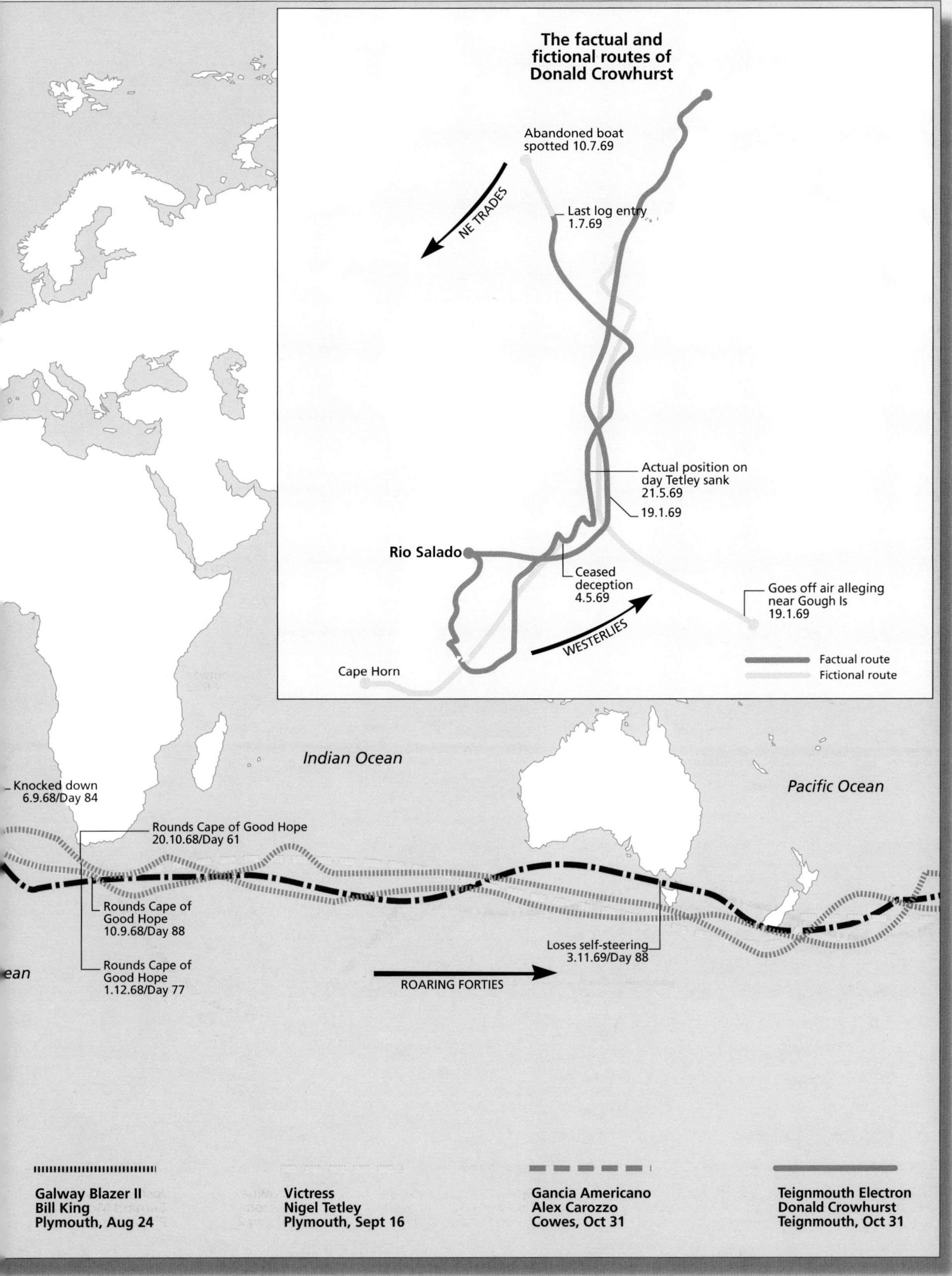
The factual and fictional routes of Donald Crowhurst
Abandoned boat spotted 10.7.69
NE TRADES
Last log entry 1.7.69
Actual position on day Tetley sank 21.5.69
19.1.69
Rio Salado
Ceased deception 4.5.69
Goes off air alleging near Gough Is 19.1.69
WESTERLIES
Cape Horn
Factual route
Fictional route
Indian Ocean
Pacific Ocean
Knocked down 6.9.68/Day 84
Rounds Cape of Good Hope 20.10.68/Day 61
Rounds Cape of Good Hope 10.9.68/Day 88
Rounds Cape of Good Hope 1.12.68/Day 77
Loses self-steering 3.11.69/Day 88
ROARING FORTIES
ean
Galway Blazer II
Bill King
Plymouth, Aug 24
Victress
Nigel Tetley
Plymouth, Sept 16
Gancia Americano
Alex Carozzo
Cowes, Oct 31
Teignmouth Electron
Donald Crowhurst
Teignmouth, Oct 31

through and by 1967 his small company, Electron Utilisation, was very nearly bankrupt. The challenge of sailing round the world, therefore, was immensely attractive on several levels. He enjoyed pottering about in his boat; still more, he loved the grand gesture, the boast of out-sailing Chichester round the world; also, it seemed to present a wonderful solution to the vexing and dreary problems besetting him in his business. Once he had been round the world there would be plenty of acclaim and money; people really would sit up and take notice. At the time it appeared to be an attractive way out of all his tribulations.

But at the moment he was unknown and had a packet of debts. His first idea was to approach the Cutty Sark Trust, who were planning to put *Gipsy Moth IV* on permanent display alongside the famous clipper *Cutty Sark* at Greenwich. Crowhurst suggested that it was a waste of a good boat to mount it in concrete, when she could be immortalised still further by a non-stop circumnavigation of the world, and he offered to charter her for a fee of £5,000. He bombarded the Trust with letters, approached Lord Dulverton, the owner, and when he proved unresponsive lobbied through the yachting press, getting a great deal of support for his request; but the Trust remained adamant and he did not get the boat. Chichester was consulted at this stage and made some enquiries about Crowhurst's sailing background, quickly discovering that he had no real ocean-sailing experience and was little more than a competent off-shore yachtsman. Crowhurst was undeterred, however, and continued to seek a boat and sponsorship.

The idea of sailing around the world non-stop had been a natural evolution inspired by Chichester's voyage, but perhaps it was inevitable that, once it became obvious that several sailors wanted to make the voyage, someone should try to turn it into a race. Robin Knox-Johnston, through his agent, George Greenfield, who also represented Francis Chichester, had approached the *Sunday Times* for sponsorship for the voyage. The editor, Harold Evans, stalled in giving a reply, having already heard that Knox-Johnston was not the only one planning to make the attempt. Murray Sayle, a swashbuckling Australian journalist who had handled the Chichester story for the *Sunday Times*, was told to have a look at the field and report back on who was most likely to succeed. He came up with 'Tahiti Bill' Howell, an Australian dentist with a good ocean-racing record who was planning to enter the *Observer* single-handed Atlantic race and then continue round the world. In the event, he abandoned the round-the-world project. Of all the contestants Sayle dismissed Knox-Johnston with his slow old boat, his down-to-earth modest manner and lack of sailing experience as the least likely to win.

It was at this stage that the *Sunday Times* decided to declare it a race, thus ensuring that, as race organisers, they would automatically get good coverage of all the contestants whether or not they had bought their exclusive stories. Their main worry was that the sailors who had already made their plans, and in some cases were sponsored by rival newspapers, might not want to play the *Sunday Times'* game. Features editor, Ron Hall, and Murray Sayle found an ingenious solution to the problem. For a start they did not require a formal entry into the race, merely laying down that departure and return should be recorded – as it inevitably would be – by a national newspaper or magazine. Boats could, therefore, set out from where and when they liked. But because it was felt dangerous to encourage anyone to arrive in the Southern Ocean before the end of the southern winter, or not to be past Cape Horn before the beginning of the following winter, starting dates were restricted to between June 1st and October 31st 1968. Obviously, the boats which set out earliest would have the best chance of getting round first, even though they might not make it in the fastest time. It was decided, therefore, to have two prizes – a trophy which was to be the Golden Globe, for the first round, and a cash prize of £5,000 for the fastest time. This would also have the attraction of extending interest in the race even after the first entrant had got home.

In the event, all the sailors tacitly accepted the race, though some were more influenced than others by the rules imposed by the race organisers. It raises the question of where adventure ends and organised competition takes over, of whether the quality of the experience was enhanced by the introduction of a formal race, admittedly with a very loose set of rules. There had been an element of a race already, since each person setting out to sail round the world non-stop wanted to be the first to do it. The situation is similar, in mountaineering terms, to the desire of climbers to be the first to achieve a particularly difficult climb. The media delighted in describing the race as 'the Mount Everest of sailing'. In the field of mountaineering, however, a direct race for the summit is barely practicable and, anyway, in expedition terms the Himalayan countries have not until recently allowed more than one expedition on any one route up a mountain at the same time. The situation can arise, however. In 1963 I was a member of a team that made the first ascent of the Central Tower of Paine, a granite tower in South Patagonia. After we had been there for about two months, having made very little progress, an Italian team who had the same objective arrived at the foot of the mountain. What evolved was undeniably a race to get to the top first, which I am glad to say we won.

There is, however, a long tradition of ocean racing, and there was certainly every ingredient of adventure in an attempt to sail single-handed non-stop round the world. The element of racing would add still further stress, for each man would need to push his boat to the utmost, yet if he pushed too hard the boat might not last the course. The test was to prove a harsh one.

first off the mark was John Ridgway, in *English Rose IV*. For sentimental reasons he wanted to start from the Aran Islands, his landfall when he rowed the Atlantic. He set out on the earliest date possible, June 1st, acutely aware that his thirty-foot sloop would need all the time he could get to beat the bigger boats which were to set out later on in the summer. Things went wrong from the start. Both the BBC and ITN had sent out camera crews to film his departure. The BBC launch nearly crashed into his stern, threatening the vital self-steering gear. Ridgway, nerves stretched, screamed abuse at them and they veered off, but then the trawler carrying the ITN crew swung in close to get a final telling shot, misjudged it and smashed into the starboard side, splintering the wooden rubbing strip that protected the hull itself. It was impossible to see if there was any structural damage, but Ridgway had a terrible feeling of ill-omen waving for the last time to his wife, Marie Christine, as the trawler swung away.

Chay Blyth had sent Ridgway a telegram 'LAST ONE HOME'S A CISSY. WHO CARES WHO WINS?' It was a conciliatory gesture, but both knew that they cared very much who got home first. Blyth set sail a week later on *Dytiscus III*. He had tried for sponsorship but his lack of sailing experience stood against him.

'They always brought in some retired naval officer,' he told me, 'and then asked very intricate questions about navigation and, of course, I had no idea at all. They'd then ask intricate questions about sailing and I wouldn't know the answers to those either. The interviews always came to an abrupt halt.'

But he had persevered, using most of the profits from his row across the Atlantic to finance the voyage. He learnt navigation at night and had a fortnight's sailing instruction, though he reckoned that in the end it amounted to little more than four days' actual practical experience. His replies to the queries of reporters about his motives and attitudes were down-to-earth:

'Out there it's all black and white. I'm not particularly fond of the sea, it's just a question of survival. I may come back as queer as a nine-bob note. But one day Saint Peter will say to me, "What did you do?" and I'll tell him. He'll say, "What did you do?" and you'll say, "I was a reporter."'

But he set out full of confidence, certain that he could beat at least one man – his old mate Ridgway.

Six days later Robin Knox-Johnston set sail from Falmouth in *Suhaili*. His little group of sponsors from the *Sunday Mirror* and the publishers Cassell, had come down to see him off. They had become a close-knit team, very confident in their man,

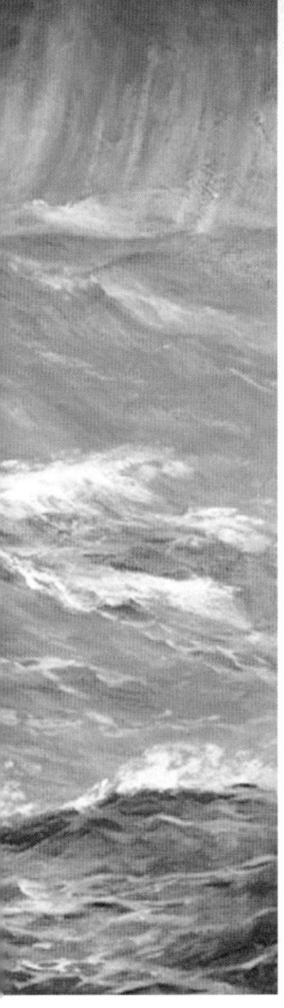

ABOVE 'I heard rather than saw this giant wave and climbed the rigging to avoid being swept away. For one brief inglorious moment there was me and two masts in sight and nothing but ocean in any direction for 2000 miles.' This painting of *Suhaili* was commissioned by Robin Knox-Johnston to show the most dramatic event of the entire voyage which could not possibly have been photographed.

Knox-Johnston, who had submitted to a going-over by a psychiatrist and been judged 'distressingly normal'. He was sure that even though his boat was not fast enough to make the quickest circumnavigation he would most certainly get round. He also displayed a healthy aggressiveness when, irritated by a *Sunday Times* reporter, he threatened to throw him into the harbour. It is unlikely that Knox-Johnston would have allowed any of the media's boats to get close enough to collide with him as he sailed for the line outside Falmouth harbour.

It would be over two months before anyone else set sail, but these three contestants needed all the time they could get if they were to stay ahead of the bigger and faster boats that were to set out later on in the season. They settled down in their different ways to the long run in down the Atlantic which provides the introduction to the rigours of the Southern Ocean.

John Ridgway found the solitude difficult to cope with, becoming almost obsessively worried about the damage done in the collision at the start as he sailed past Madeira, and then on down over the Equator into the Southern Atlantic. The boat slammed into the swell, juddering with the impact of each wave. Ridgway had already noticed some hairline cracks in the deck around the after shroud plate, which held one of the stays; but now the deck around it was bulging while the cracks opened and closed, bubbling spray. If it should pull away, the mast would probably go as well; not a pleasant prospect in the empty reaches of the Southern Atlantic. Even more serious, his wireless transmitter had failed so that there was no chance of calling for help. He did his best to repair the damage, replacing and strengthening the plate, but the deck continued to bulge ominously and the prospects of entering the Southern Ocean with a damaged boat, without wireless communication, became increasingly intimidating. At last, on July 16th, some 600 miles south of the Equator, Ridgway admitted defeat and swung westward for Recife, on the Brazilian coast.

Chay Blyth got further than Ridgway, sailing *Dytiscus III* into the great Southern Ocean round the Cape of Good Hope, but on the way down his self-steering gear was damaged and in order to radio South Africa for spare parts to be sent out from England, he took on some fuel for his generator from a yacht, *Gillian Gaggins*, which he passed near Tristan da Cunha. He reached East London, on the South African coast, on September 13th, to be told that he was disqualified from the race. He replied, 'I don't see how the *Sunday Times* can disqualify me when I never entered the race.' He was determined to go on and, having repaired his self-steering gear, set out into the Southern Ocean.

Quite apart from lacking experience, his boat was not suitable for the huge seas he encountered. He told me:

'The boat was similar to John's in that she had a bilge keel, but mine was much more buoyant in the stern; she was fine until we reached the Roaring Forties. What used to happen was that the buoyancy would lift the arse end up and so she'd go down a wave and start burying her nose. Two things can then happen; you can either pitchpole, which means the boat does a somersault, or you can broach, which means the boat swings ninety degrees to the oncoming wave and is then pushed along sideways and can go right over so that it capsizes. At least with a monohull you always come up again since there is so much weight underneath you.

'Chichester talks about being capsized once; well, I was absolutely hopeless really, hadn't a bloody clue. I capsized three times in one hour and eleven times in a day. And I thought this was part and parcel of sailing – I really did! The boat would go BANG and you'd get thrown all over the place; kit would go everywhere and I'd say, "Geez, that was pretty tough", and then you'd get up. The steering gear went again and then I thought, "You've got to make a decision." And the decision to pack it in is always much worse – I think it's easier to die really. The decision to pack up is bloody terrible.'

Chay Blyth swung back to East London, the second competitor to fail. His greatest triumph was still to come when, in the early 'seventies, he sailed the ketch *British Steel* single-handed non-stop round the world – the wrong way, from east to west against the prevailing winds and currents.

By this time Robin Knox-Johnston, in *Suhaili*, had caught up and passed Blyth. His trip down the Atlantic had been full of event, some of which might easily have forced him out of the race. On the sixteenth day out from Falmouth, on June 30th, he noticed that *Suhaili* was taking in much more water than she should. He got past the Cape Verde Islands, then donned snorkel and flippers and went over the side to discover exactly what was wrong. He found a frightening gap, more than eight feet long, along the seam where the keel was joined on to the hull; it opened and closed as *Suhaili* pitched and rolled in the water. It was easy to imagine what would happen in the ferocious seas of the Southern Ocean.

He swam back to the surface, lit a cigarette and thought out a problem that I suspect would have defeated most of the contestants in the Golden Globe race. He described his repairs in his book, *A World of my Own*.

'Having decided that caulking was the answer, I had to think of some way of doing it five feet below water. Normally dry twisted raw cotton is hammered into the seam, stopped with filling compound and painted over, but I could not do that. I decided to try and do the job with cotton anyway and hope that the fact that it would be wet would not make too much difference. We had had to do just the same thing when in the middle of the Arabian Sea, but it had not been easy, and at least I had had two other people helping me and keeping a lookout for sharks. This time I would have to do the job on my own and hope that I would notice any sharks whilst they were still circling.

'I got out the cotton and twisted up some pieces in 18-inch lengths, a convenient length to handle, although ideally I should have done the job with one piece. Next I put a long length of line on a hammer and lowered it overside near where I had to work. finally I dressed myself in a blue shirt and jeans to hide the whiteness of my body, something that sharks, great scavengers, always associate with refuse, and strapped my knife to my leg. I put the cotton on deck where I could reach it from the water and taking my largest screwdriver as the most convenient caulking instrument, I went overside.

'The job was impossible from the start. In the first place I would run out of breath before I had hammered enough cotton in place to hold it while I surfaced, and each time I came up for air I lost all the work done. Secondly, the cotton was just not going in properly, and even when I changed the screwdriver for a proper caulking iron I made no progress. After half an hour of fruitless effort I climbed back on board and tried to think of some other way of doing the job.

'A while later I was busily engaged in sewing the cotton onto a strip of canvas 1½ inches wide. When the whole strip, about seven feet of it, was completed I gave it a coating of Stockholm Tar and then forced copper tacks through the canvas about six inches apart. I went into the water again and placed the cotton in the seam so that the canvas was on the outside: I then started knocking the tacks into the hull to hold the whole thing in place. The finished job did not look too bad but it was a bit ragged at the edges and I thought that it might be ripped off when the *Suhaili* got moving again, so I decided to tack a copper strip over the canvas to tidy it up. The copper strip was, in fact, left on board by the Marconi engineers when they fitted the new radio and I am afraid that I had not drawn their attention to it when they finished.

'So far, although I had kept glancing nervously about me while I was in the water, I had seen no fish at all. But whilst I was having a coffee break, having prepared the copper strip and made holes for the tacks so that I would have an easier job under water, I suddenly noticed a lean grey shape moving sinuously past the boat. The sharks had found us at last. I watched this one for ten minutes hoping it would go away as I did not want to have to kill it. I was not being kind to the shark; if I killed it, there would be quite a lot of blood in the water and the death convulsions would be picked up by any other sharks near at hand who would immediately rush in, and I would not be able to get the job finished.

'After ten minutes though, during which the shark kept circling the boat and showing no signs of leaving, I got out my rifle and, throwing some sheets of lavatory paper into the water, waited for the shark to come and investigate. On its first run round the shark passed about three feet below the paper, but then he turned and, rising slowly, came in again. I aimed the rifle at the shape and, with finger on the trigger, squeezed the trigger. There was an explosion in the water as the shark's body threshed around but within half a minute the threshing ceased and the lifeless body began slowly to plane down until it disappeared into the blue. For the next half hour I watched carefully to see if any other sharks would appear, but apart from two pilot fish, which, having followed their previous protector down until they realised he would never feed them again, now decided to join a larger and apparently stronger master, *Suhaili* and I had the sea to ourselves. I went overside and in an hour and a half had the copper tacked over the canvas on the port side. A light wind getting up forced me to leave the starboard side until we were next becalmed. But in any case I was quite chilled from four hours' immersion, and also a little tense from constantly glancing round expecting to see a shark coming in behind me, and I was quite glad to give the job a rest for a while.'

Two days later he caulked the other side. Throughout the voyage down the Atlantic he went swimming, showing a confidence and knowledge of the sea that was to help him throughout the trip. He would dive in off the bow and swim as hard as he could, as the boat pulled ahead of him and then, in the nick of time, pull himself up on the stern stanchions. It took fine calculation not to be left alone in the middle of the ocean.

There were other crises. His battery-charging motor failed and he took the magneto to pieces, trying to find the fault. It was only when he came to re-assemble the engine that he realised he had forgotten to bring a feeler gauge for setting the gap between the points. 'I eventually got round this by counting the pages of this book – there are two hundred to the inch, therefore, one page equals 5/thousands. I wanted a gap of between 12-15/ thousands, thus three thicknesses of paper.' And the charging motor worked again.

But there were moments of doubt, when he was tempted to abandon the voyage at Cape Town. He describes his feelings:

'This, I think, was the second period of my adjustment. When I had got over the initial problems and doubts, a short period of acceptance of the new environment arrived. This was followed by a second, longer stage of deeper and more serious doubts. Surviving this, I had my second wind, and was able to settle down to things. I got through it by forcing myself to do some mental as well as physical work. For example, I began to write out a description of the Admiral [his self-steering gear, devised by himself]. The self-steering seemed simple enough, but trying to write out a description was far from easy. Anyway, the effort took me out of my depression.'

ABOVE Loick Fougeron, like Moitessier, refused to carry a radio transmitter but, after a severe storm, abandoned the race at St Helena.

Almost every sailor venturing into the Southern Ocean has his boat knocked down sooner or later; it happened to Knox-Johnston almost immediately, just three days after getting down into the Roaring Forties. His description of the event, like that of all his fellow solitary sailors, was amazingly matter-of-fact.

It was the evening of September 5th. The wind had changed during the day, blowing with increasing strength from the west, quickly building up the waves to meet the old seas created by the early wind direction. It was a conflict of waves that created a savage cross sea, with waves coming in from every direction. As night fell, Knox-Johnston reefed the mainsail down and left the boat under the tiny storm jib, which drove her along, under the guidance of the Admiral. He lay on his bunk, fully dressed, his damp waterproofs still on, with just a sheet of canvas to cover him. At last he dropped off to sleep, lulled by the roaring of the wind in the rigging and the crash of waves against the hull.

He was woken cruelly in the pitch dark, as heavy objects crashed down upon him and he became aware that the boat was lying on its side. He struggled to get out of the bunk but was pinned, as if in a strait-jacket, by the canvas sheet weighed down with the debris hurled upon him. Just as he struggled from under it, the boat heaved itself upright, throwing him across the cabin in the opaque darkness. Picking himself up, he fumbled for the hatch leading out on to the deck, dreading what he was going to find, convinced that the mast had been carried away when the boat lunged back up again against the immense clinging force of the sea. He pulled the hatch open, pushed his head out into the darkness through the wind-driven spume and could just discern the mast and boom; he could hardly believe that they were still there.

The boat was bucking like a wild stallion in the cross seas; he could see the angry gleam of the foam against the dark of the night but could barely discern the deck on which he was standing. He never used a safety harness, feeling that it restricted free movement. As he hauled himself from stay to stay, up the tossing deck, he felt every piece of rigging to make sure it was in place and got half-way up to the bow when another huge wave smashed into the boat, covering him, lifting him off his feet; all he could do was to cling on to the rigging as the roaring black waters tried to tear away his grasp. Once the freak wave had swept on its way he struggled back to the cockpit and adjusted the self-steering; he could not see in the dark whether or not it had been damaged and climbed back down into the shambles of the cabin, which was ankle-deep in water, with tins and packets of food, books, articles of clothing sloshing around in it.

The first priority was obviously to reduce the water level. He was reassured by the familiar effort and motion of pumping out the bilges; the adrenalin generated in the last few moments began to settle. Once he had pumped out most of the water he started to tidy up the appalling mess of soaked food, clothing and equipment. It was while doing this that he noticed a torrent of water pouring down from the side of the coach roof, where it joined the deck of the boat. On closer inspection, he was horrified to find that there were cracks all the way round, that the huge impact of the waves was slowly tearing the coach roof from the deck, with the frightening prospect of leaving a gaping hole nearly thirteen feet by six for the waves to thunder into. If this happened there was no way he could have saved the boat from foundering. There was nothing he could do in the dark or while the storm was at its height. He could only wait patiently for the wind to drop. The following morning, after a good breakfast while waiting for the seas to quieten down, he went through his stock of tools and spare parts to find some long bolts with which to strengthen the cabin. He spent the rest of the day painstakingly drilling through the hard teak of the deck and cabin sides to reinforce the fastening of the cabin. It was another two days before he could start repairing the self-steering gear, and even then he was completely immersed by the waves on several occasions.

Life was lonely, acutely uncomfortable and very dangerous but, more than that, it stretched out in front of him, as to any solitary sailor, for such a long time – very different from the experience of a mountaineer who, at times, is probably under greater risk but over much shorter periods of time. An expedition rarely lasts more than two or three months, of which the climb above the relative comfort of Base Camp is measured in weeks at the very most.

On September 9th, still just short of the Cape of Good hope, Knox-Johnston summed it up in his log:

'I have bruises all over from being thrown about. My skin itches from constant chafing with wet clothes and I forget when I last had a proper wash so I feel dirty. I feel altogether mentally and physically exhausted and I've been in the Southern Ocean only a week. It seems years since I gybed to turn east and yet it was only last Tuesday night, not six days, and I have another 150 days of it yet… Why couldn't I be satisfied with big ships?

'The life may be monotonous but at least one gets into port occasionally which provides some variety. A prisoner at Dartmoor doesn't get hard labour like this; the public wouldn't stand for it and he has company, however uncongenial. In addition he gets dry clothing and undisturbed sleep. I wonder how the crime rate would be affected if people were sentenced to sail around the world alone instead of going to prison. It's ten months solitary confinement with hard labour.'

Every adventurer must question his motives when the going gets rough. There was little let-up in the next 150 days, but Knox-Johnston kept going, pushing the boat as hard as he dared because he knew that he could finish the course, but he wanted to do more than that – he wanted to win. Just south of Australia, the self-steering gear finally packed in completely. Once again he thought of giving up. But his natural optimism soon bubbled back. He had come so far, was so far ahead of the field, it would be a pity to give up. He resolved to push on to New Zealand before coming to a decision. His fellow competitors were a long way behind. Moitessier and Loick Fougeron had set out on August 21st, Bill King three days later.

It is interesting to note the way the younger men, all in their twenties, had set out at the earliest possible moment, fully aware that they would be entering the Southern Ocean in the final throes of the Southern winter, while the older men in their forties and, in Bill King's case, his fifties, had chosen the later departure date which hopefully would give them an easier passage through the Roaring Forties. In addition, Moitessier and King had larger boats, being forty feet long, though Fougeron's thirty-foot cutter was no bigger than those of the younger men. Neither Fougeron nor Moitessier would carry transmitters, wanting, for aesthetic reasons, to sever all links with the land; Fougeron did start, however, with a companion, a wild kitten from Morocco called Roulis. It did not last long, for the kitten made mayhem of his cabin, pirating food and even chewing the plastic covering the wires leading to the aerial of his radio. After a few days he put it aboard a passing ship and returned, with some relief, to a solitary life. He and Moitessier were undoubtedly the most experienced long-distance solitary sailors, but Fougeron did not even reach the Roaring Forties. He was caught by a severe storm, knocked down during the night in much the same way that Robin Knox-Johnston had experienced. Afterwards he wrote:

'I curl up in the cramped bunk and wait for the unbridled sea to win its victory over me. What to do? The boat lunges sideways, driven by a frightful force. I am flattened violently against the side and then in the middle of the bubbling waters everything goes black. A cascade of kitchen materials, books, bottles, tins of jam, everything that isn't secured and in the middle of this song and dance I am projected helter-skelter across the boat. At this moment I believe that it is the end, that the sea will crush me and prevent me ever coming to the surface again.'

The boat recovered and the mast was intact, but Fougeron had had enough; he resolved to head for the nearest port and abandon the voyage.

Commander Bill King did get down into the Southern Ocean, but his speed down the Atlantic had been slow. He lacked the ferocious drive that had kept Chichester racing against himself, even when exhausted, and complained in his dispatches of feeling a lack of vitality; but it was the design of his boat that finally forced him out. The junk rig, which made it much easier for a single-handed sailor to control, had inherent weaknesses. The masts were not supported by stays and therefore terrific strains were exerted on the housing. When his boat was knocked down by a wave about a thousand miles south-west of Cape Town, the main mast was twisted by the force of the water, so he had no choice but to return to Cape Town.

This left Bernard Moitessier, who had already gained two thousand miles on Bill King's *Galway Blazer*, and was undoubtedly going faster than Robin Knox-Johnston. The *Sunday Times* even began to postulate whether Moitessier could catch *Suhaili*, whose progress so far had been steady, but slow. It is extremely unlikely that Moitessier was ever particularly interested in the voyage as a race. He commented just before setting off: 'The people who are thinking about money and of being the fastest round the world will not win. It is the people who care about their skins. I shall bring back my skin, apart from a few bumps on my head.'

He took everything the sea could do to him in his stride, even when a cargo ship, which he had closed with to hand over some mail, collided with him. He simply repaired the damage and sailed on, completely at ease with the sea, happier to be alone in the middle of the ocean than on dry land. In this respect he was different from Knox-Johnston who, though equally a seaman, was not a natural loner. Knox-Johnston was able to adapt to the situation he was in from necessity, because he had to reach his goal of being the first man round the world single-handed; but he looked forward to his return to everyday life.

Moitessier, on the other hand, embraced the experience of being alone on his boat for its own sake. He wrote: 'The days go by, never monotonous. Even when they appear exactly alike they are never quite the same. That is what gives life at sea its special dimension, made up of contemplation and very simple contrasts. Sea, wind, calms, sun, clouds, porpoises. Peace and the joy of being alive in harmony.'

Robin Knox-Johnston was approaching New Zealand as Moitessier sailed down into the Southern Ocean. Having come to terms with the total loss of his self-steering gear, in a short period free from storms Knox-Johnston had refined his system for balancing out the boat so that she would sail herself, both when running under reduced canvas and also when reaching. He had nearly crossed the Tasman Sea and was coming up to Fouveaux Strait. Soon he would be in the South Pacific, with the long clear run to Cape Horn before him. He always listened to the weather forecasts from the nearest radio station and, on the evening of November 17th, at the end of it came another message for the Master of the *Suhaili*: 'Imperative we rendezvous outside Bluff Harbour in daylight – signature Bruce Maxwell.'

Knox-Johnston knew that a cold front with its accompanying storm was on the way, but reckoned he would be able to meet Maxwell, a journalist from the *Sunday*

Mirror, before it arrived, hand over his story and, perhaps even more important, actually talk to someone in the flesh – an attractive thought after all the lonely weeks in the Southern Ocean. But the front rolled in faster than he had anticipated. The following evening, just off the Fouveaux Strait, force ten winds, heavy rain and poor visibility were forecast; all this and he was being blown onto a lee shore. He made ready the warps that would keep *Suhaili*'s stern pointing into the waves to prevent her broaching, took a compass bearing on a light he identified as the Centre Island lighthouse and then waited for the storm to strike. He wrote: 'I put the kettle on; it was still quiet outside, although as black as pitch, and I thought of Bruce sitting in a comfortable hotel lounge with a large beer in front of him. Perhaps we'd be drinking together in twenty-four hours. This last thought stuck with me and I had even begun to welcome the idea when it struck me how disloyal I was being to *Suhaili*.'

The clouds rolled in, the rain lashed down, the waves started to race past as he sailed into what he thought was the middle of the strait. He was uncomfortably close to land in this kind of weather and was being driven inexorably closer. Somehow he managed to claw his way round a headland into calmer waters, the immediate danger was over; but he still wanted to make his rendezvous with Maxwell, though he realised that he would not be able to reach Bluff Harbour in those wind conditions, especially as his engine was now completely seized up. He resolved, therefore, to head for Otago harbour, which looked as if it would be more sheltered. He reached it the following day, nosed his way cautiously round the headland and then, to his horror, realised he had run aground. He reacted immediately to the crisis; it was a sandy bottom, so would not damage the boat and, hopefully, when the tide rose again *Suhaili* would float herself off. He dived below for the anchor, grabbed it and leapt into the shallow water, walking along the bottom carrying the thirty-pound anchor. As it got deeper and the water went over his head he jumped up every few paces to get a quick breath of air, until he felt he had gone far enough and was able to dive to the bottom, to dig in flukes. He could now rest assured that the boat would not be driven further up the sand as the tide came in, though he was still faced with the problem of getting her out again. At least it was going to be easy to make his rendezvous. Some boats came out to investigate the lonely yacht, but Knox-Johnston kept them at a distance, refusing all offers of help. He was determined not to break any of the race regulations.

That night, when the tide came in, he was able to haul himself off the sandbank by pulling on the warp attached to the anchor. All he needed to do now was wait for Bruce Maxwell to find him. He arrived the following day, with plenty of news but, to Knox-Johnston's immense disappointment, no mail. Maxwell told him that since Knox-Johnston had set out, the Race Committee had got round to making some rules, one of which was that none of the competitors should be allowed to take anything on board throughout the voyage. Maxwell had read this to include mail. It seemed an extraordinarily petty restriction to Knox-Johnston and, in some ways highlights the artificial nature of the voyage. A mountaineer, in climbing a mountain, has no easy alternative. He must keep going until he reaches the top and, having decided to climb, doing it on foot is probably the easiest, probably the only feasible way. An Italian expedition raised a certain level of controversy by using a helicopter to help ferry supplies on Everest but, in the event, its payload at altitude was so poor that it was no more effective than muscle power and, in the end, it crashed near the head of the Everest Icefall. A sailor, on the other hand, is choosing to make life difficult for himself, firstly by selecting a sailing vessel rather than an ocean liner to make his journey, and then by denying himself the right to call in at ports on the way or, in this instance, the solace of mail from family and friends.

Even so, Knox-Johnston did get news of his fellow competitors and learned, for the first time, that three more had started – though one of them, Alex Carozzo, was already out of the race and the other two, Lieutenant-Commander Nigel Tetley and Donald Crowhurst, were still in the Atlantic a long way behind.

Nigel Tetley first heard of the Golden Globe race in March 1968. He was a Lieutenant-Commander in the Royal Navy, based on Plymouth, and was using his

RIGHT Victress was a production model trimaran, able to achieve speeds of up to twenty-two knots, but unable to right herself if capsized. The Southern Ocean would be her moment of truth.

trimaran, *Victress*, as a floating home for himself and his wife, Evelyn, to whom he had been married for eighteen months. Tetley was forty-five, with two sons, aged sixteen and fourteen, from his first marriage. He was approaching a critical stage of his life; he had had an enjoyable Naval career which had given him command of a frigate, a great deal of exciting and interesting travel and also the leisure to pursue his own hobby of sailing. Having entered *Victress* for the Round Britain race, he had come in a very respectable fifth place. But only a certain number of officers gain promotion to Commander and Tetley had not made it; as a result he was automatically due for retirement at the age of forty-five – a fairly traumatic period in the lives of most Service officers.

One Sunday morning Eve slipped out, a coat over her nightdress, to buy the Sunday papers. When she got back Tetley picked up the *Sunday Times*, leafed through it and then was rivetted by the announcement of the Golden Globe race.

'Round the world non-stop. To solve the problem of perpetual motion. Why had the idea always fascinated me? To sail on and on like the flying Dutchman. An apt simile even two years back; but the lost soul had since found its mate. A challenge from the past? It was now or never, like one's bluff being called in poker.'

Thoughts of packing it in came into my mind for the first time today, brought on I think by too much of my own company

He started to make plans immediately. Ideally, he would like a new boat designed for the rigours of the voyage; he wrote around to all the likely sponsors but, like Knox-Johnston, was turned down. He therefore resigned himself to using his own boat, even though it was an ordinary production model, designed more for family cruising than for solitary circumnavigation. In a trimaran the centre hull holds the living quarters, while the two outer hulls are little more than balancing floats which can be used for storage. Whereas the monohull has a heavy keel which, combined with the boat's ballast, will always bring the boat back upright even in the event of a complete capsize, the trimaran is much more lightly built and has no keel. The boat is a platform resting on three floats. This design gives it great stability and almost limitless speed, for before the wind it literally surfs on the crest of the waves, achieving speeds of anything up to twenty-two knots – much faster than the speed a monohull could ever achieve. There are snags, however, for should the boat be capsized it will not right itself. The risk was highlighted by the fact that two leading multihull exponents and designers, Hedley Nichol and Arthur Piver, had recently been lost at sea.

Tetley was not deterred by the risk; he was fully committed to multihull sailing and showed an almost evangelistic zeal in his desire to prove the capabilities of his trimaran. Eve, his wife, gave him her total support, devising for him by far the most palatable and, I suspect, nutritious menu of all the sailors. Ridgway had taken, for simplicity's sake, a uniform diet of Army rations; Knox-Johnston's was fairly limited, but Tetley's was a gourmet's delight, with braised kidneys, roast goose and duck, jugged hare, oysters, octopus and Yarmouth bloaters. He also had a good hi-fi system in his cabin and set out with a magnificent tape library. It was very appropriate that he obtained the sponsorship of a record company, Music For Pleasure. The only thing he neglected was books, and he complained on the way round of how limited was his reading matter.

He refitted the boat himself, experienced all the usual crises, but was ready to sail in good order on September 16th. Good-looking in a clean-cut, rather Naval way, he was excellent company, fitting easily into a group, and yet there was a definite reserve in his character, moulded in part, no doubt, by public school and his Naval career. This reserve is certainly perceptible in his book *Trimaran Solo*, for it reveals very little of his innermost feelings or reservations. The log of his voyage is equally inhibited, tending to cling to the surface of day-to-day sailing problems, accounts of the menu and the daily programme of music.

His achievement, though, was remarkable. Sailing down towards the Southern Ocean he must have been acutely aware of the risk he was taking. His boat was an ordinary production model; the comfortable cabin and raised wheelhouse undoubtedly made her the most comfortable boat going round the world, but they represented potential weaknesses in the structure which could prove fatal. Every solitary sailor has his moments of doubt and Tetley was no exception. The solitude and stress bore heavily upon him. This was reflected in his entry on October 2nd, seventeen days out:

'Thoughts of packing it in came into my mind for the first time today, brought on I think by too much of my own company. It would be so easy to put into port and say that the boat was not strong enough for the voyage or unsuitable. What was really upsetting me was the psychological effect – of possibly twelve months – this might have. Would I be the same person on return? This aspect I knew worried Eve too. I nearly put through a radio call to talk over the question in guarded terms. Then I realised that though she would straightaway accept the reason and agree to my stopping, say at Cape Town, we would feel that we had let ourselves down both in our own eyes and those of our friends, backers and well-wishers. It was only a touch of the blues due to the yacht's slow progress.'

Like Knox-Johnston, he overcame depression by some practical work; in this instance having a hair cut. There is never a shortage of things to do on a long-distance voyage; quite apart from sailing the boat, there is a constant round of preventive maintenance on rigging and equipment and, however thorough the sailor may be, wear and tear is relentless. Tetley had an elaborate workshop with an electric drill; a practical man, again like Knox-Johnston, he kept on top of maintenance problems as he nursed his boat down the South Atlantic and into the Southern Ocean where she was to meet her greatest test.

After failing to charter *Gipsy Moth IV*, Donald Crowhurst also decided to go for a trimaran, even though he had never actually sailed one. Since it was obvious that he would not be ready to start before the end of October, the last possible date for entering the race, it was also unlikely he would catch up with the sailors who had started earlier. He would, therefore, have to go for the fastest time if he wanted to achieve distinction, and for that he needed a really fast boat. He decided to have a trimaran built to the same basic design as *Victress*, Tetley's boat, but with a streamlined, strengthened superstructure and a host of electronic aids to increase the boat's safety.

All this needed money, though, and it was here that he effected his greatest coup. The most important creditor of his failing business was Stanley Best, a down-to-earth businessman, not easily impressed by romantic ideas. Crowhurst nevertheless succeeded in persuading Best that his surest chance of recovering his investment was to increase this still further and foot the bill for the new boat.

Now he could get started, but it was mid-May – all too little time to build a boat, especially one which was to include all the revolutionary ideas thought up by Crowhurst. It was to have a buoyancy bag hanging from the top of the mast; the electronic sensors in the hull would automatically inflate the bag from a compressed air bottle if the boat was blown over. Hopefully this would stop it capsizing. There were many other electronic aids, all to be controlled by a 'computer' installed in the cabin. Crowhurst's ideas were certainly original and might have worked; unfortunately, however, he lacked both the time and also the temperament to put them into effect. He was rushing about constantly, between boat-builders, his own home in Bridgwater and around the country chasing all the loose ends, drumming up further sponsorship and talking to the press. He had all too many bright ideas, but seemed unable to carry them through to the end and often ignored the less exciting, but essential, minor details. As a result of this and the inevitable teething troubles suffered during any form of boat construction, everything slid behind schedule. October 30th came all too quickly and Crowhurst was barely ready. The interior of the cabin was a mess of unconnected wires; there was no compressed air bottle to feed the unsightly flotation bag which hung from the masthead. More serious still, several short cuts had been taken in the construction of the boat which undoubtedly affected her seaworthiness. A team of friends helped him to get everything ready in time to beat the deadline, but it was chaotic. Crowhurst did not seem able to co-ordinate their efforts, was prey to too many conflicting demands – not least those of his energetic press agent, Rodney Hallworth, a big man with a powerful personality who handled Teignmouth's public relations.

BELOW Instead of finishing the race, Bernard Moitessier sailed Joshua one and a half times round the world 'because I am happy at sea and perhaps also to save my soul'.

At two o'clock on the morning of October 31st the decks and cabin were still piled high with stores, many of which had been bought at the last minute. Exhausted, Donald Crowhurst and his wife, Clare, returned to the hotel where they were to spend what was to be their last night together. Most adventurers have moments of agonising doubt, particularly on the brink of departure, but those of Crowhurst were particularly painful. He admitted to Clare that the boat was just not up to the voyage and asked whether she would go out of her mind with worry. With hindsight she realised that he was asking her to stop him going, but she did not see it at the time and did her best to reassure him. He cried through the rest of the night.

It was three o'clock in the afternoon of the 31st, just a few hours before deadline, that he set sail. It was a messy departure; almost immediately Crowhurst discovered that the buoyancy bag, which had been hurriedly lashed to the mast the previous day, had been tied round two halyards as well, so that neither the jib nor the staysail could be raised. He screamed invective at his accompanying escort and asked to be towed back into harbour so that the rigging could be cleared. He then managed to get away, tacking into Lyme Bay against a strong south wind, until he vanished into the misty drizzle.

As he sailed down the Channel he sorted out the shambles on deck and in the cabin, but in the next few days the hopelessness of his voyage became increasingly evident. The Hasler self-steering gear, ideal for a monohull but not really suitable for a trimaran, was giving trouble; then, even more serious, he discovered that the port bow float was shipping water. The hatches to the floats were not fully watertight. This probably brought on a further realisation. He had a very powerful pump for bailing but in the last-minute rush they had failed to get the length of Helliflex hosing needed to bail out all the different compartments. The only way he could do it was by hand, a slow and exhausting process which would be impractical in a really heavy sea because almost as much water would pour back in through the opened hatch as he would be able to bail out. (Tetley had anticipated this problem by putting permanent piping into the forward compartments of *Victress*.) Also, he discovered that a pile of spare parts and plywood patches that he would need for repairs en route had somehow been taken off the boat, even though he knew he had put them on board.

The winds across the Bay of Biscay and down the coast of Portugal were mainly against him but, even so, his progress was slow, even erratic. It was as if he were shying from commitment, trying to make up his mind what to do. The BBC had given him a tape recorder and a huge pile of tapes on which to record his impressions during the voyage. Whatever his doubts or secret thoughts, he was obviously very aware, whenever he made a recording, that this was eventually going to a wide audience and there was often a tone of bravado in his monologue which, somehow, struck a false note, when the reality was so different. For a start the boat was very bad at sailing into the wind but, much more serious, there were hosts of potentially disastrous structural faults. At last, on November 15th, he summed up the problem in his log, stating, 'Racked by the growing awareness that I must soon decide whether or not I can go on in the face of the actual situation. What a bloody awful decision!'

He went on to write a very clear, carefully thought-out assessment of his situation, listing the many faults and omissions, all of which pointed to the seeming inevitability of failure in the Southern Ocean, failure which, in all probability, would be accompanied by his own death. He then questioned whether he should abandon the voyage immediately or try to salvage something from it by going on to Cape Town, or even Australia, so that he could withdraw with greater honour and at the same time give his backer, Stanley Best, a little mileage for his investment.

Yet on November 18th, when he managed to make a radio link-up with both Clare and Stanley Best, he did not mention the possibility of abandoning the voyage. He asked Best to double-check whether or not the Helliflex hosing had been put on board and complained of his slow progress, giving his position as 'some hundred miles north of Madeira'. Talking to Best again a few days later, he still did not mention the possibility of pulling out of the race, but he did warn that he might be forced to go off the air because of problems with the charging motor. It was as if he could not bring himself to admit failure and return to the enormous problems which he knew faced him at home.

Crowhurst's fellow late entrant, Alex Carozzo, had no such inhibitions or, for that matter, very much choice. A thirty-six-year-old, flamboyant Italian, he was a very experienced sailor. Like Knox-Johnston he had a Merchant Navy background and had built a thirty-three-foot boat in the hold of his cargo ship on the way to Japan. There he had launched the boat and had sailed single-handed to San Francisco, surviving a dismasting on the way. His entry to the Golden Globe race was equally bizarre. Having already entered the *Observer* single-handed race, he set out from Plymouth and in the vast emptiness of the Atlantic, by an incredible coincidence, met up with John Ridgway, who had just set sail on his voyage. They exchanged greetings and it was this, perhaps, that influenced Carozzo in turning back to England so that he could build a boat specially for the circumnavigation. There was little time left and he had the boat built in a mere seven weeks. It was a revolutionary design, with two steel rudders and, in front of the main keel, a three-foot centre plate which could be used to adjust the boat's trim. She was by far the biggest boat to start out on the long, single-handed voyage. Provided he could manage her alone, she should have been the fastest of all the contenders. Unfortunately, however, he was overtaken by severe stomach pains whilst in the Bay of Biscay; these were diagnosed as stomach ulcers and, in the end, he had to be taken in tow to the Portuguese coast at Oporto. No doubt the nervous stress of putting together the enterprise so very quickly had been too much for him.

This was the news that Bruce Maxwell passed on to Knox-Johnston. The only serious threat seemed to be that of Moitessier, who had been making good progress as far as the Cape of Good Hope where he had last been seen on October 26th. The pundits had calculated that at his present rate of progress he could challenge Knox-Johnston to a neck-and-neck finish and would undoubtedly win on the elapsed time basis. Knox-Johnston commented, 'that was just the sort of news I needed to spur me on.'

He raised sail once again, his next sight of land to be Cape Horn. Even though he had worked out a series of sail patterns to cope with the loss of his self-steering, he still had to take the helm while sailing before the wind. This meant long hours, sixteen and seventeen at a time, sitting exposed to the elements in his tiny cockpit. *Suhaili* did not have a wheelhouse or even a canvas dodger to protect the helmsman;

Knox-Johnston did not believe in them, feeling that he had to be completely exposed to the winds and to have a real feel of what they were doing to his sails and boat. He spent the long hours clutching the helm, meditating about the world and his own future, or learning and reciting some of the poetry he had on board. He never relaxed his efforts to nurse *Suhaili* along, to get the very best he could out of her and yet to avoid straining her to the point of irreparable damage. By now his radio transmitter was out of action, so he had no chance of calling for help nor of reporting his position, though he could pick up the coastal radio stations back in New Zealand and then, as he crept across the South Pacific, on the South American coast.

There was a constant drudgery and discomfort – of damp clothes, of insufficient sleep punctuated by crises, a hand badly scalded by boiling porridge, the failure of a succession of parts on the boat, the struggle with contrary winds which came in against him from the east almost as often as they swept round from the west.

Cape Horn, which he reached on January 17th, was almost an anticlimax – he coasted past it in an almost dead calm. There was no-one to meet him, no aircraft flying out from the land: he slipped past unnoticed up into the South Atlantic, past the Falkland Islands and on up the coast of South America towards the Equator. He was on the home stretch, though still had a long way to go. The only person who had any chance of catching him up was Moitessier, who had handed some letters to a fisherman in a bay near Hobart, Tasmania, on December 18th. Moitessier was next spotted off the Falkland Islands on February 10th, but had the variables where he could expect contrary winds before him, while Knox-Johnston had reached the South-East Trades. It is unlikely that Moitessier would have caught up with Knox-Johnston, but he almost certainly would have had a faster time round the world, having set out more than two months after him.

The question was to be academic. The next time Moitessier was sighted was off the Cape of Good Hope, when the rest of the world believed he was somewhere in the mid-Atlantic approaching the Equator, nearing the final run for home. He sailed into the outer reaches of the harbour and, using a slingshot, catapulted a message for the *Sunday Times* onto the bridge of an anchored tanker. It read: 'The Horn was rounded February 5, and today is March 18. I am continuing non-stop towards the Pacific Islands because I am happy at sea and perhaps also to save my soul.'

His message was received with incredulity. How could anyone, with success and glory in his grasp, reject it like this? The *Sunday Times* tried to get a message from his wife through to him by having it broadcast on South African news bulletins: 'Bernard – the whole of France is waiting for you. Please come back to Plymouth as quickly as possible. Don't go round the world again. We will be waiting for you in England, so please do not disappoint us – Françoise and the children.'

Moitessier never heard this message, and it is impossible to guess how he would have responded if he had. He had contemplated calling in at Plymouth to claim the reward, collect all the equipment he had left there and reassure his family, but then he rejected the thought, afraid that he would be drawn back into a way of life he felt was false and into a society that he considered was destroying itself with materialism, pollution and violence. Sailing on round the Cape of Good Hope for the second time, into the savage winds and seas of the Southern winter, it was a much rougher voyage than his first through the Southern Ocean. He was knocked down on four different occasions as he sailed past Australia, past New Zealand and then on up into the Southern Pacific towards Tahiti.

Moitessier finally reached Tahiti on June 21st 1969, having sailed one and a half times round the world, further than anyone had ever done single-handed. On arrival he told journalists that he had never intended to race:

'Talking of records is stupid, an insult to the sea. The thought of a competition is grotesque. You have to understand that when one is months and months alone one evolves; some people say, go nuts. I went crazy in my own fashion. For four months all I saw were the stars. I didn't hear an unnatural sound. A purity grows out of that kind of solitude. I said to myself, "What the hell am I going to do in Europe?" I told myself I'd be crazy to go on to France.'

To him, the voyage was sufficient in itself; he did not need the embellishments of competition, rejected both the material rewards and the accolades of fame. There had even been talk of him being awarded the Legion of Honour in France. He displayed an independence that is rare. Most mountaineers, for instance, have consistently rejected formalised competition but, in most instances, have accepted any plaudits bestowed on them on their return to their homeland. Moitessier, however, was not so much rejecting the rewards of a society wanting to adulate its heroes; rather, he was saying, 'I am not going to play your games. I am going to do exactly what I want and lead my own life in the way I choose.' He preferred the simplicity of life in the Pacific Islands, the freedom to sail where and when he would.

With Moitessier out of the race there were only three left. Knox-Johnston had last been seen at Otago and now, in mid-March, should be somewhere in the Atlantic, though his family and sponsors were becoming increasingly worried about his survival; ships and planes in the mid-Atlantic were asked to keep an eye out for him. Crowhurst also had gone off the air. The only competitor still in contact was Nigel Tetley. He had made steady, but nerve-wracking progress across the Southern Ocean, nursing his trimaran through the gigantic rollers that all too easily could have capsized him with fatal results. It appears that he picked the ideal time to sail through the ocean, for the weather seems to have been kinder to him than to the others, particularly around the Cape of Good Hope where all other circumnavigators experienced the appalling storms which forced Blyth and King to abandon their voyages and which very nearly scuppered Knox-Johnston. Tetley had his narrowest escape when nearing Cape Horn; caught by a storm with sharp, choppy waves, he was very nearly pitchpoled, the cabin damaged and one of the windows smashed. In the aftermath he thought of giving up, sailing for Valparaiso, but then obstinacy set in and he turned the boat to head for Cape Horn. His passage round the Horn also was anticlimactic – he was almost becalmed.

He now turned north-east to pass the Falklands on the east, for the long run home. Tetley's achievement in sailing a trimaran through the Southern Ocean was considerable, but the stress on his boat was now beginning to tell. Both the floats and the main hull were letting in water, sure signs of structural damage caused by the months of hammering but, provided he nursed *Victress* carefully, she should get back to England and might even be the only boat to complete the voyage. Then, on April, 5th the tanker *Mobil Acme* sighted *Suhaili* to the west of the Azores. Knox-Johnston was on the home stretch and would undoubtedly be first home. Tetley, on the other hand, had a better average speed and – in all probability – would win the prize for the fastest voyage, even if he had to nurse *Victress* very carefully those last few thousand miles up the Atlantic.

Nobody had heard anything from Donald Crowhurst since January 19th, when he had reported his position a hundred miles south-east of Gough Island in the South Atlantic to the west of the Cape of Good Hope. It could be assumed, therefore, that by this time he should be somewhere in the Southern Ocean between New Zealand and Cape Horn. In fact he was still in the South Atlantic and had never left it.

We shall never know exactly what went through Crowhurst's mind as he dallied hesitantly down the Atlantic through December 1968 and the early months of 1969. The only evidence are the logs and casual notes he left in *Teignmouth Electron* and which Ron Hall and Nicholas Tomalin, two *Sunday Times* writers, sifted and analysed in a brilliant piece of detective work, described in their book *The Strange Voyage of Donald Crowhurst*. It seems unlikely that he planned his deception from the very start of the voyage – or even from the moment when he concluded that there was no way his boat could survive the seas of the Southern Ocean. Both Tetley and Knox-Johnston had had moments when they decided their voyages were no longer possible, had resolved to give up, then decided to keep going until the next landfall and to take a decision there. The big difference was that their decisions were all in the open; it never remotely occurred to either of them to practise any form of deception.

With Crowhurst, the deception seems to have built up over a period, from the original germ of the idea to final, absolute commitment. It started in early December with a spectacular claim to an all-time speed record of 243 miles in the day. (This almost certainly would have been a record, since the best run previously publicised was that of Geoffrey Williams who had logged about 220 miles in the *Observer* single-handed Atlantic race.) It certainly got Crowhurst the headlines he probably sought and was accepted, without comment by nearly all the media, though Francis Chichester was suspicious, 'phoning the *Sunday Times* to advise them that they should watch out for Crowhurst – he could be 'a bit of a joker'. At this stage it is possible that Crowhurst was still thinking of abandoning the voyage at Cape Town; the claim, which the calculations found in his cabin show was false, would have given him a bit of glory with which to face his backers on return to England.

But then, as he sailed on down the Atlantic, the moment of irreversible commitment came ever closer. He had already started a new log book, even though his existing one still had plenty of empty pages, the inference being that he intended, at a later date, to write out a false log of his imagined circumnavigation through the Southern Ocean, while he used his second log book for his actual calculations which, of course, he needed to know from day to day. He also started to mark out on his chart a series of false positions, well to the west of his actual route, which was taking him down the South American coast. He could still, however, have brought his actual route and faked course together at Cape Town and it is unlikely that anyone would have bothered to scrutinise his calculations sufficiently closely to see that there were discrepancies.

There would come a point soon, however, when if he tried to fake his voyage through the Southern Ocean there was no way that he could suddenly appear at a port in South Africa or South America without exposing his fraud. He must have devoted hours to working out all the pros and cons of trying to carry out the deceit. For a start he would have to close down his radio since any call he made would give a rough indication of where he really was. But the biggest problem of all was that of writing up the false log with all the navigational calculations he would need, in a way that would satisfy the examination by experts on his return to Britain.

There have been challenged claims in the past. There is doubt about the claims of both Cook and Peary to have reached the North Pole in 1908 and 1909. The claim of the former was widely rejected, while the latter was generally accepted, even though there were several contradictions in his account. The distances Peary claimed to have made each day in his dash for the Pole seem far-fetched. If he did fabricate, however, it was a relatively simple operation, since it represented only a few days and, after all, nobody could challenge conclusively whether or not the bit of featureless ice on which he had stood was or was not the North Pole. There have also been several cases of disputed mountaineering ascents, but these also have usually involved a push from a top camp towards a summit, as often as not in cloud or storm. One of the most notorious is that of the first ascent of Cerro Torre by Cesare Maestri and Toni Egger. They were gone from Base Camp for a week; on their way down, in a violent storm, Egger slipped and fell to his death, Maestri staggered back down and was found semiconscious and delirious. He claimed they reached the top, though this was disputed. Whether he did or not can never be proved conclusively, but if he did fabricate the story, again it was comparatively easy to do so, since he only had to imagine a few days' climbing and could be excused lapses of memory in the struggle he had for survival.

The nervous stress of living out this solitary world of make-believe must have been immense

But Crowhurst was embarking on a massive fraud. He would have to spend several months circling the empty wastes of the South Atlantic, carefully avoiding all shipping lanes, while he forged a log, day by day, across the Southern Ocean. On his return he would have to sustain the lie in all its details. From the scrap sheets he left in his cabin, he had obviously spent a great deal of time and thought in faking his speed record. Falsifying a circumnavigation represented an infinitely greater challenge. Doubtless he must have been wrestling with this as he sailed down the South Atlantic. His radio reports were consistently vague, but by January 19th he realised that the distance between his actual position, a few hundred miles east of Rio de Janeiro, and his claimed position approaching the Cape of Good Hope, was becoming too great and that it was time to close down his radio. He sent a message to Rodney Hallworth, his agent and promoter back in Teignmouth, for once giving a positive position a hundred miles south-east of Gough Island and, at the same time, warned him that the generator hatch was giving trouble, to create a reason for going off the air. This was his last call for three months – three months of complete isolation, denied the stimulus of pushing a boat to its limit or of a real goal.

He had started the journey with four log books; the first had entries up to mid-December and then, even though there were still plenty of blank pages, had been abandoned. The second was a working log, giving the day-to-day details of his actual voyage. In it he had recorded his thoughts as the voyage progressed, and it is these which give the clearest indication of his state of mind. He used the third book as a wireless log, in which he recorded not only his own messages but also detailed weather reports from stations in Africa, Australia and South America, presumably to help him falsify his log in a convincing manner. The fourth book was missing when the boat was eventually recovered. It is possible that he kept this as the false log book. On a practical level, working out the false sun sights in reverse would take considerably longer than doing it for real; also, of course, it would only be by doing it from day to day that the appearances of the log could have been at all convincing.

The nervous stress of living out this solitary world of make-believe must have been immense, but there are few records of direct introspection in his log book over this period; it is full of observations of the sea life around him, of the birds and porpoises that kept him company, and yet through these emerge glimpses of his state of mind. On January 29th an owl-like bird, which was almost certainly from the land, managed to reach the boat. He wrote a short piece about it, entitled 'The Misfit':

'He was unapproachable, as a misfit should be. He flew away as soon as I made any effort to get near him, and on to the mizzen crosstrees where he hung desperately to the shaky stays with claws useless for the task he had set himself.

'. . . Poor bloody misfit! A giant albatross, its great high-aspect wings sweeping like scimitars through the air with never a single beat slid effortlessly round the boat in mocking contrast to his ill-adapted efforts of survival.'

And then a poem:

Save some pity for the Misfit, fighting on with bursting heart;
Not a trace of common sense, his is no common flight.
Save, save him some pity. But save the greater part
For him that sees no glimmer of the Misfit's guiding light.

It is a poignant cry for understanding and sympathy, stripped of all the shallow bravado that appears in his taped commentaries for the outside world.

And then a real crisis presented itself. The starboard float of *Teignmouth Electron* was seriously damaged, letting in the water. The spare pieces of plywood he needed for repairs had been left behind. There seemed no choice; he would have to put into port to get the boat repaired. This presented a huge problem. Even had he wanted to use this as an honourable excuse for retiring from the race, he was now so far from where he had said he was, that his fraud would inevitably have been exposed. He seems to have dithered for several days, zig-zagging off the coast of Argentina, before finally summoning up the resolve to get into port, and then he chose the obscure anchorage of Rio Salado, near the mouth of the River Plate. He arrived on the morning of March 8th, repaired the damage and left two days later. Although the arrival of *Teignmouth*

Electron was noted in the coastguard log, it was not passed on but Crowhurst could not be sure of this and it must have been yet another source of worry.

As he set sail from Rio Salado, in his pretended voyage he should have been somewhere between New Zealand and Cape Horn. The time was coming close when his real self could join up with the fantasy self and, with this in mind, he started sailing south towards the Falkland Islands and the Roaring Forties. It is ironic that from March 24th, on his way south, he must have passed within a few miles of Tetley going north. He sailed to within sight of the Falklands on March 29th, but it was still too early to radio his false position approaching the Horn, and so he veered off to the north for a further ten days, zig-zagging back and forth, before sending out his first radio message for three months:

DEVONNEWS EXETER — HEADING DIGGER
RAMREZ LOG KAPUT 17697 28TH
WHATS NEW OCEAN-BASHINGWISE

ABOVE Falmouth to Falmouth. Robin Knox-Johnston is first home because he knew how to care for his boat as well as when to push her.

The broken log line covered any contradictions there might be between his actual mileage and the one he declared, while he still avoided giving a precise position, though definitely inferred that he was approaching the small group of islands named Diego Ramirez, to the south of Cape Horn. His radio call arrived just five days after Knox-Johnston had been sighted near the Azores and inevitably the world's press were concentrating on him, saving Crowhurst from a closer scrutiny that might have picked out some anomalies both in the apparent speed of his crossing the Southern Ocean and the timing of the resumption of radio communications. Once again, Francis Chichester was one of the few people to make sceptical comment.

Tetley was approaching the Tropic of Capricorn, well off the coast of South America, when he heard that Crowhurst was back in contact and heading for Cape Horn. It was unlikely that Crowhurst could get back to England before him, but of course he had set out over a month later and seemed, from his report, to have caught up dramatically. If Crowhurst kept up his present rate of progress he would have the fastest time round the world. Tetley had been stoical about Robin Knox-Johnston's reappearance, writing in his book *Trimaran Solo*:

'Robin's arrival would hive off most of the publicity and his position where expected made glad tidings. Donald Crowhurst's challenge to me from the rear was a different matter. Even so, I could by then regard the possibility of his winning without envy. At the same time, I still wanted to win; or put in another way, I didn't want anyone to beat me. . .least of all a similar type of boat.'

Tetley undoubtedly started to push *Victress* very much harder, keeping as much sail up as possible: in his words, he was now racing in earnest. But the boat was not up to it. In the early hours of April 20th, just short of the Equator and the point where he would cross his outward track, disaster struck. A frame in the bow had disintegrated, leaving a gaping hole. His first reaction was that it was all over and he started working out the nearest port he could reach, but once again his stubborn determination won through. He patched up the damage as best he could and was soon pushing his boat to the limit once again, his eyes set on Plymouth.

At the time Tetley was struggling to repair and then nurse his battered boat towards home, Crowhurst, in the South Atlantic, was still marking time; he had to calculate very carefully the moment when his false voyage could actually catch up with his real progress, when the two logs could become one, when fantasy became reality. During this period he tried, unsuccessfully, to get a telephone link-up with Clare. This was obviously tremendously important to him – not only the result of his isolation, but also of the massive strain he must now have been under. The period without any contact with the world might have enabled him to relax in his fantasy, but he was now back in contact, was perhaps beginning to wonder about the practicalities of carrying through his deception.

Robin Knox-Johnston had no such problems. He was very nearly home in his dirt-streaked, old-fashioned-looking ketch, *Suhaili*. As he came into the Channel, 'planes dipped low over him, getting the first shots of film showing his arrival; two boats came out to greet him – one carrying his mother and father which, to the embarrassment of his sponsors, the *Sunday Mirror*, had been chartered by the *Daily Express*, and the other carrying reporters and photographers of the *Sunday Mirror*. As *Suhaili* neared Falmouth the escort increased, with a Royal Naval Reserve ship to give him a formal escort and a host of yachts and small boats whose crews wanted to pay tribute to his achievement. *Suhaili* crossed the bar at 3.30 in the afternoon of April 22nd. The finishing cannon fired. Robin Knox-Johnston was the first man to sail round the world non-stop single-handed. He had taken 313 days to sail the thirty-odd thousand miles. It wasn't a dramatically fast time, but in many ways the speed was meaningless. The reason why Knox-Johnston had finished at all was because he had known how to care for his boat as well as how to push her.

The first people to board him were the Customs officers with the time-honoured question, 'Where from?' Knox-Johnston replied, 'Falmouth.'

This would have made a nice, tidy end to the story, but of course the race was not yet over and the competition, created by the *Sunday Times* was still very open. Crowhurst, who had now united his fake position with that of his real position, sent off a jaunty congratulatory cable:

> NEWSDESK BBC — TICKLED AS TAR WITH TWO FIDS SUCCESS KNOX JOHNSTON BUT KINDLY NOTE NOT RACEWINNER YET SUGGEST ACCURACY DEMANDS DISTINCTION BETWEEN GOLDEN GLOBE AND RACE = OUTRAGED SOUTH ATLANTIC OTHERWISE CROWHURST

But Crowhurst's actual log shows that he continued to sail southward for a further four days and then, even when he did turn north, his progress was spasmodic, as if he wanted to ensure that Tetley was first home, with himself sufficiently close behind to get a good share of the honour, yet be spared the close scrutiny that his logs and story would receive were he the winner. He did get in a few good days sailing and his log even registered one day's run of 243 miles – by coincidence the same as his false claim of a record the previous year.

Tetley meanwhile continued to push his damaged boat to the limit and by May 20th had reached the Azores, only a thousand miles from home. A force nine gale had blown up through the day and, as dusk fell, he took down all his sails and hove to. It was midnight when he was woken by a strange scraping sound forward. He realised instinctively that the bow of the port float must have come drift but, when he switched on the light, he was appalled to see water flowing over the floor. He went up on deck to find a gaping void where the float should have been, but somehow, in tearing away from the hull, it had left a huge hole in the main hull as well. *Victress* was sinking fast. He only had time to send out a quick emergency call on his radio, grab his log books and a few instruments and clear the life raft from the deck, before the boat sank under him in the pitch dark. For a hideous moment the raft's automatic drogue snagged something, pulling him under the three wildly rearing sterns of the boat. He managed to cut the line only just in time, shouting, 'Give over, Vicky, I have to leave you... Then the pangs set in. I had fleeting glimpses of her hull above the jagged silhouette of the waves, then all I could see was her riding light waving bravely among the tumult. As I watched, the sea reached her batteries, the light grew suddenly bright, flickered and went out.'

He spent the rest of the night, protected by the cocoon-like canopy of the rubber dinghy, tossed like a piece of flotsam by the dark waves. In the morning an American Hercules rescue aircraft flew overhead and later on that afternoon an Italian tanker, guided by the 'plane, picked him up. He had completed his circumnavigation, had come so close to completing the voyage; he was like the marathon runner who, having almost completed the course, collapses at the entrance to the stadium, a mere lap from the finish.

This now left Crowhurst in an agonising predicament. His spasmodic progress up the South Atlantic indicates that he intended to ensure that he came in second to Tetley. But now, if he kept going at his present rate, he would almost certainly beat Robin Knox-Johnston's time round the world and be subject to the inevitable close scrutiny of his logs and story that this would entail.

On the other hand, if he were to slow down, this in itself would appear suspicious – particularly in comparison with the very fast passage he had claimed for crossing the Southern Ocean. In addition, the radio messages from England were beginning to indicate both the scale and the closeness of the reception he would have to face on getting back to Teignmouth. The stress was increased still further by the failure of his transmitter – he was unable to get any messages out. He now devoted all his energy to trying to repair the transmitter, leaving the boat to sail herself while he stripped and then tried to rebuild it. The cabin must have been unbearably hot, for he was now sailing through the Tropics; it also became an untidy shambles, with bits of wire and transistors scattered everywhere. And yet, in a way, it was probably therapeutic. Even back in England, Crowhurst had frequently locked himself away for hours as he wrestled with electronic problems. This was something that he knew he could do well and, after several days' work, he managed to make the transmitter work for morse. He did not manage to make it work for voice and this meant that he was unable to get the telephone link-up with Clare that he so desperately wanted. Even so, during this period he still kept up the public front of his deception with morse messages to England and a series of passages recorded on his tape-recorder. His last recording was on June 23rd:

'I feel tremendously fit. I feel as if I could realise all those ambitions I nurtured as a boy like playing cricket for England. I feel on top of the world, tremendously fit. My reflexes amaze me. They're so fast you know. I catch things almost before they start falling. It's really very satisfying.'

And the tape ran off the spool. He did not reload it. He had had a second go at making a high-frequency speech transmitter but did not have the parts. He had even telegrammed the Race Committee to ask for dispensation to have the necessary parts sent to him, but they had stuck to the rules. There was nothing more he could do with the radio, it is easy to surmise why he could not bring himself to reload the spool.

The reality of his position must now have been too appalling for almost anyone to have borne. Crowhurst seems to have turned away from it, into the therapy of the kind of philosophical discussion that he had always enjoyed at home, particularly amongst his close friends. He started it in his second log book – a series of passages which, over the next few days, stretched into twenty-five thousand words, some of which represented reasoned, philosophical analysis, some a tortured, indirect self-justification and, towards the end, it all became increasingly obscure with more and more deletions and repetitions. His first thoughts were strongly influenced by Einstein, whose work on relativity was one of the very few books which Crowhurst had brought with him to while away the months of solitude. He gave his exposition the title 'Philosophy' and went on:

'Man is a lever whose ultimate length and strength he must determine for himself. His disposition and talent decide where the fulcrum will lie.

'The pure mathematician places the fulcrum near the effort; his exercises are much more mental than physical and can carry the 'load' – his own ideas – taking perhaps nothing but his own and kindred minds along the route. The shattering application of the idea that $E = mc^2$ is one extreme example of this activity.'

Crowhurst developed and expanded this theme to the point where he made his great discovery, that Man – and Crowhurst in particular – could escape from his body.

'And yet, and yet – *if* creative abstraction is to act as a vehicle for the new entity, and leave its hitherto stable state it lies within the power of creative abstraction to produce the phenomenon!!!!!!!!!!!! We can bring it about by creative abstraction!'

Not only could he escape from his body and from the appalling predicament in which he found himself, he could become one with God. He continued to explore this thesis and to study the last two thousand years of history, showing how some exceptional men have managed to make their impact on the world, shocking it into change. He was also becoming aware of how important were both his words and discoveries, observing: 'Now we must be very careful about getting the answer right. We are at the point where our powers of abstraction are powerful enough to do tremendous damage...'

But the outside world still intruded. On June 26th he received a cable from Rodney Hallworth:

BBC AND EXPRESS MEETING YOU WITH CLARE AND ME OFF SCILLIES YOUR TRIUMPH BRINGING ONE HUNDRED THOUSAND FOLK TEIGNMOUTH WHERE FUND REACHING FIFTEEN HUNDRED PLUS MANY OTHER BENEFITS PLEASE GIVE ME SECRETS OF TRIP NEAR DEATH AND ALL THAT FOR PRE-PRESS SELLING OPPORTUNITIES MONEY OUTLOOK GOOD REPLY URGENT THINKING ABOUT ADVERTISING

He was still able to project his public self through his morse key: on the 28th he told off the BBC and Hallworth for demanding an exact time of arrival, with the admonishment:

BECALMED THREE DAYS PUFF BOATS HAVE DESTINATIONS NOT ETAS

He was also disturbed by the thought of Clare coming out to meet him and on the 29th sent a message, through the operator at Portishead, that under no circumstances was Clare to come out to the Scillies. This was his last message, his last direct contact with the outside world.

Another subject that fascinated him was that of 'the game' as one's approach to living, but with a strong sense of self-justification of how he had played and manipulated 'the game' of the round the world race. He now began to jump from one idea to the next, at times very obviously in agony, as shown by these lines which filled a single page:

Nature does not allow
God to Sin any Sins
Except One -
That is the Sin of Concealment
This is the terrible secret of the torment of the soul
'needed' by a natural system to keep trying
He has perpetuated this sin on the tormented...

Crowhurst had lost all awareness of the passing of time, had not wound up either his watch or chronometer. There had been no practical entries into his log, no sights or positions. And then, on July 1st, he reopened the log, annotating his thoughts with the passage of time. His first problem was to work out the passage of days, in which he had ignored the time, and then to calculate the time itself. He did this by taking a sight of the moon. Initially, he made a mistake of both the day – forgetting that June has only thirty days, and of the time, but then he realised it and made his correction.

There followed his final testament which amounted to both a confession and also a conflict in his own mind. He seems to have determined to take his own life or, perhaps as he saw it, simply to leave his physical body but what was he to leave? He could destroy all evidence of his fraud and leave the falsified log, which he is assumed to have kept throughout the voyage. In all probability his story, at least publicly, would have been accepted; Clare, and more particularly his children, would have had a hero to mourn and remember. But to do this he would have had to destroy his testament, something that had become the very centre of his world; but most important of all, he probably needed to make his atonement and to do this he had to leave what amounted to his confession. His last lines, still annotated with the time were:

11 15 00 It is the end of my
my game the truth
has been revealed and it will
be done as my family requires me
to do it
11 17 00 It is the time for you
move to begin
I have not need to prolong
the game
It has been a good game that
must be ended at the
I will play this game when
I will chose I will resign the
game
11 20 40 there is no reason for harmful

ABOVE Sailors from the Royal Mail Vessel Picardy examining the abandoned Teignmouth Electron.

These were the last words he wrote. He only had two and a half minutes before the self-appointed moment of his departure. One can speculate what he did next, but the three log books and the navigational plotting sheets, on which he had fabricated his run the previous December, were stacked neatly on the chart table in a place where they would easily be found. There was no sign of the fourth log book and so, presumably to wipe away his deceit, he either threw it into the calm waters of the ocean or, clutching it, plunged over the side to watch the *Teignmouth Electron* gently slide away from him at around two-and-a-half knots – a speed which, even if he had had second thoughts, he could never have attained by swimming.

Teignmouth Electron was spotted on July 10th by the lookout on the Royal Mail Vessel *Picardy*, bound from London to the Caribbean. She was like the *Marie Celeste*, ghosting along under her mizzen sail, no-one on board; the cabin was untidy with a lived-in look, dirty pans in the sink, tools and electronic gear scattered over the work table as if they had only just been put down, and the logs, with their damning testimony, lying waiting on the chart table.

All nine contestants in the Golden Globe race had now been accounted for; only one had finished the voyage. Viewed as a single entity, the expectations, tribulations and interlinking tragedy of their stories has a quality of escalating drama one would expect to find in a classic tragedy; at the same time can be seen elements of a moral fable. Robin Knox-Johnston, the contestant who finished, showed a single-minded determination combined with fine seamanship and a level-headed

ABOVE The abandoned galley of the Teignmouth Electron.

judgement. He had been pronounced 'distressingly normal' on setting out; the verdict was the same on his return. One can assume that the psychiatrist meant that he was extraordinarily well-balanced and, at the same time, was adjusted to our own everyday life in an urbanised, consumer society.

Looking at Robin Knox-Johnston's career as a whole this would certainly seem to be the case. With that spark of adventure that exists in many people, he simply took it to extremes by sailing round the world single-handed, but even this act was carefully thought out, based on his own background as a sailor and his knowledge, both of himself and an awareness of what it might lead to. He had no trouble in adapting to everyday life; in fact he plunged into it, exploiting his success to the full, without letting the ephemeral glory go to his head. He applied his spirit of adventure and initiative to running yacht marinas and at the same time balanced this out with the excitement and satisfaction of sailing, winning the Round Britain yacht race on two occasions and still holding the record of ten days, six hours, twenty-four minutes. He also skippered *Heath's Condor*, a big ocean racer, on three of the legs of the Whitbread round-the-world race in 1977-8. His family life is back on an even keel; he remarried Sue in 1972, and with his daughter Sara, they are a close-knit and very happy family.

As Tomalin and Hall observed in their book, it is doubtful whether anyone would describe Moitessier as 'distressingly normal'. In sailing on round the world to Tahiti he rejected the behaviour patterns that society expects of its heroes. He did not want to face the razzamattaz of the media's welcome back to Europe, despised the very business of racing across oceans and, most important of all, did not wish to return to our ferociously competitive society, preferring the peace of a South Sea island.

In some ways the saddest outcome of all was Nigel Tetley's failure to finish, a failure that was undoubtedly influenced by the apparent competition offered by Donald Crowhurst. He desperately needed to complete and, ideally, win the race; on his return he maintained a very sportsmanlike front but, only two years later, he committed suicide. It is impossible to tell for certain how far this was influenced by what he felt was a failure, a failure which was only relative, since his achievement in nursing his trimaran through the Southern Ocean to complete a circumnavigation of the globe was quite extraordinary. He had shown the same high level of seamanship as that displayed by Knox-Johnston, on a boat that was less suited for the task in hand.

Of the others who withdrew from the race, three tried again, Bill King, in his revolutionary boat, *Galway Blazer*, with one stop in Australia, and John Ridgway skippering his own boat in the Whitbread round the world race, while Chay Blyth actually sailed round the world against the winds of the Roaring Forties from east to west. For them, the experience of the Golden Globe race, however painful at the time, had been a formative one from which they had been able to learn lessons and apply them as part of their lives.

Crowhurst, on the other hand, was engulfed by the experience. Enamoured of a venture that was beyond him, he found himself on an escalator built by the media and other people's expectations from which he could not escape. He had set out in a boat that was ill-prepared and, in all probability, would have foundered in the Southern Ocean, but while Ridgway and Fougeron, who had found themselves in similar circumstances, had retired with honour, Crowhurst could not bring himself to admit that his dreams of glory were over. Having allowed fantasy to lead him into fraud, when it became inevitable that his deception would be discovered, his mind escaped from reality and he committed suicide.

The way in which the ambitions of a few sailors to out-sail Chichester developed into a formalised race undoubtedly added extra pressures. It also attracted others who might never have set out without the focus given by the race and its associated publicity. There is a temptation to condemn the very concept of a formalised race, as something that sullies the purity of adventure, and yet this is an almost inevitable manifestation of the compulsive competitiveness built into so many people. The sailor or, for that matter, most adventurers, has an ego that requires the approval of others; he also needs money just to launch the venture and one way of getting it is through sponsorship or the media. They, in turn, need a story and look for ways of building one, whether it be a round the world race, the first to the top of Everest or the first across one of the Polar ice caps. And so the merry-go-round of the big adventure is built.

Some, like Robin Knox-Johnston, can ride it to attain their ambitions. Others, like Crowhurst, are not strong enough, and are destroyed.

FOUR 4

Ice Bird

David Lewis Sails Round Antarctica, 1972-74

The waves reared up, chaotic, boiling white, like huge breakers on a reef; foam and windblown sleet made it difficult to tell where ocean ended and sky began. The roar of breakers intermingled with the high-pitched scream of wind in the rigging, as the little boat was hurled up onto the crest of a wave, before lurching crabwise down into the trough, where for a few strange moments she was becalmed, sheltered by the breakers around her from the noise of the wind. But somehow that only amplified the crash of collapsing rollers; sooner or later one of these must hit *Ice Bird.*

Once already, the boat had been knocked down; the self-steering vane had vanished and what little sail he had left up had been ripped away. David Lewis was now crouched, braced on the wet bunk in the cabin, his state of mind not so much fearful as beyond fear, for there was very little he could do to control his fate. He still clutched the tiller lines, which he could operate from within the shelter of the cabin, but the boat barely answered to their call.

Then suddenly, at about two in the morning, it happened. It was like a gigantic hand that picked the boat up, tossed and then rolled it; everything went black, water roaring in, clothes, tins, books tumbling around him; he was lying on the roof, then almost in the same instant on the floor among the swilling waters and flotsam of what had been his home. By the light of the sub-Antarctic dawn he saw that the fore hatch had been ripped away, but when he struggled from under the table that had collapsed on top of him and poked his head out of the hatchway, his worst fears were confirmed. The mast had been ripped out of its seat in the huge vortex of the roll and was trailing over the side, held only by the festoons of knotted rigging.

David Lewis was as alone as anyone has ever been on this earth. He was on his way to the Antarctic Peninsula, the first solitary yachtsman ever to attempt to reach the most inhospitable coast on earth. Six weeks out from Sydney, he was about half-way there, far south of the route taken by round-the-world sailors, on the sixtieth line of latitude, nudging down towards the Antarctic Circle where cold and ice compound the threat of 100 mile an hour winds and freak waves 100 feet high. His boat was a wreck; he was without a mast and his chances of survival were minimal.

RIGHT Challenging a white wilderness. David Lewis daring the earth's stormiest seas in a bid to be the first man to sail alone around the Antarctic continent.

David Lewis was born in Plymouth in 1917, but his parents emigrated to New Zealand when he was only two. Agonisingly shy as a child, awkward at organised

games, he naturally turned to the untracked forests, mountains and white water rivers of this exciting, only partly-tamed land. At the age of seventeen he built a canoe and paddled home from his boarding school, 450 miles by river, portage and lake. He was bright academically and studied medicine; he joined the university mountaineering club and made nineteen first ascents in the Southern Alps of New Zealand.

At the start of the Second World War, like most of his generation, any adventurous instincts were absorbed by the ugly, compulsory adventure of war and he took part in the Normandy landings as a member of an airborne ambulance unit. The war left him with the compulsive need to do something socially useful so, after a short period in the West Indies, he went into practice in the East End of London. Now married with two children, he worked hard and conscientiously at his practice and regained a touch of adventure with a sailing dinghy he built himself. It was the conventional pattern of the professional man and weekend sailor but, in David Lewis, part Welsh, part Irish, the pent-up, restless passion was too great. It exploded with the break-up of his marriage and saw him acquiring the twenty-five-foot yacht, *Cardinal Vertue*, and entering the first *Observer* single-handed trans-Atlantic yacht race. Fourteen miles from the start his mast broke but he returned to Plymouth with a makeshift rig, had the mast repaired and set out once again, finishing third behind Francis Chichester and Blondie Hasler in fifty-four days.

Lewis next put everything he had into building a catamaran of revolutionary design, *Rehu Moana*, sailed her to the Arctic, then entered her in the second *Observer* race and sailed on to New Zealand with his second wife and two infant daughters, down through the Magellan Straits and on across the Pacific.

In Lewis there has always been the combination of extreme adventurer and romantic scientist. He was not content just to sail or venture for its own sake or aim towards a purely competitive goal; even the single-handed race had been for him as much an exploration of solitude as it had been a race. finishing, and what he learned from the experience, was more important than winning. His main purpose in crossing the Pacific was to try to emulate the navigational methods of the Polynesians, who had neither compass nor sextant and guided their great canoes by star paths, the pattern of ocean swells and the birds that signpost the way to land.

In many ways, the course of his life has been very close to that of Thor Heyerdahl, but in Lewis there is a harder, wilder streak of a man who courts the extreme. He had settled in Australia and was a research fellow with the Australian National University, studying the methods of the traditional star path navigators of the Pacific. He had always been fascinated by the harsh empty wastes of the Poles, and dreamt as early as 1964 of making a solo circumnavigation of the Antarctic continent. His motives were twofold, as in the case of almost every adventurer – the competitive urge to be first and the need to plumb his own personal unknown.

He had what appeared a suitable boat, a thirty-nine-foot yacht, *Isbjorn*, which had replaced his catamaran, *Rehu Moana*. *Isbjorn* was based on Tawara, in the Gilbert Islands, under the command of Lewis's son, Barry, who was doing a bit of trading between the islands and also preparing her for the Antarctic for his father. Bringing *Isbjorn* back to

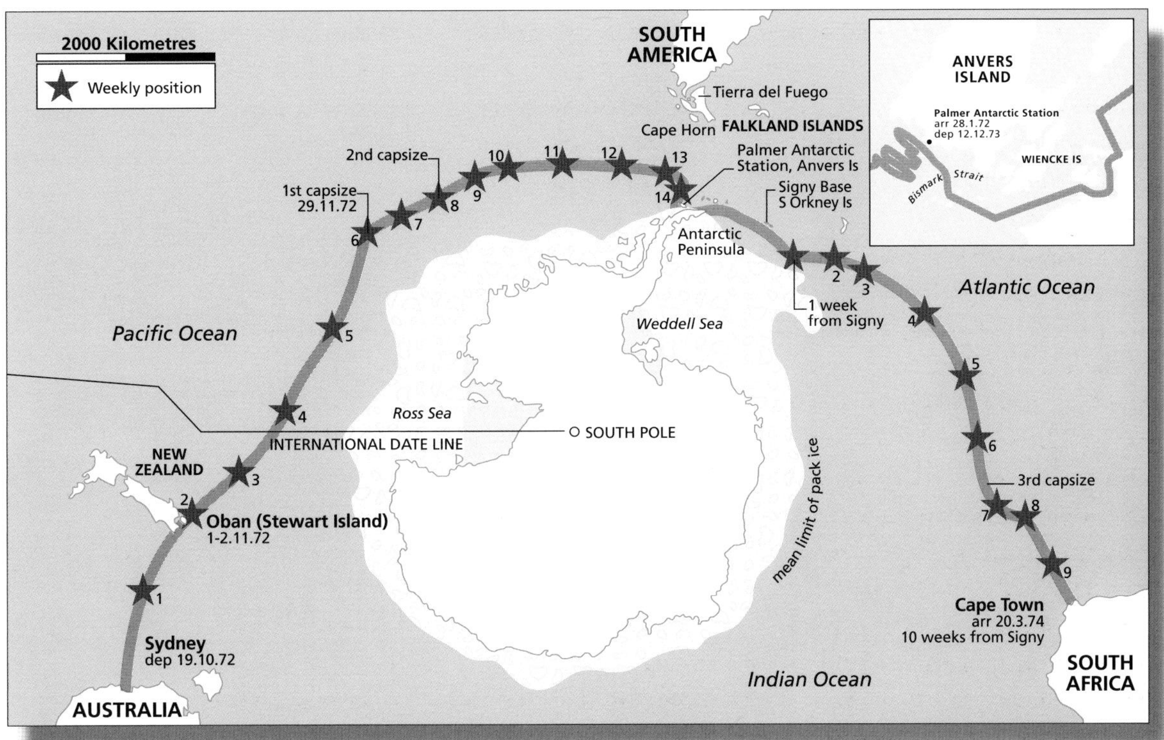

ABOVE the voyage of Ice Bird.

Sydney, Barry was caught in a severe gale and the boat foundered. The insurance had just lapsed and David Lewis had to start again from scratch.

He wanted an all-steel boat that would stand up to the huge seas and ice of Antarctica, but very few are built and Lewis had neither the time nor the money to have one specially designed. But his luck changed at last when, after searching every yard in Sydney, he stumbled upon the perfect boat. A thirty-two-foot sloop, built throughout of one-eighth-of-an-inch steel, she was tiny and yet ideal for what he wanted to do, being compact, immensely strong and easy to sail single-handed. Even more important, she was comparatively cheap – just under £4,000. If one compares this to the £60,000 that Chay Blyth's *British Steel* had cost a couple of years earlier, one can see just how small a budget David Lewis was working on. Everything had to be skimped, improvisation being the order of the day, but this was something that Lewis both excelled at and enjoyed. There were no luxuries, no heat for the cabin, the most basic of galleys, a complete dearth of electronic gadgets, except for a powerful radio transmitter and receiver. He ensured, however, that the boat herself was thoroughly sound. The hull was inspected and strengthened, every wire and rope checked and replaced where necessary, extra-strong sails were especially made. Every window was covered by a plate of one-eighth-of-an-inch steel, leaving only tiny perspex rims. This meant that the interior of the cabin was in permanent gloom, apart from a small perspex viewing dome, fitted so that he could actually steer from within the cabin, pulling on lines attached to the tiller.

Lean, muscular but slight of build, David Lewis at fifty-five was a grizzled leprechaun of the sea, with a fey quality accentuated by a dark pointed beard and deep

ABOVE
After a gale smashed the self-steering device, David Lewis devised this make-shift contraption which could be controlled from inside the cabin.

set eyes. Softly spoken, very intense yet diffident, he has a lurking sense of humour. There is a modest, yet charismatic quality to him that people find difficult to resist. Every expeditioner is indebted to a mass of voluntary helpers, and David Lewis never had any difficulty in finding and using these. It was largely due to their help that he was ready to sail on October 19th 1972.

He settled quickly to the routine of solitary sailing, irregular sleep, the constant round of make and mend, and was at one with the sea. But only a hundred miles out of Sydney, he found his new Racal radio was barely getting through, even though he had installed heavy-duty batteries to power it. So he called at Stewart Island, off the southernmost tip of New Zealand's South Island, where he replenished water and fuel, and called Sydney, warning them it was unlikely he would be able to maintain radio contact. He could not find anything wrong with his set, yet his engine failed to generate even enough power to make contact with radio stations in the South Island. When he set off once again, his next landfall was to be the Antarctic Peninsula, 5000 miles away.

Much more serious than the lack of radio contact was his next discovery, that his bilge pump would not work. He had fitted a new one in Sydney but, in the rush to get ready, had not tried it out. In Lewis's life there is a recurring theme of disasters, some great, some small, but all of which – admittedly at the cost of vast discomfort and danger – he overcomes, almost as if he wanted the challenge to his ingenuity presented by each calamity. The solution to the bilge pump failure was irksome and potentially dangerous. The wells beneath the floorboards were packed with his tinned food. This meant he had to clear the deepest well, repacking the tins into the forepeak lockers, so that he could bail out the water with a bucket. This then had to be carried down the companionway, rested on the bottom step and then heaved up at just the right moment to coincide with the roll of the boat, to be emptied into the cockpit – a slow, laborious process.

But he sailed on into the west, forever edging southward towards the Antarctic continent. It got progressively colder, flurries of snow replacing the squalls of rain. Storm followed storm and the seas got even higher. He wrote in his log:

'I have been running undercanvassed, being awed by the latitude – but not too over-awed, I know now. I was reading, the moan of the wind muted in the cabin. It rises to a shriek; we are pushed gradually but firmly over, as if by a hand and race ahead, luffing (storm trysail and storm jib only). I put the helm up from the cabin with the tiller lines, gasping in the spray showers even here. *Ice Bird* tore crashing along until the squall was past. Then I shook with reaction.'

But Lewis was still in control; *Ice Bird* was making good, if uncomfortable progress towards her goal; but everything changed on November 27th. That was the date of the capsize. The barometer had dropped so low that it went off the scale; it was a hurricane more fierce than anything Lewis had experienced in his long years at sea. In the immediate aftermath of the capsize there seemed little chance of survival. He was dismasted, *Ice Bird*'s shell ruptured by the colossal force of the water, and 2500 miles from the nearest port, which was only a tiny Antarctic base on a rocky, ice-bound coastline. And yet the instinctive will to survive immediately took over.

Lewis stuffed some rags into the split in the cabin wall, searched around for his gloves but failed to find them in the appalling shambles of the waterlogged cabin, so started bailing without them, bucket after bucketful, stumbling over the debris, trying to avoid spilling the painfully collected water in the wildly bucking boat. After five hours' continuous bailing, at last the boat was nearly empty and then – crash! *Ice Bird* had been smashed down once again, the ice-cold sea gushed in through the damaged hatchways and the partly repaired gash in the side. He had to start all over again.

At last the storm moderated to a mere force ten and Lewis collapsed in his sodden clothing onto the bunk. He had been bailing, non-stop, for ten hours. But he did not rest for long; the smash and crash of the mast against the hull got him back on deck. He had to clear the mast before it did real damage. There was no way he could recover the mast by himself; releasing it with his numbed fingers on the tossing wave-swept deck was difficult enough. The mast was imprisoned by a tangle of stainless steel wire rigging, anchored to the deck by split pins that were now twisted and jammed. Hammering and levering at them, he managed to clear all but two of the wires which fortunately sheared. His hands were torn, but he did not feel anything. He could do no more and staggered back into the ruin of the cabin.

It was only the following morning that he realised that his hands were badly frostbitten. He could now take stock and his findings were appallingly bleak. His radio receiver had packed up completely, which meant that he could not get any time signals, essential for accurate navigation. He had only the one Omega wristwatch, knew that it was gaining time, but was not sure just how much. With his frostbitten fingers he was barely able to manipulate the winder or, for that matter, use his hands effectively for the many other functions vital to his survival. He could neither handle the sextant nor even pick up a match dropped on the floor.

By now his boat was a piece of flotsam, adrift in the Southern Ocean. Somehow he had to find a way of building a jury mast. Protecting his hands with wet woollen gloves, he salvaged a ten-foot-long spinnaker pole, somehow erecting it, and staying it with what was left of the rigging and some old climbing rope. But it could only take a pathetic amount of sail, barely enough to keep him under way, as *Ice Bird* plodded crabwise, towards his haven of the Antarctic Peninsula. It was a desperate, yet hopeless struggle for survival, for he still had 2500 miles to go and, at that speed, he would have run out of water long before he got there. And yet he kept struggling on, spending up to fourteen hours at a time operating the tiller lines from the shelter of the cabin, to claw his way in the right direction, tacking painfully, first north-east, then south-east, to gain a few precious miles. The numbness of his hands had now given way to intense and growing agony. They were soft, swollen, beginning to suppurate. He took massive doses of antibiotics to stop them becoming gangrenous but even touching anything was agonisingly painful. Despite this he had to bail out twenty or thirty bucketfuls of bilge water each day, struggle with the Primus stove, go out on deck to readjust his pathetically inadequate sail or repair the fragile mast. The position was hopeless. He commented in his log:

'A shutter has closed between a week ago when I was part of the living and since. Chance of survival negligible but effort worth it in spite of pain and discomfort. These last are very great. Must go on striving to survive, as befits a man. Susie and Vickie without a daddy is worst of all.'

He continued to strive, even though the aluminium jury mast was slowly buckling and then, a week later, the barometer dropped once again. He battened down for another storm, stowing everything away, tying down the table, stuffing the ventilators with rags, and then waited.

'After watching in helpless misery while the remains of the self-steering gear broke up and was swept away, I made one more attempt to steer. It was hopeless. We lay helplessly, starboard side to, rolling the decks under. I cowered down on the port bunk, back braced against the cabin bulkhead – as if to seek companionship from the kangaroo and kiwi painted there – about as far into the depths of the cabin as it was possible to get.'

He did not have to wait for long; it was almost inevitable that sooner or later one of the huge waves would break over the helpless boat. Once again she was smashed and tumbled over, but Lewis's preparations had paid off; his sleeping bag was soaked and his typewriter smashed into pieces in a corner of the cabin, but most of the gear and food had been held in place. Most important of all, his jury mast was still standing; the hatches and roof of the cabin had withstood yet another hammering. The most serious damage was to the main hatch, which would only open a foot before jamming. For a second he was caught by panic; he was entombed in the cabin, but then common sense took over, for he could always escape from the fore hatch. But with a struggle he found that he could just wriggle through anyway. He was unable to clear the hatch, however, so his bailing problems were compounded:

I had just enough dignity left not to cry out for help when the going got a bit rough

'How on earth could I lift a bucket of bilge water past me when I was wedged in the hatchway, not to mention the far more delicate manoeuvre of lifting the toilet bucket out into the cockpit? The answer was found by trial and error. I was able to evolve a set of co-ordinated movements that, when I removed my parka and exhaled deeply, just sufficed to squeeze the bucket up past my chest and, balancing it precariously above my head lift it out of the hatch. Bilge water could then be unceremoniously tipped into the cockpit, though the toilet required further contortions before I could gain the bridge deck and empty it safely overside.'

It was so difficult to light the cooking stove and then prevent the pot on top of it being hurled to the other side of the cabin, that Lewis had hot food or drink only at intervals of several days. The temperature of the cabin was barely above freezing and his clothing and sleeping bag were permanently damp, and yet he still struggled on with a dogged, Herculean ingenuity, buoyed by his own fierce spirit of survival and the thought of his two young daughters who so depended on him. It was the kind of desperate situation in which almost anyone would be tempted to look for help from a source outside himself. Lewis wrote: 'Did I pray? people ask. No, I longed to be able to but, not being religious at other times, I had just enough dignity left not to cry out for help when the going got a bit rough. A higher power, should one exist, might even appreciate this attitude.'

But he was in a situation that seemed to be steadily deteriorating. He often omitted to wear his safety harness; there did not seem much point when the boat was almost certainly doomed anyway. While he was trying to patch up the jury mast, a breaking wave caught him unawares from behind. He was picked up off his feet and dashed cross the deck in a maelstrom of foaming water. The guard wires had vanished with the loss of the mast, so there was nothing to save him from being swept overboard. With an agonising crunch, he smashed against one of the stanchions, and was held in place as the wave poured over the side. It was a miraculous escape, but he paid a heavy price for it. Some ribs were almost certainly broken and his right arm was numb:

'I dragged myself, moaning and groaning and making a great to-do, along the side deck and down below. As the wind was from the south-west, there was no need to steer. Bilge water was overflowing the floorboards, though. Cursing mentally – drawing each breath meant stabbing pain enough without aggravating it by speech – I prised up the floor and scooped up twenty-two buckets from the well to tip them into the cockpit. The rest of that pain-fringed day and a restless, chilly night I spent on my bunk, increasingly aware of the vast difference between a merely damp sleeping bag and one still soaked from the recent capsize.'

BELOW His face a mirror of the bitter fight for survival, Lewis struggles with the wreckage of the mast.

RIGHT Dismasted and battered, Ice Bird undergoes repairs at Palmer Station.

The effort to squeeze out of the jammed hatchway and expose himself to the bitter wet and cold above decks was becoming increasingly onerous. He delayed it until the last possible minute, sought solace in an escape world of the novels he had brought with him. He could see that the jury mast was on the verge of disintegration, but put off the moment of actually doing anything about it. Another storm, another sail torn to bits, it was becoming increasingly obvious that at this rate he would run out of water, even if the boat did not founder first, before he reached any kind of haven.

But Lewis never stopped thinking out every conceivable possibility for survival. The spinnaker pole mast was obviously hopeless. He did have one other possibility, the eleven-foot-six-inch wood boom, but he had seen no way that he could possibly have raised it into position on his own in the tossing boat. Then suddenly, at his lowest moment, when he had almost given up all hope, he saw how it could be done by rigging a system of pulleys to give him some mechanical advantage. He waited for a slackening in the weather, laid out his system of tackle and ropes, eased the boom into position and was at last ready for the crucial test. It had taken him eight and a half hours of non-stop work just to get this far. Tense with anxiety, he began to turn the winch handle:

'Was the 15° angle at which the boom lay, hopefully pivoted at the mast step and supported upon the crutch at its other end, sufficient to give purchase? Yes. The boom rose a foot out of the crutch, then it slewed as the yacht lurched sharply to port and stuck fast. I could have cried. But, thank goodness, its foot had only jammed in the pin rail. On the second attempt the boom mounted steadily inch by inch to the vertical.'

The new mast was still stunted, but it was sufficiently strong to hold enough sail to attain a reasonable speed. He now had a sporting chance of reaching safety; the most obvious course was to head north, for warmer climes and kinder seas, and then to try to reach Tierra del Fuego. Lewis gave it a thought but quickly dismissed it. He did not have the charts, but, more important, he was still determined to reach the Antarctic Peninsula. The charts and pilot tables he did have had been turned into a soggy mess by constant soakings, but he dried them out carefully, and decided that a small American station, Palmer Base, on the south side of Anvers Island, gave him the best chance of survival.

His water supply still presented a problem. He decided on a drastic economy campaign, reducing his liquid intake to just over a pint a day. To accustom his kidneys to such a harsh routine, he went without any liquid at all for twenty-four hours and, after this, adjusted the fluid intake to maintain a concentrated dark urine. Whenever it became a normal yellow colour, he knew that he was wasting liquid. It was a question of disciplining his body to exist on the very edge of survival, an accomplishment at which David Lewis excelled and, one suspects, enjoyed in a strange way.

At last he was making good progress. The long hours at the tiller lines were worthwhile. And slowly his body, even under these appalling conditions, was mending. His finger nails dropped off, one by one, making his hands even more tender, but also showing that the tissue was healing. His ribs became less painful and the greatest enemy now was boredom, as day followed day, with hardly an intermission of dark to mark the passage of time. He had finished most of his books, and faced hour after hour at the tiller, in a race against the steadily diminishing level of his water containers.

As the weeks went by, he became increasingly anxious about his landfall. He had no way of knowing how accurate his only watch was. The compass had a deviation of around 20° east, because the steel framework of the cockpit had been buckled over it in the storms. If he made a quite small navigational error, he could miss Palmer Base altogether.

As he got closer to land the nervous and physical strain became progressively worse. He spent longer and longer hours at the tiller, often peering into a near white-out of driving snow. He sighted land on January 26th, piled snow peaks, rising out of chaotic glaciers that swept down to the sea, spawning great icebergs in the dark waters. It was a sight of austere, forbidding beauty, of black, ice-veined cliffs, green, gleaming walls of ice and a total lack of human life. He had had the shadowy ice birds for company for much of the voyage; he had seen whales and porpoises but, looking at that bleak coast, it was difficult to believe that there could be a human being within a thousand miles. And yet he was looking at Anvers Island, had made a perfect landfall after over 5000 miles at sea. His logic told him that the Antarctic base must be on the other side of that empty island. He was so close to warmth, comfort, the company of other people, and yet they were almost impossible to comprehend. In addition, he had entered the most dangerous phase of the entire voyage, even more so than that moment of capsize when the mast had been swept away.

For two days of increasingly wearied concentration at the tiller he dodged the jagged teeth of islands, the part-hidden threat of reefs and the more obvious ones of icebergs. He was only eight miles from safety, could even see the light of Palmer Base, but now a gale blew up with the speed and ferocity that is so typical of those climes. Close to land, particularly one so forbidding, it was infinitely more dangerous than out at sea. *Ice Bird* weathered the gale and, as the wind dropped, Lewis could keep his eyes open no longer and collapsed onto the bunk, to wake shortly afterwards by some sixth sense, just in time to see a jagged rock skerry puncturing the sea only a few yards away on his beam.

Another day and night at the tiller, tacking exhaustingly towards his goal, and he seemed nearly there – just a mile to go, when suddenly *Ice Bird* took off, tossed by a breaking wave into a chaos of spurting foam. Lewis leapt for the cockpit, but could do nothing but cling to the tiller as the boat was hurled on the crest of breaking waves over what was obviously a shoal. The keel had only to be caught once on a hidden rock and they would be tumbled, smashed, ruptured in the boiling waters. The people at Palmer Base might never even know that a yacht had come so close. And then *Ice Bird* was in smooth waters again. Somehow, she had come through the maelstrom. Another hour or so and she was in the sheltered waters of Arthur Harbour. It was January 28th 1973. The buildings, with that impermanent prefabricated look common to all structures in the far south and north, were still as silent as if they had been abandoned. A small converted minesweeper was moored to the pier. This also, was lifeless, as *Ice Bird*, rusted, battered and dirty, sidled in under her rags of sail, to drop anchor a few yards from the sleeping vessel. It was only fear that the anchor might slip that made Lewis call out, 'Is anyone awake? Do you mind if I tie up alongside?'

People erupted out of the saloon door, to see the incredible apparition. Lewis himself was even more battered than his boat. His clothes were in tatters, stained with grease and petrol; matted hair and a roughly trimmed beard framed a hollow, emaciated face, dominated by eyes that were bright yet haunted by three months of constant struggle. David Lewis was the first man ever to sail single-handed to the Antarctic; he had also come through a battle for bare survival in which, somehow, he had never relinquished his goal. Of all the stories of sea adventures, this is one of the most remarkable.

LEFT Trapped by pack ice in Penola Strait, Lewis attempts to push Ice Bird to freedom through narrow leads.

No less noteworthy was the sequel to the voyage. Even before reaching Anvers Island, David Lewis had begun to plan the repair of his boat so that he could continue the voyage. Within days of arrival, he had started work, repairing, improvising, replacing what was little more than a robust shell of a yacht. Once again his magnetic personality enlisted help, so that almost the entire staff of Palmer Base became involved in the recovery operation. The engine was stripped, cleaned and coaxed into working; two lengths of timber, used for battening down cargo, were shaped and glued together to make a longer mast; the temperamental cooking stove was stripped and cleaned. Even the bilge pump was repaired.

At this point the *National Geographic Magazine* got in touch with him, offering commissions too lucrative to turn down, so Lewis left *Ice Bird* in the Antarctic, returning to Anvers Island at the end of the year. He spent a hectic month in the final refit of his boat and set out once again on December 12th 1973. There were plenty more narrow escapes. To start with it was no easy matter coaxing a small yacht through the ice-jammed channels of the Antarctic Peninsula and then, clear of land, he was exposed once again to the fury of the Southern Ocean. He was caught in the eye of a hurricane at the end of his sixth week out, once again was capsized, once again lost his mast. Now, running out of time before the start of a new academic job, he decided to run for Cape Town. At least he would have completed his voyage, sailing both to and from the Antarctic continent, totally under his own way. He reached Cape Town on March 20th 1974, slipping unostentatiously into the Marina of the Royal Cape Yacht Club. There was no naval escort, no civic dignitaries or crowds. He would not have wanted it that way, and yet his voyage represents the most outstanding achievement of endurance, ingenuity and superb seamanship in the history of small boat sailing.

David Lewis flew back to Australia, but Barry, his son, finished off the long voyage of *Ice Bird*, sailing her single-handed across the Southern Ocean back to Sydney later on that year. For David Lewis this participation by his son was as important as his own incredible saga.

5 FIVE

The Empty Quarter

Wilfred Thesiger's Travels in Southern Arabia, 1946

IT IS NOT JUST THE THRILL OF THE UNKNOWN that has enticed Wilfred Thesiger back to unspoilt, wild country throughout his life; it is a fascination by and love of the people themselves, particularly the Bedu, who live on the edge of the savage Empty Quarter, that desert-within-a-desert in southern Arabia. He loved the harsh emptiness of the slow-moving waves of the sand dunes and the black plains of sun-blasted salt flats, was challenged by the prospect of crossing regions where no white man had been before, not so much for scientific discovery or research but rather for the pure adventure. But having crossed it once, he came back to it again by another route, and then again and again, just to live and travel with the Bedu whose life-style he admired and enjoyed so much. finally, he was forced to leave southern Arabia by the rulers and also by their English advisers who feared he might upset an already delicate balance between the nomadic, sometimes warring, tribes.

Wilfred Thesiger is the archetypal English gentleman adventurer born, perhaps, a hundred years later than ideally he would have liked. In the Victorian era there were so many more unexplored, unspoilt empty spaces; he would have been with Speke and Burton or perhaps, like Sven Hedin, would have wandered across Central Asia. Though in some ways he was born into the way of life that he eventually pursued. Son of the British Minister to Abyssinia, his infancy and early childhood were spent in that wild and colourful upland country (now Ethiopia), the only one to retain complete independence in the face of colonial domination by the great European powers. He had vivid memories of plumed warriors, rich barbaric pomp, ragged mountains and deep gorges.

Through Eton and Oxford he dreamt of African adventures. His opportunity came in 1930, when he was invited, as his father's eldest son, to attend Haile Selassie's coronation as Emperor of Ethiopia. Then, as soon as the coronation was over, he took off to the wild and lawless Danakil country to the south of Addis Ababa.

'I had everything I wanted, even more than I had dreamt of as a boy poring over *Jock of the Bushveld*. Here were herds of oryx and Soemering's gazelle on the plains, waterbuck in the tamarisk along the river, lesser kudu and gerenuk in the thick bush and greater kudu, trophy of trophies, among the isolated mountains. Here were the camp fires and voices of the night, the voices of my Somalis, the brilliant African stars, the moonlight on the river, the chill wind of the dawn, the hot still noons, mirages transforming the parched plains into phantom lakes, dust devils spiralling through the bush, vultures circling over the camp, guinea fowl calling among the trees and the loading and unloading of the camels.'

There was risk as well. The Danakil tribesmen, who gathered round their campsite at night to view the white stranger with his valuable weapons and other gear, all wore large curved daggers from which hung leather thongs, one for each man they had killed and castrated. On the first trip he reached the edge only of the Danakil desert, but it was on this little expedition that his love of adventure and the open desert spaces was formed.

On his return to Oxford he spent much of his time dreaming of the Danakil and planning another expedition, once he had graduated. In 1933 he set out with a friend hoping to follow the river Awash, which flows into the Danakil desert but then vanishes, never reaching the sea. Three expeditions had ventured into this region at the end of the nineteenth century, but they had all disappeared without trace, presumably murdered by the Danakil tribesmen. Nesbitt, an English venturer, had managed to cross the desert from south to north in 1928, but his party also had been attacked and three of their retainers killed.

Thesiger's companion was forced to drop out at an early stage in the expedition, but this in no way deterred Thesiger:

'I was glad to see him go for, though we never quarrelled, I found his presence an irritant, and was happy now to be on my own. This was no fault of his, for he was good natured and accommodating. Like many English travellers, I find it difficult to live for long periods with my own kind. On later journeys I was to find comradeship among Arabs and Africans, the very difference between us binding me closely to them.'

I was glad to see him go for, though we never quarrelled, I found his presence an irritant

This was to be the pattern of nearly all his future ventures; it was what gave him such a close understanding of the people among whom he lived. I have often been conscious of the barrier that we mountaineers inevitably erect between ourselves and the mountain people whose country we pass through, simply by being an expedition and carrying our own customs and interdependence within our own tiny, inlooking world, through Himalayan or Andean foothills.

Later Thesiger realised that on that first trip to the Danakil, where he had penetrated country from which no European had ever returned alive, 'I still had a sense of racial superiority, acquired in my childhood, which set me apart from the men who followed me. Even Omar, my Somali headman, on whom I was utterly dependent, was in no sense a companion.'

But this attitude was to change. After completing his journey down the Awash river, he made a leisurely return to Britain and the problems of following a career. He joined the Sudan Political Service, managed to get himself posted to the most isolated and undeveloped district in the Sudan, and settled down to the life of the dedicated outback colonial civil servant, using his periods of leave not to rush to the fleshpots of Europe, but to make long desert journeys into the Sahara. With the war came more ventures; involvement in the liberation of Ethiopia, frustration at the

RIGHT Thesiger's route through the Empty Quarter of Southern Arabia.

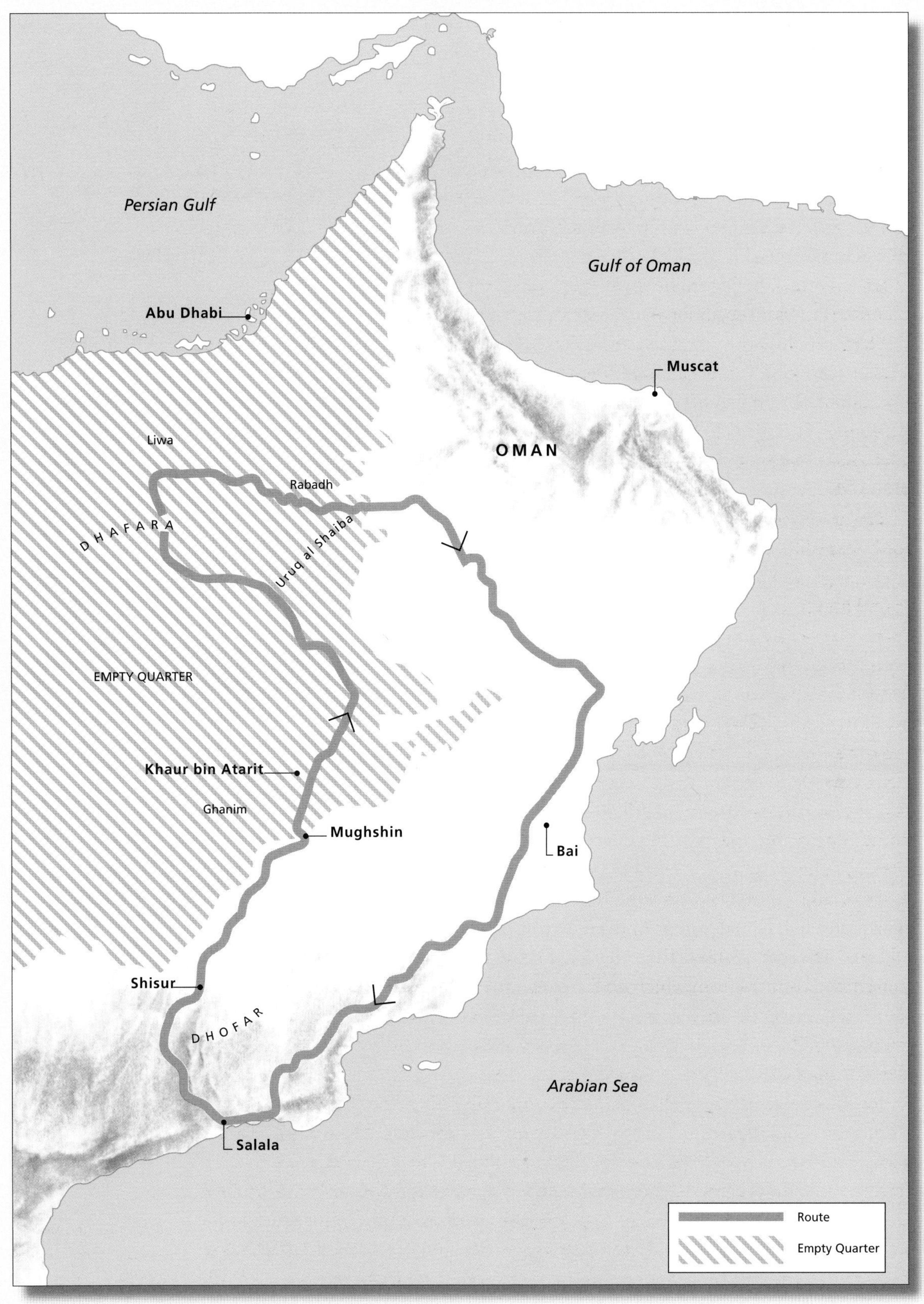
Persian Gulf
Gulf of Oman
Abu Dhabi
Muscat
Liwa
OMAN
Rabadh
DHAFARA
Uruq al Shaiba
EMPTY QUARTER
Khaur bin Atarit
Ghanim
Mughshin
Bai
Shisur
DHOFAR
Arabian Sea
Salala
Route
Empty Quarter

inevitable wastage and bureaucracy that accompanies the massive war machine and then a period in the Long Range Desert Group. At first glance, this seemed immensely adventurous and very risky as they operated in jeeps far behind the German lines, shooting up convoys, raiding supply dumps, but Thesiger found it strangely unsatisfying. 'We carried food, water and fuel with us; we required nothing from our surroundings. I was in the desert, but insulated from it by the jeep in which I travelled.'

It was in the aftermath of war, by chance, as so often happens, that the opportunity arose which was to lead him to the Empty Quarter of Arabia and a way of life he has pursued ever since. He was in Addis Ababa, just having resigned from the post of political adviser to the Ethiopian Government, when he met O. B. Lean, a desert locust specialist. Lean wanted someone to venture into the Empty Quarter to look for locust outbreak centres. Thesiger knew nothing of entomology, but was immediately attracted by the venture and accepted on the spot.

ABOVE Salim bin Kabina of the Rashid tribe was Wilfred Thesiger's travelling companion through five years of journeys in southern Arabia. His most treasured possession, his rifle, is protected against the desert sand.

Thesiger arrived in Dhofar on the southern coast of the Arabian peninsula in October 1945. Already he spoke Arabic and was accustomed to desert travel. He also knew what he wanted to do – to explore the Empty Quarter which had been penetrated by only two Europeans, Bertram Thomas in 1930-31 when he had made a crossing from south to north, and by H. St. John Philby who, in 1932, had ventured into its centre from the north and had escaped from it to the north-west. Thesiger was attracted to the ways of the desert Arab and sought to become one of them. But the barriers confronting him were formidable. In 1945 southern Arabia was still comparatively undeveloped; oilfields clung to the coast of the Persian Gulf while the desert tribes lived as they had always done, herding their goats and camels from one oasis to the next, warring and feuding with each other. Theirs was among the hardest livings in the world, comparable with that of the bushmen of the Kalahari, the aboriginals of the Australian desert, or the Eskimos.

Thesiger spent the end of 1945 and the early months of 1946 travelling on the southern edge of the Empty Quarter. He was getting to know the land and its people, finding the travelling companions for his ambitious, still secret plans. On arrival, he found that he had been apportioned a retinue of the Bait Kathir tribe, on the pretext that he would need a large party both for safety and also as a recognition of his importance. He soon realised that he was regarded as 'the rich infidel milch cow' to be milked to the very limit. Thesiger commented: 'At first glance they seemed little better than savages, as primitive as the Danakil, but I was soon disconcerted to discover that, while they were prepared to tolerate me as a source of welcome revenue, they never doubted my inferiority.'

To the Bedu, he was an Infidel or Christian; the fact that he was English had no relevance. The world beyond their arid mountains and the sea that bounded them was of little importance. They had never been colonised or conquered, though the Aden levies had made the occasional and comparatively ineffective punitive expedition against inland tribes in the Hadhramaut. As far as they were concerned this represented the total might of the Infidel, and they were not impressed. Thesiger quickly realised that he would have to capture their respect and friendship if he wanted to get away from the beaten trails and venture into the Empty Quarter.

BELOW Thesiger adopted Arab dress, went barefoot and sat in the formal Arab way, but he was still an Infidel to the Bedu, and by definition inferior. This photograph was taken by Salim bin Kabina.

'Anxious to prove their equal, I wanted no concessions and was irritated when pressed to ride while they still walked, or when they suggested I was thirsty and needed a drink. I wore their clothes – they would never have gone with me otherwise – and went barefooted as they did. In camp, especially when we had visitors, I sat in the formal way that Arabs sit, and found this unaccustomed position trying. I thought many of their formalities irksome and pointless. Sometimes we shot a gazelle or oryx and then fed well, but our usual fare was unleavened bread, brick hard or soggy, depending on how long it had lain in the embers of the fire. On the gravel plains the water from the infrequent wells tasted of camel's urine, but it was even worse when we reached the Sands, where it resembled a strong dose of Epsom salts, fortunately without the same effect.'

At the end of this period he had earned the respect of his travelling companions and had begun to master the dialect of the Bait Kathir and other tribesmen of southern Arabia. He had also started to build up the strong friendships which were to play an important part in his travels later on. Particularly important was his meeting Salim bin Kabina, a younger member of the Rashid tribe, who lived on the edge of the Empty Quarter and were familiar with its sands.

'He was to be my inseparable companion during the five years that I travelled in southern Arabia. He turned up when we were watering thirsty camels at a well that yielded only a few gallons of water an hour. For two days we worked day and night in relays. Conspicuous in a vivid red loin-cloth, he helped us in our task. On the second day he announced that he was coming with me. I told him to find himself a rifle and a camel. He grinned and said he would find both, and did. He was sixteen years old, about five foot five in height and lightly built. He was very poor, so the hardship of his life had already marked him. His hair was long and always falling into his eyes, especially when he was cooking, and he would sweep it back impatiently with a thin hand. He had very white teeth which showed constantly, for he was always talking and laughing. His father had died years before and it had fallen on bin Kabina to provide for his mother, young brother and infant sister. I had met him at a critical time in his life. Two months earlier he had gone down to the coast for a load of sardines, on the way back his old camel had collapsed and died. "I wept as I sat there in the dark beside the body of my old grey camel, the only one I had. That night death seemed very close to me and my family." Then he grinned at me and said, "God brought you. Now I shall have everything." Already I was fond of him. Attentive and cheerful, anticipating my wants, he eased the inevitable strain under which I lived. In the still rather impersonal atmosphere of my desert life his comradeship provided the only personal note.'

Thesiger had to return to Britain to report his observations on the movement and habits of the locusts. Dr. Uvarov, the head of the Locust Research Centre, wanted to know more about locust movement in Oman, at the south-east end of the Arabian peninsula, but the Sultan of Oman had already refused permission for Thesiger to enter his country. He immediately saw the chance of slipping illicitly into Oman by the backdoor and, at the same time, realising his ambition of crossing the Empty Quarter, and returned to Salala in October 1946, to find twenty-four of his former companions of the Bait Kathir waiting for him.

The problem, however, was that the Bait Kathir were not really suited to the Empty Quarter, for they rarely ventured into its vastness. The Rashid were much more at home in the desert and would have been ideal companions for Thesiger's scheme, but somehow he had to get a message to them. It was no use asking the Bait Kathir to do this, for they were jealous of the Rashid and wanted him to themselves. He was shopping in the bazaar one day when he met a young Rashid who had travelled with him the previous year; he sent a message for bin Kabina to meet him at Shisur, on the edge of the Empty Quarter, though he had no way of knowing if it would be delivered. A few days later he set out with his party of the Bait Kathir.

LEFT Watering camels. Camel urine added to the bitterness of the already brackish water.

Thesiger, in Arab dress, was an impressive sight. After a few weeks under the desert sun, he was nearly as bronzed as an Arab; his beard was dark and his curved, slightly fleshy nose had a semitic look to it, but there the resemblance ended. His eyes are a pale, greyish blue and at six-foot-two inches he towered above his companions with a natural air of inbred authority.

With their camels they trekked through the foothills, at first through grazing downs, green jungles and shadowy gorges on the southern side and then, as they passed through the mountains, it changed to a lunar landscape of black rocks and yellow sands. The inhabitants were as hard and wild as the land itself. Government control barely reached beyond the bounds of the towns on the coastal strip. Here, in the desert, every man went armed; disagreements were settled with the gun and tribe fought tribe in an endless circle of feud and counter-feud.

They reached Shisur without incident and began watering the camels. It was a bleak, ominous spot. The ruins of an old fort, perched on a rocky mound, guarded the well which was at the back of a large cave that undercut the mound. It was the only permanent water to be found in the central steppes and consequently had been the scene of many a savage fight, when rival raiding parties had surprised each other. They left a sentry high on the mound while they went to work, under the blazing sun, watering the camels:

'When we arrived at the well, the water was buried under drifted sand and had to be dug out. I offered to help but the others said I was too bulky for the job. Two hours later they shouted that they were ready and asked us to fetch the camels. In turn they scrambled up the slope out of the dark depths of the cave, the quaking water-skins heavy on their shoulders. Moisture ran down their bodies, plastering the loin cloths to their slender limbs; their hair, thick with sand, fell about their strained faces. Lowering the water-skins to the ground, they loosed jets of water into leather buckets, which they offered to the crowding camels, while they sang the age-old watering songs. Showers of camel droppings pattered on to the ground and rolled down the slope into the water, and small avalanches of sand, encrusted with urine, slipped down to add more bitterness to water that was already bitter.'

The sentry, just above them, gazing over the shimmering plain, caught sight of distant, dark shapes moving across the sand, and called the alarm. No-one could ever relax in the desert; the approaching riders could be a hostile raiding party or members of a tribe with an age-old blood feud. Quickly the camels were herded together and the Bait Kathir, rifles ready, crouched behind rocks around the well. The other party approached cautiously; there were seven riders. A couple of shots were fired over their heads; they came on steadily, waving their head cloths. Then someone called out, 'They are Rashid – I can see bin Shuas's camel.' Everyone relaxed, coming out into the open and forming a line to greet the newcomers. Thesiger's message had reached bin Kabina and he had come with six other members of his tribe.

That evening he told bin Kabina of his ambition to cross the Empty Quarter, to which Kabina replied that he thought the Rashid would go with him and that al Auf, who was one of their number, was the best guide in the tribe. It was an eight-day ride to Mughshin the last sizeable oasis before the sands of the Empty Quarter, and the journey went without incident until the day they arrived there; the camels suddenly bolted and Mahsin, one of the Rashid, was thrown to the ground. He already had a damaged leg and this was broken in the fall as it twisted under him. Fortunately, Thesiger carried with him a small first-aid kit, gave Mahsin an injection of morphine, straightened the leg and made a rough splint for it. They were close to the shelter of the few trees grouped around the well, so that they could at least take stock of the situation. Suddenly, Thesiger's scheme was threatened. There was no question of Mahsin being able to go with them. The Rashid were equally unwilling to leave him because of the risk of hostile tribesmen hearing of his predicament and coming to finish him off. He had killed many men and made many enemies in the course of his life. The Rashid said they could not move Mahsin and they would have to wait there until he either recovered or died.

RIGHT Muhammad al Auf was famous among the Rashid for his knowledge of the Empty Quarter. He sits in the typical riding posture of the southern Bedu.

After a night's sleep, however, they became more optimistic and agreed that al Auf and bin Kabina should go with Thesiger, provided he loaned the others two of his modern service rifles to guard their friend. Thesiger was delighted, and promised to stay until Mahsin's recovery was assured. He was quite glad at the reduction in the party. The fewer they were, the more unobtrusive they would be and small numbers give a greater feeling of adventure. It is perhaps a similar feeling to that of the climber who prefers to climb in a small compact party, which brings him that much closer to the mountains than he would be as a member of a massive expedition. Thesiger assumed that the Bait Kathir would not want to accompany him into the desert, but was immediately engulfed in protests. Whether it was pride or the thought of what wages they might miss, they did not want to be left out. After a lot of argument, spread over the next nine days while they waited by the well, it was decided that ten of the Bait Kathir should accompany the two Rashid and Thesiger across the Empty Quarter, while the remainder would head for the coast and meet them on their return.

At last, on November 24th, they set out from Mughshin to cross the eastern end of the Empty Quarter. They had four hundred miles of trackless, unmapped desert before them. If they ran out of water, or if the camels collapsed and died, they also would almost certainly perish. And even if they succeeded in making the crossing and reaching the wells of Liwa on the other side, they might well be attacked and killed by the tribes who lived there, particularly as Thesiger was unmistakably an Infidel. The problem was compounded by the fact that the Bedu, improvident with their food as they always were, had eaten most of the rations for the crossing.

The Bait Kathir were now frightened at the prospect of venturing into the Empty Quarter and were looking for an excuse to withdraw. Four days' march took them to Khaur bin Atarit, the last well they would encounter on the southern side of the Empty Quarter. There were no trees to give them shelter from the sun, and the well itself, little more than a depression in the sand, had been drifted over. Despite this, there was good grazing; it had rained there two years before and there was still a low ground covering of green plants providing some succulent forage for the camels. Because of this, a group of Bait Musan, a friendly tribe, were encamped nearby. That afternoon they dug out the well and watered the camels. The water was brackish, almost undrinkable, but this was something that Thesiger was now learning to accept.

The next morning he could see that something was wrong. The Bait Kathir had gathered into a circle, arguing and talking, for decisions among the Bedu were always reached democratically with everyone from the youngest lad to the oldest having his say. The leader of any group was informally recognised because of his experience and personality rather than by appointment or birth. In this case a Bedu called Sultan was the undoubted leader. He had served Thesiger well on their previous trips, was courageous and wise, but he was uncertain of himself in the empty expanses of the deep desert and told Thesiger that it would be lunacy to go on; their camels were not up to it; there was insufficient food and water.

Thesiger sympathised, understood his feelings and knew how to handle the delicate politics of this little group of tribesmen. He was still dependent on the Bait Kathir since they owned the camel he was riding, and anyway, even though al Auf and bin Kabina had expressed their determination to take him across the Empty Quarter, he now realised they would be better off with a slightly larger group. Thesiger knew that Musallim, who owned the camel he was riding, was jealous of Sultan's position in the group. He therefore asked Musallim if he would be prepared to go on with them. Musallim agreed and suggested that as Mabkhaut bin Arbain was his friend he should come too. And so the team was now down to the compact size that Thesiger had wanted at the very beginning. His role had been not so much that of leader as a catalyst whose presence and will kept the venture on its course, though it was the leadership and skill of al Auf that would take them across the Empty Quarter.

They divided the food and water once again, keeping four of the best waterskins for the journey. They also bought a powerful bull camel from the Bait Musan, to help carry their supplies and act as a spare. The little party set out into the rolling dunes of the desert the following morning. They had not gone far before al Auf suggested that they halt at the last vegetation to give their camels a final strengthening graze. That night they stopped with some camel-herders of the Bait Imani tribe and benefited from the chivalrous hospitality of the desert. Their hosts had nothing but the milk of their camels, and little enough of that, but they insisted on Thesiger's party having it all, going without themselves, for they were the hosts.

They would meet no-one else until they reached the other side of the sands. The Bait Kathir had been full of stories of parties that had vanished, never to be seen again, but al Auf was quietly optimistic. When asked by Thesiger how well he knew the sands, he simply replied, 'I know them.' He had no map or compass, had only crossed the sands on two previous occasions, each time incredibly on his own, but in his mind was a sense of direction, a recognition of tiny landmarks that no-one who had lived outside the sands could ever have. He knew where to find grazing for the camels, knew the whereabouts of the few waterholes on which their lives would depend.

The sands were like a petrified ocean of great waves that marched haphazardly from the one horizon to the next. There were stretches of calm, of flat level salt flats, and there were storm-wracked dunes that towered six hundred feet into the sky, each one of them with a long even slope on one side leading up to the crest, which then dropped away steeply into the next trough. The little party was dwarfed by its gigantic scale, creeping so slowly across its vast expanse.

At night it was bitterly cold; on his first trip Thesiger had brought three blankets with him, but the Bedu share everything and, since his companions had only a few rags to wrap round them at night, he had ended up surrendering two of the blankets and shivering through the night with them. This time, therefore, he brought out a sleeping bag which he could keep to himself so that at least during the night he was warm and comfortable.

The party began to stir at the first glimmer of dawn, anxious to push on while it was still cold. The camels would sniff at the withered branches of the tribulus shrub which was their main forage and which grew in hollows of this seemingly dead land, nurtured by rains that might have fallen some years before. As the journey went on they would become too thirsty to eat and once this happened their strength would wane rapidly. The men had nothing to eat or drink, just crept from under tattered blankets, saddled the camels, fastened in place their few belongings, the fast-shrinking sacks of flour and the vital, life-preserving waterskins, and set out across the desert. At first it was bitterly cold; the sand chilled their bare feet, causing the soles to crack – a source of pain and irritation, particularly when the sun heated the sands to an almost unbearable heat. Pain and discomfort filled their bodies through the day, the blazing sun being a harsher tormentor than the cold of the dawn. Thesiger could see the dew-covered bags full of water – water that was being lost by condensation, as the bags heated in the sun. He longed for the one moment in the day that he could take a drink, tried to ignore the length of time that he would have to wait for the evening meal, as he plodded through the sands, leading his camel or, after a few hours' walking, mounting it and swaying to the ungainly rhythm of its progress.

'We went on, passing high, pale-coloured dunes, and others that were golden, and in the evening we wasted an hour skirting a great mountain of red sand, probably six hundred and fifty feet in height. Beyond it we travelled along a salt flat, which formed a corridor through the sands. Looking back I fancied the great red dune was a door which was slowly, silently closing behind us. I watched the narrowing gap between it and the dune on the other side of the corridor and imagined that once it was shut we could never go back, whatever happened. The gap vanished and now I could see only a wall of sand. I turned back to the others and they were discussing the price of a coloured loin-cloth which Mabkhaut had bought in Salala before we started. Suddenly al Auf pointed to a camel's track and said, "Those were made by my camel when I came this way on my way to Ghanim."'

To them it was commonplace. There was nothing strange about recognising one's own camel track made two years before near the middle of this pathless wilderness. To them the price of a loin-cloth was much more interesting. They were obsessed by money, were immensely avaricious and yet incredibly generous. Their ways and values were so totally different from those to which Thesiger had always been exposed, that however much he admired and liked their way of life, the strain of becoming absorbed into it was considerable. He wrote:

'I knew that for me the hardest test would be to live with them in harmony and not to let my impatience master me; neither to withdraw into myself, nor to become critical of standards and ways of life different from my own. I knew from experience that the conditions under which we lived would slowly wear me down, mentally if not physically, and that I should often be provoked and irritated by my companions. I also knew with equal certainty that when this happened the fault would be mine not theirs.'

And at last, at the end of the day, as the sun dropped below the crest of one of the dunes, they halted for their only drink and meal in twenty-four hours. They mixed a little sour milk with the brackish water in an effort to make it more drinkable, sipped it slowly and carefully, trying to prolong the sensation of moisture, though within minutes their mouths were as dry, their tongues felt as swollen as they had been before. The evening meal was no more satisfying than their drink, just four level mugfuls of flour – around three pounds – to be divided between five men. They mixed the flour with a little water and milk to bake unleavened bread, burnt on the outside, soggy in the middle, over the fire they had built. Wherever they went in the desert they were able to find wood, even if it meant digging up the roots of long-dead shrubs that might have been nurtured by a rainfall some thirty years before. They would finish the meal with a few drops of sharp, bitter coffee. They would not eat or drink again for another twenty-four hours.

The principal barrier was the Uruq al Shaiba, a range of sand dunes through which there were no defiles or easy ways round. Towards the end of their second day they reached a sand dune that stretched across their route like a huge mountain range:

BELOW The sands were like a petrified ocean of great waves.

'Several of the summits seemed at least seven hundred feet above all the salt flats on which we stood. The face that confronted us, being on the lee side to the prevailing wind, was very steep. Al Auf told us to wait and went forward to reconnoitre. I watched him climb up a ridge like a mountaineer struggling upwards through soft snow, the only moving thing in all that empty landscape. I thought, "God, we will never get the camels over that." Some of them had lain down, an ominous sign. Bin Kabina sat beside me, cleaning the bolt of his rifle. I asked him, "Will we ever get the camels over those dunes?" He pushed back his hair, looked at them and said, "Al Auf will find a way." Al Auf came back and said, "Come on," and led us forward. It was now that he showed his skill, choosing the slopes up which the camels could climb. Very slowly, a foot at a time, we coaxed the unwilling beasts upward. Above us the rising wind was blowing streamers of sand. At last we reached the top. To my relief I saw we were on the edge of rolling dunes. I thought triumphantly, "We have made it, we have crossed the Uruq al Shaiba."

'We went on, only stopping to feed at sunset. I said cheerfully to al Auf, "Thank God we are across the Uruq al Shaiba." He looked at me for a moment and answered, "If we go well tonight we shall reach them tomorrow." At first I thought he was joking.'

They kept going through the night, hungry, tired and above all desperately thirsty. The camels had had nothing to drink for three days, were so thirsty that they would no longer eat the dried-up, desiccated foliage in the hollows of the dunes. If the camels collapsed and died, that would be the end. They stopped at midnight and Thesiger dropped into a troubled sleep, dreaming that the Uruq al Shaiba towered above them, as high and steep as the Himalaya.

Next morning they set out while it was still dark, and soon the line of sand dunes, even higher and more formidable than on the previous day, barred their route. Beyond the first wave ran another and yet another, each one higher and steeper than the last. The camels wallowed and slipped on the fine grains of sand, pulled and pushed, cajoled, but never shouted at or beaten, by the five men as they struggled up the seemingly endless, shifting slopes.

'We went down into the valley, and somehow – I shall never know how the camels did it – we got up the other side. There, utterly exhausted, we collapsed. Al Auf gave us a little water, enough to wet our mouths. He said, "We need this if we are to go on." The midday sun had drained the colour from the sands. Scattered banks of cumulus clouds threw shadows cross the dunes and salt flats, and added an illusion that we were high among alpine peaks, with frozen lakes of blue and green in the valley, far below. Half asleep I turned over, but the sand burnt through my shirt and woke me from my dreams.'

This time they really were over the Uruq al Shaiba; the dunes in front of them were just as high, but Al Auf knew the way through them. Winding sinuously through the valleys, they were now travelling with the grain of the country. It was just a question of plodding on, keeping going through the day and late into the night, to reach the nearest well before the camels collapsed. One day they caught a hare; divided between five, there was little more than a morsel each, but it tasted like a feast. Two days later, they were suddenly challenged by an Arab lying hidden behind a bush. Had he been a member of a hostile tribe he could have gunned them down before they could grab their rifles, but he recognised they were Rashid and therefore friends. They all sat down, made coffee and swapped news. He was out looking for a stray camel. He warned them, however, that raiding parties were on the rampage and that King Ibn Saud's tax collectors were in Dhafara and the Rabadh, collecting tributes from the tribes. If they ventured into any of the settlements around the oases there was a good chance that Thesiger would be arrested, imprisoned at best, but he could well be killed.

They carried on through the desert towards the Liwa oases, but resolved to turn away just short of them to avoid any contact with other Arabs. The following day, fourteen days after leaving the last waterhole of Khaur bin Atarit, they stopped just short of the oasis of Dhafara; they had completed the first ever crossing by a European of the eastern, and by far the wildest part of the Empty Quarter.

'To others my journey would have little importance. It would produce nothing except a rather inaccurate map which no-one was every likely to use. It was a personal experience, and the reward had been a drink of clean, nearly tasteless water. I was content with that.'

Thesiger still had to get back to Oman – without being identified as an Infidel, arrested or killed. They picked their way surreptitiously through the eastern foothills of the mountains of Oman and then back down the coast of the Arabian Sea to meet up with the rest of the Bait Kathir at Bai. In subsequent years, Thesiger made another crossing, of the western part of the Empty Quarter, a venture in some ways even more dangerous than his first, not so much because of the difficulty of the terrain as the hostility of the tribesmen. But it is his first crossing that he remembers with the greatest affection, for this had all the exciting novelty of the unknown.

Thesiger travelled through the breadth of southern Arabia, living with the Arabs from 1945 to 1950, when the authorities, both Arabian and British, decided to put a stop to his journeys through this increasingly sensitive, oil-rich wilderness. As he was forced to leave the land and people whom he had come to love. Thesiger felt a deep sense of loss:

'I had gone to Arabia just in time to know the spirit of the land and the greatness of the Arabs. Shortly afterwards the life that I had shared with the Bedu had irrevocably disappeared. There are no riding camels in Arabia today, only cars, lorries, aeroplanes and helicopters… For untold centuries the Bedu lived in the desert; they lived there from choice… Even today there is no Arab, however sophisticated, who would not proudly claim Bedu lineage. I shall always remember how often I was humbled by my illiterate companions, who possessed in so much greater measure generosity, courage, endurance, patience, good temper and light-hearted gallantry. Among no other people have I felt the same sense of personal inferiority.

'Bin Kabina and bin Ghabaisha accompanied me to Dubai, and there we parted. "Remain in the safe-keeping of God." "Go in peace, Umbarak," they replied. As the 'plane climbed over the town from the airport at Sharja and swung out to sea, I knew how it felt to go into exile.'

SIX

The Blue Nile

Two Very Different Expeditions, 1968 and 1972

The Blue Nile starts with a deceptive quietness, flowing low-banked, oily-smooth and brown between the tossing plumes of papyrus reeds as it leaves the wide waters of Lake Tana. A few miles on a rumble from round a bend heralds the first cataract; the river narrows, drops a few feet and suddenly the smooth waters are turned into a boiling chaos of foaming waves. For the next 470 miles to the Sudanese border the river cleaves its way into a deep-set valley that drives in a giant half-circle through the Ethiopian Highlands. Cataracts alternate with long stretches of smooth waters, whose every eddy holds its own family of crocodiles. The two-legged variety are probably the more dangerous, however, for it is a lawless region where almost every man carries a gun or spear and several parties descending the Blue Nile have been attacked by Shifta bands.

The combination of wild water and cataracts, crocodiles and bandits, make it one of the most exciting river challenges in the world. The story goes back to the early 1900s, when an American millionaire called W. N. McMillan attempted a descent in 1903 with three specially constructed steel boats. He launched them at the Shafartak bridge which carries the main road from Addis Ababa to Debre Markos and crosses the Blue Nile about a third of the way down, between Lake Tana and the Sudanese frontier. It is a convenient division, for some of the most precipitous rapids are above the bridge. McMillan did not get far, as the boats sank in the first cataract.

The river was then left well alone until after the Second World War, when a series of abortive, at times bizarre, attempts were made to descend it. On one occasion a young Austrian sculptor built himself a raft of petrol drums lashed to wooden planks, but did not get very far. In 1962 a group of Swiss canoeists started down from the Shafartak bridge and very nearly reached the Sudanese frontier, when they were attacked by Shifta bandits. Two of the team were killed but the rest managed to escape. In 1964 Arne Robin, a Swedish economist working for the United Nations, set out on his own from the Shafartak bridge and succeeded in canoeing all the way down to Khartoum in eight days. He was attacked by crocodiles, never lit a fire and only stopped when it was dark. Two years later he attempted the upper part of the river with a companion, Carl Gustav Forsmark, in a two-seater canoe. They managed only fifteen miles before being capsized in a whirlpool and very nearly lost their lives.

Then, in 1968, came the biggest and most highly organised venture so far. It was

ABOVE The most highly organised expedition down the Blue Nile was a team of fifty-six led by Captain John Blashford-Snell in 1968. They used big flat-bottomed Army assault boats, with four Avon Redshank rubber dinghies for the white water sections, and were supported by Land-Rovers, radio communication and a single-engined Beaver aircraft.

led by Captain John Blashford-Snell and was essentially an Army expedition. On the stretch of river below the Shafartak road bridge, they used big flat-bottomed Army assault boats powered by outboard motors, and on the river above they had four Avon Redshank rubber dinghies powered by paddle alone. I was closely involved, for I went out as the *Daily Telegraph* correspondent and photographer, accompanying them down most of the river. Four years later a very different party attempted a complete descent of the river, just four men in single-seater kayak canoes, led by Mike Jones, a twenty-year-old medical student. The stories of these two expeditions make an interesting contrast.

John Blashford-Snell is a big, well-fleshed man with a heavy jaw and close-clipped military moustache. He sports a sola topee, Sam Browne belt with holstered pistol, and always wears his badges of rank. He is perhaps a frustrated Victorian who would have been most happy in command of an expeditionary force venturing into darkest Africa but even today, as a comparatively junior officer, he has been extraordinarily successful in creating a series of ventures under his own autonomous command that bear a close resemblance to their nineteenth-century forbears. On the Blue Nile he had a team of fifty-six, supported by a military single-engined Beaver aircraft, Army Land-Rovers that had been specially flown out, a radio set up to make contact with headquarters in England, and a flotilla of boats.

The expedition was in the best tradition of African exploration, having aims that were both adventurous and scientific. During the first part of the trip the four big assault boats were going to ferry a band of zoologists, accompanied by an archaeologist, down the lower part of the river from the Shafartak road bridge. Once this had been achieved, a white water team was to attempt the upper part of the river in rubber dinghies. It was in the latter part of the expedition that the adventure really started. I, certainly, was more frightened and came closer to losing my life in a whole series of different ways than I have ever done in the mountains, before or since.

The white water team which set out from the source of the river at Lake Tana on September 8th 1968 numbered nine, in three Redshank dinghies named *Faith*, *Hope* and *Charity*. Leader of the group was Roger Chapman, a regular captain in the Green Howards. A quiet, serious and very thoughtful man who had done a certain amount of sea canoeing, he had very limited experience of white water – a lack we all had in common. We had had a few days' practice on rivers in Wales, but these were mere trickles compared to the Blue Nile.

The heavily laden rubber dinghies behaved sluggishly in the smooth waters immediately below Lake Tana, but when we hit our first cataract, six miles down the river, they were like pieces of flotsam at the mercy of the waves. Even so, it was quite incredibly exhilarating. As walls of white water lunged above and around us, smashing into us with a solid force, there was no time for fear – just an intense excitement. It was like skiing, surfing and fast driving, all rolled into one – a roller-coaster ride down an avalanche of white water. On that first cataract Roger Chapman's boat, the first down, capsized, thrown on its back by one of the big standing waves. There was very little skill in getting down the cataracts, our paddle power was so puny against the volume of the waters. It was a matter of luck which waves we hit.

That night we camped by the bank, just the nine of us, in an open meadow surrounded by low brush. Exhilarated by the day's run, I felt a profound sense of contentment as we sat under an almost full moon, boiling pre-cooked rice and curried meat bar which we further seasoned with garlic and chillies. Up to this point the trip had resembled a cross between a military operation and a Boy Scout jamboree, the adventure a carefully fostered illusion, but after that day on the river the adventure now seemed real enough. The following day, it was to become too real. My feelings at this point were very similar to those of Doug Scott when, on our 1975 Everest expedition, he had experienced the frustration of being a pawn in someone else's game until he found himself fully involved with the core of the adventure – in his case being out in front, near the summit of Everest. On the Blue Nile this came for me from being part of a small group that now formed the spear point of the expedition's effort to descend the river throughout its upper reaches.

I could even forget my irritation at Roger Chapman's firm, almost maternal authority. His leadership was excellent, but it was that of the platoon commander with absolute authority, rather than the much more free and easy style to which I had become accustomed in mountaineering circles since leaving the Army. I got on well with the other two crew members. Ian Macleod, a lean, slightly built Scot, was

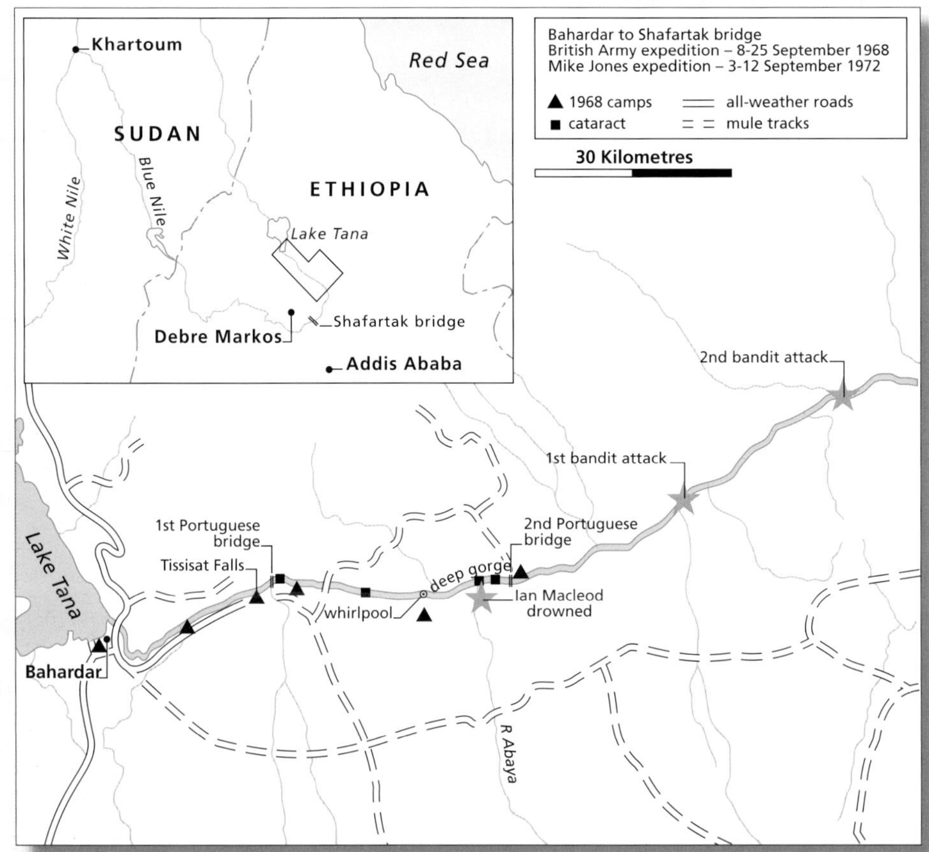

LEFT The Blue Nile

BELOW Sometimes the dinghies had to be towed and pushed along narrow channels between this archipelago of tree-covered islands whose dank undergrowth blocked the stream bed.

a corporal in the Special Air Service Regiment, Britain's crack commando and counter-insurgency force. Although one of the most junior ranks on the expedition he had the quiet authority of experience and competence that everyone from John Blashford-Snell downwards respected. My other crew-mate was Chris Edwards, a young second-lieutenant from the Infantry; six foot seven inches tall, he played rugby for the Army, was immensely powerful but also had a gentleness and breadth of imagination.

Next day we started by pushing the boats through an archipelago of tree-covered islands with spiky palms overhead and dank undergrowth blocking the stream bed. It was midday before we reached the open channel where the current raced wide and shallow over a series of cataracts, each one more dangerous than the last. There was no chance of making a foot reconnaissance, for the banks were covered by dense scrub and tentacles of marsh. We had to press on and hope for the best. In one of the cataracts the crew of *Hope* were flipped out of their boat by a wave. Jim Masters, at forty the eldest member of the white water team, was dragged under water by the undertow and only got back to the surface by inflating his life jacket. As we paused on the bank to repair the bottoms of the boats, he sat very quiet and tense, slightly away from us. At that stage we could not conceive what he had experienced nor fully understand why he was so badly shaken.

Worried by Jim Masters' narrow escape, we roped the boats down the next cataract from the bank, but this was a slow process and everyone became impatient. We could hardly see the next fall – it was just a shimmer of water in the distance, but we decided to take it. Roger Chapman went first and vanished from sight with a frightening suddenness. There was a long pause and then we saw the green mini-flare which was the signal for the next boat to follow. We let *Hope* go a few yards in front and followed immediately. They managed to get through without tipping up but were carried, barely in control, over several more cataracts before pulling into the bank.

We were less lucky: we could not see the fall until we were right on top of it. It was a shoot of foaming water, rather like a weir, leading down into the trough of a huge stopper wave – a standing wave caused by the force of water pouring over an obstacle and then rolling back on itself. The boat seemed to teeter for a second on the brink, then shot down. We were all shouting. It hit a rock, slewed round and the next moment I was under water. I came to the surface, got a glimpse of the boat, bottomside up, and was then pulled under again. Instinctively I pulled the release of the gas cylinder for the life jacket, came to the surface, grabbed a gasp of breath and then went under. It was like being tumbled round in a huge washing machine. I had no sense of fear, just an instinctive determination to breathe when I could, but then came the realisation that I was probably going to drown. A gentle feeling of guilt at having betrayed my wife, Wendy, was replaced by one of curiosity – 'What will it be like when I'm dead?'

With equal suddenness the water released me and I found myself being swept onto some rocks just below the fall. All three of us had narrow escapes. Ian Macleod somehow hung on to the up-ended boat and was swept down through some huge falls before managing to grab an overhanging branch on the bank and pull himself to safety. Chris Edwards was swept down on to the brink of another fall, and was only rescued with difficulty and considerable risk by another member of the team going out to him on the end of the line.

It took twenty-four hours for the full shock of our narrow escapes to hit me. Wendy and I had lost our first child by drowning only two years earlier and this compounded the horror. I was so badly shaken that I asked Roger Chapman to drop me from the white water team. Another member of the group also withdrew and Chris Edwards was so badly lacerated that there was now no question of his going on. Both Roger Chapman and John Blashford-Snell were faced with a major crisis. The day's events had highlighted the very real dangers of the river and the inadequacy of the rubber boats in the rapids. Roger Chapman took off on foot to make a lightning reconnaissance of the river below the Tissisat Falls, where the rapids seemed even more dangerous, while the rest of us were left to work the boats down, close to the bank, to the head of the falls. The Tissisat Falls are as impressive as Niagara, plunging in a great curtain interspersed with forested islands over a sheer wall that bounds the side of a narrow gorge, opening into a wide valley below. A modern hydro-electric station lies just below the falls, and just below this is an old bridge, one of two built by the Portuguese in the eighteenth century.

ABOVE Manhandling the vulnerable rubber dinghies down a shallow boulder-strewn channel.

RIGHT There was very little skill in getting down cataracts. It was entirely a matter of luck which waves we hit.

Since we were short of manpower I had agreed to help bring down the boats and while edging them through narrow channels, often dragging them over waterlogged grass to avoid the worst of the falls, I began to recover my peace of mind. I could not help worrying over my decision to pull out, particularly as two other members of the team who were married had elected to carry on. When Roger returned from his recce, I asked to be reinstated in the white water team, but he had already found a replacement for me and, anyway, I suspect he was quite relieved to lose an argumentative and troublesome subordinate who used his power and independence as a representative of the press to get his own way.

Roger Chapman had now reduced his white water team to six, spread between two boats. As a result of his lightning recce, he had decided that a number of stretches of the river were too dangerous. They portaged the boats to a stretch of the river some miles below the Tissisat Falls, then paddled about twelve miles to a point where the banks closed into a narrow neck, through which the entire volume of the Blue Nile was squeezed, hurtling into a cauldron of bubbling effervescent water. Below this the river plunged into a sheer-sided gorge that stretched for six miles to the second Portuguese bridge below which things appeared to become a little easier. Roger

Chapman, therefore, decided to send the boats down by themselves to be picked up by a party already in position at the Portuguese bridge, while the two crews walked round the top.

It is one of those tragic ironies that our SAS man, Ian Macleod, lost his life while taking what had seemed the safest course. We had nearly finished our march to the Portuguese bridge and had to cross the river Abaya; it was only thirty feet wide, but very deep and fast-flowing, opaque brown waters swirling past the sheer rocky banks in the bed of the gorge. Macleod went across second after tying on a safety line. He was so proficient in everything he did, we just assumed he was a strong swimmer, but before he was half-way it became obvious that he was in difficulties. The rope around his waist tended to pull him under and sweep him further downstream. Soon it was all he could do to keep his head above water. The others paid out the rope as he was swept along but in a matter of seconds they came to the end of it. If they held on, he would be pulled under; if they tried to pull him back the same would happen. Someone shouted, 'Let go the rope!' They did, and at the same time Roger Chapman, with considerable heroism, his boots still on, dived into the river to try to help Macleod. He managed to grab hold of him and towed him to the other side, reaching it just in time before the river plunged into the next cataract. But the rope tied round Ian's waist now acted like an anchor and he was torn from Roger's grasp and dragged under. We never saw him again and his body was never recovered.

John Blashford-Snell was waiting for us at the Portuguese bridge. The flotilla was now to be enlarged to three Redshanks and two inflatable Army recce boats powered by outboard motors. Blashford-Snell was to assume command once more and I had

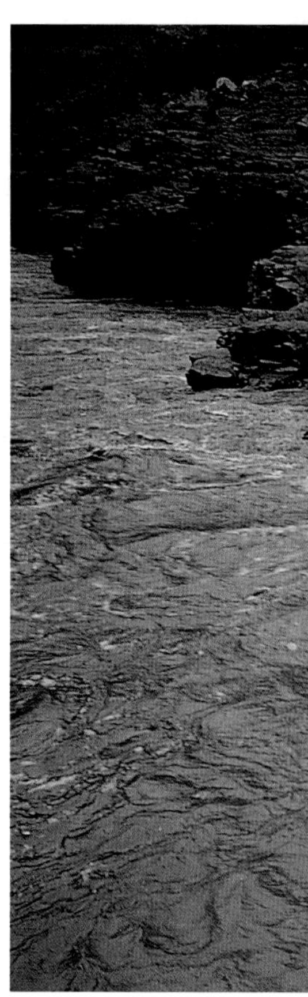

elected to return to the river. Though still badly shaken, I could not possibly cover the story from the bank.

The water was never as bad as it had been above the Tissisat Falls, but it was like going down a liquid Cresta run, never sure what was round the next bend and barely able to stop. There was no more exhilaration, just a nagging fear and taut concentration as we spun the boats out of the way of boulders or edged round the worst of the waves. Now the river began to take on a new character hurrying in a solid smooth stream between sheer rock walls. It was at last possible to relax and marvel at the rock architecture around us. Slender towers jutted hundreds of feet out of the river bed, while huge natural arches spanned its tributaries. We stopped that night in an idyllic campsite by the tree-covered banks of a side stream. The walls of the gorge towered a hundred and fifty feet above us.

We were intrigued by two caves in the sheer cliff opposite, which had obviously been inhabited at one time. Next morning we succeeded in climbing to them from the boat and discovered a number of broken pots and old grain silos well covered in bat dung. We were all excited by the discovery as we packed up camp. I was drinking a cup of coffee when John ran into the camp and shouted, 'Hurry up, it's time we got out of here.' At the same time, there was a sudden, high-pitched keening from above, followed by a volley of rifle fire. We were completely taken by surprise, finding it impossible to believe that people were actually trying to kill us.

My first reaction was that perhaps they just wanted to warn us off. John Blashford-Snell ran out with the loud-hailer shouting, '*Ternasterling, ternasterling*,' the conventional form of greeting, but one of the men on the cliff opposite replied by firing at him. I can remember running out myself, trying to wave to them, and then noticing a rifle pointing straight at me. While some of us tried appeasement others raced out from cover to load the boats. We were still arguing in the shelter of the trees about what we should do, but no-one recommended firing back at this stage. One party wanted to make a break for it; the other, of which I was one, felt we should stay put and try to reason with our attackers, or call up support on the wireless. The deciding factor was a huge rock, the size of a kitchen table, that came hurling down from above.

'Gentlemen, someone has got to make a decision,' said John Blashford-Snell, in a remarkably cool voice. 'When I say "go", run for the boats.'

The next thing I remember is pushing out our boat through the shallows. Glancing up the whole sky seemed full of rocks; bullets spurted in the water around us. We were gathering speed in the main current when I suddenly felt a violent blow on my back and was hurled across the boat. I had been hit by a rock.

John Blashford-Snell had now got out his revolver and was taking potshots at our attackers, though the chances of hitting anyone with a pistol at a range of a hundred and fifty feet, shooting upwards from a moving boat, must have been slight. It did, perhaps, cause them to duck, for it seems a miracle that not only were none of us hit but neither were the large targets presented by the boats. If an inflated side had been punctured it could have been serious.

Fortunately we travelled much faster on the river than they could possible manage on the banks and as a result were soon out of range. That night we stopped on an

ABOVE Crossing the fast-flowing river Abaya. It was here that Ian Macleod drowned while trying to take a line across.

island off the Gojjam shore. Just before dark a youngster swam the channel, chatted with us and no doubt had a good look at all our possessions. We were all nervous and, before going to bed, I made sure I had everything to hand, even contemplating keeping my boots on. Roger Chapman was standing sentry in the middle of the night. He had just walked out of the camp to check the boats and shone his torch casually at the water's edge. The light picked out the head of someone swimming across from the other bank. Then he heard a rattle of stones and swung the torch on a group of men gathered on the water's edge, spears clutched in their hands. He shouted out; one of them fired at him and suddenly it was bedlam.

I can remember waking to the shrill war-whoops of our attackers. I did not feel afraid, just keyed to a high pitch. I had been worried the previous night about the boats, which were pulled up onto the beach about two hundred feet from our camp. If the bandits managed to release or capture these, we should have no chance of survival. Grabbing my pistol and my box of cameras and exposed film, I shouted, 'For God's sake get down to the boats,' then started running, crouched, towards them. Roger Chapman heard me and did the same, while the others formed a rough line across the island, firing back at our attackers. It was a confusion of shouts and yells, of gun flashes and the arc of mini-flares which John Blashford-Snell, with great resource, was aiming at our attackers. I paused a couple of times, pointed my pistol at some of the gun flashes and fired. There was little chance of hitting anyone and

LEFT People were actually trying to kill us. John Blashford-Snell got out his service revolver and took potshots at our Shifta bandit attackers as we beat a hasty retreat.

suddenly I realised that only two bullets were left in the chamber and there were no spare rounds in my pocket. What on earth would I do if some of our attackers had sneaked up on the boats? I ran on down to them and was greatly relieved to find no-one there.

Then, as suddenly as the noise had started, there was silence – just an occasional rustle from the bank showed that our attackers were still there. We packed up in the dark and withdrew to the boats. We stayed there for a couple of hours hoping to wait until dawn before descending the river, but at 3.30 in the morning a bugle blared, almost certainly heralding another attack. John Blashford-Snell was worried about our shortage of ammunition and gave the order to cast off.

In complete silence we drifted into the main stream – it was an eerie experience, for we were able to see only the sheen of water and the dark silhouette of the banks. Then we heard the thunder of a cataract ahead and tried to pull into the bank, but were helpless in the current. Suddenly, we were in white water; we climbed a huge wave, came down the other side and were through, but the other two boats were less lucky.

'We seemed to stand on end,' Roger Chapman told me afterwards. 'I jammed my leg under the thwart and somehow managed to stay in the boat, but the other two were thrown out. I realised immediately that if I couldn't grab them we should never find them in the dark. They came to the surface just alongside the boat, and I dragged them in.'

Meanwhile, the boat which had us in tow, was sinking; the air valve had developed a fault and the front compartment was completely deflated. They had no choice but to release us and we drifted away in the dark. It was a good half-mile before we managed to pull on to a sandbank in the middle of the river where we sat until dawn, feeling very lonely and vulnerable.

The drama never seemed to end. John fletcher had damaged the propeller of his boat immediately after being thrown out in the cataract. As soon as they reached a sandbank he got out his tool kit to change propellers while the party waited for the dawn. A few minutes later he walked over to Roger Chapman.

'A terrible thing's happened. I've lost the nut holding the propeller,' he whispered.

The outboard motor was essential for our escape and they tried fixing it with a bent nail, but that was no good. Then, as a last resort, they mixed some Araldite glue and stuck it back on the shaft, but the glue needed at least an hour to stick and by now it was beginning to get light.

John Blashford-Snell waited as long as he dared before giving the order to move. John fletcher had tied a polythene bag round the propeller in an effort to keep the glue dry and the boats were pushed off and drifted down the river.

The only noise was the gurgling of the smooth, fast-flowing water. The wan light of the dawn coloured the fluted rocks and pinnacles on either side of the gorge a subtle brown. In contrast to the night's violence it was unbelievably beautiful. As we swept down the river, it was all so peaceful and yet so full of lurking threats.

Later on that morning we met up with one of the big flat-bottomed assault boats that had driven up against the current to escort us down to the Shafartak bridge. Our adventures were nearly over and, that afternoon on September 25th, we pulled the boats up onto the shore just below the bridge. We had descended most of the upper reaches of the Blue Nile, though we had avoided two long sections of difficult cataracts.

The expedition had achieved a great deal, covering more of the river than any previous expedition and completing some useful zoological work. It had also proved more adventurous than any of us had anticipated. John Blashford-Snell had tried to foresee every possible eventuality, running the expedition like a military operation with the back-up of support parties and the Beaver aircraft, but once on the waters of the upper river the back-up could have been on another continent for all the help it could give. In some ways his approach was that of the leader of a large siege-style expedition in the Himalaya, with the security of fixed ropes and camps. His management was that of a military commander with a clear chain of command, with orders being given and obeyed. It undoubtedly worked well, both in the general running of the expedition and at the moments of crisis on the river itself. It could be argued, however, that the very size and ponderousness of the party created some of its own problems. In addition, the Redshanks proved totally inadequate for the task in hand. They were too easily capsized and also insufficiently manoeuvrable to pick their way down the rapids with any kind of control.

A very different style of expedition was to attempt the Blue Nile in 1972. I became involved indirectly, when a group of young white water canoeists came to a lecture I gave on our descent of the river in 1968. They wanted to canoe down the reaches of the river Inn, and hope that I would be able to gain them the support of the *Daily Telegraph Magazine*. I took to them immediately. They had a boyish enthusiasm yet, at the same time, seemed to know what they were talking about. Next day I watched them canoe down some small rapids in Yorkshire and was impressed by the way they handled their craft. Whereas we had been bits of flotsam at the mercy of the Blue Nile, they were like water animals or mermen, encased in the shells of their canoes, flitting in and out from one eddy to the next, choosing their course down a section of rapids, capsizing just for the hell of it, and then rolling back effortlessly into an upright position.

I persuaded the *Telegraph Magazine* editor to back them and spent an invigorating and at times inspiring week in Austria, photographing them as they shot the most terrifying rapids I had ever seen and the most difficult water any of them had ever attempted. Of the five who started down the river Inn, only two got all the way down to the end of the difficult section – Dave Allen, the oldest and most experienced of the five, and Mike Jones, the youngest. Mike was sixteen at the time, had just finished doing his GCEs at school and was treated by the rest of the team as the apprentice and tea boy; but they could not keep him down. He had an irrepressible quality and this combined with a powerful physique and complete lack of fear got him all the way down the river, when some of the others were forced out either through their boats sinking or a healthy sense of caution. This tremendous feat has not, and never could be, repeated, owing to the diversion of the river from these gorges.

After leaving school Mike decided to become a doctor, going to medical school in Birmingham; but he did not allow this to interfere with his canoeing. He was in Division 1 slalom racing, but though his canoeing was extremely powerful and completely fearless he lacked the precision to get into the British team. Essentially he was an adventurous canoeist. In 1971 he joined Chris Hawksworth, an outstanding Yorkshire canoeist, on another white water adventure, this time to canoe down the Grand Canyon. It was a big team numbering fifteen canoeists. As soon as this was over he began to look round for new challenges and was immediately attracted by the lure of the Blue Nile. He was now twenty, in the middle of an exacting degree course, and yet plunged into the organisation of a full-scale expedition with the same drive and enthusiasm that had taken him down the river Inn.

He was in his element, an extrovert, a born showman with immense self-confidence and boundless energy. He wanted a lightweight trip, both for the aesthetic reason that it would be more of an adventure and also for the practical one that it would cost less. He settled on a team of six. There were to be five canoeists, three of whom were top-class white water men who had been with him to the Grand Canyon, also Mick Hopkinson, another competitive slalom canoeist from Bradford who was making a name for himself on British and Continental white water rivers. Glen Greer, a less powerful canoeist and a friend of Mike's at Birmingham University, was to be the one-man support team.

Mike flung the expedition together in six months, doing practically all the work himself, but with remarkable family support. Reg and Molly Jones, his parents, became deeply involved in Mike's adventures, supplying encouragement and practical secretarial back-up to his mercurial schemes. He was very much a one-man-band, conceiving an idea and then carrying it through with an explosive enthusiasm which made it very difficult for him to delegate jobs to others. But it was the very force of this drive, however exasperating it might have been to his team members, that overcame a whole series of hurdles which could have stopped a more meticulous and thoughtful planner.

first of all there were the problems of getting the canoes out to Ethiopia, obtaining permission to descend the river, buying firearms and pistols and finding some kind of transport in Ethiopia for the support party. He managed to get a Winston Churchill Fellowship which gave him both a cash base and an air of respectability. He also had the promise of a Land-Rover from British Leyland but was unable to get clearance to drive overland into Ethiopia. He sought help from the Royal Air Force and in a letter to the Chief of Air Staff his response to their refusal is quite revealing:

'I requested air transport out for five canoeists, (one in the fleet Air Arm, one in the Army and myself in the RAF (University of Birmingham Air Squadron) and, if possible, the Land-Rover.

'The application was turned down. The enormity of the task we are attempting, the generous support we have received from educational and charitable trusts and, above all, the fact that at twenty I should be mature enough and have the ability to set up an international expedition of this kind disgraces the RAF in their refusal, despite their vast resources, to help me explore this little-known area.

'To quote from the letter received from the Winston Churchill Trust informing me of my successful application: "Sir Winston – war leader, historian, adventurer, soldier, painter, writer, politician and statesman, had no patience with formality or red tape; he believed in action."

'In emulating Sir Winston, I hope to see more of the action and less of the Red Tape.'

He received neither reply nor the flights he wanted, but this did not deter him and he managed to get some concessions from Egypt Air. At the same time as organising the expedition he was studying for his exams and organising a tour of the British Junior Canoe Team in Europe. Then, just three weeks before departure, he was confronted with a major crisis. The Services refused clearance to join the expedition for two of his canoeists, on the grounds that the venture was too dangerous and that the political situation in Ethiopia was uncertain. The latter reason seems curious, since an expedition of Sandhurst cadets were in Ethiopia at the same time as Mike Jones and his team. Then a third man also withdrew. The reasons he gave were pressures of business and his unhappiness with Mike Jones's organisation. He had talked to John Blashford-Snell about the enterprise and felt that a stronger back-up was needed.

But Mike was not going to be beaten; he chased around and found two substitutes. David Burkinshaw, a Rotherham schoolteacher who had canoed with Mike on the slalom circuit was, in fact, more highly placed in the ratings than either Mike or the only survivor from the original team Mick Hopkinson; and Steve Nash, an electronics engineer from Reading, who was in the British white water team and, at twenty-seven would be the oldest member of the expedition.

Mike set out for Ethiopia with all the gear on July 24th. The others were going to follow a fortnight later. Looking more like a mercenary than a Winston Churchill Fellow, he arrived at London Airport with two revolvers and a shotgun under his arm. He also had the four canoes and all the expedition gear, fourteen packages in all which Egypt Air had agreed to carry out free as accompanied luggage. He managed to get everything on the 'plane, surrendering the guns to the pilot for his safe-keeping.

He had to change 'planes at Cairo and tried to persuade the pilot to carry the guns over to Customs, but the pilot wouldn't touch them. By this time the rest of the passengers had already left the 'plane and were in the airport bus. Mike, feeling very much on his own, tucked the guns under his arm and walked out onto the tarmac; he had taken only a couple of steps when there was a yell and a guard came rushing up, gun pointed at Mike. Soon he was surrounded by excited guards, disarmed, beaten up and hauled off to a detention centre. He never discovered whether they thought he was a mercenary on the way to the wars or a potential hijacker, but it took him eight hours of hard talking before he had convinced them that he was a peaceable canoeist on the way to the Blue Nile.

His troubles were not over, for when they came to change 'planes, he discovered that the canoes would not fit into the cargo bay of the Comet which flew from Cairo to Addis Ababa. He had no choice, therefore, but to leave them behind at Cairo, hoping to have them sent on by some alternative means. On arrival at Addis, he found himself plunged into a lone struggle with Ethiopian bureaucracy to get all the gear through Customs. He managed to do this in the comparatively short time of two weeks; it had taken nearly two months for Blashford-Snell's expedition to clear Customs. But the canoes were still sitting in Cairo Airport.

ABOVE Four years after John Blashford-Snell's powerful Army expedition, four young men in single-seat kayak canoes set out from Lake Tana to see how far they could get. They were led by a twenty-year-old medical student, Mike Jones, who is shooting one of the first rapids with none of the trouble that we had had.

When the rest of the team flew out to join him, Steve Nash took the precaution of sealing his .38 into the bottom of the metal box containing one of the radios and, as a result, got it through undetected. They were just about to board the 'plane at Cairo, when Mick Hopkinson noticed the four canoes which Mike Jones had brought out, lying on the tarmac where they had been dumped a fortnight before. Hopkinson insisted on the 'plane delaying its departure and Steve Nash even tried to unscrew one of the pressurised windows of the 'plane, hoping to get the canoes in that way and then to lay them in the gangway. He was stopped, very forcibly, by the pilot. In the end they left Dave Burkinshaw in Cairo, while they flew to Addis. Eventually the canoes caught up with them, flown by Ethiopian Airlines.

It was nearly six weeks from the day Mike Jones had set out from Heathrow before they were ready at last to launch their boats in Lake Tana. Inevitably the delays had got on their nerves. Although the group had met each other in the canoe circuit, they did not know each other well. For all except Mike Jones this was their first expedition and even for him there was a vast difference between joining a group canoeing down the Grand Canyon and being in Ethiopia in charge of everything.

Mike Jones was in a hurry to get going. The rainy season lasts from June to September and it was now very nearly over. As soon as the flood level began to drop, the submerged rocks would begin to reappear and the risk of tearing out the bottoms of the canoes would be very much higher. Dave Burkinshaw and Steve Nash, on the other hand, were anxious to get everything soundly organised before committing themselves to the river. Dave had spent most of the night of their arrival at Bahardar, the small town on the banks of Lake Tana by the start of the Blue Nile, fastening into position the knee clamps which would help to jam him into his canoe, to enable him to paddle and – even more important – to roll effectively. He was worried about how well he would manage to fit these and whether the fibreglass had had time to set. Steve Nash was anxious to test all the wireless equipment and opted to stay out of the water on the first day to give himself time to do this.

They pushed the canoes into the water at the Bahardar bridge on the morning of September 3rd. Glen Greer had decided to paddle Steve Nash's boat that day, since the stretch down to the Tissisat Falls did not look too serious. Nash with the Land-Rover, was going to meet them just above the falls that evening. At first everything went well. On the first big cataract, down which we had been swept out of control in 1968, they were able to pick their way. The waters were big and powerful but nothing like as difficult as some white water in Britain. Below the cataract, however, they ran into the same problems that we had encountered in 1968. Because of the number of different channels and heavily overgrown islands they were unable to inspect each cataract on foot, before going down. They had no choice but to take them blind. Mike Jones and Mick Hopkinson were out in front, taking one cataract at a time and then waiting for the others. Dave Burkinshaw and Glen Greer, less confident, were well behind. Greer was finding it particularly difficult, less at ease than the others in wild water, less adept at rolling back up once he had capsized.

The river was wide and shallow for long stretches, but then as they swept round a bend there was a roar of water; they could not see anything until they were on the very brink of the fall and completely committed. Jones, Hopkinson and Burkinshaw managed to shoot the fall, plunging down it to skirt a huge whirlpool, but Greer was sucked in, canoe and all, and vanished from sight. It seemed an age, though was probably less than a minute, before a paddle came to the surface well below the whirlpool, then the canoe itself, badly smashed, popped vertically from out of the water. And still there was no sign of Glen Greer. At last he surfaced, about three hundred feet downstream, badly shaken.

He insisted on carrying on, even though he was capsized and forced to swim for it on several more occasions. At the end of the day, still five miles short of the Tissisat Falls, they pulled into the bank and struggled for half a mile through the undergrowth to the road, where Steve Nash eventually found them and took them back to the hotel.

Dave Burkinshaw was becoming more and more worried about the whole venture. He had managed the first section without too much difficulty but was very aware that they had been paddling unladen canoes. Below the Tissisat Falls the river plunges through a series of gorges for the next two hundred miles. They would have to carry their food, sleeping bags, radios and guns with them, all of which would make the canoes heavy and difficult to manoeuvre through cataracts which were probably going to be faster and more dangerous than anything they had faced before. On top of that were the threats of crocodiles and the Shifta bandits. He wanted time to think and insisted on staying out of the river the next day to go down and look at the waters below the falls. Steve Nash also stayed out and Glen Greer had had enough of canoeing; his role was that of shore party.

The next morning Mike Jones and Mick Hopkinson returned to the river. In spite of its volume they were enjoying themselves. They made a good team, paddled at the same standard and had a similar attitude to risk. They picked their way through winding channels, past tree-clad islands, shot tumbling cataracts and saw their first crocodile – a dark shape in the murky brown water.

It was late afternoon before they reached the top of the Tissisat Falls, hauled the boats out of the river and carried them to the road. Mike wanted to return to the water at the Portuguese bridge below the hydro-electric station. Pleased with the day's canoeing and full of optimism, they rejoined the team to face a crisis. Dave Burkinshaw had announced that he was not prepared to go any further since he was convinced that they would be unable to control heavily laden canoes in the rapids. Jones disagreed and a furious argument ensued, culminating in Burkinshaw stating that he was going to return home.

The following morning Jones, Hopkinson and Nash, watched by Burkinshaw, Greer and a large group of dignitaries, set out just below the Portuguese bridge. At this point the river races down in a series of furious rapids. Heavily laden, it was difficult to manoeuvre the canoes through the torrent and they had gone only nine hundred feet when Nash hit a rock, ripped the bottom out of his canoe and was forced to bail out. The other two pulled into the bank. It was obvious that they could never get down these waters heavily laden.

Jones decided that the only course they could take was to dump as much as possible and travel down really light, living off the land – or just going hungry. After all they should be able to reach the Shafartak road bridge in four days. Nash thought this ridiculous; the risks were altogether too great. Hopkinson was happy to go along with Jones, but kept out of the argument. In the end they arrived at a compromise Nash suggested that he and Burkinshaw should act as a bank party, carrying their canoes and all the supplies round the difficult stretch of river – which they knew to be about twenty miles – while Jones and Hopkinson, travelling light, tried to canoe it. They would meet up again at the second Portuguese bridge. It also had the advantage of bringing Dave Burkinshaw back into the expedition. He agreed to join Nash on the walk and to canoe the river from the second Portuguese bridge.

It was now September 6th. Mike Jones and Mick Hopkinson returned to the river with just their sleeping bags, a radio, a cine camera, a pistol each and a little food – a bar of Kendal Mint Cake, an oatmeal block and a Rowntree's jelly. Both admitted to being scared, but were determined to complete the river. The canoes, although lighter than the previous day, were still unwieldy. fierce cataracts alternated with stretches of brown swirling waters which gave a feeling of unpredictable power. On the banks cultivated fields were interspersed with patches of forest and scrub. After twelve miles they reached a point where the huge volume of the Blue Nile was compressed into a rocky passage a bare five feet wide that led into a boiling cauldron. This was the place where the white water team of the previous expedition had pulled their rubber boats out of the river. Hopkinson and Jones did the same, but paid some men who were working in the fields to carry the canoes a short distance round the obstacle.

They returned to the river at the start of the long gorge contained by sheer walls, a hundred feet high, which we had avoided in 1968. It was the most committing stretch of water that Jones and Hopkinson had ever ventured on. There was no possibility of any reconnaissances of the cataracts from the bank; they could not escape from the river, for the racing waters had carved away the black volcanic rock of the gorge walls into a continuous overhanging lip. There were hardly any eddies for them to rest in; they had to keep going, weaving their way through the cataracts, trying to read the maze of foaming waves and tumbling water, cutting their way across the troughs of giant stoppers, skirting boiling whirlpools. They took turns in going out in front, never knowing what was going to face them round the next bend. Their necks ached from the continuous craning to see over the crests of waves; there was no release from the tension, no chance to relax. Mick Hopkinson admitted to being more frightened in this section than he has ever been before or since – they were so completely committed to a stretch of river they knew nothing about.

It was five o'clock in the afternoon; the tropical dusk was getting close when they noticed a slight bay on the right. There was some slack water and a steep watercourse cutting its way through the wall of the gorge. They swung into it, had a desperate struggle to heave the boats out of the water and then started to scramble up the boulder-strewn slope, canoes balanced precariously over their shoulders. Out in front, Mike Jones stumbled on a huge boulder which started rolling, bounding down towards Hopkinson coming up behind. He dived out of the way and just managed to avoid it.

Shaken, exhausted, they reached the top of the slope and found a thicket in which to get some shelter for the night. It started to rain, quickly soaking their clothes and sleeping bags, but they dared not light a fire for fear of attracting bandits. Munching Kendal Mint Cake and chewing through some jelly, they joked about the fact that it was Mike Jones' twenty-first birthday, then tried to settle down for the night. They both slept lightly, shivering in wet sleeping bags, frightened by every rustle in the undergrowth. Mike woke up on one occasion to find himself holding his cocked and loaded pistol, finger on the trigger, pointed at Hopkinson's head.

At last the dawn came. They could not bring themselves to put the canoes back into the gorge, particularly as the cataracts just ahead were even worse than those they had been through the previous day. Instead they decided to carry them for about a mile, round the top of the gorge, struggling through undergrowth, up and down over stream beds until the walls of the defile began to relent and they were able to return to the water. It was still very fast and threatening; they were both very tired and as a result both had narrow escapes.

Mick Hopkinson was in front as they came to the top of a fall. At first glance it did not look too bad, a shoot of brown water leading to swirling brown waters below. It was only when he was on the very brink that he realised that the water was thundering over a sheer drop of more than fifteen feet. As he plummeted down he stood on his foot rest, leaning back against the canoe to reduce the impact when he hit the water below. Fortunately there were no rocks and he arrowed down into the middle of the pool of boiling water, completely submerged, and then shot out just beyond it, his close-fitting spray deck keeping the water out of the canoe, managed to skate past the top of the fall and find an easier way down, further across. A few hundred yards further on Jones was caught in a huge whirlpool; he was spun round and round, helpless in the vortex before several minutes of frantic paddling enabled him to escape.

They reached the second Portuguese bridge that same afternoon. There was no sign of their bank support party and so they set up camp a few hundred yards above the bridge. They were careful to hide the guns and their very obvious poverty was probably their best defence. What little money they had left had been spent in paying the local people to carry their canoes round the start of the gorge. In the next two days, while awaiting the arrival of the others, they bartered the few scanty articles of clothing they had with them for potatoes. In the afternoon of the second day Nash and Burkinshaw, with nine porters, reached the bridge. They were all exhausted, for they had had to walk about ninety miles of very steep and difficult going; the porters had become increasingly nervous as they got further away from home and at one point Nash had been forced to threaten them with his loaded revolver to stop them dropping the canoes and deserting.

He glanced around to see that the crocodile seemed to be gaining on him

Mike Jones could sense an almost immediate change of atmosphere amongst the rapidly growing crowd of local people, all of them armed with rifles, now that they saw the size of the team and the amount of gear they carried. It did not seem wise to hang around longer than was absolutely necessary and so that very afternoon they loaded the canoes and pulled out into the river.

It was now both wide and deep – comparatively easy canoeing, even when heavily laden. That day they paddled a few miles downstream and stopped for a big celebration tea, lighting a fire and gorging themselves to the full. They then set off once again, paddling until it was very nearly dark before slipping into a slight inlet and bedding down amongst the bushes without lighting a fire. In this way they hoped to avoid being discovered by the local people. Using this technique they managed to get down to the Shafartak bridge in four days. They were fired upon once by a group on the bank, but their progress was so swift and surreptitious that they avoided the trouble we had encountered in 1968.

Crocodiles, on the other hand, gave them some severe frights. We had been towed down the slower, more meandering section of the river by one of the big assault boats and, as a result, had hardly noticed the crocodiles. They, however, were paddling at about the same speed as a crocodile swims and, to a crocodile, a canoe must closely resemble a very large fish. They had heard tales of crocodiles biting canoes in half and, sitting in a fragile, fibreglass shell, you don't feel like taking any chances when a fifteen-foot crocodile comes cruising through the water to take a look at you.

Dave Burkinshaw was some three hundred feet in front of the others when he noticed the distinctive V-wave coming up fast behind him. He put on speed, hoping that he could out-paddle it, having heard that crocodiles lack stamina. After about a three hundred feet he was beginning to tire and he glanced round to see that the crocodile seemed to be gaining on him. By this time he was naturally very, very frightened. He turned for the bank and paddled flat out for it. He was, of course, fastened into the canoe by his spray cover and, to make himself even more secure, he had doubled up with a second one. This meant it was always quite a struggle to free himself from the canoe, but now – with the strength of desperation – he succeeded in tearing off the covers with one hand between racing strokes of the paddle, leaping out of the canoe in a single movement as it ran aground and in three bounds reached the foot of the thirteen-foot-high wall of the bank and climbed it.

The crocodile was more interested in the canoe and, as it drifted off, he followed it downstream. The others had seen Dave's spring for the bank and followed as quickly as they could. Steve, who wore his pistol in a shoulder holster, was the only one with a gun readily available. With considerable courage, realising that he had to recover Dave's canoe, he paddled right up to the crocodile and emptied the magazine of his revolved into it at point blank range. The crocodile sank from sight, so they could not be sure whether it had been killed or not.

From this point, every stretch of slack water had its resident crocodiles who came out to investigate the intruders. Jones and Hopkinson now kept their guns at the ready, but Burkinshaw was unarmed and had to content himself with a little pile of stones. They now kept close together, but had several more encounters and had used up most of their ammunition by the time they reached the Shafartak bridge.

They arrived there on September 12th, tired and very tense from twelve days of nerve-wracking canoeing, the threat of crocodiles and the danger of possible attack by local people. They had originally planned to go all the way to the Sudan, but now all of them, I suspect, were beginning to have second thoughts. They had to wait a day at the bridge, both for Glen Greer with the support Land-Rover and also for a Reuter correspondent who had arranged to meet them there. It was a period of relaxation after tension; the bridge was somehow a natural bound to the venture and yet there was the pressure of their expressed intentions. Mike Jones, perhaps, felt obliged to urge them on, down past the bridge; after all, the expedition had been his concept. At first the other three were doubtful. Dave Burkinshaw had definitely had enough; Mick Hopkinson observed that they had very nearly run out of ammunition and that there would be even more crocodiles below the bridge than there had been above. It was not as if the river itself would provide a challenge – they knew they could manage the water. It was the threat of crocodiles and Shifta bandits and the fact that there was no road from the river once they had reached the border that deterred them now. They were not a closely knit team, had never been away on expeditions before and this, of course, was their first venture into really wild country. Steve Nash, after a night's rest, came round to wanting to complete the journey, but by now Mike Jones had swung away from it, saying that there was no point in going on if they were not united. This, I suspect, was the crux of the problem and in the end they piled their canoes into the Land-Rover and drove to Addis Ababa.

They may not have completed their objective, but they had descended more of the upper part of the Blue Nile than anyone else has succeeded doing to this day and, in so doing, had tackled some of the most dangerous white water that anyone has ever attempted.

Mike Jones went on to organise and lead an expedition which canoed down the Dudh Kosi, the glacier torrent that runs down from the Khumbu Glacier on Everest. Mick Hopkinson went with him. It was a slightly larger team than he had had on the Blue Nile and, although the waters in places were technically more difficult than those encountered on the Blue Nile, there were none of the extra risks of attacks by bandits or crocodiles. In addition, a bank support party was able to follow the river much of the way and Nepal today is becoming as much a holiday area as the European Alps. Nevertheless, this was a fine achievement which confirmed Mike Jones as the most outstanding white water expedition organiser in the world. In the course of the descent he saved the life of Mick Hopkinson, who had fallen out of his canoe, by towing him to the side through a serious of dangerous rapids.

He next went off to the Orinoco in South America and then, in 1978, with the bulk of the Dudh Kosi team, on the Braldu river running down from the Baltoro Glacier in Pakistan. Here he was drowned – once again going to the help of a member of his team who had fallen out of his canoe in a practice session. It was typical of Mike Jones that he did not think of his own safety in going to someone else's assistance. He was still only twenty-six. His immense enthusiasm and drive, combined with his boldness and physical strength, would have taken him through many more adventures had Fate spared him.

Of the 1968 expedition, John Blashford-Snell went on to organise a series of even more ambitious projects, manhandling Range-Rovers across the Darien Gap, the pathless jungle swamp that divides North America from the southern continent; descending the Zaire river with another large waterborne expedition of scientists and soldiers. He has also organised Operation Drake and Operation Raleigh, global projects to give youngsters a taste of field scientific work and adventure. In doing this he has given a large number of people a great deal of enjoyment and excitement and has made possible some useful scientific work.

There is a vast difference between the approach Mike Jones adopted and that of John Blashford-Snell on the Blue Nile. In climbing terms, it is the difference between the massive, carefully organised siege attempt on a mountain and a small party making an Alpine-style ascent. It was ironic that the big, carefully organised party had a fatal casualty and, because of the very size and so somewhat ponderous descent down river, attracted two full-scale bandit attacks, while the comparatively unorganised, lightweight dash by canoeists who really understood white water, and were using suitable boats for the upper reaches of the river, got away unscathed. It is possible that audacity has a momentum that sometimes carries its own protection.

SEVEN

Annapurna, the First 8000

Maurice Herzog's French Expedition to the North Face in 1950

One's first visit to the Himalaya is always immensely exciting. There is the anticipation of the climbing on mountains higher than one has ever been to before, the anxiety of how one will adapt to altitude or, on larger expeditions, whether one will be a member of one of the teams to reach the top. But beyond that is the fascination of the country itself, not just the mighty snow peaks that can be glimpsed, often half hidden, elusive and mysterious through the haze from the ever-ascending crests of the foothills, but of a new and different people; the women in their long cotton skirts, heavy ear-rings and gold stud in one nostril, often beautiful in a subtle, gentle way, the men, lightly built, lean from hard work, but laughing and friendly. Every inch of fertile ground is intensely farmed in terraces carved from the steep hillside, the houses, with mud walls, often with elaborately carved window frames and either thatched or slated roofs, nestle into the country with the same feeling of belonging that I've seen in English Lakeland farmhouses or the old Swiss mountain chalets.

But for Maurice Herzog and his team of eight the excitement was especially intense. It was 1950. Only one of them had ever been to the Himalaya before. Nobody had ever climbed a peak of over what has become the magic height of 8000 metres; and only one solitary mountaineering expedition had ever been into Nepal (to Kangchenjunga back in 1930), for that mountain kingdom which straddles the spine of the Himalaya for about 650 kilometres and which contains eight of the fourteen highest peaks of the world had kept its borders closed to almost all foreigners until 1949. The pre-war British expeditions to Everest had all made their approach through Tibet. Now, in the post-war period, the position was reversed. With the Chinese taking over in Tibet, that country was closed to outsiders, while Nepal was beginning to open up.

The French had played a minor part in the expeditions that had attempted the highest peaks of the world before the Second World War. But the 1950 Annapurna expedition was to be the first of a series organised centrally by the French Alpine Club which were to have a remarkably high level of success. A committee nominated both the leader and all the members of the team. Their selection was the more difficult because so few French climbers had been to the Himalaya and of course, with the gap of the war, the few that had were probably over their prime. The younger French climbers had, however, been undergoing a renaissance of hard Alpine climbing.

LEFT Maurice Herzog, leader of the French attempt on Annapurna in 1950, on the party's reconnaissance.

Before the war, pioneering the steep and difficult face routes of the Alps had been a preserve of the Germans, Austrians and Italians, who had claimed the North Faces of the Eiger, Grandes Jorasses, Matterhorn and Badile. The French approach, like the British, had been rather conservative, rejecting the techniques needed to scale the steepest walls of ice, techniques that had been developed on the sheer limestone walls of the Dolomites and Austrian Alps.

After the war, however, a new breed of French climbers had emerged, keen to catch up with modern Alpine trends. Lionel Terray and Louis Lachenal had made the second ascent of the North Wall of the Eiger. French climbers were repeating the hardest routes put up before the war and were beginning to pioneer technically hard rock routes in the Mont Blanc region. Terray and Lachenal must have been obvious choices for the team. They were very much the modern post-war climber; both had been keen and talented amateur climbers and had then decided to base their lives around climbing, becoming Chamonix guides, no easy feat for men not born in the Chamonix valley. Gaston Rébuffat came from a similar background, though born and brought up in Marseilles. He had learnt his climbing on the sun-blazed rocks of the Calanques sea cliffs, but had gone on to do many of the most difficult climbs in the Alps. Jean Couzy and Marcel Schatz, on the other hand, were talented young amateurs. Both came from the traditional middle-class backgrounds which were the hall marks of the pre-war and immediate post-war mountaineers, certainly the ones who were invited on Himalayan expeditions in both France and England at this time.

BELOW Lionel Terray, pictured here at Camp 2, and Louis Lachenal (BOTTOM) were members of the new post-war breed of French climbers.

The leader, Maurice Herzog, was also an amateur climber. His appointment caused a good deal of argument, his critics pointing out that Herzog was not at the forefront of hard climbing in the Alps. He had, on the other hand, got a broad Alpine background, was secretary of the elite Groupe de Haute Montagne, was a good organiser and committee man and acceptable to the French climbing establishment. He had climbed with all the members of the team and had the necessary force of personality, combined with tact and sympathy, to co-ordinate the efforts of a group of individualists.

The team was made up by three climbers who had more of a support role: Jacques Oudot, the doctor, Marcel Ichac as climbing camera man, and Francis de Noyelle, a young French diplomat who came along as liaison officer and in effect was their Base Camp manager. Herzog got his first glimpse of the great peaks of the Himalaya on April 10th, from the brow of a hill above the small town of Tansing. He wrote:

'The sight which awaited us at the top of the hill far exceeded anything we had imagined. At the first glance we could see nothing but filmy mist; but looking more closely we could make out, far away in the distance, a terrific wall of ice rising above the mist to an unbelievable height, and blocking the horizon to the north for hundreds and hundreds of miles. This shining wall looked colossal, without fault or defect.'

This was Dhaulagiri. They had permission for both Dhaulagiri, 8167 metres and Annapurna, 8091 metres, but first they had to find the way to the foot of their mountains. The maps of the Nepal Himalaya were particularly inaccurate, for the Survey of India had not been allowed into Nepal and consequently most of the mapping had been done from a distance. They reached the village of Tukucha on April 22nd and immediately split up into reconnaissance parties to determine which mountain to attempt and the route that would give the greatest chance of success.

Initially they were attracted to Dhaulagiri. Higher of the two and by far the most obvious, it rises in a huge isolated hump above the Kali Gandaki, steep on every side. They made three reconnaissances but were discouraged by what they found. They had judged the appearance of the difficulties by their own Alpine standards, but once they attempted the long steep ridges they quickly discovered how much greater was the scale of everything, combined with the insidious effects of the greater altitude. They then turned to Annapurna, whose upper slopes they could see were less steep, but first they had to find a way to the foot of the mountain. The map was particularly misleading, putting both the Tilicho Pass and the range of mountain peaks that sweep to the north of Annapurna in the wrong place. As a result it took two further exploratory trips to find a way to its base.

Time was now slipping past all too quickly. In a spring or pre-monsoon attempt the time available for climbing in Nepal is bounded by the end of winter, the thawing of winter snows towards the end of March and the arrival of the monsoon towards the end of May or early June, and it was now May 14th. They had spent very nearly a month on reconnaissances.

At Tukucha Herzog held a meeting. He asked everyone their opinion, let them all have their say, before summing up the consensus that Dhaulagiri was impossible, at any rate as far as they were concerned, but that Annapurna offered a chance of success. It was an agonising choice. Dhaulagiri was a magnificent challenge; they could at least see the way onto it, hard though it obviously was. They had still only had glimpses of the elusive Annapurna, by penetrating the precipitous Miristi Khola, which seemed to give the only feasible approach to the North Face, but they had only had a limited view of this and of the North-West Ridge, though these seemed less steep than those on Dhaulagiri. It was Herzog's ultimate responsibility. In Terray's words, 'Maurice Herzog hesitated before the choice. Should he abandon a prize, however doubtful, in favour of a mystery so insubstantial? Could he expose men who had sworn to obey him to mortal danger?'

In some ways I envy the level of authority that Herzog had vested in him. On my own Annapurna South Face Expedition in 1970 the members of the team had signed an agreement which included a promise to obey their leader, but I always had a feeling that this was something that would be ignored in the stress of the moment if ever my own commands were far out of line with the consensus of the expedition. In fact the authority of a leader of an expedition does not

BELOW This diagram shows the route taken by Herzog's expedition up the North Face, with the camps en route.

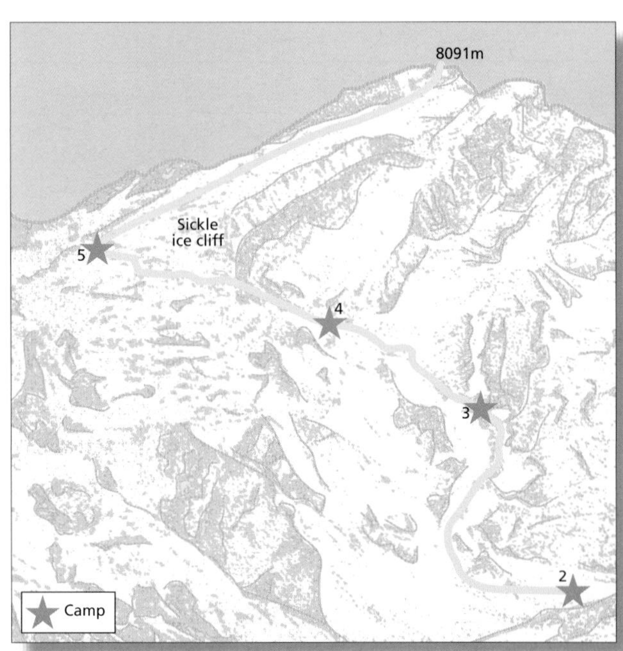

depend on a scrap of paper, or even on a formal oath, but rather on the personality of the individual concerned. Climbers tend to be individualists, accustomed to taking their own decisions, and as a result they do not respond to authoritarian leadership. A group of two or four people climbing together in the Alps, or for that matter the Himalaya, does not need a formal leader, though interestingly enough someone nearly always emerges as a natural undeclared leader in any particular situation. With a larger group, however, particularly one where the members are scattered between different camps, some kind of positive co-ordination which is accepted by the other members of the party is necessary.

It is interesting to surmise how much stronger Herzog's authority was in 1950 than that of the expedition leader of the 'eighties and 'nineties. The mood of the early 'fifties, even among mountaineers, was more amenable to the concept of authority than it is today. Even so, the morale of the team depended on very much the same ingredients as that of a modern expedition, and in this respect Herzog's approach to leadership was similar to that of John Hunt on Everest in 1953 or my own today. He believed in keeping in close touch with the feelings of his team, took an active part in the climbing and yet, when it came to decision making, took them himself rather than put the question to the vote.

The first problem was to reach the base of Annapurna. On May 15th, Terray, Lachenal and Schatz, with three Sherpas, set out up the Miristi Khola. It is an incredible switchback along forest and scrub-covered terraces, around rocky bluffs, along a series of tenuously interconnecting ledges that weave their way between the dizzy snow-clad summits of the Nilgiri peaks and the dark gorge of the Miristi Khola, 1500 metres below. They could barely hear the thunder of the torrent that hurtled down its bed, and then at last at the end of the switchback, a steep but easy couloir led down to the open sweep of the Annapurna Basin.

Annapurna was before them, but they still had to find a way up the mountain and the uncertainties weren't over. By far the safest route seemed the North-West Ridge because of being free from avalanche danger, but it was long and gendarmed. Herzog once again wanted to recce every alternative, sending parties both to the ridge and the heavily glaciated North Face. The ridge proved to be more difficult than they had anticipated, while the face proved to be easy, though threatened by huge avalanches that came sweeping down it from a great sickle of ice cliffs above. So they accepted the dangers of the easier route. It was now May 23rd; the monsoon would be upon them in another fortnight and most of the expedition baggage and part of the team were still scattered between Tukucha and their newly established Base below the mountain.

They wasted no time and started to push the route out in the manner that had already become customary on most Himalayan climbs. There are two ways of climbing a mountain: Alpine-style, where the climbers carry everything with them and make a single push towards the summit, bivouacking or camping as they go, or by siege tactics, where a series of camps are established up the mountain and all the gear needed to make a summit bid is slowly ferried upwards, the aim usually being to put two men into a top camp to make the summit bid. This pyramid approach was

developed in the face of the great scale and altitude of the Himalaya, once climbers found that they were unable to carry everything they needed on their backs for a single push. The number of camps and the distance between them is determined by how far a man, usually a Sherpa, can ferry a load in a day. The Sherpas therefore filled a vital role in this siege approach to mountaineering. Ferrying loads is both exhausting and monotonous work; much pleasanter to pay someone else to do this, while the climbers concentrate on the exciting business of finding the route. On pre-war Everest expeditions the British climbers very rarely carried a load.

ABOVE Camp 2 of the 1978 American women's expedition, which was in approximately the same place as Herzog's, with the North Face towering above in the moonlight.

Back in France, Herzog and his team had discussed the possibility of making an Alpine approach, of moving swiftly, lightly laden up the mountain, as they had done on many multi-day climbs in the Alps. It seemed aesthetically more pleasing and, on a practical level, would have meant that they could complete the climb much more swiftly. But they were ahead of their time and now, in the great bowl of Annapurna, they were confronted with the realities of Himalayan climbing, the savage heat of the midday sun, the afternoon snowfall that covered their tracks each day, and most of all the effects of altitude, exaggerated by the fact that it was their first visit to the Himalaya. With subsequent visits the speed of acclimatisation undoubtedly improves.

They found that they had no choice but to resort to the siege-style expedition – though they approached it with considerable élan, sharing the task of load carrying with the Sherpas and pushing the route out as fast as possible.

The six climbers alternated out in front, picking their way across the dangerous basin below the Sickle ice cliff, up the steep gully that led into the upper reaches of the mountain. They were full of optimism, yet their differing abilities and characters emerge. Herzog, probably the least capable technical climber of the six, emerged as an extremely strong goer at altitude. The other driving force of the team was Lionel Terray, dogmatic, single-minded, immensely determined, not so much for himself, but for the expedition as a whole. He was prepared to do that little bit extra, to go back down with the Sherpas, to escort them through a dangerous stretch of glacier, rush back up with a heavy load the next day, push the route out a little bit further when others were exhausted. They had already heard that the monsoon had reached Eastern India, and was expected to hit Nepal on June 5th. May was now very nearly spent and they were running out of time.

At last, on June 2nd, they seemed poised for their bid for the summit. Who goes for the summit depends as much on their position on the mountain at the time as their fitness. Herzog had hoped to make his bid with Lionel Terray, but they had got out of phase with each other, through Terray doggedly stocking Camp 4, knowing it had to be done, even though it would mean he would be in the wrong place to made the summit bid with Herzog. As a result it was Terray's closest friend, Lachenal, who teamed up with Herzog to climb up to the top camp. Lachenal, a volatile, impetuous personality, was always restless, at times wildly optimistic, but he could also be easily depressed. On Annapurna he had swung from demonic pushes to moments of pessimism, but now, making his way with Herzog and two Sherpas, above the Sickle ice barrier, across the long slope that stretched up towards the summit, it didn't look as if anything could stop them. They were climbing at over 7300 metres; every step took a separate effort of will as they ploughed through the freshly fallen snow; high above, the snow-laden wind blasted through the crenellated summit ridge as through the teeth of a comb, trailing long streamers of mist across the sky above them. They plodded on through the afternoon, the ridge never seeming to get any closer, and then, almost before they were aware of it, it was there in front of them, smooth ice-plastered rock.

BELOW A Sherpa crossing the ice slope above Camp 2. The monsoon was almost upon them and they were running out of time.

They hacked out a tiny ledge in the hard snow, erected the tent and, wishing them luck, the two

Sherpas hurried back down to the security of the lower camps. The tent was barely big enough for two and already, before dusk, the spindrift hissing down the slope had started to build up between the snow and the tent wall, inexorably pushing them towards the abyss. At altitude there is a terrible lethargy that makes every movement, every task an almost insurmountable challenge. That night they couldn't face cooking any food, just brewed some tea and swallowed the array of pills that Oudot had prescribed. Through a combination of excitement and discomfort they didn't sleep much. It had now begun to snow and the wind was tearing at the tent, threatening to pluck it from its precarious perch. By morning the tent had very nearly collapsed; they were both half suffocated, the rime-covered walls pressed down onto their sleeping bags. Dulled by the altitude, it was just too much trouble even to light the stove; it was hard enough wriggling out of their sleeping bags, forcing on frozen boots.

And so they set out, having had only a cup of tea the previous night and nothing at all to eat or drink that morning. The slope looked straightforward so they left the rope behind, but Herzog did push into his sack a tube of condensed milk and some nougat. They struggled upwards through the day, one foot in front of the other, several pants for every step.

Lachenal insisted on stopping and took off his boots to massage his feet; he had lost all feeling, they were so cold.

'What'll you do if I turn back?' Lachenal asked Herzog.

'Go on by myself,' was the reply.

'I'll keep going then.'

And they plodded on, the mountains around them slowly dropping away below their feet, each of them in a world of his own. Herzog, in a state of euphoria, described it. 'I was living in a world of crystal. Sounds were indistinct, the atmosphere like cotton wool. An astonishing happiness welled up in me, but I could not define it. Everything was so new, so utterly unprecedented.'

And at last the summit rocks came in sight; there was a short gully leading through them; they climbed it and suddenly the savage wind was tearing at their clothes and faces, the slope dropped away on all sides. They had reached the summit of Annapurna; they were the first men to climb a peak of over 8000 metres. Herzog had a wonderful sense of joy as he gazed across at the new vistas, now unfolded. The South Face of Annapurna dropped away dizzily below his feet; he could gaze down at the shapely fish-tailed summit of Machapuchare, nudging through the dark, banked clouds marching in from the south. They had got there only just in front of the monsoon.

Already Lachenal was impatient to start down, but Herzog, wanting to savour their moment of victory, dug a tiny silk flag from his rucksack, tied it to the ice axe and handed it to Lachenal for the vital photograph. Herzog stayed on the summit for another few moments after Lachenal had started descending the gully and then, almost in a dream, began to follow him down. It was all so miraculous, after being rebuffed by Dhaulagiri, the long search for the way onto Annapurna, and then their race up the mountain. He was hurrying to catch up with Lachenal who was already

RIGHT Climbers just below the Sickle ice cliff.

a tiny dot making the long traverse below the summit rocks. Out of breath, he paused, took off his sack and opened it, he could never remember why. To do this he had taken off his gloves; suddenly, out of the corner of his eye, he saw two dark shapes roll and bounce down the slope – his gloves. He watched them with a growing awareness of the significance of their loss as they vanished into the dazzling white of the snows around him.

He had a pair of socks in his rucksack, but it never occurred to him to use them as gloves. Terray and Rébuffat should be at the top camp by now; they'd look after him; he had to get there as quickly as possible and set off once more. He felt as if he was running, but in fact he was desperately slow – a few slow-motion steps, sit down in the snow for a rest, then a few more steps in the daze of euphoric exhaustion. The clouds were now racing over the top of Annapurna, a bitter, penetrating wind lashing down the slope, but his hands were no longer cold, there was no feeling at all.

The tendrils of cloud wrapped around him. Lachenal had been somewhere in front, but his tracks were covered. Herzog kept going, and at last the tents came in sight. Two tents, when there had only been one that morning. Terray and Rébuffat must be there; his problems were over. He plunged into the tent with a shout of relief, excited to tell them of their successful ascent. They were as delighted as he, but then they noticed his hands; they were like blocks of ice, white, hard and cold. Where was Lachenal? He should have been down in front of Herzog, but he hadn't arrived. Terray poked his head out of the tent and listened, but heard nothing beside the howling of the wind, and then there was a distant cry.

ABOVE Maurice Herzog on the summit of Annapurna, the first 8000-metre peak to have been climbed, June 3rd 1950.

He got out of the tent and gazed around him, but the cloud had closed in and he could see nothing. He shouted into the mist but there was no reply. Lachenal was one of his best friends, they had done so many hard climbs together. He broke down crying, and then the mists parted, and about a hundred metres below, he saw the body of his friend lying motionless in the snow. He didn't wait to put on his crampons, just grabbed an ice axe and leapt into a glissade down the steep, hard snow, stopping himself with a jump turn as he came level with Lachenal. It was a rash, but incredibly courageous act.

Fortunately Lachenal had not broken any bones in his fall, but he had lost a crampon and his ice axe, and he was obsessed with worry about his feet which were now frozen hard. He wanted to go straight down that night to reach the doctor, terrified at the prospect of amputation and never again being able to climb. It was all Terray could do to persuade him to climb back up to the tents.

They had a terrible night, Terray and Rébuffat spending most of it massaging and beating the frostbitten limbs of Herzog and Lachenal. In fact they probably did quite a lot of damage, for it has since been found that it is better to avoid any kind of abrasion on frostbitten areas and to use steady body heat to warm up the injured parts. It would in fact have been better to have left the limbs frozen until they got back down to Base Camp. Even so by the morning some life had come back to their limbs but with it also came inflammation and swelling. The storm had now built up to a furious crescendo, spindrift avalanches pouring down the face, crushing the tents, penetrating every chink in the entrance and ventilators. Getting ready in the morning is bad enough in perfect conditions. In a storm with two exhausted, injured men, it must have been desperate. In these circumstances, someone nearly always assumes command; in this instance it was Terray. He shouted at the others to get ready, started to dress Lachenal for the descent and was immediately confronted with an appalling problem. In thawing out, Lachenal's feet had now swollen and he couldn't force them into his boots. There seemed only one solution; Terray's were two sizes larger, and Lachenal could get these on, but then, what about Terray? It would mean forcing his feet into boots that were much too small. He realised the significance of what he was doing, probably condemning himself to severe frostbite, but he didn't think twice, and taking off his spare socks, managed to squeeze into Lachenal's boots. He stuffed their sleeping bags into the rucksacks and climbed out of the tent, shouted at Rébuffat to hurry up, and then at last they were all ready and started down the slope.

It was a white out. They couldn't see where they were going, couldn't recognise the séracs and crevasses through which they had weaved on the way up. Herzog was terribly weak, but kept going; Lachenal was almost hysterical with worry about his feet; his natural impatience exaggerated by the crisis. At one moment he fought with Terray to keep rushing downwards, no matter if it was in the wrong direction, and the next demanded they stopped where they were and waited till the weather cleared. The day crept by; no sign of the tent at Camp 4; no sign of the vital gully that led back down through the Sickle ice wall. They were lost, exhausted and almost helpless, faced with the prospect of a night out in the storm without any kind of shelter. Terray began trying to dig out a snow cave with his ice axe; Lachenal had wandered off to look at a part-covered crevasse a few metres away. Suddenly there was a yell; he vanished from sight. They raced over, and there was a shout from its dark depths.

'It's all right. I've found just the place. There's a bloody great cave in here.'

Soon they were all down in the cave, sheltered from the tearing wind and cold above. At least they had a chance of surviving the night. Terray pulled out his sleeping bag, longing to snuggle into it, looked across at the others. Rébuffat and Herzog had that look about them that told him they didn't have their bags; in the rush to get down that morning they had wanted to travel as light as possible, convinced that they could get all the way down that day. Terray shared his bag with the other two, all three squeezing their legs into it.

They shivered and dozed through the night, as the spindrift seeped down into the cave, covering them and all their equipment. At last the dawn arrived. In an ice cave you can't tell what is happening outside; you can't hear the howl of the wind and the light filtering through the snow gives no indication of whether it is bright sunlight or thick cloud. Lethargically, they started to hunt for their boots and other gear, hidden under the mantle of icy spindrift. Rébuffat was the first to find his boots, get them on and climb out of the cave. It took him a moment to realise that he was snow blind; the previous day, he and Terray had removed their goggles in an effort to see through the driving snows of the white out. They were now paying the price for their mistake.

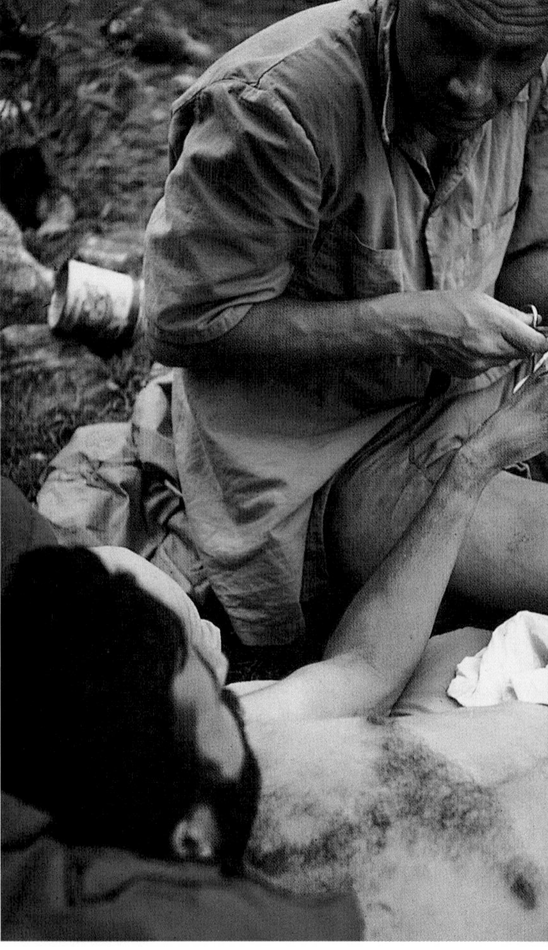

ABOVE 'Tell me if it hurts'. Dead tissue didn't hurt, but it meant Oudot amputated the ends of all Herzog's fingers and toes without anaesthetic during the retreat from the mountain.

Their spirits dropped; they must all have secretly wondered about their chances of survival. It was a case of the blind leading the lame. Lachenal was the next out; as he poked his head out of the hole he let out a cry of joy. It was a fine, clear day. They might yet survive. Terray also climbed out but Herzog stayed below searching for all their boots and belongings in the snow, digging away with his bare, feelingless hands. At last he found all the vital items and then Terray had a desperate task trying to haul him up the steep snow shoot that led out of the cave. Herzog had lost the use of his hands; his fingers were frozen stick-like talons. There was no feeling at all in his legs. With an enormous struggle he managed to crawl out of his icy tomb.

'I'm dying,' he told Terray. 'You'll have to leave me'.

Terray did his best to reassure Herzog, and then suddenly there was a shout. It was Schatz; the Sherpas were there too. The previous night they had stopped only a couple of hundred metres short of the camp. They were saved, but their adventures were by no means over. They had a long way to get down. They were involved in an avalanche and only saved because Herzog fell into a crevasse and was caught like an inert anchor, holding the others from the rope tied round his waist. At last, that afternoon they staggered into Camp 2. The other members of the team and, most important, Oudot, the doctor, were there. They had come through it alive, but the pain had only just begun. Then came the agony of intravenous injections given by Oudot in the cramped confines of a two-man tent, of being manhandled down the mountain, and then, in the monsoon rains, back over the switchbacks of the Miristi Khola, down through the foothills. There were days of pain and worry, of amputations by the wayside without the benefit of anaesthetic and wondering how they would adapt to lives without fingers and toes, deprived of the joy of climbing.

Lionel Terray and Gaston Rébuffat had escaped with no more than frost-nipped fingers and toes, and snow blindness that soon wore off. It was undoubtedly a miracle that the four survived at all; there had been so many narrow escapes. With the hindsight of the present day it is easy to pick out mistakes, to observe that the north side of Annapurna was technically easy, but this is to forget how little was known of Himalayan climbing in 1950, how sparse was the level of success up to this time. Considering the problems they had had in trying to find a way onto the mountain and then the limited time they had to climb it, their achievement was all the greater. They displayed élan in their approach to the climb that in many ways was ahead of their time. The team had worked well together. One can't resist wondering what would have happened had Terray not sacrificed his chance to be on the summit bid. He might well have stayed with Herzog, given him a spare pair of gloves to ensure he got back to their top camp without frostbite, but that is pure conjecture. After getting back, Herzog ended his book with the following words: 'Annapurna, to which we had gone empty-handed, was a treasure on which we should live the rest of our days. With this realisation we turn a new page: a new life begins. There are other Annapurnas in the lives of men.'

They had come through it alive, but the pain had only just begun

Herzog found his Annapurna in spite of losing all his toes and fingers. He could never climb again but he sublimated his energies in his business and the work of the French Alpine Club, eventually becoming Minister of Sport for France. Today he is an urbane, relaxed man who one feels has led a full and profoundly satisfying life. There are no signs of any discontent or frustration. Lachenal, on the other hand, found it less easy. Terray described it:

'The curtailment profoundly changed his character. Once he had seemed magically immune from the ordinary clumsiness and weight of humankind and the contrast was like wearing a ball and chain. This slower kind of mountaineering no longer gave him the old feeling of moving in a fourth dimension, of dancing on the impossible and he sought desperately to rediscover it elsewhere.'

He had always been a fast driver, as many climbers are and the recklessness of his driving became legendary. He died four years later in a skiing accident.

Terray was killed in 1965 on the limestone cliffs of the Vercors in Central France. Only a few weeks before, I had climbed with him and the famous Belgian solo climber, Claudio Barbier, on the very same cliff. It had been a joyous, light-hearted day, climbing on the sun-warmed limestone, the wooded valley with its nestling fields and farmhouses down below. It all seemed so peaceful, so free from threat. Terray's death brought home to me how constant is the risk in climbing, not so much in the moments of acute and obvious danger, as on Annapurna, when fighting for life, every nerve stretched to the limit, but in moments of relaxation on easy ground, when a loose hold, a falling stone, can cause a slip which might end in a long and fatal fall.

8

EIGHT

The Challenge of Everest

The First Ascent Led by John Hunt, 1953

FROM THE SOUTH, MOUNT EVEREST (8848 METRES) resembles a medieval fortress, its triangular summit, the keep, guarded by the turreted walls of the outer bailey; Lhotse, fourth highest mountain in the world, is a massive corner tower linking the high curtain wall of Nuptse. The gateway to this fortress is the Khumbu Icefall, portcullised with séracs, moated with crevasses. Few mountain peaks are better guarded or have resisted so many assaults. There was no doubt concerning the whereabouts of the mountain or even of how to approach it from the south, as there had been in the case of Annapurna and Dhaulagiri, but there was a great deal of doubt as to whether it could be climbed from this direction.

British climbers had reached the Lho La before the war and had seen the entrance to the Khumbu Icefall, but the way to the peak itself was barred by the outlying spurs of the West Ridge and the South-West Face. The first westerners to approach Everest from the south were Bill Tilman and Charles Houston, who had attempted Everest and K2, respectively, in 1938. As members of a small trekking party, for them it must have been like venturing into an incredible Aladdin's cave of treasures, of unknown, unclimbed peaks, of unspoilt villages that were the homes of the Sherpa people, of turbulent glacier torrents, lush vegetation, high pastures, mani walls and prayer flags. It is hardly surprising that they took little more than a cursory glance at the approach to Everest, walking a short way up the Khumbu Glacier to peer round the shoulder of Nuptse into the Icefall and Western Cwm. They could only see the steep buttresses of the South-West Face of Everest, which appeared to reach the South Col; as a result, their report was discouraging.

But even as they made their reconnaissance, a young, unknown climber of the post-war generation was also thinking of Everest. Mike Ward had started climbing in North Wales during the war, while still at school, had gone to Cambridge in 1943 to study medicine and climbed at every opportunity. With the end of the war, he was able to go out to the Alps. He had already shown himself to be a brilliant natural rock climber, and the thoroughness with which he researched and then pushed through his plans for a further Everest reconnaissance, despite Tilman's unfavourable report, displayed his capacity as an organiser as well as a climber. Yet he was in the traditional mould of pre-war climbers, essentially amateur, knowing that however great his enthusiasm for climbing his career in medicine would always take priority.

RIGHT Aerial view of the South-West Face of Everest. The route of the first ascent goes up the right-hand skyline from the South Col (just off the picture).

He realised he was short on big mountain experience and therefore invited Bill Murray, a Scot who had led an expedition to the Garhwal Himalaya the previous year and had climbed extensively in Scotland both before and after the war. Murray's books *Mountaineering in Scotland* and *Undiscovered Scotland* have become climbing classics. The other member of the team was to be Tom Bourdillon, one of the most outstanding of all the post-war young climbers.

ABOVE Mike Ward was the young, newly qualified doctor who pushed through the first post-war Everest Reconnaissance.

Pre-war expeditions to Everest had been sponsored through an organisation called the Everest Committee, formed from members of both the Royal Geographical Society and the Alpine Club. It was coming into existence once again, under the name of the Himalayan Committee, and was to play a very important role in the Everest expedition, but for the time being Mike Ward simply wanted its approval and blessing which, after some hesitation because of Tilman's unfavourable reaction, was finally given.

Only a short time before they were ready to depart, Eric Shipton came onto the scene. Undoubtedly Britain's most eminent mountaineer at this time, he had established himself, with Tilman, as an outstanding mountain explorer, surveying and exploring the Himalaya with small, lightweight expeditions. Shipton was more mountain explorer than technical climber for whom reaching the top of a mountain was just part of the experience as a whole and not an end in itself. Of average height and build, with bushy eyebrows shielding piercing blue eyes, he seemed to gaze straight through you to some distant mountain range. There was also a slightly absent-minded distance in his manner, not cold or aloof, for he was essentially a kind man, but a distance born, perhaps, of shyness, a certain inhibition of emotion. He did not enjoy the hurly-burly of big expeditions, their politics and ponderous slow movement, but he had been unable to resist the lure of Everest and had taken part in four pre-war Everest expeditions. His books were an inspiration to countless youngsters, including myself, who were just starting to climb. During the war he was British Consul-General in Kashgar, in Sinkiang, and had gone on to Kunming in China, but this had ended with the victory of the Communist forces and he arrived back in Britain, not at all sure what to do next. He was promptly invited to lead the Reconnaissance expedition.

Mike Ward and Bill Murray had already set out by sea when Shipton received a telegram from the President of the New Zealand Alpine Club, saying that four of his countrymen were climbing in the Garhwal Himalaya and asking if two of them could join the Everest Reconnaissance. Up to this point Shipton, who always favoured the smallest possible numbers, had resisted several applications to join the expedition, but on impulse, mainly because of good memories of climbing with New Zealander Dan Bryant on Everest in 1935, he accepted the proposal – even though it meant taking on two climbers whom none of them knew.

This also gave the four New Zealanders a very real problem – which two of the four should accept this opportunity. Ed Hillary, a big, raw-boned bee-keeper, was an obvious candidate. Although having only started climbing at the comparatively late age of twenty-six, his physique was superb and, on the expedition in the Garhwal, he had been outstandingly the strongest. The second place in the team was open to question, however. The leader of the party, Earle Riddiford, was determined to go, even though George Lowe, a primary school teacher who combined a rich sense of humour with a great deal of climbing ability and determination, felt that not only was he stronger, but also that he and Hillary made a particularly good team. Nonetheless, it was Riddiford and Hillary who joined Shipton.

And so there were six climbers on the Everest Reconnaissance. They had a tough approach through the height of the monsoon from Jogbani in the south to reach the Upper Khumbu Valley on September 29th 1951. Bourdillon, Riddiford and Ward ventured into the Icefall, while Shipton and Hillary climbed a spur of Pumori to look into the Western Cwm. The view they got showed that Everest was undoubtedly climbable from the south, for they could now see right up the Cwm, the long easy slope of the Lhotse Face and the comparatively easy angle of the South-East Ridge leading down to the South Col. The way into the Western Cwm, however, lay through the daunting obstacle of the Khumbu Icefall.

ABOVE Eric Shipton, undoubtedly Britain's most eminent mountaineer and mountain explorer, pictured here in 1951 when he led the Everest Reconnaissance.

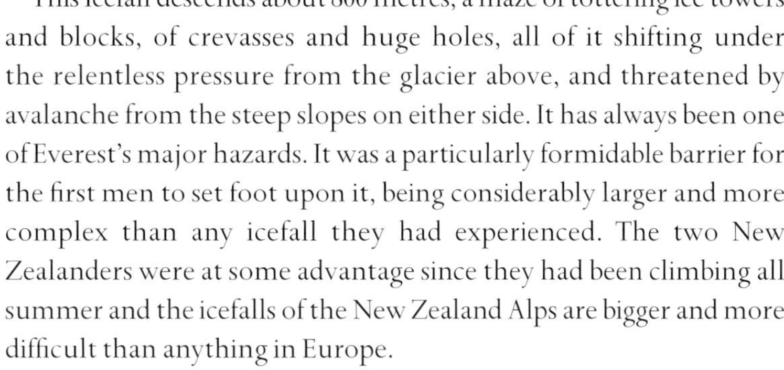

This Icefall descends about 800 metres, a maze of tottering ice towers and blocks, of crevasses and huge holes, all of it shifting under the relentless pressure from the glacier above, and threatened by avalanche from the steep slopes on either side. It has always been one of Everest's major hazards. It was a particularly formidable barrier for the first men to set foot upon it, being considerably larger and more complex than any icefall they had experienced. The two New Zealanders were at some advantage since they had been climbing all summer and the icefalls of the New Zealand Alps are bigger and more difficult than anything in Europe.

Their progress must be judged against this background. On their first attempt they got about three-quarters of the way up when they were hit by an avalanche and were lucky to escape without serious injury; they decided to leave the Icefall for a fortnight, in the hope of letting the snow settle. This also gave Shipton an opportunity to explore the mountains to the south of Everest, which I suspect he found much more intriguing than the challenge of the Icefall.

Returning to the fray, on October 19th, they were undoubtedly shaken when a complete section, which had seemed fairly stable, collapsed during the night, leaving behind an area of chaotic debris. When, at last, they reached the top of the Icefall they found that the way into the Western Cwm was barred by a huge crevasse that stretched from wall to wall. This was the place where Camp 1 is usually situated. Now a long way above their last camp, they were tired, stretched to the limit by the very level of the unknown, but the younger members of the team were keen to press on, while the older and more experienced decided that the risks were too high and they had seen enough. In retrospect, Shipton regretted this decision but, at the time, it seemed sensible. They had proved that Everest was feasible by this route.

Unfortunately, however, the British had lost the opportunity to confirm it. The Himalayan Committee, perhaps over-confident that Everest was a 'British' mountain, had not applied for permission for 1952 in time. A Swiss expedition had got in first. There was some discussion about making it a Swiss-British effort under joint leadership, but this came to nothing. The Swiss were given first chance and they nearly made it, with what was really a very small expedition. Although the team numbered twelve, only six of them were hard climbers; the rest were scientists or had a support role such as doctor or cameraman.

The Sherpa force numbered twenty, led by Tenzing Norkay, who had already gained a considerable reputation, not only as a sirdar, or foreman, of the Sherpas, but also as a climber in his own right. He was thirty-eight years old, tall and heavy by Sherpa standards, weighing over 63 kilograms. With his swept-back hair, strong, square-cut chin and broad smile, he had an almost European look which was reflected in his attitude to the mountains. Most of the Sherpas still regarded mountaineering purely as a job; Angtharkay, Herzog's sirdar on Annapurna, whose experience was even greater than Tenzing's, declined an invitation to go to the summit. His job was to supervise the efforts of the high-altitude porters and he saw no point in the struggle to reach the top. Tenzing, on the other hand, had the same driving ambition as a European climber to reach the summit. Already he had been to the top of Nanda Devi East with the French in 1951; he wanted to reach the summit of Everest in 1952. With Swiss climber Raymond Lambert, he got to within 250 metres, high upon the South-East Ridge, just 165 metres below the South Summit.

The Swiss had shown the way to the top; almost all the route was known. Their failure to finish was partly the result of the comparative lightness of their assault, in the face of the huge gulf of the unknown that they had to penetrate, through the mysteries of the Western Cwm, the Lhotse Face and the final Summit Ridge; but, most of all, it was because the oxygen sets used by Lambert and Tenzing were ineffective, feeding them insufficient oxygen to compensate for the weight of the cylinders they were carrying. The sets were so primitive that they could use them only while resting, which meant having to carry the extra load of the oxygen bottles without getting any benefit from them while actually climbing. The Swiss did not give up; they made another attempt in the autumn, after the heavy snows of the monsoon, but the savage cold and high winds of the winter overtook them and they got no higher than the South Col.

Meanwhile, the British had to sit it out, praying secretly that the Swiss would not succeed. This did at least give them more time to work on some of the specialised equipment, particularly oxygen systems which seemed a vital ingredient for success. A rather abortive expedition to Cho Oyu (8153 metres) under Shipton's leadership gave further altitude experience to some potential members of the next British attempt on Everest, which was now scheduled for 1953.

It was generally assumed that Shipton would lead this attempt, but he himself had some doubts about the suitability of his temperament for such a role, as he confessed in his autobiography, *That Untravelled World*:

'It was clear that the Committee assumed that I would lead the expedition. I had, however, given a good deal of thought to the matter, and felt it right to voice certain possible objections. Having been to Everest five times, I undoubtedly had a great deal more experience of the mountain and of climbing at extreme altitude than anyone else; also, in the past year I had been closely connected, practically and emotionally, with the new aspect of the venture. On the other hand, long involvement with an unsolved problem can easily produce rigidity of outlook, a slow response to new ideas, and it is often the case that a man with fewer inhibitions is better equipped to tackle it than one with greater experience. I had more reason than most to take a realistic view of the big element of luck involved, and this was not conducive to bounding optimism. Was it not time, perhaps, to hand over to a younger man with a fresh outlook? Moreover, Everest had become the focus of greatly inflated publicity and of keen international competition, and there were many who regarded success in the coming attempt to be of high national importance. My well-known dislike of large expeditions and my abhorrence of a competitive element in mountaineering might well seem out of place in the present situation.

'I asked the Committee to consider these points very carefully before deciding the question of leadership and then left them while they did so.'

The Chairman, Claude Elliott, and several members of the Committee already had doubts about Shipton's leadership, particularly in the light of his failure to push through into the Western Cwm and his seeming lack of determination on Cho Oyu, but they could not bring themselves to dispense with him altogether – the main problem being that there was no other obvious candidate. It was felt, however, that a more forceful climbing leader was needed for the final push on the mountain, together with a good organiser to co-ordinate preparations in Britain, so that Shipton could remain a figurehead for the expedition while the two most vital executive functions of leadership were hived off. It was a compromise decision with all the weaknesses that this involved.

The Committee liked the idea of a military man with a proven ability in organisation and management. Two soldiers were particularly discussed – Major Jimmy Roberts, a Gurkha officer who had climbed extensively in the Himalaya, and Colonel John Hunt, who had also served in India and had had both Alpine and Himalayan expedition experience, but was almost completely unknown in British climbing circles. The previous summer, however, Hunt had climbed in the Alps with Basil Goodfellow, who was secretary at this time of both the Alpine Club and the Himalayan Committee. Impressed by Hunt's ability as a mountaineer, combined with his obvious drive and capability as an organiser, Goodfellow pushed Hunt's case very strongly and it was decided that he was the ideal choice as assault leader and organiser.

On being told of the Committee's suggestion that there should be an assault leader, Eric Shipton concurred but suggested that 'deputy leader' would be a better title and that Charles Evans who had been on Cho Oyu with him could best fill this role. There was no question of Evans, a busy brain surgeon, being able to take on the job of full-time organiser, however, so this left an opening for Hunt.

But Elliott and Goodfellow were determined to go much further than this and the day after the Committee meeting, without consulting Shipton, Elliott wrote to Hunt asking whether he would be available for the expedition as assault or deputy leader, and also to act as full-time organiser. A few days later Goodfellow telegrammed Hunt, inviting him to come over to England to discuss his role with Shipton. It must have been downright embarrassing for all concerned. Shipton was under the impression that he was interviewing Hunt for the job of expedition organiser, while Hunt had been given the impression that he was to be deputy leader – a role that Shipton considered was already held by Charles Evans. The meeting was a failure and Hunt returned to Germany where he was serving at the time. Charles Wylie, another Army officer, was made full-time organiser and set up an office in the Royal Geographical Society building.

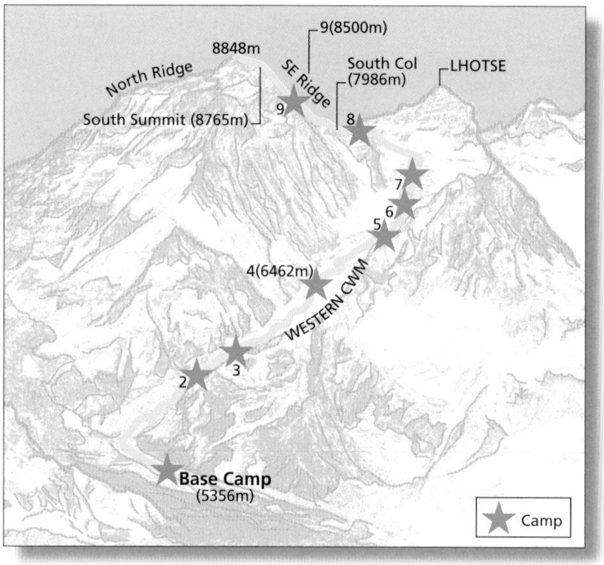

But Goodfellow, convinced that Hunt was essential to the success of the expedition, was not prepared to let the matter drop. At the next Committee meeting on September 11th, the question of deputy leadership was at the top of the agenda. Shipton was asked to leave the room – an extraordinary slight to the leader of the expedition – while the Committee discussed it. When Shipton was asked back in, he was told that the Committee had decided to make John Hunt not deputy leader but co-leader, something that they must have realised would have been unacceptable to Shipton, who felt he had no choice but to resign.

ABOVE The route taken by the 1953 expedition.

Inevitably, there was uproar throughout the world of mountaineering and within the team. Eric Shipton was by far the best-known and most popular mountaineer in Britain at that time. Nobody had ever heard of John Hunt. Bourdillon, loyal as always, said he was going to withdraw from the expedition and it was Shipton who persuaded him to stay on. Evans was very distressed though, ironically, he received the title deputy leader. Hillary, first hearing about it in a newspaper report, was indignant, saying that Everest just wouldn't be the same without Shipton, but he never thought of withdrawing from the expedition.

Were the Committee right? Would Everest have been climbed under Shipton's leadership? Certainly several members of his team thought so, arguing that Charles Evans and Charles Wylie would have ensured that the organisation was sound and that the determination of the climbers out in front, men like Hillary and Lowe, could have carried the expedition with its own momentum, even if Shipton had left it to look after itself. I experienced something like this when I went to Nuptse, the third peak of Everest; the leader of the expedition believed in letting the climbers out in front make their own decisions, without actually appointing anyone in authority. We had no radios, but left each other little notes at the various camps with the plans that each member had made. We climbed the mountain in a storm of acrimony, which might have had a certain dynamic force of its own. But in the case of Everest, I suspect the problem was so huge and complex, the need for careful co-ordination so great, that it required a firm and positive overall leadership. This can only come from one person who has this responsibility vested in him, is prepared to use it, and at the same time has the acceptance and respect of his fellow team members. From this point of view, the expedition almost certainly had a higher chance of success under John Hunt's leadership than it would have done under Shipton who, apart from anything else, never seemed totally committed to the enterprise or happy directing a single-minded thrust up a mountain. It was very unfortunate, however, that the decision was made in such a messy way.

Shipton was cruelly hurt by this rejection. It is one thing to be allowed to stand down from an expedition, quite another to be manoeuvred into an impossible position. It triggered off a series of personal crises that had a traumatic effect over the next five years and it was only in 1957, through an invitation by a group of university students to lead their expedition to the Karakoram, that he returned to the mountains. In his fifties he then had a renaissance, which he described as the happiest years of his life, exploring the wild, unmapped glaciers and mountains of Patagonia in the southern tip of South America. This was the style of mountaineering in which he excelled and in which he could find complete commitment and happiness.

In the meantime, John Hunt had been given the opportunity of his life. Shipton and Hunt, who were so very different in personality, had very similar backgrounds. Both were born in India – Shipton in Ceylon in 1907, the son of a tea planter, Hunt in Simla in 1910, the son of a regular Army officer. Both lost their fathers at around the age of four, both were sent to prep schools in England, but here the similarity ended. Shipton was a slow learner, perhaps suffered from dyslexia, for he was a very late reader. As a result, he failed the common entrance examination to public school, and after a sketchy schooling took up tea planting in Kenya; for him this led naturally to a life of individual adventure.

The young Hunt, on the other hand, was brought up from a very early age to the idea of a life of serious and dedicated public service. He went to Marlborough, then followed family tradition by going to Sandhurst, where he distinguished himself, becoming a senior under-officer and winning both the Sword of Honour and the Gold Medal for Top Academic Attainment. He was commissioned into the fashionable Rifle Brigade and posted to India. But here he ceased to be the stereotyped young subaltern; he was not happy in the claustrophobic pre-war Army officer's life of polo, cocktail parties and mess gossip. He preferred playing football with his soldiers, and already had a sense of social responsibility combined with a strong Christian belief that made him much more progressive in his political and social attitudes than the average Army officer. Tiring of the fairly aimless routine of garrison life, he applied for a temporary transfer to the Indian Police to work in intelligence and counter-terrorism. Already he was addicted to mountaineering, having had several Alpine sessions before going out to India. With the Himalaya on his doorstep, he took every opportunity to escape to the mountains with adventurous ski tours in Kashmir and more ambitious climbs on Saltoro Kangri and in the Kangchenjunga region. Hunt was considered for the 1936 Everest expedition but, ironically, failed the medical test because of a slight flutter in his heart-beat. He saw active service during the war, commanding a battalion in

BELOW Colonel John Hunt, almost completely unknown in British climbing circles, but the man for the job.

Italy, where he was awarded the Distinguished Service Order, and then getting command of a brigade in Greece at the end of the war. He went to Staff College and served on field-Marshal Montgomery's staff at the end of the 'forties, at Fontainebleau, getting to know French climbers and being invited to join the Groupe de Haute Montagne. He married Joy, who was a Wimbledon tennis player, in 1935. Theirs was a very close relationship and between an exacting career and raising a family, they did much of their mountain adventuring together.

Hunt certainly looked the part of the professional soldier, but he was no martinet. He plunged into the job of organising the expedition, but in doing so fully involved everyone around him, overcoming any initial resentment. One commentator, Ingrid Cranfield, summed up what has become a popular interpretation of Hunt's approach, writing: 'To Hunt an "assault" merely meant a concerted, military-style operation; whereas to Shipton "assault" sounded more like a criminal offence.' In fact, this was hardly fair, for Hunt's approach to climbing was essentially romantic, with an almost spiritual undertone. Wilfrid Noyce remembered Hunt commenting how mountains made him want to pray. Hunt undoubtedly saw Everest as a romantic, perhaps even spiritual, challenge, but used his military training to approach a task that needed careful planning. He could see that the basic principles of ensuring success on a mountain are very similar to those of success in war, and one finds oneself using similar terminology.

Dr Griffith Pugh, the physiologist who had accompanied the Cho Oyu expedition, played a very important part in the preparations. The way the human body adapted to altitude was still a mystery and it was largely Griff Pugh's work that determined the need for acclimatisation to altitude and, perhaps even more important, the need to drink a lot to avoid dehydration. The diet of the expedition was carefully worked out and the equipment, with specially designed high-altitude boots, tentage and clothing, was better than anything that had been used before.

There were plenty of strong incentives demanding success; the fact that the French had permission for 1954, the Swiss for 1955, so that if the British failed this time they were most unlikely to have another chance; the fact that it was the year of the Queen's Coronation; the amount of money and effort involved; the controversy over the change in leadership; but, most important of all, Hunt – and for that matter most of his team – wanted success for its own sake. If you set out on a climb, there is a tremendous drive to succeed in what you are attempting. On Everest, certainly in 1953 when six serious attempts had failed (five on the north side and one on the south), the chances of success seemed slim, however large and well-equipped the expedition might be.

Hunt settled on a slightly larger team than perhaps Shipton would have taken, making it up to a total of twelve climbers, plus thirty-six high-altitude porters. Evans, Bourdillon, Gregory, Hillary and Lowe, had been in the Cho Oyu party, Michael Ward, had been on the 1951 Reconnaissance as a doctor, and George Band, Wilfrid Noyce, Charles Wylie and Mike Westmacott were newcomers. Even the Cho Oyu men were thin on real high-altitude experience; Charles Evans had reached 7300 metres on Annapurna IV in 1950, while Hillary and Lowe had collected a fine crop of

ABOVE Acclimatisation camp at Thyangboche, showing just part of the array of stores and manpower needed by a siege-style expedition.

peaks around 6400 metres and had been to about 6850 metres on both Mukut Parbat and Cho Oyu, but they had not climbed any really high mountains. In this respect John Hunt was the most experienced, for he had been to 7470 metres on Saltoro Kangri and had made a bold solo ascent of the South-West Summit of Nepal Peak (7107 metres) in East Nepal. It was Tenzing Norkay, however, who had more high-altitude experience and knew Everest better than any of the other members of the party and, because of this, he was made a full team member as well as being sirdar of the porters.

The British part of the expedition came from traditional Oxbridge or military backgrounds, the only exception being Alf Gregory, a northerner who ran a travel agency in Blackpool. The selection, however, was a natural one, for the climbing explosion that hit Britain in the early 'fifties, spearheaded by the tough Mancunians of the Rock and Ice Climbing Club, had only just got under way. In completing the selection of the team, Hunt had looked for compatibility as much as a record for hard climbing. This certainly worked out, for the team functioned well together under Hunt's firm, but tactful direction.

Preparations were complicated by the fact that the Swiss were having their second try for the mountain that autumn, which meant that Hunt and his team could not let go at full bore until the end of November, when the Swiss finally admitted defeat. The British had just three months to put the expedition together; much of the equipment had to be specially designed and manufactured and, although some work had already been started, they had not been able to place any firm orders until they knew the outcome of the Swiss attempt. It is unlikely that they would have been able to raise the financial support for a second ascent of the mountain.

All the gear and food was ready to leave by sea on February 12th 1953. The team reached Thyangboche, the Buddhist monastery a few kilometres south of the Everest massif, on March 27th. This was early in the season, but Hunt was determined to allow an acclimatisation period before the start of the serious climbing. This was a concept fashionable in pre-war expeditions and in those of the early 'fifties, though later expeditions tended to concentrate all their efforts on the climb itself, acclimatising by working on the lower slopes of the mountain.

The story of the Everest expedition, like that of all siege-type expeditions, is a complex yet stereotyped one, of establishment of camps and different parties moving up and down the mountain, as the route is slowly pushed towards the summit.

The first barrier is the now famous Khumbu Icefall; the route then relents through the Western Cwm; it is a long walk, skirting crevasses which tend to force the climber into the sides, and the consequent threat of avalanche from the steep, crenellated walls of Nuptse. At the head of the Cwm is the Lhotse Glacier, a giant series of steps, steep ice walls alternating with broad platforms, leading up towards the summit rocks of Lhotse. From near the top of the glacier, a long traverse across snow slopes leads to the South Col of Everest, the springboard for a summit bid up the South-East Ridge, soaring for 860 metres past the South Summit, which, deceptively, looks like the top from the South Col, and then beyond it to the summit itself.

Throughout, John Hunt pressed himself to the limit, determined to be seen to be working as hard, if not harder, than anyone else on the expedition, either in carrying a load while escorting porters, making a reconnaissance in the Western Cwm or on the Lhotse Face, as well as coping with the detailed planning and day-to-day administration needed for the expedition. On several occasions he pushed himself too hard, as he struggled, grey-faced, to complete the day's task. There was a strong competitive element in his make-up, noticed by Hillary on the approach march and recorded in his autobiography:

'I learned to respect John even if I found it difficult to understand him. He drove himself with incredible determination and I always felt he was out to prove himself the physical equal of any member – even though most of us were a good deal younger than himself. I can remember on the third day's march pounding up the long steep hill from Dologhat and catching up with John and the way he shot ahead, absolutely determined not to be passed – the sort of challenge I could not then resist. I surged past with a burst of speed and was astonished to see John's face, white and drawn, as he threw every bit of strength into the effort. There was an impression of desperation because he wasn't quite fast enough. What was he trying to prove, I wondered? He was the leader and cracked the whip – surely that was enough? I now know that sometimes it isn't enough – that we can be reluctant to accept that our physical powers have their limits or are declining, even though our best executive years may still be ahead of us.'

Mike Ward had an uncomfortable feeling in his presence, noting, 'My first impression of John was of some disturbing quality that I sensed but could not define. Later, I understood this to be the intense emotional background to his character, by no means obvious, and yet an undercurrent came through.' George Lowe commented, 'He greeted me most warmly and said how much he was depending on me – his assault on personal susceptibilities was impossible to resist.'

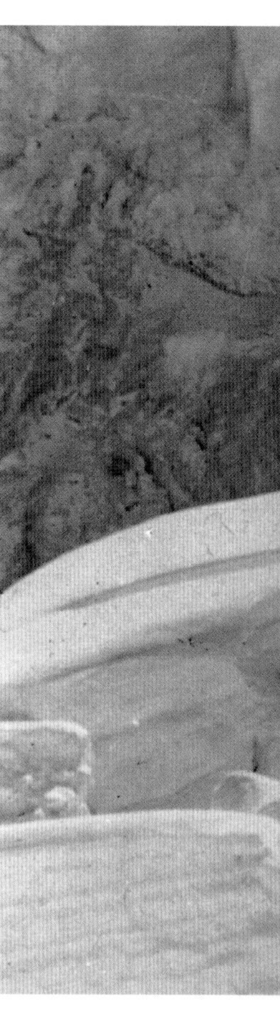

ABOVE A climber crosses a crevasse in the immensity of the Everest Icefall, gateway to the Western Cwm and one of the most dangerous parts of the mountain.

This was an experience that everyone I have talked to remembered. At the same time, however, both through his own personality and also from his position as leader, he kept a certain distance from his fellow members and had an air of authority, very similar to that Thor Heyerdahl inspired in his crew on *Kon-Tiki*. Even when members of the team disagreed with him they always ended up complying with his wishes.

From the very start Hunt had thought Hillary and Tenzing potentially his strongest pair, though they had never met before the expedition and climbed together for the first time in the lower part of the Western Cwm. Hillary was immediately impressed by Tenzing's energy, competence, enthusiasm and, above all, his determination. He wrote later:

'If you accept the modern philosophy that there must be a ruthless and selfish motivation to succeed in sport, then it could be justly claimed that Tenzing and I were the closest approximation we had on our expedition to the climbing prima donnas of today. We wanted for the expedition to succeed – and nobody worked any harder to ensure that it did – but in both our minds success was always equated with us being somewhere around the summit when it happened.'

Another strong pairing was that of Charles Evans and Tom Bourdillon. Although Bourdillon was younger than Evans, and had climbed at a much higher standard in the Alps, they had much in common. Both had a scientific background and Evans, though initially sceptical, became deeply involved in Bourdillon's brainchild, the closed-circuit oxygen system, which his father had specially developed for the 1953 expedition in the hope of avoiding the wastage of the conventional open-circuit set. In theory it should have been the best system, but in practice it proved to be less reliable than the open-circuit system and the other members of the team were not impressed. Privately, Hunt felt the same way, but gave his support to the closed-circuit trials all the same. Bourdillon and Evans had been the two members of the team closest to Eric Shipton, Bourdillon having actually resigned from the expedition, and only brought back in after a great deal of persuasion. Hunt had been very touched on the walk in, when Bourdillon had told him how happy the expedition seemed to be. He wanted to keep it that way.

Hillary, down-to-earth and practical, preferred the look of the open-circuit oxygen system and felt that too much time was being expended in trying to prove the closed-circuit equipment. At 6.30 a.m. on May 2nd, Hillary and Tenzing set out from Base Camp, using the open-circuit set, carrying a load that totalled 18 kilograms. They reached Camp 4, the Advanced Base in the Western Cwm, 1525 metres of climbing with about six kilometres in lateral distance, breaking trail most of the way through soft snow. It was as much an affirmation of their fitness and suitability for the summit as a vindication of the open-circuit system. Hunt was already thinking of them as his main summit hope, and this confirmed his choice.

By modern standards, Hunt's approach to the assault was slow if methodical, not so much a blitzkrieg as a steady siege. But there was a great deal more that was unknown in 1953 than there is today. Only one mountain of over 8000 metres had been climbed and Hunt had no desire to repeat the desperate, ill-supported summit bid, followed by the near-disastrous retreat from Annapurna experienced by Herzog's expedition, nor the failure, through an inadequate oxygen system and cumulative exhaustion, of the Swiss. It was believed climbers deteriorated physically, even while resting, at heights of over 6400 metres, and it was not known how long anyone could survive and function effectively above this height. Hunt, therefore, was determined to nurse his team, particularly the climbers he was considering for the summit.

It was on May 7th, with most of the team down at Base Camp, that he laid before them his final plan of assault. He felt that he had only the resources, both in materials and man-power, to mount one strong attempt on the summit. If this failed they would all have to come back down, rest and think again. But his thinking for the summit bid was consistent with his policy up to that point; it was one of reconnaissance, build-up of supplies and then the thrust forward. To do this, he first had to reach the South Col and he gave this job to George Lowe who, with Hillary, probably had the greatest all-round snow and ice experience of the expedition. With him were to be George Band and Mike Westmacott, two of the young newcomers to the Himalaya, and a group of Sherpas. Once the route was made to the South Col, Hunt planned a big carry to the Col, supervised by Noyce and Wylie, after which Charles Evans and Tom Bourdillon would move into position and make a bid for the South Summit, using the closed-circuit sets. Since, in theory, these sets were more effective and had greater endurance than open-circuit sets, they should be able at least to reach the South Summit from the South Col, a height of around 780 metres, and it was just conceivable that they could reach the top. In this way Hunt could satisfy the two exponents of the closed-circuit system as well as making what he felt was a vital reconnaissance, opening the way for the main summit bid. In this respect one must remember just how huge a barrier that last 250 metres on Everest appeared to be in 1953. Just one day behind them would be Hillary and Tenzing, with a strong support party consisting of Hunt, Gregory and two Sherpas. They would establish a camp as high as possible above the South Col on the South-East Ridge, and then Hillary and Tenzing, using open-circuit sets, would make their bid for the summit – hoping to benefit from the first party's tracks and with that indefinable barrier of the unknown pushed still higher up the mountain.

Subsequently Hunt modified his plan so that he, with two Sherpas, would move up with Evans and Bourdillon to give them direct support just in case anything went wrong and, at the same time, to make a dump for the high camp. Hunt hoped to stay up on the South Col throughout the period of the summit attempts, since this was obviously the place of decision and the only place from which he could effectively influence events.

It must have been a tense moment for the entire team when they assembled for the meeting that was to give them their roles in the final phase of the expedition. Up to this point, Hunt had used a low-key approach to leadership, consulting with people as far as possible, often sowing the germ of an idea in others' heads so that they could almost believe that it was their own; but now he had to lay down a series of roles for the team, knowing all too well that some of its members would be bitterly disappointed.

Ward came out very strongly against Hunt's plan on two counts. He could not understand the logic of making an initial bid from the South Col, when only a slightly greater porter effort would be needed to establish a high camp for Evans and Bourdillon's attempt which, of course, could also be used by Hillary and Tenzing. He also challenged Hunt's plan to take charge of the carry to the top camp himself on the grounds that he was not physically fit for it – a heavy charge, coming from the expedition medical officer. But John Hunt weathered both attacks, which were delivered with great vehemence, and stuck to his guns.

I myself have always wondered at the thinking behind John Hunt's decision to allow Bourdillon and Evans to make their attempt from the South Col which meant, in effect, that there would be only one strong attempt on the summit itself. Had Bourdillon and Evans been granted that top camp, in all probability they would have been the first men on top of Everest. It is easy, however, to be wise after the event. Hunt was probably the only member of the team fully aware of just how thin was the ferrying capability of his Sherpas, particularly once they were above the South Col. Had Hillary and Tenzing failed in their summit bid, and the British team not climbed Everest in 1953, then no doubt the post-mortems would have been long and furious – but no-one is too interested in a post-mortem after success.

Whatever reservations some members of the team might have had, they all settled into their roles and worked themselves to the limit in the next three weeks. But things began going wrong almost from the start. It needs ruthless determination to keep the momentum of a climb under way. At altitude time seems to be slowed up by the very lethargy of the climber himself and the chores that have to be done. Struggling with a recalcitrant Primus, washing up dirty dishes in cold snow water and fighting with frozen crampon straps can eat into a day and somehow dominate it so that the real aim of the climber, in this case to reach the South Col, becomes obscured. This is what happened now.

At Camp 6 on the night of May 15th, Lowe took a sleeping tablet for the first time. It had a disastrous effect. The next morning he just couldn't wake up. Noyce pleaded with him, cursed him, pummelled him, but it was not until 10.30 that Lowe staggered out of the tent and they were able to start up the tracks he had made the previous day. They didn't get far; he was falling asleep while he walked; they had no choice but to return, a precious day wasted. On May 17th, fully recovered and now well-rested, Lowe went like a rocket and at last they established their seventh camp, about half-way up the Lhotse Face at a height of 7315 metres. They still had 670 metres to go to the South Col. Noyce now dropped back, for he was going to be responsible for supervising the first big carry up to the South Col. Mike Ward went up to join Lowe that day, but he had a struggle just reaching the camp. Next day an icy wind blasted across the slope; Ward felt the cold bite through him. He went more and more slowly before being forced to turn back after less than a hundred metres' progress. They stayed in the tent on the 19th and barely reached their previous high point on the 20th. The forward drive of the expedition seemed to have come to a grinding halt.

Hunt now made a bold decision, pressured no doubt by desperation. Even though they were still far short of the South Col, he resolved to send Wilfrid Noyce up to Camp 7 with the Sherpa carrying party to try to push the route out and make the carry at the same time. In Hillary's view, Wilf Noyce was the best and most determined mountaineer of all the British contingent. A school master and a poet, he had a diffident manner, but once on the mountain he was a very different person, with a single-minded drive and the immense determination of a man who had been one of Britain's most outstanding young rock climbers before the war.

Hunt, still desperately worried, uncharacteristically snapped at Lowe when he came back down after his marathon ten days out in front on the Lhotse Face. In Mike Ward's words 'he was excessively rude' – an outburst caused by strain and very quickly rectified. Hunt now realised, though, that he had to reinforce the push for the South Col, but who could he send without weakening his summit assault? That night he resolved to send two more climbers up to Camp 7 the following day.

On the morning of the 21st things looked bad at the top camp. The Sherpas with Noyce had eaten something

BELOW George Lowe, who with Hillary, his New Zealand climbing partner, probably had the greatest all-round snow and ice experience of the party, was chosen by Hunt to push the route out up the Lhotse Face.

that disagreed with them and were all sick. There seemed little chance of getting up to the South Col, particularly on a route that was still unclimbed. Noyce, therefore, decided to set out with Anullu, a powerfully built young Sherpa who chain-smoked and enjoyed his chang, the local beer, brewed from fermented rice, maize or barley.

Back at Advanced Base, Hunt watched the slow progress of the two tiny dots and decided that Hillary and Tenzing would have to go up to the front and lend a hand. Hillary had come to the same conclusion already. Tenzing, more than anyone, would be able to encourage the Sherpas and Hillary had a huge and vested interest in getting the camp on the South Col established. In addition, he was confident that he had the fitness to make this lightning push up to the Col, come back down, rest a day or so, and then make his summit bid. So Hillary and Tenzing set out from Advanced Base that afternoon and surged straight through to Camp 7.

Meanwhile, Wilf Noyce and Anullu had passed the high point reached by Lowe and Ward and were now working their way across the steep snow slope that swept down in a single span to the floor of the Western Cwm 900 metres below. They reached a crevasse that stretched its barrier right across the slope, and cast in either direction to find a snow bridge; but there was none:

ABOVE Wilf Noyce achieved his own personal summit by completing the route to the South Col.

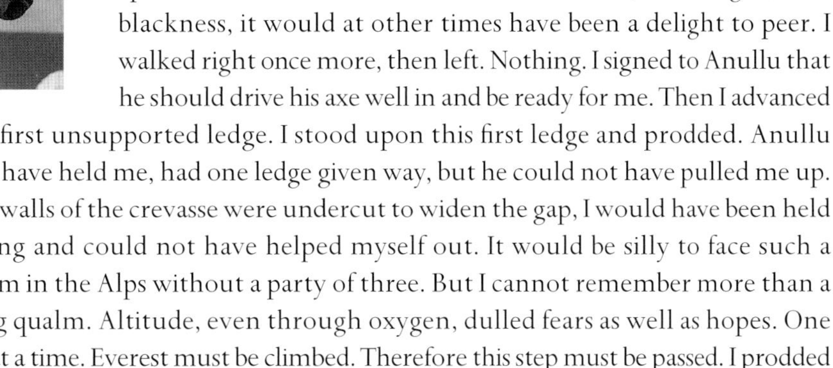

'I looked at Anullu, and Anullu, behind his mask, looked back at me. He was pointing. Where he pointed, the crevasse, some eight feet wide had narrowed to perhaps three. The cause of narrowing was the two lips, which had pushed forward as if to kiss over the bottle green depths below. The lips were composed, apparently, of unsupported snow, and seemed to suspend themselves above this "pleasure-dome of ice" into whose cool chasms, widening to utter blackness, it would at other times have been a delight to peer. I walked right once more, then left. Nothing. I signed to Anullu that he should drive his axe well in and be ready for me. Then I advanced to the first unsupported ledge. I stood upon this first ledge and prodded. Anullu would have held me, had one ledge given way, but he could not have pulled me up. As the walls of the crevasse were undercut to widen the gap, I would have been held dangling and could not have helped myself out. It would be silly to face such a problem in the Alps without a party of three. But I cannot remember more than a passing qualm. Altitude, even through oxygen, dulled fears as well as hopes. One thing at a time. Everest must be climbed. Therefore this step must be passed. I prodded my ice axe across at the other ledge, but I could not quite reach deep enough to tell. I took the quick stride and jump, trying not to look down, plunged the axe hard in and gasped. The lip was firm. This time the Lhotse Face really was climbed.'

Slowly, they plodded on towards the wide gully that led to the crest of the Geneva Spur, which in turn would lead them easily to the South Col:

'Strange, how breathless I could feel, even on four litres a minute. Anticipation was breathless too as the crest drew near, backed by the shadow of Everest's last pyramid, now a floating right-handed curve from which snow mist blew. I was leading again, and hacked the last steps on to the crest. Still no view, and no easy traverse; we must go on up to the widening top. first boulders, up which we stumbled easily, then more snow, the broad forehead of the Geneva Spur, and then suddenly nothing was immediately above us any more. We were on a summit, overlooked in this whole scene only by Lhotse and Everest. And this was the scene long dreamed, long hoped.

'To the right and above, the crenellations of Lhotse cut a blue sky fringed with snow cloudlets. To the left, snow mist still held Everest mysteriously. But the eye wandered hungry and fascinated over the plateau between; a space of boulders and bare ice perhaps four hundred yards square, absurdly solid and comfortable at first glance in contrast with the sweeping ridges around, or the blank mist that masked the Tibetan hills beyond. But across it a noisy little wind moaned its warning that the South Col, goal of so many days' ambition, was not comfortable at all. And in among the glinting ice and dirty grey boulders there lay some yellow tatters – all that remained of the Swiss expeditions of last year.'

Wilf Noyce had achieved his own personal summit; he knew that for him the expedition was probably over. He had fulfilled his role in John Hunt's master plan, had established one vital stepping-stone for others to achieve the final goal, but that goal was denied him, as it is to the vast majority of members of a large expedition. Some are better than others at suppressing ambition and envy; in his book, *South Col*, Wilf Noyce only allowed: 'Yet when I looked up and saw John's trio setting out for the Face, a demon of suppressed envy pricked me, now that my job was done.'

On May 22nd, Ed Hillary and Tenzing helped cajole and encourage Charles Wylie's carrying party to the South Col; Charles Evans and Tom Bourdillon, with John Hunt in support, were on their way up to the Lhotse Face to put in the first tentative assault or reconnaissance of the South Summit, though I am quite sure that as Bourdillon and Evans plodded up the long slopes, enclosed in the claustrophobic embrace of their chosen oxygen sets, they were dreaming and hoping for the summit. In theory, the closed-circuit system should give them the speed and the endurance to get them to the top, but what if it failed or ran out near the summit? They had talked endlessly about this eventuality. The sudden withdrawal of a flow of almost pure oxygen could have disastrous effects. Would it be like running out of oxygen in a high-flying aircraft? Could they adjust to the complete loss of oxygen in time to get back down the mountain There was no way of knowing for certain.

Until now, Wilf Noyce, George Lowe and all the others had been pursuing a series of limited adventures, limited not so much by their own strength, determination and acceptance of risk, as by the roles imposed upon them by the leader of the expedition. Bourdillon, however, had been given the opportunity of seeking out adventure in its fullest sense, for not only had he an outside chance of getting to the top, but also he was putting on trial his own oxygen system.

It is often argued that the use of artificial aids reduces the level of adventure; it certainly does with the indiscriminate use of expansion bolts, drilled and hammered into a rock wall to aid an ascent, for this dramatically reduces the level of uncertainty experienced by the climbers. In this respect, perhaps, had the closed-circuit oxygen system been perfect in every respect, lightweight and reliable, reducing Everest's summit to the height of Snowdon or Scafell, the feeling of adventure would have been lessened, though no doubt the satisfaction to Bourdillon the scientist would have been enormous. As it was, the system was by no means perfect. With fully-charged bottles and spare soda lime canisters (which absorbed the carbon dioxide), it weighed about 23 kilograms; it was temperamental in the extreme and uncomfortable to use. Charles Evans went along with Bourdillon out of friendship, coupled with his own scientific interest in the outcome of the experiment. It was a loyalty and enthusiasm that was to be severely tried.

Initially, their route went up a snow gully on the side of the ridge. They reached the crest, at a height of around 8290 metres, just after nine o'clock, having taken only an hour and a half to climb 400 metres. At that rate they had a good chance of not only reaching the South Summit, but getting to the top; but the going now became much more difficult. Fresh snow covered the rocks of the ridge; the clouds rolled in and soon it began to snow; their pace slowed and it took two hours to cover the next 245 metres. They had now reached the high point achieved by Lambert and Tenzing the previous year and were confronted by a difficult decision. The soda lime canisters had a life of around three and a half hours; they were slightly awkward to change and there was always a risk of valves freezing up immediately after the change. On the other hand, they could probably get another half hour or so out of the canisters that were in place – something that could make a big difference later on. They had a muffled conversation through the masks clamped around their faces. They decided to make the change.

Once again, they set out, now on new ground. The cloud swirled around them, the angle steepened and the snow was unstable, a fragile crust overlying loose deep snow beneath. There was a serious risk of avalanche. Even more serious, Evans' set now developed a fault which caused laboured, rapid breathing. Slowly, they forced their way upwards and, at last, reached the crest of the South Summit. The cloud was milling around them, clinging to the eastern side of the ridge like a great banner, but the crest of the ridge was clear.

Now higher than any man had ever been before, for the first time they were able to examine the final ridge to the summit of Everest. It did not look encouraging. Looking at it head-on made it appear much steeper and more difficult than it actually was; it also looked very much longer, a phenomenon noticed by Doug Scott when he arrived just below the South Summit in 1975. It was one o'clock in the afternoon; they had already been going for five and a half hours; they were tired and were now well into their second canister. To go on or not? The summit was within their grasp; they could almost certainly reach it, but could they get back? They would undoubtedly run out of oxygen, might well be benighted. Bourdillon was prepared to risk all; he had that kind of temperament, had made a whole series of very bold and committing climbs in the Alps. Evans, however, whom John Hunt had put in charge of the pair and who was that little bit older, resolved that the risk was too great. They had a furious argument, muted no doubt by their oxygen masks, but Evans stuck to his point and Bourdillon, reluctantly, agreed to retreat. They only just got back, falling in their exhaustion on several occasions and tumbling, almost out of control,

ABOVE Bourdillon and Evans return from the South Summit. They had been higher than any climber before. The main summit had been within their grasp, but their oxygen supply was low and they could not risk the return.

down the final gully leading back to the South Col, only saved by Bourdillon taking braking action with the pick of his axe. Had they pushed on to the summit, it seems most unlikely that they would have managed to get back alive.

Back on the South Col, there had been a moment when the onlookers, who now included Hillary and Tenzing, thought that Bourdillon and Evans were going to be successful. It was something that Hillary and Tenzing must have watched with mixed emotions. Whatever he felt, Hillary was able to muster a show of Anglo-Saxon team spirit. Tenzing, however, was both visibly and vocally agitated as he saw his chances of being the first man on top of the world starting to vanish.

Bourdillon and Evans, lying exhausted in their tents, had done a magnificent job; had they started from a higher camp they would almost certainly have reached the summit of Everest. As it was, they had opened the way for Hillary and Tenzing, though the story they brought back, understandably, was not encouraging.

John Hunt, who was also exhausted after his carry, felt a deep sense of satisfaction. His oxygen set had given trouble and, as a result, he had received a flow rate of only two litres per minute – half of what he really needed to make up for the weight of the oxygen cylinders and then to give him real help. Even so, he had struggled on to a height of around 8336 metres before dumping his load. For the leader of an expedition it is very important psychologically to make this carry to the top camp; in doing so he can feel that everything possible has been done to make the ascent viable and in some measure, I suspect, have a stronger sense of vicarious involvement in the final summit bid. The expedition as a whole becomes an extension of the leader's personality and ego. Because of this, it is not a huge sacrifice to forego the summit bid, for the success of the expedition overall is very much his handiwork, bringing a satisfaction that is as much intellectual as purely egotistical. On the other hand, the other expedition members inevitably experience frustration on many occasions because they are being held back, given humdrum tasks or denied the chance of going to the summit. On a large expedition, some can lose the sense of personal adventure they would have experienced on a smaller venture.

Not so the irrepressible George Lowe who, as Hunt returned to the Western Cwm, had bobbed back up to the South Col, after the very minimum of rest from his herculean efforts on the Lhotse Face. He had no thought and little chance of making a summit bid himself; he just wanted to get as high up the mountain as he could, and was all too happy to do this in a support role.

After a day of storm the 28th dawned fine, though bitterly cold at -25°C, and still very windy; but they had no choice, they had to start the final push for the summit. Of their two Sherpas only Ang Nyma, another hard-drinking, chain-smoking young man, was fit, so Gregory, Lowe and Ang Nyma had to take on heavy loads, but the heaviest of all were those carried by Hillary and Tenzing, who each took around 23 kilograms. They reached the place where John Hunt and Da Namgyl had dumped their loads, but decided that this was too low and therefore picked up everything, sharing it out among themselves. Hillary was carrying the heaviest load – more than 27 kilograms.

RIGHT Hillary and Tenzing at the top of the Lhotse Glacier. Tenzing, behind, has the summit flags wrapped confidently round the shaft of his ice axe.

Slowly, they clambered on up the ridge to a height of around 8494 metres, before finally stopping. Hillary and Tenzing started digging out a platform for their tent, while the others dropped back down towards the South Col. Both Hillary and Tenzing were in superb condition, finding they could work at the platform and put up the tent without using oxygen. That evening they dined well off endless cups of hot, sweet lemon water, soup and coffee, which washed down sardines on biscuits, a tin of apricots, biscuits and jam.

They woke at 4 a.m. on the morning of May 29th. It was a brilliant, clear dawn and, even more important, the wind had almost vanished. Tenzing was able to point out the Thyangboche Monastery, 5180 metres lower and 20 kilometres away. It took them two and a half hours to get ready for their bid for the summit, melting snow for a drink, struggling with frozen boots and fiddling with the oxygen sets.

At 6.30 they set out. In the event, they got little benefit from the previous party's tracks. They did not like the look of the route taken and therefore waded up through steep, insubstantial snow that felt as it if could slip away with them any minute. It was only nine in the morning when they reached the South Summit, and the view was magnificent. Makalu in the foreground, Kangchenjunga behind, were almost dwarfed from their airy viewpoint; little puffballs of cloud clung to the valleys, but above them the sky was that intense blue of high altitude, while to the east it was traced with no more than light streamers of high cloud. Hillary looked with some foreboding at the final ridge, about which Evans and Bourdillon had made such a gloomy forecast.

'At first glance it was an exceedingly impressive and indeed frightening sight. In the narrow crest of this ridge, the basic rock of the mountain had a thin capping of snow and ice – ice that reached out over the East Face in enormous cornices, overhanging and treacherous, and only waiting for the careless foot of the mountaineer to break off and crash ten thousand feet to the Kangshung Glacier. And from the cornices the snow dropped steeply to the left to merge with the enormous rock bluffs which towered eight thousand feet above the Western Cwm. It was impressive all right! But as I looked my fears started to lift a little. Surely I could see a route there? For this snow slope on the left, although very steep and exposed, was practically continuous for the first half of the ridge, although in places the great cornices reached hungrily across. If we could make a route along that snow slope, we could go quite a distance at least.'

They had a short rest and Hillary changed both his and Tenzing's oxygen bottles for full ones. Then they set out, Hillary out in front, cutting big steps for their ungainly, cramponned high-altitude boots, down a slope of good firm snow leading to the col between the Main and South Summits. Tenzing kept him on a tight rope, and then followed down. From the col they followed the heavily corniced ridge, moving carefully, one at a time. Hillary noticed that Tenzing had slowed down badly and was panting hard; he checked Tenzing's oxygen mask and saw that one of the valves was iced up so that he was getting hardly any oxygen. Quickly, he cleared it and they carried on, cutting steps, edging their way round ledges, ever-conscious of the dizzy drop down into the Western Cwm, 2438 metres below.

RIGHT Hillary and Tenzing whose achievement caught the imagination of the world. 'Well, we knocked the bastard off!' Hillary greeted his compatriot, Lowe.

The most serious barrier was a vertical rock step in the ridge. At first glance it looked smooth and unclimbable, but then Hillary noticed a gap between the cornice that was peeling away from the rock on the right of the ridge and the wall of the rock itself.

'In front of me was the rock wall, vertical, but with a few promising holds. Behind me was the ice wall of the cornice, glittering and hard but cracked here and there. I took a hold on the rock in front and then jammed one of my crampons hard into the ice behind. Leaning back with my oxygen set on the ice, I slowly levered myself upwards. Searching feverishly with my spare boot, I found a tiny ledge on the rock and took some of the weight off with my other leg. Leaning back on the cornice, I fought to regain my breath. Constantly at the back of my mind was the fear that the cornice might break off, and my nerves were taut with suspense. But slowly, I forced my way up – wriggling and jamming and using every little hold. In one place I managed to force my ice axe into a crack in the ice, and this gave me the necessary purchase to get over a holdless stretch. And then I found a solid foothold in a hollow in the ice, and next moment I was reaching over the top of the rock and pulling myself to safety. The rope came tight – its forty feet had been barely enough.'

Tenzing then followed.

'As I heaved hard on the rope Tenzing wriggled his way up the crack and finally collapsed exhausted at the top like a giant fish when it has just been hauled from the sea after a terrible struggle.

'I checked both our oxygen sets and roughly calculated our flow rates. Everything seemed to be going well. Probably owing to the strain imposed on him by the trouble with his oxygen set, Tenzing had been moving rather slowly but he was climbing safely and this was the major consideration. His only comment on my enquiring of his condition was to smile and wave along the ridge.'

Above The footmarks of Hillary and Tenzing coming down left of the ridge, May 29th 1953. The Hillary Step goes up between the rock and snow just above and to the left of the top of the footprints.

They had now overcome the last real barrier and at last, at 11.30 in the morning, Hillary, with Tenzing just behind him, reached the highest point on earth. Suddenly everything dropped away around them. They could gaze down the North Ridge of Everest, across the endless and brown hills of Tibet, across to Kangchenjunga in the east and the serried peaks of the Himalaya to the west. They shook hands, embraced, flew their flags in those few moments of untrammelled delight, of complete unity in what they had achieved. Then they started the long and hazardous way down.

The first ascent of Everest caught the imagination of the entire world to a degree as great, if not greater than, any other venture before or since. Only the arrival of the first man on the moon, a victory of supreme technology, perhaps surpassed man's reaching the highest point on earth. But the very scale of the interest and adulation brought its accompanying problems the moment the expedition reached the Kathmandu valley. Nepalese nationalists wanted to adopt Tenzing as a standard-bearer for their own cause; the adulating crowds pounced upon him, shouting, '*Tenzing zindabad*', long live Tenzing! They ignored Hillary and waved placards which depicted Tenzing arriving at the summit of Everest hauling behind him a fat and helpless white man. Hunt and Hillary were awarded knighthoods, Tenzing the George Medal. The fact that, as an Indian or Nepalese citizen, he was not allowed to accept a foreign title was ignored and, inevitably, the Indian and Nepalese press tried to exploit what they described as a racist slight to Tenzing.

Hillary, perhaps extra-sensitive to the implications that he was hauled to the summit by Tenzing, wrote a frank description of what he thought happened on the day of the summit bid. Tenzing was affronted by the suggestion, which I suspect was true, that Hillary took the initiative on the push to the summit, particularly from the South Summit onwards. In his autobiography, *Man of Everest*, compiled by the American novelist, James Ramsay Ullman, Tenzing stated:

'I must be honest and say that I do not feel his account, as told in *The Ascent of Everest*, is wholly accurate. For one thing he has written that this gap up the rock wall was about forty feet high, but in my judgement it was little more than fifteen. Also, he gives the impression that it was only he who really climbed it on his own, and that he then practically pulled me, so that I "finally collapsed exhausted at the top, like a giant fish when it has just been hauled from the sea after a terrible struggle". Since then I have heard plenty about that "fish" and I admit I do not like it. For it is the plain truth that no one pulled or hauled me up the gap, I climbed it myself, just as Hillary had done; and if he was protecting me with the rope while I was doing it, this was no more than I had done for him.'

In their own ways both accounts are probably true, but it is noticeable that Hillary toned down his account of how Tenzing climbed the step, both in his own personal story of the expedition, *High Adventure*, and in his autobiography, *Nothing Venture, Nothing Win*.

The other members of the expedition, who had helped Hillary and Tenzing reach the top, got only a fraction of the acclaim. The public needs easily identifiable heroes and is little interested in whole teams. The team itself, however, has held together, meeting regularly for reunions and, in various combinations, joining each other for other climbs or expeditions. Perhaps this is the ultimate tribute to the leadership of John Hunt.

Charles Evans avoided the fanfares of the return journey, going off trekking to the south of Everest. Two years later he led a small, low-key expedition to Kangchenjunga, third highest mountain of the world, and George Band, the youngest of the Everest team, who had had difficulty in acclimatising, reached the summit with Joe Brown, the Manchester plumber who was the representative of a new driving force in British climbing. Wilf Noyce, too, went on to climb other mountains in the Himalaya, until he was killed in the Pamirs in 1962 with the brilliant young Scottish climber, Robin Smith. George Lowe made the Antarctic crossing with Vivian Fuchs, meeting Ed Hillary who led the New Zealand contingent coming in the opposite direction, and ended up marrying one of John Hunt's daughters.

John Hunt's career was undoubtedly helped, as in fact was that of most of the others, by his experience on the Everest expedition, but he has always remained a distinguished public servant rather than an adventurer. After retiring from the Army, he ran the Duke of Edinburgh's Award Scheme for some years, before becoming Chairman of the Parole Board. He has also taken part in several public enquiries and became a Life Peer in reward for his many and varied public services. Ed Hillary, also, has put a great deal back. His greatest work and contribution has undoubtedly been with the Sherpas, running a Sherpa Trust which has brought them a number of small hospitals and schools, helped them to build bridges and adapt in general to a changing world.

Everest has held its fascination, attracting climbers from every climbing country in the world, to repeat the route made by the 1953 expedition or to try to find a new way to the highest point on earth. It is a focal point of adventure that draws the participant as much as the onlooker, through the irresistible attraction of its supreme height, in which the sense of discovery, the challenge of risk, the sheer beauty of what can be seen from so high and the drive of ego-satisfaction all play their parts.

NINE

Annapurna, South Face

Big Wall Climbing in the Himalaya, 1970

We projected the two-metre-square picture onto the wall of the living room and gazed and gazed – excited and then frightened. 'There's a line all right,' said Martin, 'but it's bloody big.' The South Face of Annapurna – I don't think I remember seeing a mountain photograph that has given such an impression of huge size and steepness. It was like four different Alpine faces piled one on top of the other – but what a line! Hard, uncompromising, positive all the way up. A squat snow ridge, like the buttress of a Gothic cathedral, leaned against the lower part of the wall. That was the start all right; perhaps one could bypass it by sneaking along the glacier at its foot – but what about avalanche risk? The buttress led to an ice ridge; even at the distance from which the photograph had been taken one could see it was a genuine knife-edge. I had climbed something like it before, on the South Face of Nuptse, the third peak of the Everest range – in places we had been able to look straight through the ridge, thirty metres below its crest. That had been frightening; this would be worse. The knife-edge died below a band of ice cliffs.

'I wonder how stable they are?' asked Nick.

I wondered too and traced a line through them with only partial confidence. And that led to a rock band.

'Must be at least a thousand feet.'

'But what altitude is it? Could be at 23,000 feet. Do you fancy some hard climbing at that height?'

'What about that groove?' It split the crest of the ridge, a huge gash, inviting, but undoubtedly more difficult and sustained than anything that had ever been climbed at that altitude.

That had been frightening; this would be worse

The rock band ended with what seemed to be a shoulder of snow that led to the 8091-metre summit. It was difficult to tell just how high the face was, but you could have fitted the North Wall of the Eiger into it two, perhaps even three, times. The expedition was barely conceived, and I don't think any of us fully realised then the significance of what we were trying to do. The South Face of Annapurna was considerably steeper, bigger and obviously more difficult than anything that had hitherto been attempted in the Himalaya. Our decision to tackle it, first arrived at in autumn 1968, was part of a natural evolution, not only on a personal level but also within the broad development of Himalayan climbing. It is significant that around

Above Climber approaching the Whillans Box at Camp 4 with Hiunchuli, 6442 metres, in the background.

the same time groups of German and Japanese climbers, without any contact with ourselves or each other, were planning similar expeditions – the Germans, under Dr Karl Herrligkoffer, to the huge Rupal Face of Nanga Parbat, and the Japanese to the South-West Face of Everest.

I had been a member of two conventional Himalayan expeditions in 1960 and '61, making the first ascents of Annapurna II (7937 metres) and Nuptse (7879 metres). This was very much part of the first wave of Himalayan climbing, when climbers were attempting first ascents of the myriad of unclimbed peaks. By 1969, however, the Himalaya was in the same state of development as the European Alps had been in the mid-nineteenth century, with most of the highest peaks achieved and climbers now turning their attention to the challenge of harder and harder routes. In the Alps there had been a gradual development of skills and techniques, enabling pioneers to climb successively more difficult ridges and then faces, slowly filling in all the gaps of unclimbed ground.

Inevitably, however, this gradual evolution was accelerated in the Himalaya where climbers had skills developed on the rock and ice of the Alps as a reference. For political reasons, the Himalaya had been closed to climbers from 1965 to 1969. Nick Estcourt, Martin Boysen and I had been talking about going off on an expedition somewhere – anywhere, probably to Alaska – when we heard that Nepal was going to open its frontiers once again. The selection of an objective was strongly influenced by my experience on Annapurna II and Nuptse. All the highest peaks in Nepal had been climbed, and although we could have gone for an unclimbed 7500 metre one, I felt that this would have been a lesser experience than the peaks I had already climbed. A big unclimbed face, on the other hand, would give an altogether new dimension – the combination of a North Wall of the Eiger with all the problems of scale and altitude. At the time I did not stop to analyse my motives; it was more a gut-feeling, a rejection of the familiar in favour of the new, unknown experience which, after all, is the very essence of adventure.

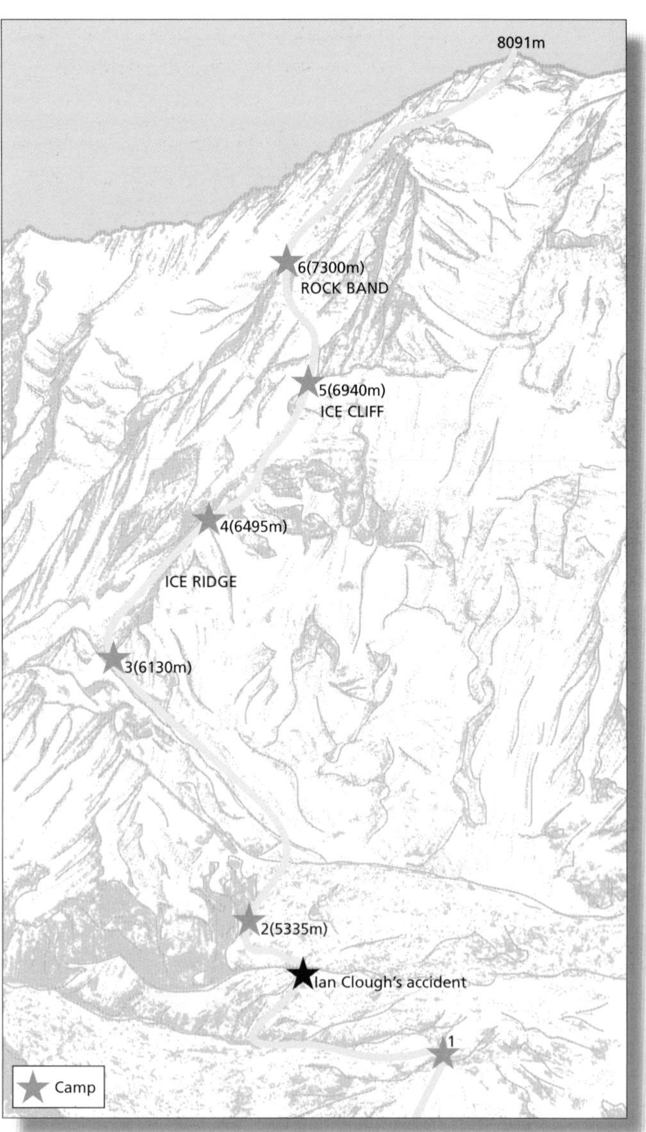

ABOVE The route taken by the 1970 Annapurna South Face expedition.

It was at this stage that I first saw a photo of the South Face of Annapurna and showed it to Martin Boysen and Nick Estcourt. During the following months the team grew as I began to put together the expedition. For me it was an adventure on two levels, both in terms of the mountain challenge and also grappling with the problems of organisation and leadership. I had never before led an expedition, had never considered myself to be the organising type. In fact, my lack of organisation was becoming a bad joke among my friends. I was unpunctual, forgetful and absent-minded. Although I had held a commission in the regular Army, my military career was hardly distinguished. I had detested all the administrative jobs that I had been given as a junior officer and one commanding officer had even refused to recommend me for the almost automatic promotion to captain because of my poor personal administration – there were never enough lamp bulbs in the barrack room I was responsible for.

And now I was trying to organise and lead the largest and most complex expedition since the 1953 Everest expedition. Some of my antecedents might have been similar to those of John Hunt – we had at least both been to Sandhurst, but there is a vast difference between commanding a brigade in battle and misdirecting a troop of three tanks on Army manoeuvres in North Germany. However, I did have the experience I had gained both on hard Alpine climbs and also in the past few years when I had earned a living as a freelance writer and photographer, joining projects like Blashford-Snell's Blue Nile expedition and going off to Baffin Island in the middle of winter to hunt with the Eskimos. It had taught me to be more organised in myself and also to understand how the media worked, a thing that was essential if you wanted to finance an expedition.

There were many moments in the months of preparation when I knew a blank despair, either appalled by organisational mistakes I had made, by personality problems or, most of all, by the fear of the whole thing being a complete flop. After all, we had only seen a photograph of the face. We had been given the sponsorship of the Mount Everest Foundation, we would have a TV team with us, every move would be reported. What if the route proved impossibly dangerous, if it were swept by avalanche so that we could barely make a start on the face? Could I really control and co-ordinate this group of talented, strong and at times bloody-minded individuals?

I had finally settled on a team of eleven, of whom eight were hard climbers, each with the ability and drive to reach the summit, and three with more of a support role. Of the eleven I knew eight extremely well; we had climbed together, knew each other's ways, strengths and weaknesses. At the same time, though, there were elements of stress within the make-up of the team, a factor that was perhaps inevitable and even useful as a spur and irritant that was to be important later on. Undoubtedly the most experienced member of the party was Don Whillans, the tough, stocky ex-plumber from Manchester who, with Joe Brown, had revolutionised British rock climbing in the early 'fifties. I had had some of my best climbing with Don. Of all the people I have climbed with, Don had the best mountain judgement and, at his peak in the early 'sixties, the greatest climbing ability. We had got on well in our two seasons in the Alps mainly, I suspect, because I had been prepared to yield to his judgement; it was Don who undoubtedly had the initiative in our relationship. Through the rest of the 'sixties our paths rarely crossed. Don had seemed to have lost interest in rock climbing on his home crags, had little interest, even in the Alps. He had been on an expedition to Gauri Sankar in 1965 and had climbed in North America, but lack of exercise and a fondness for his pint while at home in Britain had given him an impressive gut. I had had serious reservations about inviting him to join the expedition; knew that there would be a tension between us but, at the same time, felt sure that once he got going he had a judgement and drive that would increase our chances of success.

The feeling was mutual, Don commented in an article after our return:

'Chris has developed from an easy-going, generous, haphazard lieutenant in the Army to a high-powered, materialistic photo-journalist, to all outward appearances motivated only by money. (Chris believes we must tell the truth about each other regardless of feelings, as long as he is doing the telling!) However, I knew him well enough to know that when the crunch point is reached his sense of proportion always returns to more normal standards, so I had no real decision to make about accepting his offer.'

The others were easier choices. The only other member of the team who had been to the Himalaya was Ian Clough, who had climbed the Central Pillar of Frêney with Don and myself and had been with me on the Eiger and with Don on Gauri Sankar. Warm-hearted, unselfish and easy-going, Ian was both a brilliant and a very safe climber, as well as being a perfect member of any team. Of the newcomers to the Himalaya, Dougal Haston was undoubtedly the strongest. A quiet, introverted Scot, he had a single-minded drive that had taken him to the top of the North Wall of the Eiger by its direct route and had already established him as Britain's most outstanding young climber. Mick Burke from Wigan had a very similar background to Whillans, the same dry Lancashire humour, and a readiness to speak his mind. The two frequently clashed. Martin Boysen was a brilliant rock climber, easy-going, indolent but completely committed to climbing. He and I had had many delightful days' climbing on British crags but had never been together further afield. I had also climbed a lot with Nick Estcourt, a steady rock climber and very experienced Alpinist. He was a computer programmer by profession and, unlike many of his fellow climbers, understood the need for systematic planning. He always saw my problems in trying to organise an expedition and gave me a steady, loyal support throughout our expeditioning.

ABOVE Our 140 porters in the foothills on our way to Annapurna.

So far, I knew everyone well, but my choice of an eighth climber was influenced by commercial considerations. Our expedition agent, George Greenfield, with whom I had just started to work, suggested that perhaps we could have an American climber in the team. It would be such a help in selling American book rights. Today I don't think I would agree to let such a consideration affect team selection, but back in 1970 none of us was particularly well-known, and fund-raising was a very much more serious problem. I did not know any American climbers personally, but both Don Whillans and Dougal Haston knew several. finally, we settled on Tom Frost, a brilliant rock climber who had taken a leading part in the opening up of the great rock walls of Yosemite and who also had some Himalayan experience. It was only at a later date that I discovered he was a practising Mormon, a very strict religion that forbids drinking, smoking and swearing – vices pursued to a greater or lesser degree by almost everyone else in the team. In the event he proved to be very tolerant and, though he did not succeed in converting any of us, we co-existed happily.

I now had eight outstanding climbers in the team and it seemed essential to have someone whose sole function was to look after Base Camp and ensure that the right supplies started their passage up the mountain. In military parlance I wanted a combination of Chief of Staff and Quartermaster General, who would look after headquarters, leaving me free to get up into the front line to get the feel of the action. Who better for this role than a military man? I made enquiries through the Gurkhas, because it would obviously be a tremendous advantage to have a Nepali-speaker. As a result, Kelvin Kent, a captain in the Gurkha Signals, became our Base Camp manager. A dynamic hard worker, he took on all the organisational work in Nepal and was to fill a vital role on the expedition.

The final two members of our team were Dave Lambert, our doctor, and Mike Thompson, another ex-military man and one of my closest and oldest friends. A good steady performer, he was invited along as the other support climber, someone who would be happy to help in the vital chore of humping loads between intermediate camps without expecting to go out in front to make the route or have a chance of a summit bid.

We had our share of crises in putting together the expedition. Through inexperience, I had failed to delegate nearly enough, but my worst mistake was to send out all the expedition gear by sea to Bombay with an uncomfortably tight margin for error in a boat that broke down in Cape Town. Fortunately for us, a British Army expedition was attempting the North Face of Annapurna at the same time that we were trying the South. Generously, they agreed to loan us some of their rations and fly out enough gear for us to get started on the South Face while we waited for our own supplies to catch up with us.

BELOW Team sorting out climbing gear at Base Camp, with the South Face of Annapurna in the background. The route went up the left-hand buttress.

We reached Base Camp on March 27th. The route to the South Face of Annapurna is guarded by outlying peaks; the beautiful Machapuchare, or 'fish's tail', Hiunchuli and Modi Peak. At first glance they seem to form a continuous wall, but the Modi Khola, a deep and narrow gorge, winds sinuously between Hiunchuli and Machapuchare to reach the Annapurna Sanctuary, a great glacier basin at the head of which towers the South Face of Annapurna. Don Whillans, having gone ahead to make a reconnaissance, met us in the gorge of the Modi Khola.

'Did you see the face?' I asked.

'Aye.'

'What was it like?'

'Steep. But after I'd been looking at it for a few hours, it seemed to lie back a bit. It's going to be hard, but I think it'll go all right.'

The following day we emerged from the confines of the gorge and were able to see the South Face for ourselves. It was certainly steep and difficult, but it did look climbable.

For the next two months we were to be involved in the complex, at times repetitive manoeuvres of a siege-style climb. For me, the juggling of logistics – devising a plan and then trying to make it work – was as fascinating as the climb itself, but for most of the team the exciting role was to be out in front, actually selecting, then climbing the route up the next few feet of snow, ice or rock. The very steepness and difficulty of the face made this all the more satisfying; but only one person of the team of eleven could be out in front at any one time. The rest were either humping loads up the fixed ropes or resting at Base Camp. We had six high-altitude porters with us – a very small number by standard custom, but I had felt that the Sherpas were unlikely to be able to cope with such steep ground. As there had not been any climbing expeditions in Nepal since 1965 they would be out of practice, and it was also most unlikely that they had ever been asked to use fixed ropes on anything as steep as the South Face of Annapurna.

Most of the inevitable tensions of a siege-style expedition are caused by the frustration of spending so much time in a support role, and in worrying about one's prospects of personally getting to the top of the chosen peak. Back in England I had hoped to get over this by alternating the lead climbers so that everyone had a fair turn, but now reality was forcing me to adopt pragmatic courses, to abandon the notions of equality. The problem is that people's talents are not the same, yet each person involved sees his abilities in a different perspective. Already, I felt that the two strongest climbers in their different ways were Don Whillans and Dougal Haston, even though Don, at the start of the expedition, was anything but fit. Don's canniness and Dougal's fitness, drive and climbing ability made a powerful combination but also created an imbalance, for the other pairings just did not have the same drive or experience – at any rate in my eyes. I was never quite as confident when one of the other pairs was out in front.

BELOW Ian Clough, crossing steep snow on fixed ropes above Camp 4.

At times this lack of confidence was barely justified. Martin Boysen and Nick Estcourt forced the steepest and most difficult section of the Ice Ridge that guarded the middle part of the face. It was an incredible cock's-comb of ice, to which clung great cornices of crumbling, aerated snow. Martin burrowed his way through a narrow tunnel which went right through the ridge and then climbed a stretch of vertical ice leading up into another cornice of soft snow. It was probably the most demanding lead of the entire climb.

Ian Clough and I took over from them. Perhaps through over-confidence in myself, a desire to be where the most vital part of the action was, I stayed out in front for what was probably much too long. The snow arête which linked the lower part of the face with its upper reaches proved to be a critical barrier. It just never seemed to end – fragile ice, little rock steps, endless traverses on insubstantial snow. I spent a week at Camp 4, the only place where the ridge relented into a small half-moon of angled snow. It would have been no good for an ordinary tent, but Don had designed a special box tent, based on our experience in Patagonia in 1963 where we had found that no normal tent would stand up to the savage winds. The Whillans Box, a framework of alloy tubing with a covering of proofed nylon, had the advantage of being a rigid structure that could be fitted into a slot cut into a snow slope and, unlike a conventional ridge tent, would not collapse under the weight of snow. Camp 4 was a spectacular but uncomfortable eyrie and the climbing each day was both exacting and wearing. Somehow we had to make a route up which we could ferry loads. This meant finding suitable anchor points for the fixed rope and, because our line traversed along the side of the ridge, these anchors had to be every metre or so. The weather did not help. It was bitterly cold and windy, with the cloud rolling in from below and engulfing us before mid-morning; with the cloud came snow and more wind.

In many ways I was in the wrong place, for out in the lead your entire concentration is taken up with the snow and ice in front of your nose. It was difficult to take a long-term view of the climb, to keep track of the flow of supplies and people up the mountain behind us. I had become obsessed with reaching the end of the arête. My partner, Ian Clough, who had stayed behind at Bombay to escort all our late-arriving baggage across India by truck, was barely acclimatised. He was forced to go down and Don, who was now running the lower part of the mountain, sent up Dougal Haston instead of Mick Burke or Tom Frost, whose turn it was to go out in front. Don felt that neither of them was going strongly enough.

Dougal certainly brought a fresh drive to our daily struggle, though we were still making little more than thirty metres or so progress each day. But at last, on May 3rd, Dougal Haston and I reached the top of the Ice Ridge. Back in England we had allowed a mere three days for climbing it; after all, it was only forty-five and a bit metres of vertical height and had looked in the photograph like a fragile but elegant flying buttress between the lower and upper parts of the face. It had taken us three weeks. By now I had been out in front for just over a week. It doesn't sound much, but I was desperately tired, as much, I suspect, a nervous tiredness from worrying about the climb as a whole, as the actual fatigue of the climbing. I had not yet learned how to pace myself while running an expedition.

When Dougal and I had arrived back at Camp 4, Don Whillans, with Mick Burke and Tom Frost were already there. They had dug out another notch for a box tent and were cosily installed. I dropped back down the ropes to Camp 3, hoping to stay there for a few days' rest rather than go all the way back to Base Camp. This had been Whillans' idea. Harder, more ruthless than I, he was worried by the amount of time being wasted by climbers moving up and down between camps to rest at Base Camp, and had decreed that none of the climbers should go below Camp 2. It had sounded a good idea at the time, and I was to be the first guinea pig. I spent two days lolling in my sleeping bag, and then set off for Camp 4, got about half way up but felt the strength ooze out of me. I decided to go down, turned round and slid a few metres down the rope but the thought revolted me. How could I expect others to grind their guts out if I wasn't prepared to do it myself? A spasm of coughing hit me, and I hung on the rope, amidst tears and coughs, trying to bolster my resolve.

Above Climber load carrying on the fixed ropes on the Ice Cliff just below Camp 5.

I turned back up the rope and made a few steps. It had taken a matter of seconds to drop back nine metres on the rope. It took me a quarter of an hour to regain those few metres. The contrast was too much. My body was screaming to go down, my logic told me that I could do no good by going up, yet a sense of duty, mixed with pride, was trying to force me on. I felt torn apart by two conflicting impulses, weakened and degraded by my own indecision. There seemed no point in stopping at Camp 3. I felt I had learnt the hard way that if you get over-fatigued, rest at 6000 metres does very little to help you recover. I therefore dropped all the way down to Base Camp.

It is interesting that on Everest in 1972 and 1975, I never went back below our Advanced Base, once it had been established. This meant staying there for periods of as much as six weeks, at a height of 6615 metres, without any ill effects. On Annapurna South Face we undoubtedly pushed ourselves much harder than we ever did on the Everest. expeditions. Wracked by serious coughing, I spent very nearly a week at Base Camp, watching through binoculars the drama that was being enacted on the great wall opposite.

Don and Dougal were able to make fast, spectacular progress up the long, comparatively straightforward snow slopes above the ridge. On May 6th they established a camp just below the sheer Ice Cliffs that formed the next barrier but, on the following morning, Dougal found a gangway that led – dizzily but surprisingly easily – through them. Tom Frost and Mick Burke, impatient to have their turn in front, now went up to the foot of the Rock Band. We had always thought that this feature would prove to be the crux of the entire climb, steep rock and ice at an altitude of around 7000 metres.

Don and Dougal shot down the ropes for a rest, leaving Nick and Martin at Camp 4 with the unenviable task of supporting Tom and Mick. I was lying, frustrated, on the sun-warmed grass at Base Camp. I had tried to go back up but had only reached

Camp 2 at 5335 metres, where Dave Lambert, our doctor, was staying. I had a stabbing pain in my chest every time I coughed and he diagnosed pleurisy. Clutching a bottle of antibiotics, I returned disconsolately. There was no way that you could lead or even effectively co-ordinate an expedition from down at Base. You had no feel for what it was like high up on the rock and ice of the face, even though you had been there just a few days before. On an expedition of this kind, undoubtedly the best place for the leader is in the camp immediately behind the lead climbers. In this way he maintains a direct contact with the people out in front and, being at the penultimate point in the line of supply, can feel how effectively this is working.

The carry from Camp 4 up the Ice Ridge and then up the endless snow slopes to the foot of the Rock Band was particularly savage. The ropes were too steep and difficult for our Sherpas, and anyway we needed them for the carries between the lower camps. We were now so short of manpower that we were using local Gurkha porters, who had never been on a mountain before, for ferrying loads from Base Camp, across the glacier to our bottom camp. We even ensnared casual visitors with the promise of a good view from the lower part of the face as a reward for ferrying a load up to Camp 1, 2 or even 3. One party of trekkers, two men and a couple of girls whom we named the London Sherpas, stayed for several weeks and became honorary members of the expedition. But it was the climbers doing the carry from Camp 4 to 5 who were becoming exhausted and it was at Camp 4 that I should have been at this stage.

BELOW Mick Burke led most of the Rock Band, crux of the entire climb, often in bad conditions.

The Whillans Box at Camp 5 was tucked into the bergschrund itself. This gave some protection from the spindrift avalanches that came pouring down the slopes from above but as it also blocked out the rays of the early morning sun, the interior rapidly became an icy coffin. The ice on its walls never melted, the spindrift that had poured down each afternoon and night covered everything that had been left outside. And the climbing was hard, much harder than anything we had encountered so far.

And while those at Base Camp theorised and criticised, out there in front Mick Burke did some of the most difficult climbing that had ever been carried out at such an altitude. Icy runnels led onto steep rock. He had to take off his crampons, balancing on a tiny foothold some thirty metres above Tom Frost, as he struggled ungloved with frozen straps on the almost holdless rock.

But we were running out of time. It was now mid-May; the monsoon was close upon us and we were barely a quarter of the way up the Rock Band. I was impatient to push the route out, fully confident only of Don and Dougal as a lead climbing pair. Everyone else was beginning to tire, largely because they had all been exhausting themselves on the long carry from Camp 4 to 5. I decided to push Don and Dougal into the front as quickly as possible, even though this meant upsetting the rotation of lead pairs. I put the plan across on the radio. And then all hell broke loose. It's never easy having an argument by radio – Nick, at Camp 4, very rationally pointed out the appalling bottleneck that we now had at the start of the long carry to Camp 5. Mick Burke, at Camp 5, urged the need for Don and Dougal to make a carry from 4 to 5: 'The thing is, Chris, you don't realise what it's like up here. It's much easier to lead than to carry loads.'

Then Don came on the air.

'Dougal and I left that place Camp 5 a week ago. Camp 5 isn't even consolidated and the progress of all towards Camp 6 is so poor that it's had me and Dougal depressed all the way up the mountain. I don't know what Mick thinks he's playing at, but Camp 5 is short and we want to get the route pushed out and unless they get their fingers out, push it out and establish 6 or at least find a site, they should make way for someone else to try. He's had a week and progress seems very poor.'

The reaction from the two higher camps to this remark was violent. It was just as well, perhaps, that the various contenders in the argument were separated by several thousand metres of space! In fact, both parties were partly right. Ferrying loads up behind the lead climbers was a desperate problem, but if we had slowed down in an effort to build up our supplies I suspect we would have come to a grinding halt.

The following day Mick, who always responded to a challenge, particularly one set by Don, was determined to prove that he could do as much as – if not more than – any other pair on the mountain. Mick and Tom ran out 240 metres of rope up some of the steepest and most difficult climbing we had yet encountered. It was certainly the best bit of climbing that had been done on the expedition to date, but it was also their last fling, for they were now on their way back down to Base Camp for a rest. Martin Boysen helped Don and Dougal get established in Camp 6, half-way up the Rock Band, but he also was forced to retreat, exhausted by his long stint of carrying, his morale undoubtedly dented through being passed over by Don and Dougal.

I was now on my way back up the mountain, but our effort was like a rickety human pyramid: Don and Dougal at Camp 6 at around 7300 metres, Nick Estcourt at Camp 5, Ian Clough and Dave Lambert at Camp 4, Mike Thompson and the Sherpas at Camp 2 and a growing number of exhausted climbers and Sherpas recuperating at Base Camp. I joined Nick Estcourt at Camp 5 on May 15th, finding it all I could do to struggle up those long slopes leading up to the Rock Band. Every time I coughed I had to hold my ribs to try to control the stabbing pain.

The carry from Camp 5 to 6 was the wildest and most exhausting so far. The ropes went diagonally across the face, over a series of ice fields and rocky walls. It was impossible to build up any kind of rhythm and the ropes stretched away, never seeming to come to an end. I did that carry, and most of the other carries I made in the next week, on my own. In spite of my exhaustion I could not help marvelling at the wild beauty of the scene. In the distance was the shapely pyramid of Annapurna II which I had climbed ten years before; to the south Machapuchare, now almost dwarfed as we looked down onto it, the great spread of the Annapurna Sanctuary, patterned with its crevasses into a crazy mosaic far below, and then round to the east the retaining walls of Hiunchuli, Modi Peak and the Fang. We were now almost level with their tops. But fatigue and altitude were taking their toll and it took me six hours to climb the 365 metres to just below Camp 6. I was so exhausted on getting within shouting distance of the camp that I dumped my load and yelled for Don to come down and pick it up; after all, he had had a rest that day.

I was at Camp 5 for a week. Nick, exhausted by his long stint in a support role, was finally forced to drop back down to Base. I had two lonely days by myself before Ian Clough came up to join me; exhausting carries in the teeth of the driving wind and swirling spindrift; moments of hope and elation, moments of utter despair. I still had dreams of reaching the summit, was warmed by Dougal's invitation to join them after they had forced a way up a long snow gully that led to the top of the Rock Band. I even set out from Camp 5 with my personal gear plus the tent, rope, spare food and cine camera that we needed to make the summit push, and got only a few metres above the camp before realising that there was no way I could manage such a heavy load. In addition, I was using oxygen to reach them, while Don and Dougal were doing without. I could not possibly do it and so dropped back to the empty camp to dump my personal gear. In my despair I sat down and cried and then, ashamed at my weakness, shouted at the walls around me, 'Get a grip on yourself, you bloody idiot,' repacked the sack and set out once again.

In a way, it was much easier for me to suppress my own personal ambition to reach the top; after all, having conceived the idea of the expedition, having co-ordinated it and, for most of the time, held it together it was possible to sublimate my own desires in the success of the team as a whole. This was very different for the other team members. Nick Estcourt summed it up when he got back to Base Camp, saying: 'It's

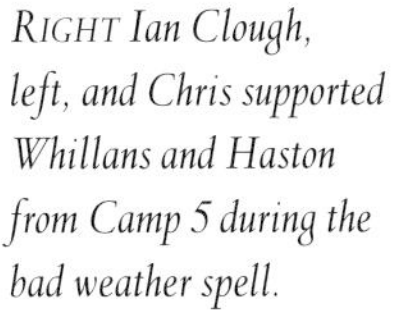

RIGHT Ian Clough, left, and Chris supported Whillans and Haston from Camp 5 during the bad weather spell.

all very well talking about the satisfaction of contributing to the success of the team, but it's a hell of a sight better if you manage to kick the winning goal.'

Don and Dougal stuck it out at Camp 6, surviving on the trickle of food and gear we were able to funnel up to them. The monsoon now seemed to be upon us – day after day of cloud and storm, of fierce winds and billowing spindrift. Don and Dougal had one abortive attempt at establishing Camp 7, but were unable to find anywhere to pitch a tent, very nearly failed to find the way back to the top of the fixed ropes and finally struggled down to Camp 6, where Ian Clough and I had moved up in support, hoping to have a go for the summit ourselves. The four of us spent a hideously uncomfortable night crammed into one small, two-man tent, pitched precariously on a tiny spur of snow. Next morning, there was no discussion about who should stay and who should go down – Don and Dougal were so much more fit than Ian and I.

ABOVE Don Whillans, who with Dougal Haston pushed the route out from Camp 6 and sat out the bad weather waiting for a break.

Tom Frost and Mick Burke were on their way back up, eager to have a go for the summit and prepared to support Don and Dougal up at the front, so Ian and I dropped back down to Camp 4. We knew that we had used up most of our reserves, but were determined to hang on until Don and Dougal had either made their bid for the summit, or had given up. Until that happened, somehow we all had to keep them supplied with just enough food to keep going.

On May 27th we were storm-bound at Camp 4, the snow hammering at the box tent throughout the day. That evening I called Camp 5 and asked Dougal if they had managed to get out at all.

He replied: 'Aye, we've just climbed Annapurna.'

Don and Dougal had set out that morning, hoping to establish a top camp. Higher up on on the mountain it wasn't quite so bad as it was on the lower slopes. They made fast progress on the fixed ropes up the gully, reached the top of the Rock Band where they had left the tent but, with hardly a word between them, they set out up the crest of the long ridge leading up towards the summit. They had reached a level of communication over the weeks on the mountain that hardly needed words. They were going for the top, Don out in front breaking trail and picking the route, Dougal behind carrying the rope and cine camera. They were both going superbly well; Dougal wrote: 'The wonderful thing was that there was no breathing trouble. I had imagined great lung-gasping efforts at 26,000 feet [7925 metres], but I was moving with no more difficulty than I had experienced 4000 feet lower down.'

There was a steep wall of snow-plastered rock at the top but they climbed it unroped, and then Dougal filmed Don as he plodded those final metres to the summit of Annapurna, to stand where Herzog and Lachenal had been twenty years before. Their descent in a storm could easily have been more disastrous than that of their predecessors, but so superbly attuned were they to their environment that they picked their way back down the mountain, still unroped, through the gusting spindrift, down over icy steps and snow-plastered rocks to the haven of the top of the fixed ropes.

There was a moment of sheer, unrestrained joy throughout the expedition; there was no more recrimination, no envy for their achievement; but for me the euphoria was very short-lived, for the expedition was not yet over. Tom and Mick, up at Camp 5, naturally wanted a go at the summit and, the following day, moved up to the top camp. I was filled with foreboding. The pair in front were very much on their own. If anything were to happen to them none of us had the strength to go back up the face to help them. I listened to the radio all day; at midday Mick Burke came on the air. His feet had lost all feeling and he had dropped back to the tent, but Tom was going on by himself for the summit. I was even more worried. Then, at last, the radio came to life again. Tom, also, had returned.

Although sorry for their sakes that they had not made it to the top, I was even more relieved that they were down in one piece. I must confess here that the feeling was not entirely humanitarian. I was guilty of a feeling that I suspect is common to almost every leader of any enterprise – of wanting the expedition as a whole, as a projection of the leader's ego, to be successful both in terms of achieving its objective and reaching a satisfactory conclusion.

BELOW Don Whillans on the summit of Annapurna (from a 16mm film camera frame), the only camera they took to the summit.

Next morning it was with a profound sense of relief that I raced down to Base Camp to start the heady job of writing the expedition reports and co-ordinating our return to civilisation. I was sitting inside the tent, typewriter on an upturned box, when I heard someone rush up to the tent calling, 'Chris, Chris!' The rest of what he said was incomprehensible. I ran out and found Mike Thompson sitting on the grass, head between knees, sucking in the air in great hacking gasps. He looked up, face contorted with shock, grief and exhaustion.

'It's Ian. He's dead. Killed in an ice avalanche below Camp 2.'

Everyone had run out of their tents on hearing Mike's arrival; they just stood numbed in shocked, unbelieving silence as Mike gasped out his story.

Mike, Ian and Dave Lambert had decided not to wait for Mick Burke and Tom Frost, who were on their way down from the top camp, but set out from Camp 3 early that morning, hauling down as much gear as they could manage. They passed Camp 2, and carried on down the side of the glacier, onto a narrow shelf below an ice wall. This was a spot that we had always realised was dangerous, but the most obvious threat, an overhanging ice cliff, had collapsed earlier on. There was still an element of risk from some ice towers further up the glacier, but their threat was not so obvious and it seemed unlikely that these would collapse in the space of the few minutes it took to cross the danger zone. Even so, we all tended to hurry across this part of the glacier.

Ian was in front, Mike immediately behind. Dave Lambert was about five minutes behind them. There was practically no warning, just a thunderous roar and the impression of a huge, dark mass filling the sky above. Mike ducked back into the side of an ice wall, where a small trough was formed. He thought that Ian, slightly further out than he, had tried to run away from the avalanche, down the slope. But Ian hadn't a hope and was engulfed by the fall.

'It went completely dark' said Mike. 'I thought I'd had it; just lay there and swore at the top of my voice. It seemed such a stupid way to die.'

When the cloud of ice particles had settled and the last grating rumble had died away into the silence of the glacier, Mike picked himself up and, with some Sherpas who had been on their way up to meet them, started searching through the debris, finding Ian's body part-buried by blocks of ice. They carried Ian down and we buried him just above our Base Camp, on a grassy slope looking across at the face on which we had striven all those weeks. Shortly after the climb, I wrote:

'I can't attempt to evaluate the worth of our ascent balanced against its cost in terms of the loss of a man's life, of the time devoted to it or the money spent on it. Climbing and the risks involved are part of my life and, I think, of those of most of the team – it was certainly a very large part of Ian's life. It is difficult to justify the risks once one is married with a family and I think most of us have stopped trying. We love climbing, have let a large part of our lives be dominated by this passion, and this eventually led us to Annapurna.'

Although I had been climbing for nearly twenty years, Ian was the first close friend I had lost in the mountains, but the next ten years between 1970 and 1980 were to see a terrible toll. Mick Burke was killed on Everest in 1975 when he went for the summit on his own. Dougal Haston died in an avalanche near his home in Leysin, Switzerland, the day before I was due to meet him to go winter climbing. Nick Estcourt, the closest of all my friends, died on the West Ridge of K2, swept away by an avalanche, during our attempt on the mountain in 1978. Mike Thompson has compared the sadness of lost friends to being prematurely old; so many of one's contemporaries have died that one knows the loneliness of an older generation. Of the eight lead climbers on the South Face of Annapurna, four have died in the mountains, a frightening statistic that is mirrored among almost any other group undertaking extreme climbing over a long period of time, particularly at high altitude.

The mountaineer is exposed to some level of risk at almost all times he is on the mountain, but it is fairly rare for a good climber to be killed because the climb is too hard, or even when caught out by bad weather or some other kind of emergency. Then, his concentration is complete, with every nerve stretched towards survival. It is on easy ground that accidents occur; that momentary lack of concentration, a slip where there happens to be a long drop; a hidden crevasse and, most dangerous of all, the risk of avalanche.

And yet we go on; it has certainly never occurred to me to give up climbing – I love it too much; the challenge and stimulus of playing a danger game, the beauty of the mountains in which there is so much peace alongside the lurking threat are all tied in with the gratification of ego, the enjoyment of success, of being good at something. I do worry about the responsibility I have to a family I love, but then the pull of the mountains is so great that perhaps selfishly, I could never give up climbing – I will always want to go back to the mountains.

BELOW Memorial plaque for Ian Clough, placed at the site of Base Camp by team member Kelvin Kent in November 1999.

10

TEN

Diamir – Messner on Nanga Parbat

The First Complete Solo Ascent of an 8000-Metre Peak

ONLY THE GENTLE ROAR OF THE GAS STOVE disturbed the silence. The tent, with its chill moss of hoar frost festooning the walls, was sepulchral in the dim, grey light of the dawn. Yet it had a reassuring, womblike quality, for those thin walls protected him from the lonely immensity of the sky and mountains outside. And then another noise intruded; an insistent, rushing, hissing rumble that came from all around him. It sounded like a gigantic flood about to engulf his shelter. Panic-stricken, he tore at the iced-up fastenings of the entrance to see what was happening. The whole mountain seemed to be on the move, torrents of ice pouring down on either side, while below him the entire slope, which he had climbed the previous day, had now broken away and was plunging in a great, tumbling, boiling wave to the glacier far below, reaching out and down towards the little camp at its foot where he had left his two companions.

And then the sound died away. A cloud of snow particles, looking no more substantial than fluffy cumulus on a summer's day, settled gently, and it was as if the avalanche had never happened, the icy debris merging into the existing snow and ice. Once again, the only sound was the purr of the gas stove. Somehow it emphasised his smallness, inconsequence, the ephemeral nature of his own existence.

Reinhold Messner was at a height of around 6400 metres on the Diamir Face of Nanga Parbat. Having set out the previous morning from a bivouac at the foot of the face, he was attempting the first solo ascent of a major Himalayan peak, all the way from its foot to the summit. It meant complete self-sufficiency, carrying all his food and equipment with him, facing the physical and mental stresses of high-altitude climbing on his own, also facing the risk of accident, of falling down a hidden crevasse, with no-one to help him.

Although he could see the site of his Base Camp, some 2000 metres below and eight kilometres away, he was as much alone as a solitary sailor in the Southern Ocean or as isolated as an astronaut in orbit on the other side of the moon. That sense of isolation was now even more extreme; his line of descent having been swept away by the avalanche, he would have to find another way back down the mountain.

Others had, of course, reached Himalayan summits on their own. Hermann Buhl had made the first ascent of Nanga Parbat in a solitary push – an incredible achievement, but he had been part of a large expedition which had worked together to reach the top camp. It was just the final, if most challenging, step that he had to make on his own – a very different concept from that of starting at the foot by oneself. Some had tried. In 1934 Maurice Wilson had slipped into Tibet and attempted to climb Everest from the north, leaving his porters behind at Camp 3. Comparatively inexperienced, he had wanted to climb the mountain for the mystic experience, but perished fairly low down. Earl Denman, a Canadian climber, got no further than the North Col before accepting the futility of his attempt in 1947, while four years later the Dane, Klaus Becker Larson, did not get as high. Both these climbers had employed Sherpas. Messner himself had attempted Nanga Parbat solo on two previous occasions, but on the first barely started the climb before the immensity of the challenge overcame him, and on the second did not even reach the foot of the mountain.

But unlike Wilson, Denman and Larson, most of Messner's life had been devoted to the mountains, to stretching himself to the extreme, forever striving to discover new ground, new experience. Attempting an 8000-metre peak solo was a logical step in his own personal evolution.

Born in 1944 in the village of Vilnoss which nestles among the Dolomite peaks of South Tyrol, he was the second of eight children, seven boys and a girl. His father, the village schoolmaster, was from the same peasant stock as the children he taught. There was not much money, but it was a secure and happy, if disciplined, upbringing within the tight circle of his large family. Joseph Messner loved the mountains and each summer they moved up to a hut among the high pastures where they could wander and climb. Reinhold Messner was taken on his first climb, up Sass Rigais, the highest peak of the Geisler Alps, at the age of five.

As he grew older he began climbing with his younger brother, Günther, exploring the Geisler peaks around his home and steadily expanding his own climbing ability. By the time he went to the University of Padua he was already an extremely capable and forceful climber and quickly developed his prowess, spurning the use of artificial aids, particularly the indiscriminate use of expansion bolts. He made a series of very fast ascents of the most difficult routes and also some outstanding solo ascents, among them the North Face of the Droites, long considered the most difficult mixed ice and rock route of the Western Alps, and the Philipp/flamm route on the North Face of the Civetta, one of the hardest free rock routes in the Dolomites. By 1969 Messner was established as one of the boldest and most innovative climbers in Europe, with a stature very similar to that of Hermann Buhl in the early 'fifties.

It was Karl Herrligkoffer who was going to offer the opportunity of going to the Himalaya. This Munich doctor had an obsession with Nanga Parbat ever since his idolised half-brother Willy Merkl had died on the mountain during a disastrous 1934 expedition. Herrligkoffer was to organise and lead no less than eight expeditions to Nanga Parbat. In 1961 he attempted the mountain from the west, by its Diamir Face. This is the side from which Mummery, the British pioneer who was swept away in an avalanche, made the first attempt in 1895. Herrligkoffer failed in 1961 but returned the following year, when Toni Kinshofer, Siegi Löw and Anderl Mannhardt reached the top by a difficult route skirting round the huge ice cliffs in the centre of the face.

Herrligkoffer turned next to the forbidding south aspect, the Rupal Face, at 4500 metres one of the highest mountain walls in the world. He had made three attempts on this face between 1963 and 1968, each time getting a little higher. The year 1970, however, seemed destined to be the year of the big walls in the Himalaya. It was the year our British party climbed the South Face of Annapurna and the Japanese were attempting the South-West Face of Everest. Messner had reservations about joining a large expedition, very few of whose members he knew personally, but the opportunity was too good to miss.

He approached the climb with characteristic seriousness, very different from the attitude of British climbers of this period. In Britain there was undoubtedly an ethic against formal training outside the process of climbing itself; it was a tradition of climbing by day and boozing in the pub at night. Messner, on the other hand, approached his climbing with the dedication of a competitive athlete. He trained on the walls of an old saw mill near his home, traversing along the wall, back and forth until his arms and fingers gave out. This is very similar to the climbing training undertaken by leading British rock climbers today, but in Britain this approach was only developed in the mid-'seventies. Messner's training went a lot further. It encompassed a regime of cold showers in the morning, a careful diet in which he ate only fruit for one day of the week to accustom his body to deprivation, and a routine of four hours' distance running each day as well as exercises designed to build up his stamina.

BELOW The forbidding Rupal Face which, at 4500 metres, is one of the highest mountain walls in the world.

Before going to the South Face of Annapurna, I can remember being invited by a sports medicine research unit to submit my own group of climbers to the same series of tests for fitness as those which had recently been given to the England football team. I found an excuse for declining the invitation, knowing that we should almost certainly compare unfavourably and, if we failed to climb the South Face, could then be pilloried as unfit. As it happened Don Whillans, who had a substantial beer gut before the expedition, got himself fit during the climb and reached the top. Messner could have taken such a test with impunity and, I suspect, would have compared in lung capacity and fitness with any Olympic athlete. His pulse rate was down to forty-two beats per minute and he could gain a thousand metres of height on his training runs in under an hour. The Rupal Face was to prove a crucible in which to test his fitness and drive.

Herrligkoffer himself was an organiser rather than a climber and he led from Base Camp, a recipe for dissension on many of his expeditions. This time the dissension focused on Messner, who wanted to make a solo bid for the summit. The story around this is still clouded in confusion and ended in court actions.

ABOVE Reinhold and (RIGHT) Günther Messner. When Reinhold's younger brother joined him on the summit bid their success was overshadowed by the problem of finding a way down for the overstretched Günther.

Just three climbers were at the top camp; Reinhold Messner, his younger brother, Günther, and a German climber and film cameraman, Gerhard Baur. They had no radio, so the previous day on the radio at the camp below Messner had made an agreement with Herrligkoffer that if the weather report were good, the three at the top camp would fix ropes in place for a summit bid to be made by Felix Kuen, Peter Scholz, Günther and himself. But in view of the lateness of the season and the approaching monsoon, if the weather report were bad, Messner should make a fast solo bid for the summit. The signal was to be a rocket fired from Base Camp – a red one for a bad weather report and a blue one for good.

It was June 26th and that evening at Base Camp the weather forecast was good for the next few days. It should have been a blue rocket. This was to become the subject of a violent controversy, for a red rocket was fired. Apparently it had a blue marking on its cover and Herrligkoffer, assuming that all the remaining rockets were also red, did not attempt to fire any others for fear of confusing the issue still further.

To Messner it seemed quite clear. He could see the great cloud bank in the distance; the rocket signal indicated that it was rolling up towards Nanga Parbat, but his eyes and experience told him that he just had time to reach the summit and get back. It was a challenge that inevitably part of him welcomed, daunting, huge but something that he had confronted before, on the steep walls of the Alps. He set out at three in the morning, climbed swiftly and steadily upwards, into the Merkl Gully. After a mistake in route finding he was forced to drop back and take another line and then, just after dawn, he saw a dark shape coming up from below. It was Günther, who had been unable to resist the temptation to follow his brother and share in the summit. He had made extraordinary progress, catching Reinhold up in only four hours of climbing over a distance that was to take Kuen and Scholz a full ten the following day.

The two brothers climbed on together. It had been a bitterly cold night when they started, but now the enervating glare of the sun was their main problem. Making steady, continuous progress, they reached a shoulder on the ridge, and suddenly Reinhold realised that success was within their grasp. He could see across the Silver Saddle, the long weary way that Hermann Buhl had crossed on the 1953 first ascent. The summit pyramid was just a short way beyond; nothing could stop them. And then in the late afternoon they were at the top, relishing the momentary euphoria of slopes dropping away on every side, of endless peaks around them in the warm yellow light of the late afternoon sun, but then came the nagging awareness of their position. They had to find a way down.

On the way up fear becomes anaesthetised by the summit goal, the focal point of all one's effort and desire, but once attained, reality floods back and for the Messners, the reality was daunting. They had no rope, no bivouac gear except a thin silver foil space blanket, no stove for melting snow and practically no food. Reinhold had been confident he could return by the way he had come, but Günther was an unforeseen circumstance. Younger, less experienced than his brother, he had stretched himself to his limit on the way up and knew with a horrible certainty that he could not climb back down those desperately steep walls of the Merkl Gully. The Diamir Face swept away to the west, lit by the setting sun, seemingly easy-angled, inviting, less daunting than the steepness of the wall from which they had only just escaped. But it was completely unknown ground. Kinshofer, Löw and Mannhardt's route had been well to the right of the apparently easy summit slopes the brothers could see below them. But what of the route lower down? Messner had examined photographs and knew all too well how complex were the icefalls through which they would have to find their way. And so he compromised; there was only an hour or so before it was dark and a bivouac was inevitable. They could at least lose some height by climbing down to the col below the summit pyramid. From there it might still be possible to go down the Rupal Face and it was just feasible that someone might come to help them. It took them a long time to reach the col. Günther was desperately tired, slumping into the snow every few metres to get some rest.

Huddled into a tiny rock niche on the col, wrapped in the space blanket, they shivered through the night, exposed to the icy wind blasting through the gap. In the chill dawn Reinhold scrambled over to the ridge of the col; he could see where they had left the Merkl Crack to reach the shoulder about a hundred metres below. There was no way they could climb down without a rope. If only someone would come up from below. He shouted for help, but his voice was snatched away by the wind. For two hours he called, to no avail. And then, far below, he saw two figures slowly working their way up towards them. A great wave of relief – they were saved.

The two figures were a hundred metres below when Reinhold recognised Felix Kuen and Peter Scholz. He shouted down to them and Felix looked up, but their words were torn away by the winds. Messner took it for granted that they would climb up the steep and broken rocks leading to the col but saw that Kuen had turned away and was following their track leading to the shoulder. He shouted that it was much quicker for them to climb up to the col, that all he and Günther needed was the use of the rope to get down to where Kuen was now climbing, that Kuen and Scholz could then go on to the summit. But Kuen did not appear to understand or hear properly, merely shouting, 'Everything OK?'

Messner thought he was simply asking if they were all right, so said yes. After all, they only needed a rope. So he was stunned when Kuen turned away and continued up the shoulder. When Kuen looked back Messner pointed to the west, the Diamir side, to which he now seemed irrevocably committed.

In Felix Kuen's account, there is no mention of the wind or any difficulty in communication:

'The Merkl Gully continued vertically above. We left the gully by the right and crossed towards the South Shoulder. The traverse led over a snow slope of about fifty degrees in easy terrain, where I was able to carry on a conversation with Reinhold Messner. He stood on the ridge where the top of the Merkl Crack met the South Shoulder, some seventy to a hundred metres distant. It was ten o'clock and he spoke of the possible routes to the summit, as well as the time they would require. Reinhold reported that he and his brother were on the summit at 17.00 hours the previous day and that they were now about to descend in a westerly direction [Diamir side!]. To my question whether everything was OK, he replied "yes". A great weight lifted from my heart for I had feared he was calling for help. As yet I had no presentiment that the tragedy had already begun the day before when Günther had followed in the wake of his climbing brother. From that moment the two were without a rope, without bivouac sack, without sufficient survival equipment. Reinhold was prepared only for a solo climb with an NRC-blanket and some food in his pocket. And now he charged me to tell the others he was going down the reverse side of the mountain and would soon be back at Base. I strongly advised him against this, whereupon he broke off with a "Cheerio" and disappeared over the ridge.'

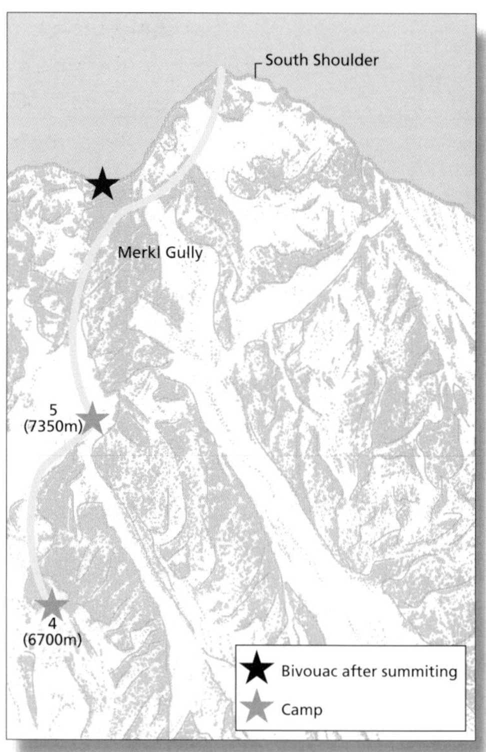

ABOVE Rupal Face ascent route.

The two versions have the bare skeleton in common but the interpretation of the detail is very different. It certainly seems unlikely that Reinhold Messner would have chosen to go down the Diamir Face, as Kuen implies. Although an extraordinarily bold and innovative climber, he has always displayed very sound judgement and practical common sense. Heading down an unknown face on the other side of the mountain, with no gear, food or support, accompanied by his exhausted brother, seems completely out of character.

He was in a desperate state, he stumbled and fell a few times, tearing his hand on his crampons, and eventually leant on his ice axe and cried. It was not until the exhausted Günther rallied his brother that Messner took charge of the situation.

Reinhold knew that Günther would never survive another night at this altitude and was not capable of climbing back up to join Kuen and Scholz. He was desperate to get down those easy-looking slopes on the western side and so, at about eleven o'clock in the morning, they set out down the sunlit snow of the Diamir Face.

Reinhold went first, trying to pick out the best route, never easy from above, for it is impossible to see the ice cliffs until you are right on top of them. And then the afternoon clouds crept up the slope, engulfed them in their tide, flattening out all perspective as they groped their way down. Suddenly the mist parted, revealing a dark hole plunging into the depths of the Diamir Valley far below. They came to a barrier of ice, steep, sheer, impossible. Skirting it, Reinhold found a chute of smooth, polished ice at an angle of around fifty degrees. It was just possible. Facing in, kicking in with the front points of their crampons, penetrating only a few millimetres, they teetered down the hard, smooth surface.

Reinhold felt the presence of a third person with uncanny clarity, just outside his field of vision, keeping pace with him as he carefully kicked downwards. They climbed on into the dark. A few rocks appeared. They were now on the Mummery Rib. They stopped at last around midnight. Exhausted, chilled, desperately thirsty, for they had had nothing to drink for two days, they crouched on a tiny ledge.

They set out before dawn, by the light of the moon. It was ghostly, mysterious with the thin gleam of the snow and the opaque black of the shadows lit by the occasional spark of crampons striking rock. Forcing themselves through the last levels of their exhaustion, they finally realised in the dawn that they had reached the glacier at the bottom of the Diamir Face. They had come through the worst; exhausted as they were, still far from safety, they knew the momentary elation of what they had achieved – of having made the first traverse of Nanga Parbat, the first ascent of the Rupal Face, the first direct descent of the Diamir Face – and of being alive.

BELOW Diamir Face: routes taken on the Messner brothers' descent in 1970 and Reinhold's solo ascent in 1978.

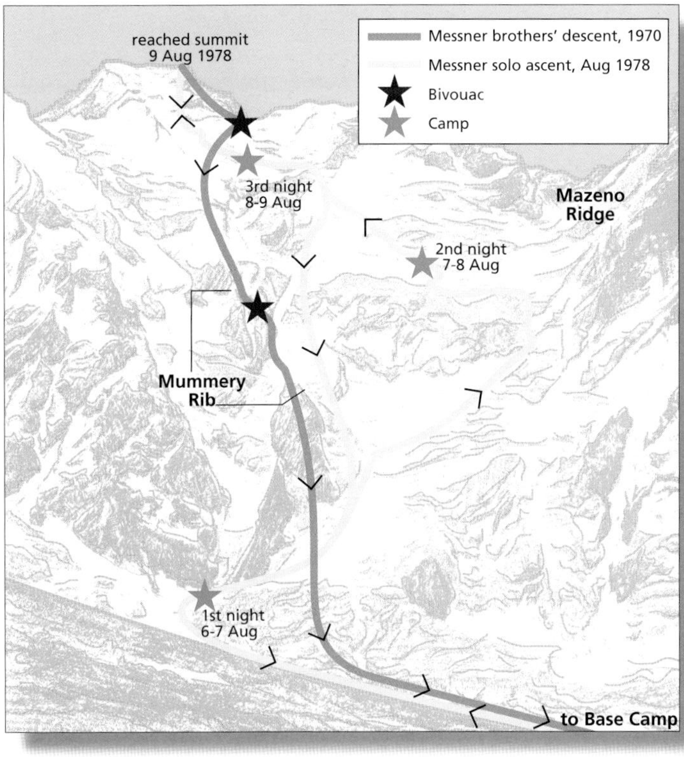

In a dream, they wandered on down the glacier. Reinhold out in front picking out the route, Günther coming on behind. The glacier was bare of snow, the crevasses exposed, no longer a threat, and then as the sun rose little rivulets of water began to trickle on every side. Reinhold lay down, drank and drank, then sat basking in the sun as he waited for his brother. He heard voices, saw a horse silhouetted against the sky, cattle grazing, people leaning against a wall. He focused his eyes and the horse turned into a crevasse, the cattle into great blocks of snow, the people into stones.

But there was no sign of Günther. He waited for another hour – still no sign. Increasingly worried, he forced his body back up the glacier, retracing his route, forgetting his exhaustion as he made his frantic search. There were no footprints, for it had been frozen hard as they walked down, but there was the great piled debris of an ice avalanche that had swept down only a short time after he had last seen his brother. Slowly, the realisation sank in that Günther had almost certainly been caught by it and was somewhere underneath thousands of tons of ice. Unable to accept it fully, he continued searching throughout the day, shouting himself hoarse. He slept out on the glacier, searched the next day as well, and only towards evening at last began to admit what had happened. In a daze, almost unconscious, he staggered down the glacier to its end, to spend his fourth night in the open without food or shelter.

The following morning was cold, clear, still and silent, the Diamir Face inscrutably in shadow, the teeth of the Mazeno Ridge just catching the rays of the early morning sun. It was as if there were no-one left alive in the entire world. Messner shouted his brother's name yet again into the silence. There was not even an echo. He left his gaiters on top of a rock in case a helicopter was sent in to search for him, and started down the long, empty valley. His progress was desperately slow. Accompanied by spectres, he staggered from boulder to boulder, spending three more nights in the open before stumbling upon the high grazing camp of local villagers. He was emaciated, burnt by the sun, with torn, frostbitten feet.

He was emaciated, burnt by the sun, with torn, frostbitten feet

For Messner it had been an Armageddon that I suspect very few people would have survived, let alone have gone on from to even greater challenges. There were not only his injuries – the amputation of one big toe and the loss of parts of all the others except the two little ones, but also the emotional wounds. As if that were not enough, a series of law suits were brought by Herrligkoffer against Messner for breach of contract and libel. Messner described the impact of his experience in his book, *The Big Walls*: 'The Nanga Parbat Odyssey has given me the strength to face any future hazards squarely and accept or reject them, and every single hazardous enterprise I now undertake – whether it is successful or no – is an invisible ingredient of my life, of my fate.'

In every way, 1970 was a year of crisis for Messner. He was befriended by Baron von Kienlin, a wealthy German aristocrat who had played a minor role on the Rupal Face expedition and had taken Messner's side in the protracted legal wrangling which followed. He also invited the climber to convalesce at his castle in Württemberg. It was during this period that Messner and von Kienlin's beautiful young wife, Uschi, fell in love. Uschi left her husband and three children to be with Messner. They were married in 1971 and together returned to the Diamir Valley to search for the body of Günther. They did not succeed.

In 1972 Messner climbed Manaslu (8156 metres), his second 8000-metre peak, as a member of an Austrian expedition led by Wolfgang Nairz, but once again disaster struck his climbing companion. Franz Jäger, who was making the summit bid with Messner, turned back, while Messner pressed on to the top alone. On his way back down from the summit, Messner was caught in a violent snow storm, and when he reached the top camp was appalled to learn Jäger had not arrived. Two other climbers at Camp 4 immediately set out in search of him and one of these, Andi Schlick, also lost his life. Inevitably there was some controversy, though there was no way

Messner could have foreseen the events that followed his decision to go for the summit alone.

Around this time Messner began to dream of the possibility of climbing an 8000-metre peak solo, and the Diamir Face seemed to act as a magnet. He returned in 1973 to make his first solo attempt, described in his book, *Solo Nanga Parbat,* camping below the rocky spur of the Mummery Rib, quite close to where he had bivouacked in despair after his brother's death. But his heart was not in it. Before leaving his little Base Camp, he had confessed in his diary:

'Long after midnight and I cannot sleep. The few mouthfuls of food I managed to force down last evening weigh heavily on my stomach. I think of Uschi and sob violently. This oppressive feeling that robs me of hunger and thirst won't go away. It is not my Grand Plan that prevents me from eating and sleeping, it is this separation from my wife. I am not mentally ready to see such a big undertaking through to the end.'

Even so, he had set out and, that morning of June 3rd, he packed his sack, put on his boots and started climbing the lower slopes of the Face in the ghostly light of the dawn. He did not take the decision to turn back consciously. He simply found himself heading back down the slope. The jump into the unknown was too big and, equally important perhaps, his own ties on the ground were too strong.

No sooner did he get back to Funes than he began to dream and plan for other climbs; it is a syndrome which I, and almost every other addicted climber, have been through, the longing to be home when on the mountain, and the restless plans within a few days of getting back.

In 1975 Messner went on two expeditions which provided extreme examples of two different climbing philosophies. In the spring he joined a siege-style Italian expedition to the huge South Face of Lhotse, one of the most complex and dangerous faces in the Himalaya. The party was led by Riccardo Cassin, one of the great climbers of the pre-war era. Messner liked and respected Cassin and, on the whole, got on well with his fellow team members. Though he had done much of the climbing out in front, he found this type of expedition uncongenial, commenting in his book, *The Challenge*:

'On the one side it offers greater safety, back-up, the possibility of substitution in case of illness, comradeship. On the other hand you must offset the restricted mobility, the long discussions and the team spirit, which under some circumstances can strangle all progress. With careful preparation and the necessary experience, a two-man expedition would not only be quicker and cheaper, but also safer. On any quite large mountain everyone must be self-reliant. It is much easier to find a single well-matched partner than ten or fifteen.'

Cassin's team did not succeed and already Messner was planning a very different kind of expedition, a two-man attempt on Hidden Peak (Gasherbrum I, 8068 metres) in the Karakoram. No mountain of over 8000 metres had yielded either to a two-man expedition or, for that matter, to a purely Alpine-style attempt. Hermann Buhl's expedition to Broad Peak had been extremely compact and had not used high-altitude porters, but they had ferried loads up the mountain, establishing their camps in the traditional way.

The evolution of mountaineering is influenced strongly by a conflict between basic instincts. On the one hand there is the spirit of adventure, the desire to pitch skill and judgement against the unknown, with the spice of risk to sharpen the experience, but on the other hand is the instinct for survival and also a need to increase the chances of success. The siege approach gives a greater chance of success, with its big teams and lines of fixed ropes, and at the same time reduces the psychological commitment, though in some ways the risks are just as great, if in different guises. The climber on a siege-style expedition can become over-complacent, confident in his camps and ropes. But he is going back and forth over potentially dangerous ground many times, and is therefore increasing the chances of being caught by avalanche stone fall or hidden crevasses. A weaker climber can, perhaps, get higher on the mountain than he ever would have done had he started from the bottom without the fragile scaffolding of a siege-style expedition.

ABOVE Reinhold Messner (left) and Peter Habeler (right) who teamed up to tackle Hidden Peak Alpine-style and went on to be the first to climb Everest without supplementary oxygen.

And so, the move towards an Alpine approach, while psychologically much more daunting, had some sound, practical merit, as pointed out by Messner. He had talked this over with Peter Habeler, a talented Austrian guide with whom he had climbed in the Andes and made a very fast ascent of the Eiger. He learned that he had permission for Hidden Peak during the Lhotse expedition. The timing was tight, for it was unlikely that they would have finished on Lhotse – successfully or otherwise – before mid-May, the start of the climbing season in the Karakoram. Nevertheless, he resolved to go and, as soon as he got back to the Tyrol, plunged into preparations for the expedition. This introduced another conflict between his relationship with Uschi and his driving urge to climb. She could see an endless series of expeditions, with the period between devoted to preparations for the next one, to lecture tours, to a constant preoccupation in which their life together would be forever subordinate. Messner could see signs of trouble, but the need to go to Hidden Peak was all-consuming; he could not give it up and Uschi would never have asked him to, knowing all too well that this in itself would forever have put a shadow over their relationship.

So a few hectic weeks after getting back to Europe, Messner was back in the Himalaya, this time in Skardu. He and Peter Habeler had a mere twelve porters to carry in the expedition gear, and reached their Base Camp below Hidden Peak near the end of July. They spent a fortnight reconnoitring the approach to their chosen route and then, on August 8th, set out in a dramatic dash for their objective. They bivouacked at the foot of the North-West Face and then, on the following day, climbed the 1200-metre ice and rock wall. It was as steep and committing as the North Face of the Matterhorn, with all the problems of altitude thrown in. To reduce weight and commit themselves to fast movement, they had decided to leave the rope behind which meant, in effect, that each was climbing solo; a mistake would mean almost certain death. Even so, the psychological reassurance that each could give the other was tremendously important. This is what Messner had lacked in that first solo attempt on Nanga Parbat.

They climbed through the day, steep ice, rocks piled loosely upon each other, with the uncomfortable knowledge in the backs of their minds that they also had to get back down. Calves ached with the constant strain of being on the front points of their crampons; their lungs ached with the fatigue of their exertion as they thrust slowly upwards from a height of 5900 metres to 7100. And then, at last, they were above the face in a great snow basin on the upper part of Hidden Peak. The summit ridge, another thousand metres high, stretched invitingly, less steeply above. They camped in their tiny two-man tent and next day set out for the summit. Never had a mountain of this height been climbed with such élan, and complete commitment.

But Messner was to pay a high price for his single-minded devotion to the mountains. In 1977 Uschi left him. On returning to Nanga Parbat later the same year, once again hoping to make the solo ascent, he did not even reach the foot of the mountain – so great was his sense of desolate loneliness.

But there were other challenges. No-one had ever reached the summit of Everest without oxygen, though people had got very close. In 1924, Colonel Norton had reached a height of about 8570 metres on the north side of Everest and then, in 1933, Wyn Harris, Wager and Smythe reached the same height. The difficulty of the ground,

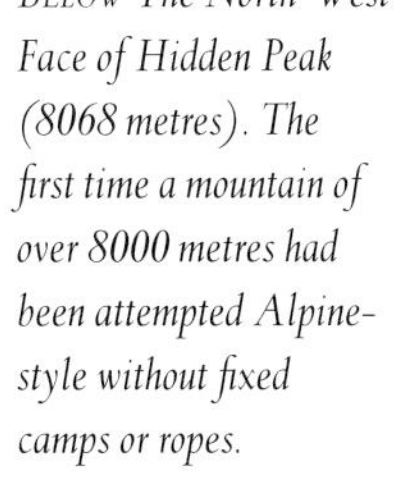

BELOW The North-West Face of Hidden Peak (8068 metres). The first time a mountain of over 8000 metres had been attempted Alpine-style without fixed camps or ropes.

as much as the lack of oxygen, finally forced them to retreat. The Chinese on their ascent from the north in 1975, made only partial use of oxygen, carrying a couple of bottles and passing one round whenever they rested, so that everyone could have a whiff. But nobody reached the top without using it at all.

There were many unanswered questions. Was the human frame capable of working at 8000 metres without the help of an extra oxygen supply? It was certainly very close to, if not above, that critical height when there just is not sufficient oxygen in the atmosphere to sustain life. And what about the threat of brain damage? For Messner, however, the challenge was immensely appealing; it fitted into his philosophy of reducing all technical aids that intrude between the climber and the actual experience to the very minimum. It was also a unique dramatic statement. He described his attempt as being an attempt on Everest by fair means, implying that everyone else who had climbed the mountain had, in some way, been cheating.

But it is not easy to get permission to climb Everest. The mountain was booked for years ahead. An Austrian expedition, led by Messner's friend Wolfgang Nairz, was going there in the spring of 1978, and he agreed to Messner and Habeler joining the expedition, almost as a self-contained mini-expedition within his own. In return, Messner was able to raise funds which would not have been available otherwise.

They worked well together as a team on the climb, with Messner and Habeler helping to make the route up through the Icefall, the Western Cwm and up onto the Lhotse Face. They abandoned their first summit bid without oxygen, Habeler because of a stomach upset and Messner defeated by a storm. At this point Habeler had momentary second thoughts and tried to join an oxygen-using team for his second bid, but the rest of the party's arrangements had already been made and there was, anyway, a level of resentment among the others, since part of the deal had been that the oxygenless pair should have first go for the summit. Habeler's resolution returned and on May 8th he and Messner reached the top of Everest without oxygen.

It was an extraordinary achievement and yet Messner felt a sense of anticlimax; he was already thinking about going back to Nanga Parbat: 'When we were back in Base Camp again and I didn't feel any joy in our success, but rather an inner emptiness, I filled this emptiness with the conception of this eight-thousander solo ideal.'

He had already applied again for permission for Nanga Parbat and he learned he had got it while on Everest. He returned to the Tyrol to spend a hectic month writing his account of his Everest climb, giving interviews and arranging the new trip. One advantage of making a solo attempt is that it requires delightfully little organisation. At the end of June the expedition set out. It consisted of Messner and Ursula Grether, a medical student in her final year who had trekked on her own to the Everest Base Camp where she had meet Messner. She was to be companion and doctor on the expedition.

In Rawalpindi they acquired a liaison officer, Major Mohammed Tahir, bought some local food and set out for the mountain. The challenge awaiting Messner was probably greater, and certainly very much more committing, than the one he had faced on Everest. He had made two attempts already and had failed because he had not been ready psychologically for so great a commitment. This time, perhaps, he

RIGHT Diamir Face of Nanga Parbat – the fact that Messner had climbed down it in the desperate circumstances of 1970 did not lessen the challenge. This would be his third attempt at an ascent.

had managed the right mix. His ascent of Everest must have given him still greater confidence in his own ability to keep going. With Ursula's companionship as far as Base Camp, he would not know the debilitating loneliness that he had experienced on both his previous attempts, and he had come to terms with the break-up of his marriage, writing: 'I still suffer from depression every now and then, but it does me good to think about her. I certainly don't want to forget her.'

The approach to the mountain was delightfully relaxed; it was more like a trekking holiday than an expedition, with the little team of three becoming absorbed into the atmosphere of the society around them. Quickly they formed a close and easy friendship with their liaison officer; each took turns at cooking and the other minor chores as they walked through the foothills. At the foot of the Diamir Glacier, where Messner had now been on three separate occasions, they set up their tiny camp and looked up at the face. The fact that he had climbed down it in 1970 did not lessen the challenge, the quality of the unknown. It is the concept of being totally alone on that huge mountain, the obvious risk of falling into a hidden crevasse or bergschrund, the less obvious one of facing the appalling upward struggle of high-altitude climbing without encouragement, without the sustaining presence of another.

They had been at Base Camp for ten days before Messner felt ready for his attempt. He had the residual acclimatisation and fitness left over from his ascent of Everest as well as the ten-day approach march, going up and down between two and four thousand metres. Yet, even as he packed his rucksack that afternoon, there was a nagging doubt at the back of his mind. That night it was worse; thoughts and images galloped through his mind in that hazy, frightening realm that lies between wakefulness and uneasy sleep:

'In my torment I sit up. Suddenly the vision of a body falling down the mountainside flashes before me. It comes straight at me. I duck out of its way. Fear engulfs my whole body As it falls, this whirling body almost touches me, and I recognise its face as my own. My stomach turns over. I think I am going to be sick. It no longer makes any difference if I fall or cling on, live or die I must have uttered a cry for Ursula wakes.'

He did not set out the following morning. Instead, he and Ursula climbed a small peak above their camp and through this he gained the self-confidence he needed, together with a feeling of being in harmony with the face that was his objective and the peaks and the sky surrounding him. A few days later he was ready to start. As on Hidden Peak, he was basing his plan on speed; the longer he was on the mountain, the more likely it was for the weather to break, the longer he would be exposed to objective dangers of avalanche or stone fall. He therefore carried with him the bare minimum – a lightweight tent, sleeping bag, ice axe, crampons, gas stove and a few days' food. The lot came to fifteen kilos. This meant that he had to climb the 3500-metre face in just three or four days, whereas a conventional siege-style expedition might have taken as many weeks, or even longer.

Setting out from Base Camp on August 6th, he walked up the easy dry glacier to the foot of the Mummery Rib; Ursula accompanied him and, that night, they camped beneath a large rock which Messner hoped would guard them from the effects of any avalanche from the face. The following morning he set out in the grey dawn up the glacier guarding the lower part of the face, picking his way through the crevasses and round the steep sérac walls. As on his fateful descent with Günther eight years before, he felt another presence and could actually hear its voice guiding him, telling him to go left or right to find the best route. He was making good progress, heading for the hanging glacier that turned the huge ice wall that barred the centre of the face. To be safe, he had to get above it that day.

The face was still in shadow, the snow crisp and firm under foot and he was above the great ice wall. He had climbed 1600 metres in only six hours. Although still early in the day, he decided to stop where he was and trampled out a small platform immediately below a sérac wall which he hoped would protect it from avalanches. He put up his tent and flopped inside. At altitude the contrasts are almost as great as those on the moon. In the shade it is bitterly cold, but in the sun, particularly inside a tent, it is like being in an oven, so warm that the snow packed into the tent bag, hanging from the roof, steadily melted through the day providing him with precious liquid and thus conserving his fuel. He heated the water and made soup, swallowed some cold corned beef and was promptly sick. The heat, the fast height gain, exhaustion had all played their part, but in being sick he had lost precious fluid, something that he could not afford. He sipped the melt water through the day, had another brew of soup that night, and then snuggled down into his sleeping bag for his first night alone on the Diamir Face. So far everything was under control, progress as planned.

And then came the morning of the huge avalanche. Much later he learned that this had been caused by an earthquake whose epicentre was in the knee-bend of the river Indus in its serpentine course through the mountains. All he knew was that the route he had followed the previous day had been swept away, that if he had started one day later, he would have been at the bottom of the face, in the direct path of the torrent of ice and snow. The size of the catastrophe emphasised his own lonely vulnerability. But it never occurred to him to start trying to find an alternative way back; his whole being was focused on the summit.

He packed his gear, neatly folded the tent and set out once again in the bitter cold of the early morning, heading for the next barrier – a broken wall of rock and ice stretching down from the crest of the ridge. He was going more slowly than on the previous day, each step taking a separate effort of will. There was no question of racing the sun, and once this crept over the shoulder the bitter cold changed to blazing heat and the snow soon turned into a treacherous morass. And still he kept going, getting ever closer to the great trapezoid of rock that marked the summit block. He stopped just beneath it. He was now at a height of around 7500 metres, another thousand metres gained, another long afternoon to savour his isolation. Intermittently he was again aware of another presence, this time a girl; tantalising, he could almost glimpse her at the extreme edge of vision. They talked. She reassured him that the weather would hold, that he would reach the summit the following day. And through the afternoon the clouds, strange mountains of cumulus, shifted and changed in shape and tone as the sun dropped down over the western horizon. That night in the lee of the long day, Messner felt at peace with himself, but the following morning was very different:

'This sudden confrontation with such utter loneliness immediately envelops me in a deep depression. In the months after my break-up with Uschi it was often like this when I woke up. The sudden pressure which threatens to dash me to pieces, a well of despair bubbling up from deep sources and taking possession of my whole being. It is so strong I have to cry.'

But action has its own quality of reassurance. He peered out of the tent to see what the reality of the day would bring:

'The play of the dark clouds below me both worry and fascinate me. Now and then, between the surging clouds, a mountain top emerges. It is like being witness to the Creation. Like seeing everything from the outside. It doesn't occur to me to be surprised at the threatening bad weather. It is a strange sensation. *"Tike"* [All right] I say; just that, a word that slips into my mind unbidden. I could blow soap bubbles and suspend the tent on them. For a tiny moment something warm passes through my dog-tired body.'

ABOVE Reinhold Messner on the summit of Nanga Parbat. A screw set into his ice axe shaft turned it into a monopod for delayed-action photography.

Now within striking distance of the top, he could hope to get there and back in the day; indeed, he had to, for he could no longer carry a fifteen-kilo load on his back; could not afford to spend any more nights at that altitude and continue to toil upwards. He left his tent, sleeping bag and food and, just carrying his ice axe and camera, started out for the top.

He was now well above the altitude where snow thaws and then freezes. Even in the early morning cold it was a deep slough in which he wallowed up to his thighs. After three hours' struggle, he had made hardly any progress – the day and his own strength were racing away. There seemed only one chance, to take the steep rocks leading direct to the summit, even though this meant infinitely greater insecurity. He teetered around narrow ledges, no wider than a window sill; no chance of hard rock climbing at this altitude, in clumsy double boots with crampons.

The act of balancing on crampon points was bad enough. Snow-filled gullies alternated with rocky steps; his rests became more frequent as his limbs grew more and more leaden. There is no physical exhilaration in climbing at altitude; it is will-power alone that can keep you going, make each leg move forward with such painful slowness that the goal never seems to come any closer. He could hear his lungs roar, his heartbeat hammering at a furious rate and still he kept plodding on.

It was four o'clock when, at last, he reached the top. Suddenly, the snow dropped away on every side; the view was the same as he had seen eight years before and yet so different, for that ascent had been in the freshness of his experience. It was his first Himalayan peak and his brother had been with him to share that momentary euphoria. Messner writes:

'I wander around in a circle, repeatedly looking at the view, as if I can hardly believe I am really here. There is no great outrush of emotion such as I experienced on Everest; I am quite calm, calmer than I have ever been on any eight-thousander. I often thought about that later and wondered why these swelling emotions which on Everest wracked me with sobs and tears, should have been absent on Nanga Parbat. I

have come to the conclusion that being alone, as I was on top of Nanga, I could not have borne such a strong surge of feeling. I would have been unable to leave. Our bodies know more than we understand with our minds.'

He spent an hour on the summit, and took a series of photographs with his camera mounted on a screw head specially fitted to his ice axe. Using the timer and an ultra-wide-angle lens, he could include himself in the picture. A great mass of cloud covered the Karakoram; ominous tendrils chased across the sky, reaching out towards Nanga Parbat, yet Messner felt very little anxiety about his chances of getting back down by a different route from his ascent in the face of the threatened storm. No doubt his reactions were deadened by fatigue and lack of oxygen but, more important, so at one with the mountain did he feel that the very strength of this feeling gave him a calm confidence.

But it was time to descend. He picked a different route down and was able to make relatively fast, easy progress back to the lonely tent at the foot of the summit pyramid. That night he could sense the gathering storm. There was not yet any wind, but he could almost feel the cloud pressing in on the tent and then, next morning, with a banshee wail came the wind and snow. There was no question of moving now, for he could never have found his way down in the driving snow. But the storm might last a couple of days, a week, or even longer. If he conserved his fuel and food he could last for five days, and so he settled down in his sleeping bag to try to wait it out. But it wasn't just a question of supplies, for at that altitude the body is slowly deteriorating. Already badly dehydrated, he was also exhausted and knew that he could only get worse, that even rest would do him little good. He was becoming clumsy in his movements, upset the stove a couple of times and burnt his sleeping bag. There was plenty of time in which to ponder his predicament, to try to work out the best line of descent.

All that day he was pinned down in the tent, but the next morning the cloud around him cleared, although the sky was still overcast with a high scum of grey. He realised that he had to get down that day and so abandoned tent, sleeping bag and food, knowing that if he failed to escape from the face before dark he would have little chance of survival. He set out, heading down the long snow slopes towards the ice runnel running down the centre of the face between the Mummery Rib and the great ice wall – his only hope of descent, for the rocks on the rib were plastered with a thin layer of ice. But it was also the natural avalanche line. Messner had no choice, he just had to hope for the best. He slipped on the way down, knew that once he fell he would be out of control and so raced down the slope in a series of giant strides, crampons biting into the ice as he tried to regain his balance and get back control.

Lungs heaving, trembling with shock, he managed to do it. And so it went on through the day, the whole time at the edge between extinction and survival, of accepting exhaustion and forcing himself on, each step on the hard ice needing all his concentration as he teetered down, seeming to go little faster than he had on the way up.

And then he was down; almost without realising it, the angle had eased. He was on the dry glacier at the foot of the face and just had to put one foot in front of the other. Ursula came out to meet him. The climb was over.

'Somehow I have overstepped my limitations; my strength, the loneliness. A year ago feeling I was alone was my weakness. I am not saying that now I have got over it, no, I was only totally alone for a few days. But it was beautiful. I don't know everything about loneliness yet – that too is reassuring.'

The following year Messner climbed K2, this time as part of an expedition and then, in 1980, he climbed Everest solo, once again without oxygen, from the Chinese side. The pattern, in many ways, was very similar to that of Nanga Parbat. A girlfriend, this time Nena Ritchie, from Canada, accompanied him to Base Camp and, like Ursula in '78, went with him to his advanced camp. Once again he took the mountain by storm, climbing it in just three days by the North Ridge, the route attempted by the British before the war and first climbed by the Chinese in 1960. It was an amazing feat. To put it into perspective, there had been twenty-five successful expeditions to Everest between 1953 and 1980, none of them with fewer than thirty climbers and Sherpas, none of them without oxygen and not one of these expeditions had taken less than a month to climb the mountain. Since Messner's solo ascent there has been an explosion of activity, due both to the Nepalese and Chinese allowing any number of expeditions on to Everest at the same time, and the growth of commercial expeditions. Messner showed what can be done.

He went on to climb all fourteen of the 8000-metre peaks, finishing with Lhotse in 1986. In doing this he gave birth to a sub-sport in mountaineering – that of 8000-metre peak bagging – before giving up serious mountaineering and turning to what he describes as 'ice walking' in Antarctica and in the Arctic. But in the mountains there are still infinite opportunities. Climbers, using Alpine-style tactics have tackled ever steeper and technically more difficult climbs on the highest peaks, not only in the summer season, but in winter as well. One of the most impressive in this genre was the first ascent of the West Face of Gasherbrum IV (7925 metres) by Voytek Kurtyka and Robert Schauer in 1985. Today no face or line can be dismissed as impossible but it was Messner who opened up the possibilities of climbing the highest peaks solo and in Alpine-style.

BELOW An exhausted Messner, back at Base Camp, has an injection to aid circulation.

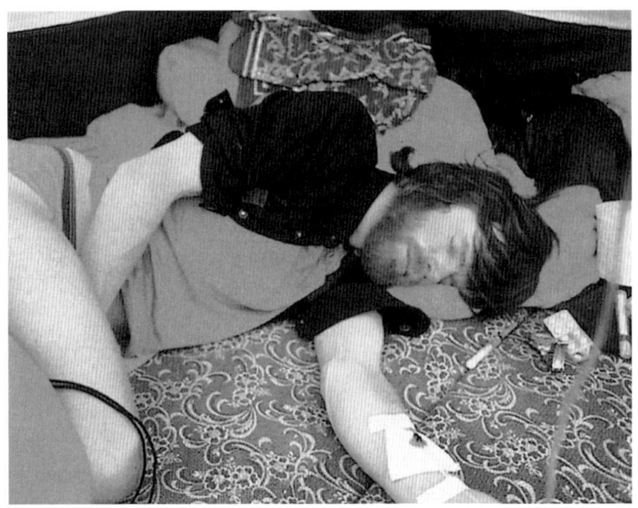

11

ELEVEN

A Vertical Desert

The Challenge of El Capitan

El Capitan soars above the pine trees of Yosemite Valley in a single sweep of light grey granite. It is difficult to get an idea of its huge scale. The lines are so clean, the rock, on first glance, so featureless. Arguably, it is the most beautiful and dramatic rock feature in the world. There are walls as big, or bigger, in Baffin Island and the Karakoram but none has the same cleanness of line. It is a place of contrasts. Long gone is the unspoilt beauty and peace of the valley bottom for it has become a tourist honey pot with a network of roads, adjacent campsites, lodges and hotels, and yet from a distance it still has that pristine beauty.

The story of the development of climbing on El Capitan mirrors the history of climbing as a whole and yet retains a unique quality of its own. Compared to Europe its development, like that of the west coast of America, is essentially young. Although the valley was discovered by white pioneers in the mid-1850s, serious climbing only began in the 1930s, inspired by a few people who had visited Europe. El Capitan and the other great blank-looking walls seemed unattainable, indeed unthinkable, and the early pioneers sought out tree-filled gullies and broken features.

It was after the Second World War, as with so many other aspects of climbing and adventure, that the breakthrough began to take place, although initially the pace was slow. There was still a tiny number of climbers, many of whom had served in the war and had seen something of climbing in Europe. They began creeping out onto the more exposed faces using the nylon ropes, alloy karabiners and soft iron pitons that were becoming available.

It was to be a European whose name is immortalised by one of the finest rock climbs in the world – the Salathé Wall. John Salathé was born in Switzerland in 1899 and settled in California in the early 'thirties, setting up a blacksmith's business making garden furniture. It was only in 1945 that he discovered climbing. After a long period of ill health he had a vision of an angel who told him to become a vegetarian and shortly afterwards, on the advice of his doctor, he moved up into the hills behind Yosemite, saw the handful of climbers in action and decided to have a go. He wasn't a natural free climber and was a little late in starting, but he saw the need for strong steel pitons that could be driven into the thin, often bottoming cracks of Yosemite granite. He also began developing the aid techniques which were to become so much more sophisticated than those used in Europe.

The great challenge of the 'forties was a magnificent blade of solid crackless rock, the Lost Arrow. Its summit had been reached with some clever rope trickery, but its ascent in 1947 by Salathé and Ax Nelson was the first major big wall climb executed in the valley. They took five days to complete the climb and had to carry sufficient water for the duration – a mere six quarts to give them a pint each per day – which, in the event was not enough. By modern standards they had a very small rack consisting of eighteen rock pitons of hardened steel, from thin knife blades to one-inch angle pitons, and eighteen expansion bolts for the blank tip of the Lost Arrow. This ascent opened up the huge potential for climbing on the great walls of the valley, but El Capitan still seemed impossible.

Through the 'fifties the numbers of climbers increased. A new young generation emerged who realised they could earn enough in the winter with casual jobs to spend summers climbing. As a result they achieved a level of fitness and expertise that led to rapidly improving standards. With this development came the eternal debate on ethics, of how far it was justified to use expansion bolts and pitons for aid. The nature of the rock and the gear available at the time meant that there seemed to be no alternative to hammering pitons into cracks for protection. The purism of English climbing, which had always spurned the use of pitons, did not seem an option but the extensive use of bolts and siege tactics using fixed ropes was a matter for debate.

Two strong personalities had just come onto the scene. Royal Robbins, a lanky serious youngster, had had an unsettled childhood and brushed with the law. He was rescued by the Scout movement and found an outlet for his sense of adventure back-packing in the High Sierra. He then discovered climbing so dropped out of school at sixteen to get odd jobs at ski resorts and pursue the sport for which he had a natural affinity. His approach was disciplined and structured. He saw the need for a rationalised grading system as standards soared yet were only covered by one all-embracing grade. From the start he took a strong ethical stance on the style of climbing, feeling that the use of siege tactics on the big blank walls of the valley would destroy the spirit of adventure and uncertainty that is so much part of the sport.

He demonstrated his belief with the first ascent of the North-West Face of Half Dome, a magnificent towering wall that was bigger and steeper than anything before climbed. It took five days and involved the longest and wildest pendulum yet attempted to change from one crack system to another. One of the features of Yosemite granite is the way crack lines stretch up the faces and then tend to fade into holdless rock. Robbins wasn't averse to using bolts to link natural lines but he tried to keep their use to a minimum both on aesthetic grounds and also because drilling the holes in which to hammer the expansion bolts took a long time. The pendulum was a way round this need. The lead climber would get as high as he could on one crack line, have himself lowered some feet and then start running back and forth across the sheer rock, like the weight on the end of a pendulum, until he managed to snatch a hold or crack line at the extremity of his swing – a frightening manoeuvre a thousand feet up a vertical wall.

The other person who was to dominate the Yosemite scene was very different from Robbins. Warren Batso Harding was a maverick, larger-than-life character,

ABOVE Warren Harding, wild man of American climbing, in action on the South Face of Half Dome.

representing in many ways the free-spirited individualism that is so much part of climbing. He had a healthy contempt for rules, be they those of society or the ethics observed and argued over by the climbing world. Brought up in California during the depression, ironically he was turned down for military service during the war because of a heart murmur and ended up working in the Highways Department. He made his mark tackling first ascents and yet in some ways remained outside the climbing scene, very much his own man.

Steve Roper, historian of the era and long-term habitué of Camp 4, the place in the valley where all the climbers stayed, describes his first meeting with Harding. It was at a bouldering area in the suburbs of Berkeley. Roper saw a flashy Jaguar roar up and park in the nearby street.

'"It's Warren Harding," someone then whispered. Out stepped a handsome devilish fellow with a young woman draped on his arm. Short and classically wiry, he strolled over to our group, a furtive gleam in his eye. I stared closely, trying to measure the man.

'I thought I would see him swarm up our practice routes, but instead he sat down and began drinking a jug of wine and telling stories. A sociable chap, I thought, but why doesn't he climb? Though he wore army fatigue pants, like most of us, he had dyed his black. Looking at his black flashing eyes, his wild black hair, his jet-black pants, his sultry moll by his side, his wine, and his lack of interest in what anyone was climbing, I couldn't believe my eyes. I was fascinated, mainly because the other climbers I knew were spectacled scientists, staid folk who would never have dreamed of wheeling up to a rock with a sports car and a jug and a flashy dame.'

Warren Harding had been involved in an earlier attempt on the North Face of Half Dome with Robbins and some others, but hadn't felt comfortable with Don Wilson, the self-appointed leader who gave the impression of being in charge and called a retreat on the grounds they were going too slowly. Harding returned some time later with Mark Powell and Bill Dolt Feuerer, with whom he felt more at home and who, I suspect, were happier to concur with his views, only to find that Robbins was already part way up the coveted North Face. Harding's reaction was: 'Well, shit, we're here with all this gear – might as well climb something!' There certainly were plenty of attractive new routes to be done, but everything else seemed to represent some sort of put down compared to Half Dome. All but one, that is.

And so they went for the Nose of El Capitan, the mass of compact rock which until that moment climbers had glanced at but reckoned impossible. It was altogether

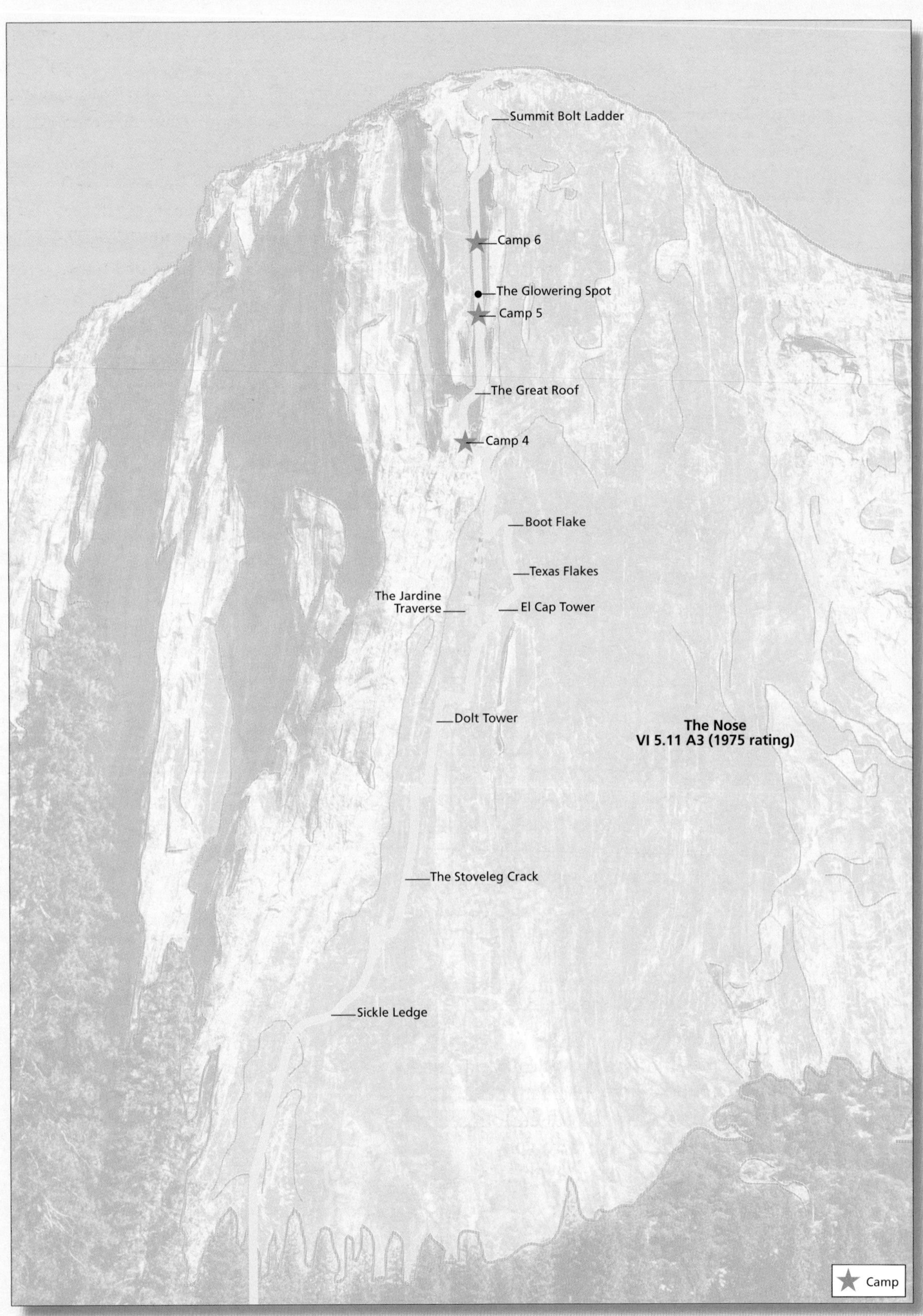
Summit Bolt Ladder
Camp 6
The Glowering Spot
Camp 5
The Great Roof
Camp 4
Boot Flake
Texas Flakes
The Jardine Traverse
El Cap Tower
Dolt Tower
The Nose
VI 5.11 A3 (1975 rating)
The Stoveleg Crack
Sickle Ledge
Camp

bigger, steeper and smoother than anything anywhere in the world that had so far been climbed, so it was perhaps inevitable that that first attempt should have employed siege tactics, nibbling away at the wall over a period of time, slowly gaining height, but returning to ground for rests, provisions and more gear. Up to this point climbs had been made Alpine-style, bivouacking on the way up. The most time Harding had ever spent on a climb was four days and the longest anyone had spent was five. It was a matter not just of carrying food and gear, but water as well. This was to be the first major siege climb and at the time was not particularly criticised. It seemed the only way of doing it. The criticism was reserved more for the extent of the media interest. Suddenly, this very private minority activity was being adopted by the national media.

They started on July 4th 1957, but could have had little idea it was going to take eighteen months to reach the top. Their first objective was a clearly defined ledge about 550 feet above the start. It was technically hard from the beginning, a sweep of smooth steep holdless slabs with vanishing unlinked crack lines that demanded pendulum tactics to swing from one line to the next. It took three days to reach the Sickle Ledge, which was to become their base of operations for the next section. Everything then became steeper and more serious with off-width cracks (ones too wide to jam a hand in, yet not wide enough to insert one's body). There were more pendulums and the exposure was becoming ever more frightening.

Today it is something of a trade route with a queue of climbers stretched up it through the season. It is all too easy to forget what a challenge it was in 1957-58 both because they were reaching into the unknown and also because of the gear and techniques available at that time. Although they had hawser-laid nylon ropes, these were so expensive that they were using hemp for their fixed rope. The jumar clamp was not yet in existence, so they ascended the ropes with prusik knots, which were awkward to handle. Although they had hardened steel pitons, these were still basic in design and there were no big angle pitons for use in the wide cracks. One of their secret weapons was a set of stove legs, rescued from a rubbish dump, which acted as wide, but very heavy, angle pitons, to be immortalised in the notorious Stoveleg Crack. They only had four stove legs and the crack was 300 feet long and of uniform width. This meant that Harding had to leapfrog the devices upwards, a frightening procedure, since it entailed removing the intermediate pitons. If the four he was clipped into had pulled out, he would have had a very long fall, and falls were frequent. They used 125 expansion bolts for protection and belays over the entire climb, but even this represented a huge amount of work, drilling by hand the three-eighths of an inch diameter hole needed for the bolt. Harding was using aid practically all the way. Apart from anything else, he was not a brilliant free climber, being steady, but without the natural genius of Robbins.

They had been on the wall for a week, were tired and had run out of food, water and gear. It was time for a break, so they abseiled to the ground. This in some ways was an easy option but even the abseils and the prospect of prusiking all the way back up were frightening, particularly on the frayed hemp ropes. Once back at ground level other problems arose. Their climb had become a tourist spectacle causing traffic

LEFT The Nose of El Capitan.

ABOVE Surprisingly, they found a few commodious ledges on the way up. Wayne Merry grabbing a much needed rest.

jams on the road below El Capitan. The Park rangers had even tried to order them down, shouting through bullhorns, but Warren chose not to hear. After being hauled in front of the chief ranger, 'a salty old devil who wasn't keen on rock climbing or anything else that might disrupt the otherwise smooth operation of Yosemite National Park', they reached an agreement with the Park authorities that they should stay away until the end of the tourist season.

They got back onto the Nose on Thanksgiving Day, when the November days were getting short and the nights were cold. Mark Powell, a key member of the team, was out of action after a bad fall so Harding invited Robbins to join them. But Robbins declined, later telling an interviewer that he felt it was Harding's scene and that he didn't want to use fixed ropes, even though the route probably couldn't be completed by any other means. Bill Dolt Feuerer was still keen and Harding recruited Wally Reed, a steady climber working the season at Yosemite Lodge, and the legendary Al Steck, who had made the first ascent of Sentinel, but hadn't climbed for some years. He had a young family and was teaching at Berkeley but couldn't resist Harding's persuasive tongue and the assurance that he could prusik all the way and act as a belayer and hauler.

It was a frightening re-introduction. It took them a day and a half to prusik up the fixed ropes to the previous high point. In addition the manila rope was showing serious signs of wear, as Reed was to discover when he found himself plummeting earthwards. The rope had abraded through and he was very lucky to be a short distance above a ledge on which he landed. It's a tribute to his determination that he kept going. Henceforth all fixed ropes would be nylon and expense be damned. Once at the high point, Harding only managed to make another sixty feet and that night they had their first ever bivouac in slings. There were no ledges and the exposure was terrifying. Steck was beginning to regret being involved. Sitting in slings is hideously uncomfortable, circulation is restricted, you get cramp and it is difficult to shift position. Harding was dangling about fifteen feet above Steck, suspended from a huge home-made T-bar piton hammered in with a heavy oversize hammer. Half way through the night it shifted, dropping a significant distance before becoming jammed once again. Steck was shaken as badly as Harding by the incident, though they all did their best to laugh it off. If that wasn't enough, Harding had to answer a call of nature during the night and ended up peeing on Steck.

Next morning Harding managed to nail ninety feet up the crack to the top of what became known as the Dolt Tower where they found a commodious bivouac site. They experienced another near miss as Harding heaved on a huge chock stone in that awkward transition from aid climbing to free. The boulder started to roll outwards and Harding instinctively let go to fall onto his top piton. Fortunately the chock stone re-bedded itself, since it could have wiped them all out had it come away. Harding had now climbed a third of the Nose. Early the following spring he and Dolt Feuerer replaced all the manila fixed rope with nylon. Prusiking up the manila ropes after six months of winter storms and the consequent abrasion of the ropes must have been a nerve wracking experience. By April the team was ready once again. Steck had had enough, but Mark Powell, even though his ankle hadn't healed, decided to come along to act as a belayer. Feuerer, the engineer, had designed a two-wheel cart to make the chore of load-hauling a little easier. It wasn't. It required four people and thousands of feet of rope to run the thing. With just a weekend to spare, it took them most of their time to get themselves and their gear to the high point and they only managed sixty feet of fresh ascent.

They returned a month later, had a little more time and made better progress, reaching and establishing Camp 3, a dump of gear, food and water on a large ledge on top of El Cap Tower. They even made quick progress above up an easy chimney behind Texas flake and then bolted up a blank stretch to the foot of the infamous Boot flake, a wide crack up a slab. Being behind a flake, there is always the possibility of the crack expanding as each angle piton is hammered in, with the risk of the pitons below becoming loose or even falling out. Harding was in his element as he hammered his way cautiously up the precarious crack. It was a fine bold lead, but once again time had run out and they had to return to the ground. The Park authorities were getting restive and the siege had to be put on hold for the summer tourist season.

They returned again in early September, after the Labor Day weekend. They were now a team of six. Powell had relented and was back yet again, to be joined by Wally Reed and a relative novice, Rick Calderwood. Wayne Merry, a summer ranger, and John Whitmore, who had made the first ascent of the North Buttress of Middle Cathedral with Harding, made up the team. This was to be a nine-day push. Just reaching the high point with the hardware and provisions was a major undertaking. They were soaked and frightened by thunderstorms. The newcomers were intimidated by the ferocious unrelenting exposure, but slowly progress was made.

The most challenging section of the entire climb was at the top of Boot flake. There were no more crack lines above and the next line of weakness was a long way to the left across smooth blank walls. They had already used the pendulum technique, but this one was going to be bigger and longer than anything before attempted. Merry took a belay on the ledge above the flake and lowered Harding off about fifty feet, level with the foot of the flake. It took him five swings to grab the edge of a crack which was out of sight behind a shallow corner. He managed somehow to hang on, tap in a piton and then take stock. He was disappointed. The crack petered out after only a few feet but there was another crack system that did seem continuous another twenty feet or so further to the left. He passed the rope through a karabiner, clipped in to the piton, yelled to Merry to lower him once again so that he could make another pendulum. They were out of sight of each other, could barely hear each other's yells, yet Harding kept going, managing the final pendulum to reach the elusive crack line.

ABOVE The long and difficult pendulum from Boot Flake to reach the crack line leading into the upper part of the face. This was avoided by Ray Jardine who controversially chiselled a line of finger holes across the blank wall at a lower level. These were used by everyone, including Lynn Hill, attempting free ascents.

Merry then had to join him by a series of terrifying prusiks and abseils, in their way both more frightening and exacting than the initial pendulum. So many things can go wrong with the possibility of frayed ropes, faulty knots or clipping. At the end of nine days' hard and nerve-jangling work they had only increased their vertical height by a few feet. It was time to retreat yet again. There were two more attempts in October, but they were hindered by storms and the sheer distance that had to be covered each time on the fixed ropes. Consequently they made no more upward progress. The Park authorities were becoming impatient and issued an ultimatum that the climb had to be finished by Thanksgiving Day.

Warren set out on one last push. The team was now down to four, Harding, Calderwood, Merry and a newcomer, George Whitmore. They had at least fully stocked their top camp, called Camp 4, in their two previous forays. This meant it took just a day to prusik the 1900 feet to their high point. The Great Roof, a huge overhang, loomed above them but it went surprisingly easily up a perfect peg crack that slid round it. Above, the difficulties relented. Steve Roper memorably describes the upper third of the Nose: 'Planes of marble-smooth granite shoot upwards towards infinity. The various dihedral walls, dead vertical at this stage, converge in broad angular facets, and climbing through this magical place is like living inside a cut diamond.'

Harding and Merry were sharing the leads. It was straightforward aid climbing with good cracks into which they just had to pound their pitons, clip in a karabiner and stirrup, step into the top loop and hammer in another piton. But it all took a long time and they were making little more than a hundred feet a day, dropping back to their top bivouac, Camp 6, each night. It demanded constant concentration, checking and rechecking every knot and interlinked sling in an environment more daunting then ever before experienced by climbers.

Calderwood and Whitmore were acting as Sherpas, ferrying the supplies up the fixed ropes behind the assault team. In many ways theirs was the more exacting role, for there was none of the excitement of making the route, just the grinding hard work of hauling heavy loads and endless terrifying prusiks when every moment the rope gave a few inches they felt it was their last. They were running out of gear, particularly bolts and drills. Calderwood abseiled all the way down to the ground to phone the Ski Hut in Berkeley for more gear to be sent to Yosemite by special delivery and then prusiked all the way back up to Camp 6, where he had a narrow escape. Camp 6 was a fairly commodious ledge, so he hadn't bothered to tie himself into a safety line as he moved around, and very nearly tumbled over the edge. It was all too much. He packed his sack and headed for home.

This just left three of them, Merry and Harding out in front and Whitmore leading a solitary existence, often on a lower bivouac, relaying supplies up the face. The days were getting shorter, the nights longer and colder. On November 10th they were hit by a blizzard and made no progress at all, but they knew they were close to the top and could even hear the shouts of friends waiting to greet them. Harding worked through the next night by the light of a head torch, drilling his way up a blank wall above the black void. To save time and effort he only drilled every third hole deep enough for the bolt to go all the way in. He drilled twenty-seven bolts through the night and in the dawn of November 12th pulled over the lip of the wall to scramble

BELOW Wayne Merry using aid climbing on the crack line above the Great Roof leading to Camp 5.

up the summit slabs and be greeted by a crowd of friends and representatives of the media. He looked even more than usually the wildest of wild men, with his unkempt black hair, hands torn and bloody, as, with a wolfish smile, he accepted a swig of red wine.

They had lived for twelve days on the wall on that final attempt, longer than anyone had been on such a face before. He had spent altogether forty-five days spread over eighteen months on the wall – a tribute to his dogged tenacity. He had always been the driving force, for the most part climbing with people of less experience. It was the longest, steepest, hardest climb in technical terms to have been completed anywhere in the world. At the same time, within the American climbing community, it was also the most controversial on a number of fronts. The purists had reservations, not only about the siege tactics employed, but also about the publicity that they felt Harding had sought. It was claimed that his girlfriend made regular calls to the media, keeping them up to date on the progress of the climb.

Steve Roper commented: 'Climbing publicity is not intrinsically sinister. Yet for those who regarded climbing as a type of pure sport, as many in those halcyon days were wont to do, publicity was something to be shunned. Outsiders couldn't possibly understand our motives, so you climbed for yourself. You wanted peer recognition of course, but you never went outside the immediate group for acceptance.'

It was Robbins who made the second ascent, just two years later, with three of the leading climbers of the day, Tom Frost, who would join me on the South Face of Annapurna in 1970, Joe fitschen and Chuck Pratt. They were determined to climb it Alpine-style, in a single push, and took just seven days. But it must be remembered that all 125 bolts were in place and, more important, that intangible barrier of the unknown had been removed. A year later, in 1961, Robbins, Frost and Pratt turned their attention to the huge face to the left of the Nose, to make the first ascent of the Salathé Wall. The challenge was so enormous they can be forgiven making an initial three-and-a-half-day sortie on a long diagonal traverse towards a natural line of weakness leading straight to the top. They then abseiled straight down, leaving the ropes in place. A few days later, on the climb proper, they removed the ropes as they ascended and threw three of them to the ground, keeping just three for the climb. Thus they cut the umbilical cord safeguarding their retreat in order to commit themselves totally to the climb. They topped out in six days after some of the most difficult free and aid climbing ever done on a big wall at that time.

Robbins expressed his approach to the climb and his attitude to adventure in the *American Alpine Journal*: 'It was perfectly clear to us that given sufficient time, fixed ropes, bolts and determination, any section of any rock wall could be climbed.'

Should Warren Harding have left the Nose to his climbing betters? I don't think so. Climbing needed the catalyst, the irritant, that he provided with such flare. Harding's contempt for rules, for the 'Valley Christians' as he described the purists, is typical of the individualism of so many adventurers and innovators. He struck out at them in his 1975 book, *Downward Bound, a Mad Guide to Rock Climbing*. Part light-hearted instruction, part spoof, part story of his climbs, part self-justification, he had this to say to Steve Roper, author of a new guide to Yosemite climbing, which contained a section on ethics: 'This material reads like a religious catechism. (I've often wondered about what sort of uh- religious training these fellows enjoyed during their formative years.) I found this quite amusing, for Roper and the others as well, seemed to project an image of rebelliousness toward society and all its mores. So now, in great logic, these fellows exhibited a strong desire for something to be righteous and moral about, something to conform to, a longing to proselytise.'

Harding went on to confound the purists in 1970 with his ascent of the Dawn Wall, a huge stretch of blank rock to the east of the Nose. He tackled it Alpine-style with Dean Caldwell, spending three weeks on the wall, itself a record, battered by storms, running out of food, but keeping going. Even so, they were criticised because they weren't following a natural line. There being few cracks, they used a huge number of bolts, drilling 330 holes in all, though many of these were used for bat hooks, a precarious means of ascent, whereby a hook is placed in a shallow hole to allow the climber to stand in the sling attached to it. You could do several moves like this before needing to drill a deeper hole and hammer in a bolt.

Initially Robbins was magnanimous, stating: 'good to have a man around who doesn't give a damn what the establishment thinks. As our sport becomes rapidly more institutionalised, Harding stands out as a magnificent maverick.' In making the second ascent with Don Lauria, however, he could not resist the urge to eradicate the route, hammering out the offending bolts. In doing this he was defying climbing etiquette which holds that one is only justified in removing a bolt if one has managed to lead that particular stretch of rock without using it. They became so impressed, however, by the extreme difficulty of some of the aid climbing using natural features in the rock, that they relented and in the upper part left the offending bolts alone.

BELOW A mellowed Warren Harding in later years – he repeated the Nose in 1989 at the age of sixty-five.

Asked recently about Robbins' action, Harding replied, 'That whole thing was blown up. Everyone thought that I'd be all bummed out about the bolt chopping. Nothing could have been further from the truth! I thought it was funny!'

This was his last major climb, though he made a couple of lesser new routes in 1975 and, in 1989 at the age of sixty-five, he repeated his route on the Nose, climbing with Mike Corbett and Ken Yager. Today, in his mid-seventies he still lives in California with his partner Alice, enjoys his red wine and on occasion acts as ground crew for a ballooning friend.

Within a few years the Nose was to change from being the impossible to being a classic test piece for any competent big wall climber. It was also to act as a yardstick for extreme climbing development. There were three challenges – trying to climb it in an ever faster time, climbing it solo and climbing it entirely free without pulling on any pegs or bolts, an aspiration which seemed impossible until very recently. Speed and advances in climbing technique were undoubtedly helped by improvements in climbing gear, particularly the adoption of ever more sophisticated metal wedges and camming devices, originally introduced in Britain, and footwear with ever stickier rubber soles.

In 1967 Jim Bridwell, a brilliant and colourful climber, freed the notorious Stoveleg Crack. Henry Barber, who came from New Hampshire, climbed the route in three days, saving a lot of time by doing much of it free and using hand-inserted protection. In 1975 Bridwell returned with Billy Westbay and John Long to become the first to climb the Nose in a day. In 1990 Peter Croft and Dave Schultz climbed the Nose and Salathé Wall within an incredible eighteen hours, while in the previous year Steve Schneider had soloed the Nose in 21 hours 22 minutes.

The greatest challenge of all was to climb the Nose free. The 1980s, with rising rock-climbing standards around the world, saw many routes going free that had originally been climbed using extensive aid, and 1980 saw the first serious free attempt on the Nose by Ray Jardine. He was the inventor of the Friend, an adjustable camming device which revolutionised protection in wide parallel cracks. The main crux was the completely blank section above the top of El Cap Tower. Jardine chiselled a sparse line of holds to link the two lines of weakness, but the Great Roof defeated him. Repeated insertion and removal of chrome molybdenum pegs in the thin crack snaking up the side of the huge overhang had left widened pockets into which fingers that were not too large could just fit, but it was too much for Jardine.

It was another thirteen years before the Nose was climbed free in its entirety, although there were plenty of attempts. It was a trip not so much into the geographical, as into the athletic and personal unknown and in many ways epitomises the challenge and dilemma of the modern adventurer when all the obvious geographical firsts have been attained. It was Lynn Hill who found the solution and in doing so not only established herself as the best woman rock climber in the world, but broke through the sex barrier, emerging as one of the best, if not the best, all round rock climbers in history.

At only five foot one, she made up for lack of height with a superb power to weight ratio, gymnastic ability and, most important, focus of mind. Born in 1961 her apprenticeship was very much a traditional one that inevitably took her to Yosemite with an ascent of the Nose and other test pieces. One of her climbing partners was John Long who had made the first ascent of the Nose in a day.

She visited Europe for the first time in 1986 at the invitation of French climbers and was impressed by the standards that had been developed on the limestone walls of southern France. Sport climbing, as it has come to be known, using bolts for protection but climbing the rock without using any aid, had progressed to a high level. In a way it was a retreat from adventure for the element of risk had been minimised to allow the climber to develop his or her athletic skill to the ultimate. It also marked the birth of formalised competition climbing. Lynn Hill was invited to Bardonecchia in Italy for one of the early competitions. She was the only American there, it was all strange to her, but she ended up very nearly winning, being runner up to Catherine Destivelle from France.

These two women dominated the burgeoning competition climbing circuit for

RIGHT Lynn Hill making the only free lead ever accomplished of the Great Roof on the Nose of El Capitan.

the next few years. It gave them the means of earning a very good living around the activity they loved, enabled them to stretch their skills to the limit and reach the clearly defined summit of that sport. Both, however, grew tired of the limitations of competition climbing, always indoors on artificial walls with the pressure of intensive training. Each returned to traditional adventure climbing, Destivelle making a series of remarkable ascents in the high mountains, which included a solo new route on the South-West Pillar of the Dru and an ascent, with Jeff Lowe, of a new route on the Trango Tower in the Karakoram. Lynn Hill, meanwhile, returned to Yosemite and the challenge of the Nose of El Capitan.

While climbing at Cave Rock near Lake Tahoe she happened to meet up with Simon Nadin, a British climber who had also been on the competition circuit, becoming first ever world champion at the 1989 finals in Leeds. He, like Lynn, came from a traditional climbing background and like her had returned to it. When they discovered that they were both intrigued by the challenge of climbing the Nose free, Simon postponed his return flight to Britain and three days later they were in Yosemite.

They reached the foot of the Great Roof on their third day without incident, but were beginning to feel the fatigue of not only free climbing 2000 feet but also of hauling their provisions and carrying a heavy rack of nuts and camming devices. Lynn commented: 'After climbing from 5.30 a.m. until midnight the previous day, I had gained a great respect for the amount of time and energy the route demanded. The force of gravity seemed to multiply the higher we climbed.'

They were sharing the lead and Simon had first try on the Great Roof pitch, but quickly backed off. It was now Lynn's turn She laybacked up the sheer open corner, the tips of her fingers barely fitting into the thin crack, to where the roof thrust out above her. This was the crux, with a series of tenuous undercut holds in the back of the bulging overhang and even more tenuous smears on the granite wall for her feet. She was nearly at the end, when she miscalculated a move, her foot slipped and she was off, hurtling head first towards the ground 2000 feet below. Ironically, the very steepness and smoothness of the wall was her protection and she ended dangling, unhurt, at the end of the rope. Her running belay had held and Simon lowered her to the ledge.

She was now very tired, realised that she had used up almost all her energy, but was determined to have just one more try, summoning what reserves she had, this time pushing beyond her previous high point, reaching for the very last hold, when her foot slid off what was no more than a smear. Miraculously, her head touched the roof just at the right moment to enable her to maintain equilibrium and she propelled herself on. She extended her arm as far as she could and reached her fingers into a small under-cling lock. A few relatively straightforward moves and she was on the ledge to join some Croatian climbers who were tackling the route by conventional means.

Next morning she and Simon shared their last morsels of food, half an energy bar and a date each, and then set out on their fourth day with some hard climbing ahead. Simon led the notorious pitch round the Glowering Spot, so named by Warren

Harding because he had broken his hammer there in a particularly awkward bit of aid climbing and there is a lump of rock that looks like a grumpy face.

Lynn was hoping to conserve her diminishing stock of energy for the final extreme section just above Camp 6 where others had tried and failed. It was reputed to be very blank, needing a long reach, something that Lynn most certainly did not have. A brief investigation was enough to show there were no intermediate holds. The way Harding had originally gone was up a sheer groove to the right with a hairline crack in its back. Just getting into it was desperate. At least, at its base was a pocket where she might have got a finger lock, but it was filled by the stub of an old broken off piton. She tried everything, trying to brace herself in the smooth flared holdless corner, but she could make no upward progress and eventually admitted defeat, using aid to complete the climb and reach the top.

BELOW The thirtieth pitch, and arguably the hardest , with almost non-existent holds requiring immense concentration.

But she could not let it go and constantly thought of ways and means of solving this seemingly impossible problem. Sponsorship crept into the equation, but in an indirect kind of way. One of her sponsors was so impressed by her free ascent of the Great Roof, a major achievement in its own right, they wanted her to repeat it in front of a professional photographer in order to get some really good advertising shots. She could do this and try to complete the section that had defeated her as well.

She invited Brooke Sandahl, who had been exploring free climbing possibilities on the upper part of the Nose the previous year, to join her. They started by abseiling in from the top to investigate and, to a degree, prepare the critical pitch above Camp 6. Lynn removed the broken off piton, to free up a hold to start with and then spent three days trying out various permutations of moves to climb the pitch. 'As I became engrossed in exploring unusual techniques and body positions on this pitch, I was increasingly appreciative of its extraordinary nature. Climbing it free would involve an ingenuity and technical finesse that I rarely, if ever, encountered on any other route.' She eventually managed to complete the pitch with only one fall, but felt that to claim the entire climb as a free ascent, she had to start at the bottom and go all the way to the top.

This time they had more food, slipped into a better rhythm, enabling Lynn to lead the Great Roof in a single push. They pressed on past Camp

5, up the pitch round the Glowering Spot, which this time she led to reach Camp 6 and get a good night's sleep before the final challenge. She dreamt of the moves that night and the following morning it all came together as if in the dream. The final pitch casting to left and right for tenuous holds to either side of Harding's bolt ladder, led them to the top and the completion of a climb that established Lynn Hill's position as one of the most extraordinary rock climbers of all time.

But it still wasn't quite enough for her. Could she complete the climb in a day? It wasn't so much to make a speed record as to climb it in as elegant a way as possible, to travel light without the need of hauling food and water. 'It not only represented a kind of marathon linkage of this monumental route but provided a new focus and evolution in my life.'

Her climbing partner was to be Steve Sutton, who was happy to take on the role of belayer, jumaring all the way up the route. His role was similar to that of a caddy to a top professional golfer. He was even being paid. Lynn welcomed the encouragement he gave her. On her first attempt she made the mistake of co-producing a documentary film of her ascent and, not surprisingly, found she was losing that very focus she sought. By the time she reached the Great Roof after twenty-two pitches of climbing, she had run out of chalk, nearly run out of water, was tired and flustered, and after five attempts and five and half hours' struggle, they completed the climb using aid.

She was back again a fortnight later, this time without filming commitments and fully focused on the climb ahead. They started at 10 p.m. climbing in the ethereal light of a full moon and were at the Great Roof by 8.30 in the morning. She took a rest, dozed for what seemed no time at all but suddenly realised that the sun was creeping round the corner. It was vital to climb the Great Roof while it was still cool. This time she made the daunting pitch in a single push, laybacking the open corner to the roof with an easy rhythmic movement, placing the occasional nut and clipping into in-situ pitons. Then as she came to the overhang with its tiny undercut holds, she had a moment of self-doubt. To save on energy, she hadn't bothered to clip a piton just below, suddenly realised that if she did fall, she'd swing hard into the corner. She thrust away the moment of doubt, focused on the rock in front of her, taking each move steadily, to pull out onto the ledge at 10.25.

It was getting ever hotter. Pitch followed pitch. The next major challenge was the Glowering Spot, which she reached at midday. She was beginning to tire and her hands were sweaty. She'd reached the hard moves, placed a stopper (small metal wedge) in the crack, but before she had time to seat it, it slipped out. She didn't have another of the right size. Had she fallen she would have hit the ledge some thirty feet below. She kept cool, found another placement for one of her two remaining pieces of gear, and pulled up and over the crux to easier ground.

It was only one o'clock in the afternoon when she reached Camp 6 but the hardest pitch of all was ahead. The holds in the open groove were so tenuous she needed the rock to be as cool as possible for better friction for her climbing shoes and the complex pressure holds she would be using. She tried to doze through the afternoon, waiting for the groove to go into the shade. She waited four and a half hours but, impatient to get going, started before the rock had had time to cool and, as a result, had her first fall. The moves were so complex, convoluted, and tenuous, requiring precise body balance and muscular pressure. She got it wrong and once again went hurtling down. She rested on the belay, refocusing and trying to keep the doubt from sliding into her mind, but she was getting tired. This third attempt could be her last chance. She started up the complex opening moves again but had not even got as high as on her previous attempt before her foot slipped and she was off once more. It wasn't life threatening; she could afford to fall, but she had put in so much effort.

She went into the fourth attempt. She concentrated everything she had on those next moves. This was the concentration of the Olympic athlete going for gold but there was no audience, just the huge void below and a smooth sheer rounded arête in front which she was pinching with her fingers as she frictioned her feet precariously up its edge. This time she made it, reached a positive hold and pulled up to the belay ledge.

This was the concentration of the Olympic athlete going for gold but there was no audience, just the huge void below

She still had four pitches to climb. The last two were difficult and strenuous, although nothing like as hard as the one she had just completed. The top pitch, the section on which Harding had hammered a bolt ladder, gave a last challenge with the final overhang. She knew her reserves of strength were very nearly finished. She made one last dynamic irreversible lunge for the final hold on the final roof, caught it, heaved and swung up onto the easy slabs that led to the top of the Nose. She had achieved her objective, thirty-three rope-lengths, more than three thousand feet of supremely hard climbing in just twenty-three hours.

There have been similar free ascents on other routes on El Capitan. The Wyoming climbers Paul Piana and Todd Skinner climbed the Salathé Wall free in 1988. It was repeated by the Huber brothers from Berchtesgaden in Bavaria, who then went on in 1997 to make a remarkable new route completely free up the line of the North America Wall to the right of the Nose. This was repeated some days later by two young British climbers, Leo Houlding and Patrick Hammond on their first visit to Yosemite and their first big wall. But no one has repeated Lynn Hill's achievement. The closest has been a local climber, Scott Burke who in 261 days of actual climbing over a three-year period , managed to lead all but the Great Overhang, which he top-roped.

Lynn Hill's free ascent was nearly thirty-six years after that of Warren Harding's first ascent. Both were extraordinary achievements in their different ways from such very different people. Warren, an anarchic individualist and free-wheeling maverick, not remotely bothered by the Puritan mores of his peers, defied ethical stances and yet was very much the climbers' climber, the stuff of legends. Perhaps it needed all of that to get the seemingly impossible climbed in the first place. In contrast, Lynn Hill, with her finely tuned self-discipline perfected the climb, in effect making a new and fresh route, arguably the longest and most difficult free rock climb in the world.

TWELVE 12

Changabang

Triumph and Tragedy on Changabang's North Face

Although all the 8000-metre peaks and most 7000-metre peaks have long since been climbed, and mountains like Everest or K2 now have as many different routes up them as Mont Blanc or the Matterhorn, there are still literally hundreds of faces and ridges in the greater ranges that remain unexplored. It is a tiny group of mountaineers from around the world that are attracted to these technically challenging lines on unclimbed routes. By and large, their achievements are ignored by the media who are still obsessed with Everest and the 8000-metre peaks, even though most ascents on these mountains are by what have now become trade routes.

Today the world is more accessible than ever before with roads penetrating ever deeper into wild regions and travel by helicopter available to many places. Mountains remain one of the areas where the individual can truly explore and where helicopters cannot reach (their ceiling is around 6000 metres). The story of the first ascent of the North Face of Changabang is an outstanding example of this style of climbing. The history of the mountain reflects the way climbing has evolved on the smaller peaks of the Himalaya. It also features some of the leading British climbers of the last sixty years. The first attempt to climb it was by a joint Indian-British expedition which I co-led in 1974.

Changabang forms part of the northern ramparts of the legendary Sanctuary of Nanda Devi which, at 7816 metres, is the highest peak entirely within India and the highest to be climbed before the Second World War – by Bill Tilman and Noel Odell. Just finding a way to the foot of Nanda Devi proved a major challenge, and Eric Shipton, that great exploratory mountaineer who found the way into the Sanctuary with Bill Tilman in 1934, described how he sat for an hour fascinated by the gigantic white cliffs of Changabang. He also was the first person to set foot on the mountain when he climbed a gully out of the Sanctuary leading onto the col to the immediate south of Changabang, only to find there was a precipitous drop down to the Rhamani Glacier on the other side.

The following year Frank Smythe, who made the first ascent of Kamet, gazed up at Changabang from the Dunagiri Col and wondered at, 'The terrible precipices of Changabang, a peak that falls from crest to glacier in a wall that might have been sliced in a single cut of a knife.'

RIGHT The climbers on the North Face – Brendan and Andy's fourth day, leaving their third bivouac to climb up the side of the second icefield with Mick and Steve on their second day on the steep icy slabs.

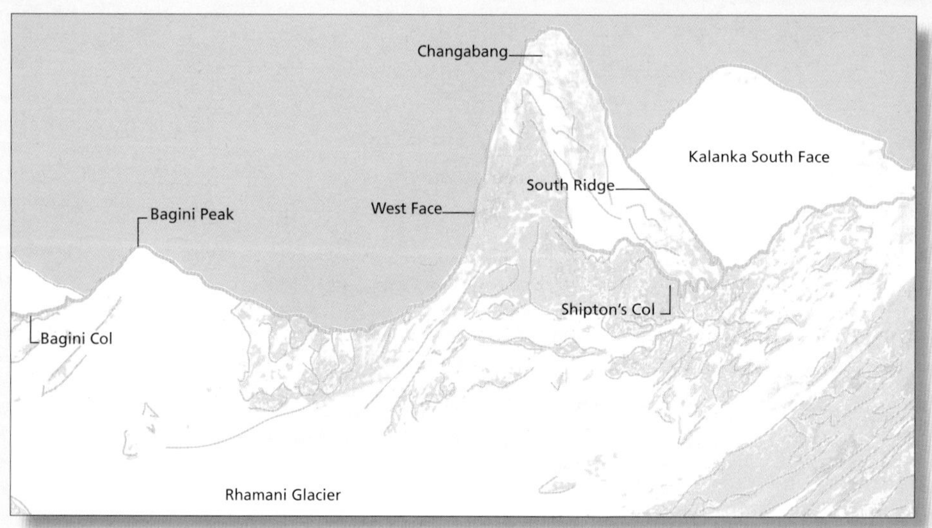

ABOVE Changabang and the Rhamani Glacier from the side of one of the peaks on its south-side flank.

LEFT Diagram of Changabang, Kalanka and Rhamani Glacier

W.H. Murray, leader of the Scottish Himalayan Expedition of 1950 which made an impressive series of first ascents in the Garhwal and Kumoan ranges, was the most lyrical of all:

'By day like a vast eye-tooth fang, both in shape and colour – for its rock was a milk- white granite – Changabang in the moonlight shone tenderly as though veiled in bridal lace; at ten miles distant seemingly as fragile as an icicle; – a product of earth and sky rare and fantastic, and of liveliness unparalleled so that unaware one's pulse leapt and the heart gave thanks – that this mountain should be as it is.'

It was these descriptions that inspired me to apply for permission to attempt the mountain in 1974. There were ten of us, five from Britain and five from India.

Reaching our mountain proved almost as much of a challenge as the area had been for Shipton and Tilman, as we turned off up the Rhamani Glacier to approach Changabang from the west, its steepest and most spectacular side. It proved a trifle too spectacular for a team that had a wide range of experience and ability. We therefore decided to find an easier way to the top by crossing Shipton's Col from the opposite side to Shipton, and then climbing the huge, but comparatively easy snow face and glacier of Kalanka to reach the col between it and the South-East Ridge of Changabang. It was a long and committing route but one with little technical difficulty that six of us, Martin Boysen, Dougal Haston, Balwant Sandhu, Doug Scott, Tachei and I completed successfully.

The following year a remarkable expedition took place, comprising two young British climbers, Joe Tasker and Dick Renshaw, who had an impressive alpine record that included a winter ascent of the North Wall of the Eiger. They decided to go to the Himalaya, bought a second-hand clapped-out Ford van, packed their expedition gear into it and set out for Dunagiri, a 7066-metre peak to the immediate west of Changabang. Their liaison officer, unused to such small and frugal expeditions, turned back before they even reached Base Camp. They treated the mountain as they would have done an Alpine climb, set out up its long unclimbed South-East Ridge with six days' food, took seven days to reach the top and a further four, very hungry and thirsty days, to get down.

They had plenty of opportunity to examine the massive West Face of Changabang, and Renshaw, on their precarious descent, to Tasker's horror, even suggested they had a go at it after they had had a short rest. But there was no question of that. Tasker was exhausted and Renshaw had frostbitten fingers and a sprained ankle. On returning to Britain, however, Joe could not stop thinking of that huge West Face. Dick could not join him the following year since he was still having treatment for his fingers. Joe therefore invited Peter Boardman, who had just got back from my own expedition to the South-West Face of Everest. At twenty-three he was the youngest member of the group but proved to be a very strong, focused climber and reached the summit with our team's sirdar, Sherpa Pertemba, on the second ascent. After that huge expedition, the thought of a two-man trip against such an obstacle was irresistible and he accepted Tasker's invitation.

Their trip was only a little less frugal than the previous year's. They set out in mid-August to climb in the post-monsoon period, took more climbing gear and food and had a slightly more comfortable Base Camp, although their liaison officer once again decided to stay in the valley. There were just the two of them confronting what was arguably the most formidable rock wall ever to be attempted at that altitude. It soars from the col at the head of the Rhamani Glacier for nearly 1500 metres of pale grey granite, broken only by scanty ice smears up steep grooves and gangways. They started to fix-rope the route, encountering ferociously hard climbing on rock and ice, returning each night to a camp on the col, but the higher they got, the longer and more laborious became the chore of reaching the high point. Temperatures were bitterly cold, –25°C at night and the wind rarely ceased blowing.

They tried to break loose from the fixed ropes but, after three extremely uncomfortable bivouacs in hammocks, they were forced to retreat to Base Camp with only half the face climbed. Time was running out. Many would have been tempted at this stage to give up, but they reassessed their plans, even climbed to Shipton's Col to salvage some of the rope we had left in place two years earlier, and returned to the fray, establishing a second camp at around 6100 metres. They pulled most of the fixed rope up behind them and, from this marginally more secure base, fixed some further rope and made their push for the summit, reaching it on October 15th 1976.

ABOVE The North Face of Changabang.

The South Face, a sweep of rock with ice slicks soaring up into a steep head wall, was climbed in 1978 by a powerful Polish-British team comprising Voytek Kurtyka, Krzysztof Zurek, Alex MacIntyre and John Porter. Technically the climb was as hard, if not harder, than the West Face but it had the great benefit of being in the sun. They climbed it in elegant, if painful, Alpine-style in a single push from bottom to top over eight days, running out of food on the fifth. Alex MacIntyre went on to make a very impressive Alpine-style new route on the East Face of Dhaulagiri, this time with Kurtyka, Ludwick Wilczyczynski and René Ghilini from France. In the spring of 1982 he made yet another bold first ascent with Doug Scott and Roger Baxter-Jones on the South-West Face of Shisha Pangma, and then tragically was killed by a single falling stone near the foot of the South Face of Annapurna that same autumn.

Changabang still held challenges. The North Face is the biggest and possibly the most formidable of all its facets but until very recently it was unattainable, being too close to the Chinese frontier and within the Inner Line and therefore forbidden to foreigners.

It took the political skills of Roger Payne to get permission for 1996. He has that quality, rare among talented climbers, of not only being a first-class administrator but actually enjoying the process. His love of climbing led him to train as a mountain guide but he then changed course to become National Officer of the British

Mountaineering Council, a role that both Peter Boardman and Alex MacIntyre had held before him. He was so good at his job that he became General Secretary – senior civil servant of British Mountaineering.

Unlike some climbing bureaucrats he has always remained very much a climber, going on lightweight exploratory climbing trips each year with his wife and climbing partner, Julie-Ann Clyma. They had undertaken two expeditions in the Garhwal area, climbing the eastern summit of Nanda Devi in 1994 and the following year making an attempt on Trisuli West, as well as a couple of first ascents of peaks at the head of the West Bagini Glacier. A glimpse of the formidable North Face of Changabang was enough to determine them to attempt it. Getting permission and then weaving his way through the barriers built by Indian bureaucracy was a major challenge, but Roger Payne persevered and achieved what had seemed the impossible.

In contrast the approach to the mountain was easy – just two days from Delhi to the roadhead and an easy two-day walk up the Bagini Glacier to establish Base Camp at 4000 metres. The face was still out of sight some eight kilometres away but it dominated the head of the glacier, a huge sweep of featureless granite to which clung improbable ice formations. A series of ice-filled gangways and grooves crept up the left-hand side of the wall, converging on an icefield about half way up the face. From there just one line of weakness reached up towards the crest of the North-East Ridge of Changabang, the route by which we finished our climb in 1974.

Roger had invited two other climbers. Brendan Murphy, although short and wiry, made up for any lack of size with a quiet yet intense determination. He was a scientist who successfully managed to juggle climbing with an academic career. Andy Perkins was more ebullient and worked for Troll, manufacturers of climbing harnesses. Murphy and Perkins had made a very impressive attempt on a formidable unclimbed peak called Cerro Kishtwar (6200 metres) in the Indian Himalaya, spending seventeen days on it using capsule tactics. The pair had climbed the steepest section but had run out of food, fuel and energy and were forced to retreat only 150 metres from the summit. Roger thought that a similar approach would be necessary on the North Face of Changabang, the two pairs taking turns with one out in front pushing out the route, while the other came up behind, ferrying all the gear.

They started with a couple of forays to acclimatise and get some good views of the face, reaching both the Bagini Col and the col immediately below the West Face of Changabang where Peter Boardman and Joe Tasker had had their camp. The route they chose followed a groove line leading to the right side of the conspicuous icefield. It took them three days of hard ice climbing with two uncomfortable sitting bivouacs to the side of the gully. Once the sun hit the face, snow and ice began melting and the base of the gully became a torrent, soaking the climbers. Their third bivouac was on the edge of the icefield but it took several hours of exhausting work to hack out two narrow ledges for their tents. At least now they could lie down.

They were all tired after three hard days' climbing and two appalling bivouacs. As if that wasn't enough, Andy Perkins went down that night with violent gastro-enteritis, a nightmare half way up a Himalayan face. They had already decided to take a rest the following day. They needed it and hoped that this would give Andy time to

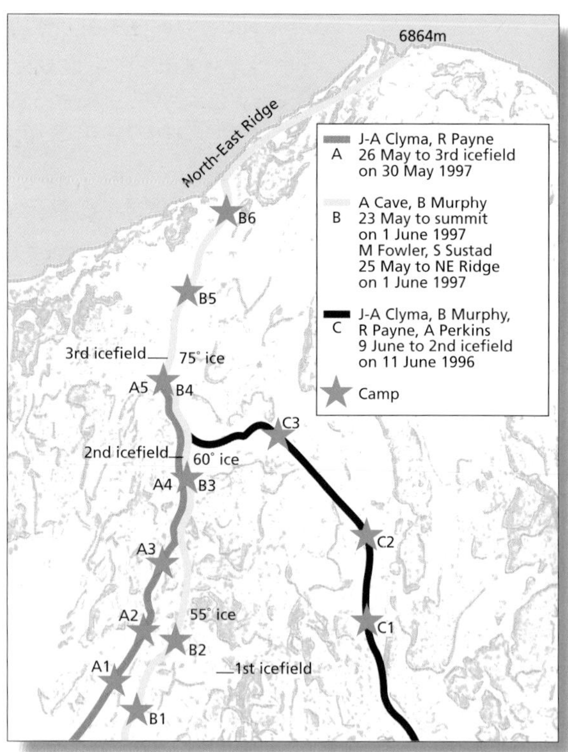

ABOVE North Face route.

recover. But next day Andy was too weak to move and the weather had deteriorated, so they took another rest day.

They were running out of time and food, since they reckoned it was going to take at least three days to reach the crest of the ridge. Andy was still desperately weak, but very determined, so they decided to keep going. They now had to cross the steep icefield to the beginning of the line of weakness at the other side. Their capsule approach, in effect having a line of fixed rope, was now an encumbrance rather than a help. Traversing on fixed rope with heavy loads across ice is a slow exhausting business.

Roger took the lead, running out three pitches across the bottom of the icefield. Once they had removed the ropes behind them a retreat was going to be difficult since they would either have to traverse back the way they had come or launch themselves down unknown ground. In addition, the icefield was swept by spindrift avalanches whenever it snowed. Andy was getting progressively weaker and the weather was showing signs of breaking. They discussed what to do and there seemed no alternative but for all of them to retreat. That night they got back to the site of their camp at the start of the icefield. It snowed all night and was still snowing in the morning. They abseiled to safety in a torrent of spindrift avalanches. They had been defeated by Andy's illness and the weather but even as they walked out of Base Camp Roger was already planning another attempt. The reputation of the face was becoming known and other talented climbers were looking at it hungrily.

One of these was Mick Fowler, the most successful innovative mountaineer of the last twenty years. He has never climbed an 8000-metre peak, unwilling to take the length of time off work, but most years he goes to the farther ranges of the earth to snatch steep and challenging climbs on peaks of around 6000 to 7000 metres.

Mick was born and brought up in north-east London by his father George, who did a bit of climbing and was a keen hill walker, taking young Mick with him on his adventures in a three-wheeled Reliant Robin. Mick, like me, started his career on Kentish sandstone, was a natural climber and was attracted by tottering rock walls which others had ignored or been afraid to tackle. He quickly established a reputation for bold new routes, particularly on the sea cliffs of Devon and Cornwall. He also revelled in transporting ice climbing techniques to the crumbling chalk cliffs of the south-east coastline.

While many climbers of his ability found ways of making a living around their climbing he pursued a more conventional course, ending up as a tax inspector, ascending the upper reaches of the Inland Revenue, despite the lack of a university degree and taking every possible day's leave, and a few extra, to go climbing. In the 'eighties he was the driving force in a group of London climbers who took off most winter weekends for the far north of Scotland. They drove through the Friday night, snatched an unclimbed ice line in the far north-west of Scotland from under the eyes of the local Scottish experts, and then drove back on the Sunday night to be at work in body, if not in mind, first thing on Monday morning.

A British apprenticeship was accompanied by hard climbs in the Alps and then further afield – Taulliraju South Pillar in Peru and the superb Golden Pillar of Spantik in Hunza Pakistan. Taking a different line from Brendan Murphy and Andy Perkins, he reached the top of Cerro Kishtwar with Stephen Sustad in 1993 and made an impressive ascent of the North-East Buttress of Taweche in 1995 – all first ascents – an extraordinarily high success rate. Marriage and fatherhood had not diminished his appetite for hard climbing.

He was already thinking of trying the North Face of Changabang during the first attempt – just in case they didn't get up – and had invited Steve Sustad to join him. Steve came from Seattle but had settled in Britain in the mid-'eighties, making a living as a joiner and spending as much time as possible climbing. Easy to get on with, yet totally focused on his climbing, he had joined Doug Scott and the French climber Jean Afanassieff in an attempt to traverse Makalu, fifth highest mountain in the world, very nearly getting to the top before making a desperate retreat. He was making a solo attempt on the huge South Face of Aconcagua, when the snow hole in which he was sheltering was avalanched and swept away most of his gear, yet somehow he managed to make a hazardous descent. He was just hooked on climbing, but he had no desire to write or lecture about it. For him it was a very personal experience.

As well as these potential candidates Roger Payne had his original team to think about for his second attempt on the North Face. Andy Perkins, who was training to be a guide, felt he couldn't get away, but Brendan Murphy was keen and had been talking to Andy Cave, another academic who had started his working life as a coal miner and was now completing his dissertation for a PhD on 'The Linguistic Heritage of the Yorkshire Coal fields'. It became a team of six for their attempt in the early summer of 1997.

Mick Fowler was mildly bemused by the sheer efficiency of the organisation:

'I had not been on a Payne-Clyma expedition before. Previous jaunts in the big mountains always had been on the basis of a sort of communal responsibility, vaguely steered by one person. Here, though, Roger and Julie-Ann were clearly in complete control. Prior to leaving for India, I had wondered about this. Roger and I met on the crag, only to discover that we hadn't enough equipment to climb...but now, organised computer lists of things to do in Delhi appeared with alarming efficiency

'In fact, in retrospect, things had been different from usual the moment we arrived at the airport. Instead of the chaos and confusion followed by the cheapest possible transport to Delhi, we were met by a luxury mini-bus complete with curtains, which whisked us away to comfortable pre-booked accommodation. A whole new experience for me.'

And so it went on. Roger steered them adroitly through bureaucratic pitfalls, ensured that their porters were adequately equipped and guided his flock to Base Camp with the minimum of fuss or inconvenience. They had already agreed that they would operate as three independent self-contained pairs. The problem, however, was that although there was a choice of routes to the icefield where they had turned back the previous year, beyond it there seemed only one reasonable line. In addition, the face had a very different look. In 1996 there was plenty of snow ice, easily identified by its creamy white colour, but this year the icefields were a dirty grey-green, signs that the climbing was going to be very much harder.

first they had to acclimatise. They set out to establish an Advance Base and make a recce over the Bagini Pass, intending to leave a dump of food on the Rhamani Glacier which they could pick up on their return if they made their descent down the other side of the mountain. But it was not to be; the snow was soft and deep, it was ferociously hot on the glacier and they camped well short of the Bagini Pass. For someone who has specialised in cramming Himalayan climbs into limited leave periods, Mick has the disadvantage of being slow to acclimatise. Feeling nauseous and lethargic, he and Steve Sustad took it very gently, spending a couple of nights on the glacier, before making a half-hearted attempt on Dunagiri Parbat, having two more nights at around 5500 metres. They then decided they had had enough of acclimatisation and hoped that by returning to Base Camp, they would be at the head of the queue and get onto Changabang first. They had been beaten to it, however, by Brendan Murphy and Andy Cave, who had also been on Dunagiri Parbat, had acclimatised faster and were bent on being out in front on the main objective. They had both selected the same line. Mick wryly commented, 'I made a mental note to think about ensuring that I am surrounded by slow and unhealthy companions in the future.' Roger and Julie-Ann were still acclimatising and had chosen a line to the left of the one selected by the others.

I made a mental note to think about ensuring that I am surrounded by slow and unhealthy companions in the future

Andy and Brendan were ready to set out next morning. Quite apart from the satisfaction of route-finding, there is a practical advantage in being first – there is nobody above you to dislodge rocks or lumps of ice. Because of this hazard, Mick and Steve opted to delay their departure for two days. Andy and Brendan set out for the foot of the climb at two in the morning on May 21st, each weighed down by 20 kilograms of climbing hardware, bivouac equipment and food and fuel for about eight days. They had two 60-metre ropes and a lightweight tent which they hoped to pitch on ledges hacked out of the snow arêtes they could see clinging to the face. They had chosen a route well to the left of the one used the previous year to take them, by a series of ice-filled grooves, to the left-hand end of the icefield. This would cut out the awkward traverse, giving them a much more direct line. They had reckoned it would take three hours to the foot of the real climbing. As so often happens they had underestimated the difficulties. It took them thirteen hours to reach what they had thought was the start. What had looked like an easy plod turned out to be soft snow lying on very hard ice. By the time they reached the start of the 'real' climbing they had broken two of their six ice screws, were tired from humping heavy loads and it had started to snow.

Brendan set off up an ill-defined, ice-smeared shield of rock, trying to avoid two cataracts of spindrift thundering down chutes on either side. Progress was now even slower and more precarious. By the time he reached the top of the pitch it was nearly dark but there was no sign of a bivouac ledge. Andy had to lead through the left-hand chute exposed to the full torrent of spindrift which penetrated his clothing, filled his gloves and got behind his goggles, nearly blinding him. The ice was steep and it was difficult to place any protection with their dwindling stock of ice screws. Axe and crampon placements were tenuous and he was encumbered by the weight and bulk of his sack. The climb had barely begun and they were already pushed to the limit.

He reached easier ground, searched around in the twilight, fingers numb with cold, to find a narrow ledge for a bivouac. It was dark by the time Brendan reached him and they had to go through the laborious process of clearing the ledge, unpacking sacks and preparing for the night. There was no room to erect the tent, so they just got into their sleeping bags, tied into their anchor point in case they fell out of bed.

Shivering and parched with thirst, they were longing for a warm drink. Their stove was a Heath Robinson affair. Andy had been unable to find his usual Markil Stormy hanging bivouac stove before leaving England, so they had made one with bits of wire that they could suspend from a loop in the top of the tent. They called it Metal Mickey and it worked amazingly well – better than the production model which tends to starve the burner flame of the meagre amounts of oxygen present in the confines of a tent sealed from spindrift and the elements.

The following morning dawned fine but bitterly cold. They brewed up, delayed getting out of warm sleeping bags as long as they could, and then faced the slow painful

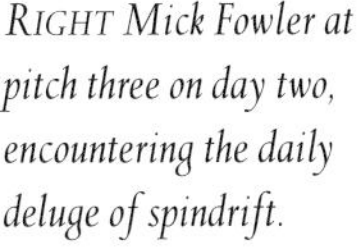

RIGHT Mick Fowler at pitch three on day two, encountering the daily deluge of spindrift.

process of forcing on cold plastic boots, pushing sleeping bags rimed with frost into stuff sacks, all the time terrified of dropping something. It was well after dawn when they were ready to set out on the first pitch. The climbing remained steep and demanding. Progress was slow and once again it started snowing shortly after midday, so their line of ascent became a cataract of rushing spindrift. On the third day, after a testing start, the difficulty relented slightly and they made better headway, reaching the left-hand end of the first icefield. This was like 'a giant skating rink, tilted at 55°, with an impenetrable skin of steel that shattered and splintered until the sun softened it up'.

They were now down to three working ice screws. The ice was so tough that even for belays they could only sink a screw about half way in, tying it off with a length of tape close to the surface, and backing this up by tying into the ice tools, whose picks penetrated little more than a centimetre. They couldn't afford a fall.

This day took them to the foot of the big icefield which Brendan and the others had reached the previous year. It was an important landmark. They made good progress up one side to its top where they had the choice of very steep ice on the right or mixed rock and ice to the left. They chose the former despite their shortage of ice screws. Brendan led the first pitch and then it was Andy's turn. The afternoon storm had started and quickly rose to a more intense pitch than on either of the previous days. Spindrift was pouring down the face, streaming across and even upwards as it blasted around them. The rumble of thunder and crash of wind over the summit merged in a roar of sound.

Brendan was hanging from a tied-off ice screw, which left Andy with only two – one for a runner and one that he would have to keep for a belay. The snow pelted him with ever increasing force as he teetered up, crampon points and the picks of his ice tools barely penetrating the steely surface. Twenty metres above the belay he tried to place a screw. It is not easy on steep ground at the best of times, but with avalanches of snow pouring over him, the weight of his sack pulling him backwards and the blunted bent teeth of the screw failing to bite in the ice, it was desperate. He was tiring rapidly, clipped into one of his ice tools and hung on it so that he could use both hands. It held for a few seconds and then ripped out. He toppled backwards, his crampon points flicked out and he fell onto his remaining tool, which miraculously held. Panting with exhaustion and fear, blinded by clouds of snow blown upwards into his face, hampered by the weight of the sack, he managed to kick in the front point of his crampons and stand up in balance once more. At last he managed to engage the teeth of the screw and keep turning until it was embedded half way in. He tied in thankfully and brought Brendan up through the deluge of snow to join him. Brendan, usually the most stoic of climbers, was retching with the pain of frozen fingers and toes. The spindrift had penetrated everywhere, into gloves, down their necks, behind their goggles.

Brendan hardly paused at the stance, but just battled on up a brittle, ice-filled corner. At least movement created some warmth, but Andy, now belaying, was quickly frozen to the bone, shivering uncontrollably as he tried to keep himself warm by flapping his arms. Progress was desperately slow and it was getting dark. Andy climbed up to Brendan on a tight rope, screaming that he had to have something to

RIGHT Brendan climbing the headwall on day six, a crucial part of the climb linking the ice tongue to the upper grooves.

eat. As he arrived, Brendan thrust him a food bar, which Andy bit into with the wrapper still on.

There was no sign of a bivvy ledge, so it was Andy's turn to press on. The angle eased slightly and he was able to move faster, traversing to a snow arête which would at last provide a good bivvy site. He had already used all the functioning ice screws and spent twenty minutes pounding one of the broken ones into the ice, tied off on it and his ice tools and shouted down into the darkness for Brendan to come up, warning him, 'The belays are shit.'

The rope pulled in all too slowly and jerkily, and then he felt a sudden violent heave. He was pulled straight off his stance. For an agonising moment he wondered whether the belays would hold. They did. He could just discern a blob of light through the driving snow and darkness as Brendan pendulumed 20 metres across the slope to a point where he was suspended directly below Andy's belay. Fortunately he was able to climb straight up to rejoin his climbing partner. The only comment he made was, 'That was lucky, I could have lost my torch.'

It took them another two weary hours to hack out a platform, pitch the tent and get a brew on. They were both frost-nipped, chilled to the bone and ravenously hungry and thirsty. Neither of them in their long and challenging climbing careers had encountered a day like this. They were undoubtedly lucky to be alive.

Next morning they decided to take a day off – they didn't have much choice; they were so debilitated. They didn't talk much. Brendan was a self-contained person, good to climb with, considerate and yet someone who was difficult to get to know.

BELOW Andy Cave after the seventh bivouac – the most uncomfortable yet. There was no room to put up a tent and barely room to sit on the ledge.

Meanwhile, the others also set out. Mick and Steve had been surprised at the slowness of Andy and Brendan as they watched them from Advance Base, but once they started climbing on May 25th they discovered why. They made no better headway each day and suffered the same restricted bivvy ledges, but they were better placed on the afternoon of the storm that had hammered Andy and Brendan, being at the second bivouac in plenty of time to get into the shelter of their tent. Roger and Julie-Ann fared less well. They had set out on their independent line to the left on the day of the storm and, caught on steep ground, were forced into a standing bivouac, with their tent draped over them. It was a long bitterly cold and very uncomfortable night. It says something for their determination that they all kept going.

On May 28th, after a day lying in their tent drinking hot brews and eating, Brendan and Andy felt better. Brendan led three hard pitches but again there was no sign of a good bivvy ledge, so they abseiled back down to the previous night's campsite, leaving their ropes in position. This led to a complication since Mick and Steve, who had been using the same bivvy sites, but had not taken a day off, now caught them up. Mick and Steve had mixed feelings. While they got on well with Andy and Brendan, they also believed in travelling as fast as possible with the freedom to stop where and when they liked. On terrain like this good bivouac sites were at a premium and whoever was in the second party would have second choice.

They discussed what to do and decided, at least on a temporary basis, to join forces. Andy and Brendan would stay out in front, take Steve and Mick's ropes and push the route, then the second pair could pick up the two fixed lines to use for their ascent. Since each party still had their own protection gear and slings, they could easily revert to climbing independently. Another factor was that Brendan and Andy were on their sixth day and had only brought eight days' food, while the other pair were not only just on their fourth day, but found they had a surprise surplus of mashed potato. This particular brand went further than any other they had used before, giving about six times the finished bulk, which meant they would have more than enough to feed all four members of the team.

That morning, day seven for Andy and Brendan, it took a long time to jumar up the ropes and they only started climbing at around midday. There had been ominous streaks of high cloud at dawn and the weather looked as if it was going to close in even earlier than usual. Mick and Steve delayed their departure, even enjoying the lie in. The climbing up above looked hard and was obviously going to take a long time. There didn't seem much chance of getting one good bivvy ledge, let alone two, so they decided to stay where they were for the day and night and to follow on independently the next day.

It was inevitable that Andy and Brendan were going to dislodge blocks of ice as they hacked their way up, but Mick and Steve hoped that they were out of the line of fire, ensconced on the crest of a little snow arête. They were soon disillusioned. A roaring whirr signalled something much more solid than an ice block and a rock tore through the wall of the tent to miss Steve's head by five centimetres. They screamed up at the others and spent the rest of the day wearing their crash helmets, cowering as close to the back wall as they could. Two more blocks of ice tore holes in the tent and the spindrift poured in covering their sleeping bags, mats and everything. They even discussed retreat, worried by the damage to the tent and the prospect of their being in the firing line for the rest of the climb but neither Steve nor Mick retreats easily. They decided to keep going.

It had been Brendan who had dislodged the rock and he felt terrible, but there was nothing he could do about it. The ice was hard and brittle, breaking off into blocks as they swung in their tools. Andy led the next pitch, probably the hardest and most elegant on the entire climb, up a thin and intermittent smear of ice plastered on smooth almost holdless granite. Pitch followed pitch, all of them formidable, up the iced groove line, seemingly the only way up this vast wall of granite with its huge corners roofed by massive overhangs and tenuous cracks that petered out. It was like El Capitan at altitude, but much bigger, with ice and snow. There were no forest glades, winding roads and Camp 4 in the valley below – just the crevasse-seamed glacier and empty snow peaks.

But Andy and Brendan were beginning to revel in their isolation and the unrelenting quality of the climbing. They were getting ever closer to the top of this huge wall. Two more bivouacs, the first on the narrowest ledge yet, more difficult and committing climbing, and at last they reached a steep snow-plastered slab which led to a cornice. They cut through and were standing on the crest of the ridge that we had climbed back in 1974, which finally led to the summit of Changabang.

It was nearly dark and they hacked out a platform from a mushroom of snow. Next morning dawned cloudy and it was snowing by eight. They decided to sit the weather out. Andy had quite forgotten that it was his birthday. Brendan had not and produced six Snicker bars which he had stored away. They shared them and settled down to a day of hungry rest, feeling a deep sense of contentment at having fought through the eight days they had spent on that huge face in such appalling conditions. Andy wrote: 'We had grown close on the climb and had become like an eccentric couple. We knew what soup or type of tea the other preferred, knew each other's aspirations and fears. Philosophising high on that twisting corniced ridge seemed a luxury after the grinding face.'

ABOVE Mick and Steve at their last bivouac where they were able to find a small spur on which to pitch their tent and have a comfortable night.

They finished their food at their evening meal, but were looking forward to Mick and Steve's arrival and to sharing their mashed potato surplus. Next morning they started up the ridge in a clear dawn. It was a delight to be on comparatively easy ground, though it was narrow and corniced. They were travelling light but felt weak from lack of food as the cloud rolled in and it took them an hour to wade through deep snow between the two horns of Changabang's summit to reach the top. Then, as if the gods wanted to give them a reward, the cloud cleared away and they gazed at the magnificent twin peaks of Nanda Devi rising out of the mist-filled Sanctuary. But it was time to descend and they had a long way to go. They heard a shout and could just discern the figure of Steve Sustad as he came up onto the ridge.

Mick and Steve had followed a slightly different route, joining the summit ridge higher than the others. They had used the same bivvy ledges and had had a glimpse of Roger and Julie-Ann, far below but still climbing upwards. They could see Andy and Brendan's tracks dropping back to the tent and decided to follow these down so that they could camp together that night, hoping to go for the summit themselves the following morning.

Steve was already starting down and Mick was just picking up the loose coils of rope, when Steve slipped. The wet afternoon snow had balled up between the points of his crampons, his boots skidded from under him, and he was off, sliding down on the south side of the ridge, his cumbersome rucksack stopping him from rolling into position to use the pick of his axe as a brake. He was gathering speed and the slope was steepening. Mick's first reaction was to jump down the other side of the ridge, but the crest was too far above him. His axe, sunk in soft snow, was not much good but he quickly took the rope round his waist and braced himself: 'To begin with, I felt I was in with a chance. I could feel my crampon points biting home and see Steve swinging around below me. But the farther he swung, the more the slope steepened and the more the strain grew. Ultimately, I crumpled to one side and came on to the axe. I felt just a token resistance as I was dragged down. My feelings were of total despair. All those promises to my wife and children.'

He was now free-falling in mid-air. There was a huge thump. He felt a sharp pain across his face and, almost to his surprise, he realised he had stopped. He explored himself cautiously. His nose was bleeding but he did not seem to have broken anything. He called Steve. There was a painful pause and then Steve croaked, 'My ribs hurt, I don't feel too good.'

They quickly ascertained that he had broken several ribs. It was now five in the afternoon and they had fallen about 60 metres below the crest of the ridge. They were very lucky that it had not been further. A broad snow ledge had saved them. It was the best campsite in days but they had a disturbed night, Steve gurgling and groaning, both wondering how they were going to get back to Base Camp. The following morning they climbed up to join the others, who had spent their third night on the crest of the ridge.

BELOW Steve, Brendan and Mick (left to right) sheltering under an ice-cliff, with the ever-present danger of avalanche, during the descent of the south side of Changabang a few hours before Brendan was killed.

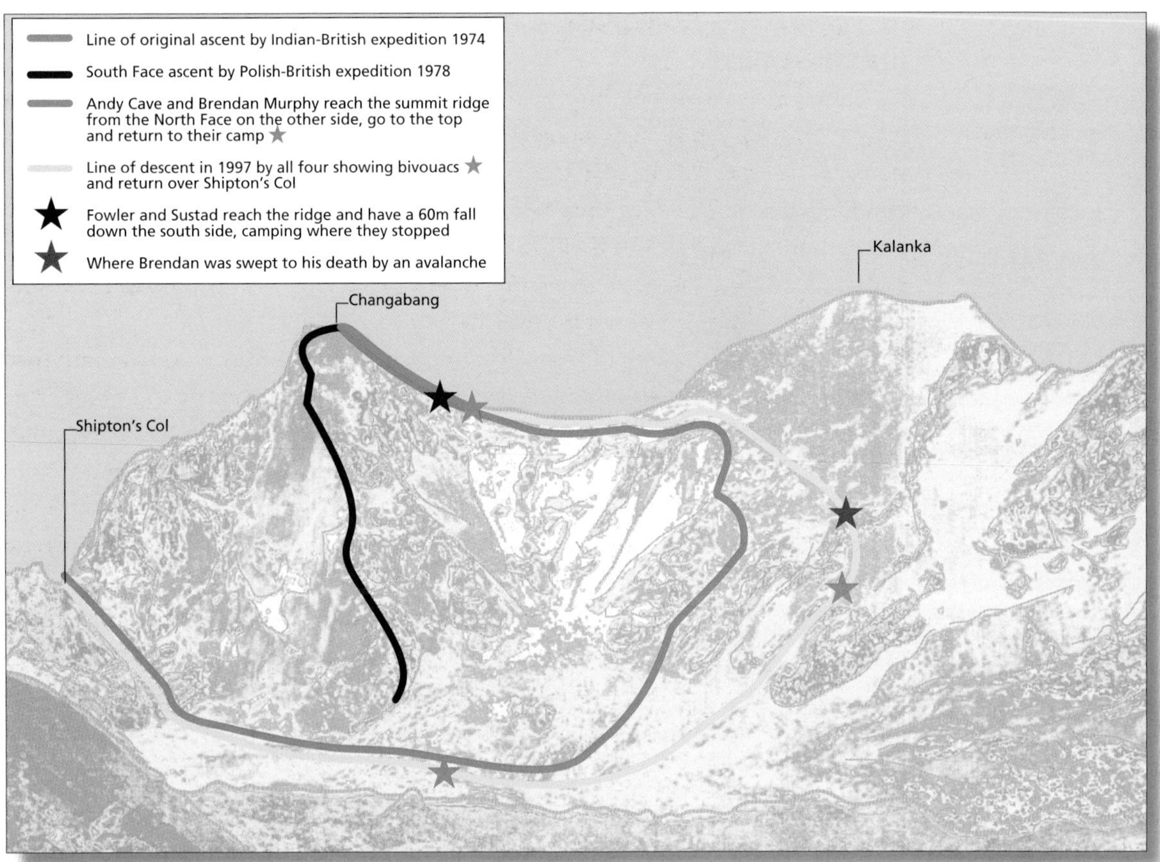

ABOVE The South Face of Changabang, showing the original route (1974), South Face route (1978) and the line of descent of the 1997 North Face expedition.

Thanks to Mick's potato surplus they at least had some food, but they were in a precarious situation. They had two choices: either to abseil down the face they had just climbed, the option that Steve favoured, or to take the easier but much longer descent down the south side. This would entail crossing Shipton's Col, abseiling down onto the Rhamani Glacier, climbing up that and over the Bagini Col to get back onto the Bagini Glacier and their Base Camp. The others favoured this longer route and they set off taking the rest of the day just to reach the col between Kalanka and Changabang. Steve was in considerable pain from his ribs and one of Andy's fingers was frostnipped. Next morning they started down the Kalanka Face in near white-out conditions, following a broad gangway diagonally across it. It was blowing hard and bitterly cold. The ropes were frozen and they were moving slowly in their exhausted state, feeling their way down in unfamiliar territory. A break in the clouds showed they were on the right line and did not have far to go to reach easier ground but, just as they were getting their bearings, the cloud rolled in once again.

Mick was the first to abseil down. It was over an overhanging sérac wall, and would have been hell for Steve. There seemed a better line out to the right. Brendan volunteered to go across and fix an anchor. It was easy ground and he traversed across the snow slope unroped. It took him twenty minutes to find a good placement and screw in the piton. Andy and Steve chatted while he worked A muffled rumble interrupted their conversation. They glanced up to see a series of avalanches triggering each other off far above and then sweeping down in an ever-growing cloud towards them.

'Brendan, Brendan!' Andy screamed to warn his climbing partner, as he drove his own axe into the snow and clipped himself to it with a sling. Brendan had no sling, no rope, not even his axe. He tried to grab onto the ice screw as the snow silently engulfed him. Avalanches are very different from what you see on television. There is practically no sound, but their power is vast. Brendan was swept away out of sight and a few minutes later it was as if the avalanche had never taken place. They were left in a numb horror at what had just happened.

They camped a very short way below on a small spur and the next day continued down, looking at the huge ice cliffs over which Brendan had been swept. They shouted his name again and again but the sound was absorbed by the still silent ice walls and snow slopes of Kalanka. There was no reply, no sign of their friend.

They spent that night on the Changabang Glacier and set out at one o'clock the following morning to make the long climb up the gully leading to Shipton's Col. It was tough going in crusty snow that sometimes held their weight but would then give way, causing legs to plunge deep into the soft powder below. It was agony for Steve. Once at the col, the face on the other side is steep and sheer, comprised mostly of rock. The abseils were once again painful and very time-consuming. They camped on the Rhamani Glacier and ate what little was left of their food, and they still had another 1000-metre climb over the Bagini Col. They dumped practically all their gear as they went and reached the site of Advance Base the following afternoon. Mick and Steve decided to stay there but Andy wanted to share the dreadful news with Roger and Julie-Ann. He was also worried about his finger which was now black, swollen and suppurating, so he pressed on to Base Camp.

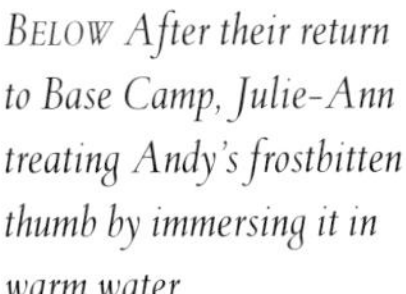

Below After their return to Base Camp, Julie-Ann treating Andy's frostbitten thumb by immersing it in warm water.

Roger and Julie-Ann had only got back the previous day and were still asleep, exhausted by their adventure, when Andy arrived. They had spent ten days on the face, joining the route the others had taken just below the second icefield and reaching the upper icefield on the day the fierce storm hit the others on their way down. They had sat out the storm, buffeted by avalanches, and then made their own precarious retreat.

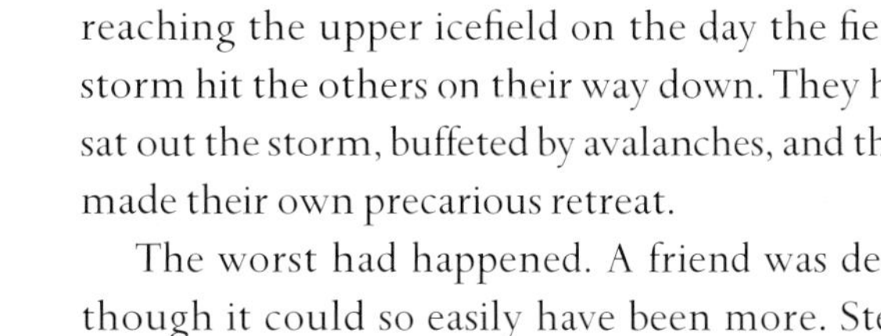

The worst had happened. A friend was dead, though it could so easily have been more. Steve could have died on the face when the rock missed him only by inches. Mick and Steve were lucky to survive their fall on the summit ridge and all six of them had been pushing the limits, often with negligible protection in appalling weather throughout the climb.

It was a magnificent piece of mountain exploration, adventure in its fullest sense. Did they push the risks beyond reasonable limits? Perhaps, but that is in the nature of adventure.

13

THIRTEEN

The Crossing of Antarctica

Fuchs, Hillary and the Commonwealth Trans-Antarctic Expedition, 1957-58

The Antarctic continent is an icy desert – the coldest, most arid place on earth. Here is no grass, no vegetation except a little lichen on the rocks by the coast in summer. Inland, only the highest mountain peaks emerge from the ice and snow. The ice cap is over 14,500 feet thick in some areas. The penguins and seals, the only wild life on the continent, are dependent on the sea for their sustenance. There have been no human inhabitants and even today, the shifting population of scientists with their support staffs are totally reliant on the outside world for supplies. Yet the Antarctic can get a hold on people as tenaciously as any mountains, ocean or desert. Men who have worked in the Antarctic return again and again, and even after settling down in their home countries with wives and families, they still yearn for that harsh, empty but incredibly beautiful land.

I am not sure whether a certain kind of personality is attracted to the Antarctic or if life in polar regions moulds the man, but a very definite type of person seems to emerge. You need a resolute, almost plodding sense of endurance to survive. Everything takes a long time. An expedition is going to take a year, perhaps longer, to complete; it is not a question of surmounting a spectacular mountain peak, but rather one of sheer survival, of just keeping alive, of plodding over endless icy wastes, carrying out a task of survey, meteorology or some other scientific aim. It may entail wintering together in one tiny hut. And so the successful polar man is a great survivor with a lot of self-control; often quiet and self-contained, immensely tenacious, a steady plodder, he is not the athletic star with whom many mountaineers could be compared.

Vivian Fuchs, who was to lead the Commonwealth Trans-Antarctic expedition, summed up the difference saying: 'I see mountaineering like a hundred yards race, where it is a quick, tremendous exertion of effort that counts; whereas the Antarctic thing I see as a cross-country race. You will always win against nature if you hold your position and then, at the right moment, press through.'

In many ways Vivian Fuchs epitomises the polar explorer. Of medium build and height, he has a compact strength, both of physique and personality. He is a singularly self-contained man who rarely shows emotion and projects an aura of complete self-control. Like Thor Heyerdahl, he sees himself not so much as an adventurer, but as a scientist whose insatiable curiosity might take him into areas of risk, but the risk of adventure is in no way an end in itself. Born in 1908, Vivian Fuchs had a classic,

RIGHT A Sno-cat straddles a crevasse, pontoons slewed at crazy angles. Some crevasses were deep enough to house St Paul's Cathedral.

NTARCTIC
PEDITION
A

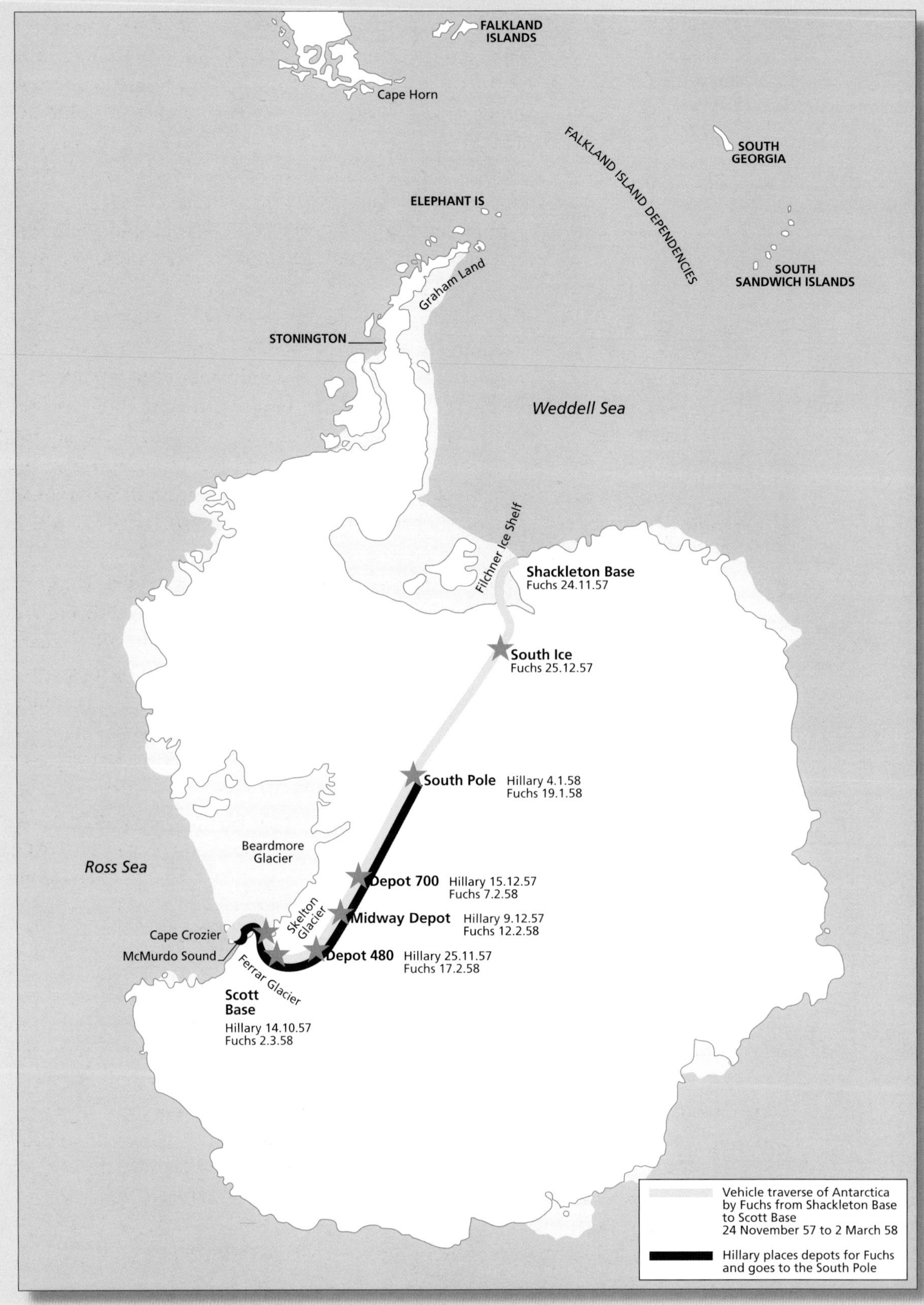
FALKLAND ISLANDS
Cape Horn
FALKLAND ISLAND DEPENDENCIES
SOUTH GEORGIA
ELEPHANT IS
SOUTH SANDWICH ISLANDS
Graham Land
STONINGTON
Weddell Sea
Filchner Ice Shelf
Shackleton Base
Fuchs 24.11.57
South Ice
Fuchs 25.12.57
South Pole
Hillary 4.1.58
Fuchs 19.1.58
Beardmore Glacier
Ross Sea
Depot 700
Hillary 15.12.57
Fuchs 7.2.58
Skelton Glacier
Midway Depot
Hillary 9.12.57
Fuchs 12.2.58
Cape Crozier
McMurdo Sound
Depot 480
Hillary 25.11.57
Fuchs 17.2.58
Ferrar Glacier
Scott Base
Hillary 14.10.57
Fuchs 2.3.58
Vehicle traverse of Antarctica by Fuchs from Shackleton Base to Scott Base 24 November 57 to 2 March 58
Hillary places depots for Fuchs and goes to the South Pole

middle-class upbringing, going to Brighton College and then St John's, Cambridge. At school he was reasonably good at games and fairly bright, without being brilliant academically. From an early age he had a passion for natural history, collecting butterflies, beetles, flowers and odd-shaped pieces of wood. He was also practical and built his own radio set in the very early days of radio. As an only child he had a close, warm relationship with his parents and, as a result, grew and developed in a very secure environment.

At Cambridge Fuchs studied geology and went on his first expedition, to Arctic Greenland. This did not lead to an instant devotion to polar regions for his next opportunity arose in equatorial Africa, with another Cambridge expedition to the African lakes. At the end of this trip there were still some unanswered questions and so other opportunities arose and he spent the period before the Second World War taking part in, and leading, a series of geological expeditions in Africa, collecting a PhD on the way. He would probably have become an African expert and was already negotiating for a job with the Colonial Government of the Sudan, but the war changed all that. Commissioned, he was sent to Staff College where his administrative abilities were both noticed and undoubtedly developed. With the end of the war coincidence, as so often happens, was to lead him into the career for which he was so singularly qualified.

Antarctica was still a huge, empty continent of unknown potential. The great powers and the countries closest to it had already put in their claims and Britain, even during the war, had established a few scientific outposts on the islands off Graham Land, the peninsula that juts out from the Antarctic continent, reaching up towards the southern tip of South America. After the war the British immediately planned to widen their programme and advertised for personnel. Vivian Fuchs was one of the men who applied for a position with the Falkland Islands Dependencies Survey and, because of his qualifications gained in geological surveying in Africa and his administrative experience in the Army, was offered the post of Director in the field of all the British bases then in Antarctica. It was decidedly not a desk job and during the next three years Fuchs journeyed many thousands of miles with dog teams, learning how to travel and live in Antarctica.

It was while on a survey trip that Fuchs first thought of making the trans-Antarctic crossing. He told me:

'I remember the moment well. It was in a tent and we were about four or five hundred miles out from Stonington and couldn't go any further because we were running out of food and had all that way to go back. We'd been stuck there for four days by a blizzard. We could see some mountains further on and wanted to know what their geology was. I said that there must be even more peaks beyond, but we did not know at that time what happened inside the continent. There had been very little aerial survey at that stage. I said to Adie, "The only way to do this is to make a trip all the way across the continent and then we shall know, shan't we?" I sat down then and there, with a stub of pencil and worked out that it should be a joint effort of all the Commonwealth nations with claims in the Antarctic and that it would cost a quarter of a million. In the event, it cost three quarters.'

LEFT The route taken by Fuchs to cross Antarctica from the Weddell Sea to Scott Base, and Hillary's mission to establish depots from Scott Base towards the Pole.

This was in 1948, but the idea lay dormant for a little longer. Fuchs was advised to wait – something he was very good at doing; and as Director of the Falkland Islands Dependencies Survey Scientific Bureau back in Britain, he remained in an excellent position to seize the right opportunity for advancing his plan.

It was not a new idea. In 1914 Ernest Shackleton had sailed into the Weddell Sea in *Endurance*, planning to winter on the coast before making his attempt to cross the continent the following summer. It was an almost unbelievably bold project, considering they were totally dependent on their dog teams and their own strength, that they would have to establish their own supply depots on the way to the Pole before setting out on their journey, and that they would have no form of radio communication with the outside world or their support party, coming in from the other side to lay depots up the Beardmore Glacier. Caught in the ice through the winter of 1914, *Endurance* drifted further and further in towards the centre of the Weddell Sea and was finally crushed. They were in a desperate predicament, hundreds of miles over ice and ocean from the nearest settlement with very little chance of anyone being able to come and look for them, since the first World War was now well under way. But for Ernest Shackleton's extraordinary powers of leadership, the twenty-seven men under his command would almost certainly have died. They set out to save themselves, hauling two of the ship's boats over the ice of the Weddell Sea, through the bitter cold of the winter, till the summer thaws stopped their progress. Then they drifted on an ever-decreasing ice floe through the long summer, towards the Atlantic Ocean until, at last, they could push the boats into open waters and row towards the dubious haven of Elephant Island, a bleak and rocky bump, buffeted by Atlantic storms. Had they stayed there they would have starved to death and so Shackleton, with five seaman, sailed one of the boats to the island of South Georgia, 700 miles away over some of the stormiest seas in the world. It took them sixteen days, half-starved, their clothes soaked and rotten, the boat covered in ice and filled with water for most of the time. And still it wasn't over. Having landed on the uninhabited side of the island, they had to cross its glaciers and mountainous terrain without maps, food or any kind of climbing equipment to reach the whaling station of Stromness. Shackleton then sailed back with the rescue party to pick up the remainder of his crew. It was an extraordinary achievement, something that the modern polar explorer, with his radios, air support, modern food and equipment, would never be called upon to perform.

Vivian Fuchs' plan was almost identical to that of Shackleton. He, too, wanted to sail into the Weddell Sea, establish a wintering base on its shore and then make his dash for the Pole, with a support party to lay down depots at the other side. The plan was the same; the available equipment was vastly different. He would have a powerful, almost unsinkable ice-breaker to penetrate the Weddell Sea, aircraft to spy out a route and stock his depots, motor-driven, specially designed tractors to make the crossing. It could be argued that Shackleton's plan, with the knowledge and equipment available at that time, was a forlorn hope, but it also held the very essence of adventure, a challenge against vast odds and unknown dangers, while that of Fuchs had an element of over-kill; but then, Vivian Fuchs was not interested in adventure for its own sake. He was undoubtedly an adventurous man. He would not have chosen the course of life he had adopted had he been anything else, but he was essentially a scientist. 'I have to have a reason for everything I do,' he told me. His main aim in making the crossing of the Antarctic was to increase man's knowledge of that continent; the adventurous side of the concept, which was something he most certainly enjoyed, was still secondary to the scientific.

In 1954 Vivian Fuchs had his chance. The International Geophysical Year was going to be from 1957 to 1958, when the governments of the world would be concentrating on scientific exploration and research, and would be amenable to a project which would be extremely expensive but also prestigious. Fuchs was not the only Briton who dreamed of making a trans-Antarctic crossing. Duncan Carse, the childhood hero of my generation in the guise of 'Dick Barton – Special Agent' (in a radio series of the late 'forties and early 'fifties), had grown tired of fantasy adventure and had joined the Falkland Islands Dependencies Survey. Now he produced a plan for an Antarctic crossing which he submitted to the Polar Committee. Vivian Fuchs also produced his, and from the position he held and with the backing he had from the establishment it was almost inevitable that his would be accepted. He then succeeded in gaining the enthusiastic support of Winston Churchill, presented his plans to the Conference of Commonwealth Prime Ministers in 1954, and the expedition was fully under way.

Fuchs needed a support team to come in towards the Pole from the other side and, since this was in New Zealand's sphere of influence, a New Zealand party was the

BELOW The eight-man advance party lost vital stores in a storm but survived the Antarctic winter of 1956 in their Sno-cat crate.

obvious choice. He had already met Sir Edmund Hillary and, as New Zealand's most eminent adventurer, Hillary seemed best qualified for leader, even though he had no polar experience. The two men provided an interesting contrast, which was to cause a great deal of trouble as the expedition unfolded. Fuchs was primarily the scientist and brilliant bureaucrat, with the plodding patience and determination that so many polar explorers have developed; Hillary, on the other hand, regarded the South Pole as a mountain to be climbed for its own adventurous sake. He was extrovert where Fuchs was self-contained; Hillary spoke his mind, whereas Fuchs carefully chose his words. But in those early days of preparation they each got on with their own sides of the huge and complex job of organisation without coming over much into contact or conflict.

In November 1955 the advance party of the expedition set sail in the ice-breaker *Theron*, with both Fuchs and Hillary on board. They shared a cabin, but this did not bring the two men any closer together, perhaps even accentuated an awareness of their differences in temperament and motive. Hillary remembered:

'I was treated with an unswerving friendliness but it was made very clear that I was only an observer and I was never permitted to attend the regular meetings of his executive committee (although both of my expedition members were invited to these meetings on various occasions). I suppose I shouldn't have resented this, but I did. I felt an outsider, not to be trusted with expedition responsibilities, and this was probably an uncomfortable foundation on which to build our association over the next couple of years.'

I felt an outsider, not to be trusted with expedition responsibilities

Most of the voyage was very relaxed, since they were little more than passengers, their only duties being to take turns in cleaning out the dogs. They played various deck games to while away the hours and maintain some level of fitness. In these games Fuchs showed another side of his character; although fifty years old and the oldest man in the party, he was furiously competitive and would always do more skipping or press-ups than anyone else on board. He was determined to win every rough game they played and was the champion arm wrestler of the voyage. He had to be leader in every respect, commanding his team by physical as well as intellectual dominance.

The object of the voyage was to establish an advance party on the permanent ice shelf of the Weddell Sea, to prepare for the main party which would set out the following year. Only one other boat had ventured into the Weddell Sea since *Endurance* had been trapped forty years before. Even with the power of modern engines and the help of their Auster aircraft, it was all *Theron* could do to penetrate the piled floes and reach the filchner Ice Shelf. They were late in reaching their destination, barely had time to unload all the supplies onto the ice floe abutting the main ice shelf, before setting sail in a rush to avoid being trapped as *Endurance* had been.

The eight members of the advance party, under the leadership of Ken Blaiklock, an experienced Antarctic hand, had the task of ferrying all the supplies from the floe edge to the relative safety of the permanent ice. They had the advantage of tractors and Sno-cats, but even these were of little use against the power of the elements.

A violent storm blew up shortly after the departure of *Theron*, broke up the sea ice on which most of the stores were still stacked and the lot were swept out to sea.

The advance party's hut was not yet built and they were still living in tents. The Antarctic winter was close at hand. Blaiklock kept his nerve, calmly suggesting that they return to the big crate which had contained their Sno-cat, and which they were now using as a living shelter, to have a cup of tea and take stock. It was a very different situation from the one that had faced Shackleton some forty years before, for the nearest base – an Argentinian one – was only fifty miles away down the coast. Even though they had lost most of the fuel for their tractors, they had plenty of fresh dog teams and could undoubtedly have reached safety. But Blaiklock quickly dismissed this option. He had had the foresight to bring up to their camp a carefully balanced selection of stores which were just enough to last out the winter. True, there was no fuel for heating but there was just enough for cooking. He was determined to get the hut built and Shackleton Base established before the return of the main party.

The discomfort and the feeling of isolation experienced by Blaiklock's party was no less acute because it was self-chosen. Several of them, particularly the ones without Antarctic experience, had difficulty in adjusting to their circumstances. Hannes La Grange, a South African meteorologist, suffered particular stress, spending long hours by the floe edge gazing out into the pack ice for a relief ship that, logically, he should have known would not be arriving until after the winter. He would shout out, 'A ship! A ship!' at the sight of a distant iceberg, only to be told by the others to shut up and not to be so bloody stupid! Then he took to walking out of earshot, so that he could shout out in the cold, empty spaces, 'A ship! A ship!' without irritating his companions.

Eventually he and the other members of the advance party overcame their troubles and settled down in their bleak environment. In talking to polar people, I gather Blaiklock ran a no-nonsense set-up, where individuals were encouraged to keep a stiff upper lip, keep their emotions to themselves and sort out their own troubles. Perhaps this was the only way for a small group to survive, living on top of each other in fair discomfort over a long period of time.

It took them most of the winter to build the hut. It was prefabricated into hundreds of pieces that bolted together. Unfortunately, however, laid out on the uneven surface of the ice with the snow constantly drifting in, few of the bolt holes could be lined up together. As a result, assembling the hut was a painfully slow process which occupied the entire winter, with the men working in temperatures which went down to –50°C and having constantly to dig out the wind-driven snows. They had no fuel for heat, slept in their tents and used the Sno-cat crate, which was also unheated, as a kitchen and living room.

And yet, at the end of the winter, when the main party returned in the ice-breaker *Magga Dan* their spirits were high, for the hut was built, their initial fears overcome, the small group welded into a tight team. Fuchs, with George Lowe, an easy-going New Zealander who had been a member of the 1953 Everest expedition and was now official photographer for the venture, flew into Shackleton Base in advance of the boat to bring in their mail and a few luxury items. The advance team had made a special feast for their visitors, enormous cakes, home-made biscuits and sugared dough cakes, all cooked on an oil drum stove. *Magga Dan* arrived the following day and the stores were unloaded in the next few weeks. At the same time, on the other side of the continent, Ed Hillary was establishing Scott Base on the Ross Sea, whence he was going to lay out his line of depots for the traversing party.

The pattern of polar exploration is so very much more deliberate than that of mountaineering. You arrive one summer, build a base or camp in which to survive through the winter and be poised at the beginning of the following summer to carry out an adventure or do scientific work. Antarctic bases very quickly resemble one another, each with a big living hut containing workshops and laboratories, and a work shed for the vehicles nearby. The Antarctic explorer has to be a thoroughly practical man, able to set his hand to building, vehicle maintenance, sewing and taking his turn at mass catering, in this instance for sixteen hungry men. There is also a tradition of structured work and routine, established partly by the scientific disciplines that have always dominated polar adventure and partly by the fact that everyone taking part in the Falkland Islands Dependencies Survey had been doing it as a job of work, admittedly a highly vocational one, but nonetheless one for which they were being paid.

This was a difference in approach that George Lowe noticed particularly. Used to the free and easy ways of a mountaineering expedition, he began to see the difference that winter in Shackleton Base. They had a record player in the communal living-room, but the rule was that this could only be played on Saturday nights and Sundays, the argument being that it would disturb people who were working and that not necessarily everyone would want to have music – or like the music that had been chosen. It was a logical rule, but it was also a fact that Fuchs was not particularly musical, considering the music as an 'infernal din', and that the decision had been reached by Fuchs without any kind of consultation with the others. This was undoubtedly his style of leadership. A self-contained man, who knew exactly what he wanted, he governed every feature of the expedition with a firm hand. It had to be done his way. He did not encourage any kind of discussion, even casual, of expedition matters. George Lowe described one incident that brought this out.

'One day, a group of three or four were listening with interest while Geoff Pratt held forth on the subject of the gloves he wore. "These things are no bloody good," said Geoffrey. "I wouldn't mind betting that I could design a far more efficient glove for conditions like ours." Bunny [Fuchs] glanced up sharply from his book, took off his glasses, laid them on the open pages and spoke, "When you know a good deal more about Antarctic conditions," he said quietly, "you'll also know more about gloves. These gloves have been designed after years of experience – and I think you'll find they will do the job they were intended for."'

On the other side of the continent, Ed Hillary had no such inhibitions. He knew very little about the Antarctic, had very few preconceived notions and therefore had looked at each piece of equipment with fresh eyes. He foresaw the problems that the prefabricated huts could present and completely redesigned the ones he was going to use, having them made in very much larger sections that could be more easily bolted together. He was also flexible on the question of clothing, bringing to bear the experience he had gained climbing in the Himalaya. Fuchs distrusted down gear, feeling that the down would get wet, then freeze and lose all its insulating properties. Hillary, on the other hand, went for down suits and jackets, since they had worked so well on Everest.

Although Fuchs' rule was autocratic, he had the personality to gain acceptance. The morale of the group was high because they felt that the venture was worthwhile and that, under Fuchs' command, they had a very good chance of success. He was totally competent, consistent and quietly determined; also, equally important, his team were accustomed to this kind of discipline and were, in Lowe's view, very much more amenable than a group of mountaineers would have been.

The period before the arrival of winter had been spent in organising both the Shackleton Base and establishing their forward depot, to be known as South Ice; it was on the Antarctic plateau, about 300 miles south of Shackleton and 500 miles from the Pole. This was done entirely by air, using the single-engined Otter, to make both their initial reconnaissance and then to ferry in the parts of the prefabricated hut. Three members of the team, led by Ken Blaiklock, whose appetite for lonely outposts was in no way diminished by his experience of the previous year, were to stay there through the winter, to carry out a scientific programme.

Winter and summer in Antarctica are merely relative terms. Summer means continuous glaring light, cold, snow and wind. Winter is continuous, unrelenting dark, even greater cold, with yet more winds and snow. Fuchs and his party sat out the winter, filling their time with scientific research and the preparations for their long journey next year. The vehicles were overhauled, modified and improved in a large engine shed which was even heated. The huts, partly buried in drifting snow, had an ugly, impermanent look, as if they did not belong to this pure, bleak, empty world, having a radio that was sufficiently powerful to reach England, with an arrangement to link in with the telephone network. This meant that they could call anyone in Britain for a modest ten shillings and six pence a minute. It was a strange mixture of the traditional and the new – on the one hand the huge, empty continent, a hut which was very similar in design to the ones built by Captain Scott or Shackleton at the beginning of the century, a diet that was very similar to the one that the early explorers had had, even a rhythm of life that was not so very different, and yet combined with this were the aircraft, the big powerful Sno-cats, wireless communication that could reach anywhere in the world and the knowledge that there were other, similar bases littered over the continent, even at the Pole itself.

The sun nudged over the northern horizon towards the end of August, a sign that they would soon have to start moving, but although it crept higher each day, there were few other signs of a let-up in the winter. The temperature dropped to -50°C and there were winds of up to sixty-three miles per hour. Fuchs had prepared an ambitious programme of reconnaissance, aerial exploration and survey work in the area before the departure of the main party on the traverse, but this very soon had to be modified. Most important was the reconnaissance on the ground of the terrain between Shackleton and South Ice.

It was October 8th before Fuchs, with deputy leader David Stratton and his two engineers, David Pratt and Roy Homard, set out with four vehicles to make the reconnaissance. They had three types of vehicle on the expedition, the largest and most sophisticated of them, the Sno-cat, rode on four-tracked pontoons; then there was the Weasel, an oblong box on two tracks, and finally some modified tractors. One of the Weasels, driven by Homard, broke down within eight miles of Shackleton Base and, although they made a temporary repair, there was no question of taking the vehicle all the way. Roy Homard drove it back to Base, leaving the others to press on.

It was discouraging, nerve-wracking work as they edged their way over the crevassed ice shelf. Walking across a crevassed region is bad enough, but cooped in the cabin of a vehicle it must have been much worse, with the ever-present thought of hurtling downwards into the black pit of a crevasse, trapped in the cockpit. Roped together, it needed precise driving to ensure that there was enough slack cable to allow the front vehicle to surge forward if it started to go into a hidden chasm (and thus, perhaps, manage to bridge it), and yet not so much slack that it could fall into the crevasse and become irretrievably jammed or perhaps even break the rope. The cabins of the vehicles were unheated, for Fuchs believed that the interior should be a similar temperature to the outside to avoid the driver becoming cocooned from the environment, but it meant being perpetually cold, encumbered in furs or down clothing at all times. Some days they made little more than two or three miles' progress, spending most of the time hauling vehicles out of crevasses or backtracking to find a better way round a particularly bad area. Time was now slipping by. They had set out a week late anyway, and were now badly over time. It took them thirty-seven days to reach South Ice; they had lost one vehicle and were forced to abandon another temporarily.

Back at Shackleton Base, the morale of the team had reached a low ebb. In the absence of the two most experienced engineers, they were badly behind in their maintenance programme and several of the vehicles were still buried in the snow. Several members of the crossing team had never even camped on Antarctic ice before; there was a feeling of unpreparedness and even of a haunting failure, not eased by the constant barrage of queries over the radio from the world's press, asking when they were going to start, or for news of Hillary's progress on the other side of the continent.

With three modified Ferguson farm tractors and a Weasel loaned by the American polar station, Hillary's party had climbed the Skelton Glacier, the major obstacle barring their way to the polar plateau, and had established their second depot for Fuchs' polar crossing. Viewing the efforts of the two parties, there seems a dynamic energy about everything that the New Zealand support party did, while the main party seems to have had a slow, cumbersome quality about its approach and progress. The difference was noticeable from the very start. While it took most of the energies of the main party just to erect their complex jigsaw of pre-assembled huts, Hillary's simplified structures left his team with the time and the energy to start their reconnaissance programme before the arrival of winter. He wasted no time in getting his dog teams out to find a way up onto the Antarctic plateau. first they looked at the Ferrar Glacier, but the lower part was too badly broken up by crevasses and ice towers,

ABOVE Mount Erebus, Antarctica's only known active volcano, was climbed by members of Shackleton's party in 1908. Hillary drove around it while trying out his transport.

so they turned their attention to the Skelton Glacier and, in spite of deep snow, managed to climb it before winter. They established a depot at the top of it which was stocked by air. Hillary was still not content, however. He wanted to try out his farm tractors and decided to make a journey to Cape Crozier, repeating the incredible winter journey made by Wilson and described by Apsley Cherry-Garrard on Scott's expedition in 1910.

They had set out in the middle of winter to investigate the nesting habits of the emperor penguin. In Cherry-Garrard's words, 'And so we started just after midwinter on the weirdest birdsnesting expedition that has ever been or ever will be.' For nineteen days three of them had hauled a heavily laden sledge through the bitter cold and dark of the Antarctic winter. They had then built a tiny stone hut at Cape Crozier as a shelter while they observed the penguins. I remember reading the account while I was on an expedition to Nuptse, the third peak of Everest. Whenever I thought the climbing was getting at all rough, all I had to do was to read Cherry-Garrard's description to know that our Himalayan expedition was a holiday compared to what they had gone through.

Hillary's experience was also very much easier. Having set out on March 19th with two tractors, they took three days to cover the distance that had taken Wilson and his party nineteen. It did give them an insight, however, into some of the drawbacks of the tractors and produced ideas for modification to improve both their performance and comfort. As a result of their experience, Hillary built a canvas shelter for the driver of each tractor and a caravan or caboose on runners, so that the team could use it for cooking and sleeping in during their journey the following year.

As on the other side, the New Zealand team spent the winter preparing for the summer's activities and doing scientific work. Hillary, in consultation with the scientists, had prepared an extensive programme for the following year but was then amazed – indeed, outraged – when the Committee of Management back in New Zealand vetoed many of his plans as being too ambitious or risky.

'I had no particular desire to offend the committee but I was confident that the programme was well within our powers. I continued as though the exchange of messages had never occurred, made a few worthwhile modifications to the plans and reintroduced the idea of a push towards the Pole if I could get enough extra fuel at Depot 700. It was becoming clear to me that a supporting role was not my particular strength. Once we had done all that was asked of us and a good bit more – I could see no reason why we shouldn't organise a few interesting challenges for ourselves.'

Hillary's approach to his venture was as a mountaineer. The summit was the South Pole and he wanted to get there. His three team members, like himself, had had no previous Antarctic experience. Pete Mulgrew was a petty officer in the New Zealand Navy and an expert on wireless communications. He was also a climber and he and Hillary formed a close friendship from the very start. Mulgrew's original role had been to remain at Base, controlling the rear link back to the outside world, but he had set his heart on the Pole from the very beginning, was irrepressibly adventurous and, anyway, Hillary needed a good wireless operator for their polar journey. The other two members of the 'Old firm', as they called themselves, were Jim Bates, a brilliant mechanic and inventor who was also an expert skier, and Murray Ellis who was an engineering graduate with sound mechanical knowledge. Hillary was the only member of the team who knew anything about celestial navigation, and so he would have the sole responsibility for pointing them in the right direction.

They set out from Scott Base on October 14th with their one Weasel and three tractors towing the cumbersome caboose they had made and the heavily laden sledges. No-one had much confidence in the tractors, since they had not been designed for the task in hand and the modifications were of a makeshift character. Two dog teams, with Bob Miller and George Marsh, one of the two English polar experts with the expedition, were flown in to the foot of the Skelton Glacier, so that they could lead the route which they had already completed the previous year. With the constant threat of concealed crevasses, the four drivers took turns in going out in front to make the route, each trusting the ability of the others. This was in marked contrast to Fuchs' approach. He insisted on being out in front the whole time, physically leading the expedition, taking the major risk, but also taking the satisfaction of actually finding a route. Hillary's policy of sharing the lead among the team certainly increased the enjoyment of the individual team members and also enabled them to make better progress. In a matter of days, Hillary had reached the Antarctic plateau, ready to establish his depots and then, once free of this responsibility, make his push for the Pole. He set out across the plateau on November 12th, just one day before Fuchs reached South Ice – still on the reconnaissance. The main party had not even left Shackleton Base, and were still not ready for their part of the expedition.

ABOVE Fuchs' convoy on the polar plateau.

Vivian Fuchs now announced that, come what may, they would set out on November 24th. It meant working round the clock to get all the vehicles ready in time but, on the 24th at 6.45 pm, they were ready at last and set out with three Sno-cats, two Weasels and a converted Muskeg tractor. There were eleven men in the party and they were going to pick up the vehicles used in their recce at South Ice, also the two dog teams which had found the route up on to the plateau. It was a very much larger team than Hillary's and, of course, had further to go. The atmosphere and discipline of the party was also very different. Fuchs made the decisions. The only person with whom he consulted closely was his deputy leader, David Stratton, an Antarctic veteran from an Antarctic-experienced family background; he had been to Harrow School and concealed behind a relaxed, easy-going manner, immense determination and an extremely well-ordered mind. He did much to soften and warm Vivian Fuchs' cool, unemotional – at times apparently insensitive – approach to his fellow expedition members.

From the very start it was slow going. They were not making much better progress than had the reconnaissance. The vehicles regularly smashed into concealed crevasses or were forced to make long and painful diversions. By November 29th, five days out from Shackleton Base, they had covered only forty miles. On that same day, Ed Hillary reached Depot 480 on the plateau; he was 480 miles into his journey, some 770 miles from the South Pole.

But now they were on the move, the morale of the Fuchs party was high. Lowe commented:

'I had always been critical of the lack of cohesion, of bad communications, of being kept in the dark about expedition plans, of the failure to give both men and vehicles at least a taste of rehearsal before the big journey began; and I tended also to be the

ABOVE *Sub-zero gales lash the camp, scouring snow from the surface. Ventilators project from tent peaks.*

channel through whom Bunny would receive the grievances of others in the party. As I followed the yellow tail of Bunny's Cat into the wilderness, I felt a little contrite and resolved to be more reasonable.'

Other members of the team, the old polar hands, were less critical than George Lowe. Hal Lister, who shared a tent throughout the expedition with George, had already had a two-year stint on the Greenland Ice Cap. He was a glaciologist and accepted the discipline and structured command which prevails in polar circles. Indeed, he even found Bunny Fuchs to be positively easy-going compared with the Naval Commander who had been in charge of his Greenland expedition. He had that

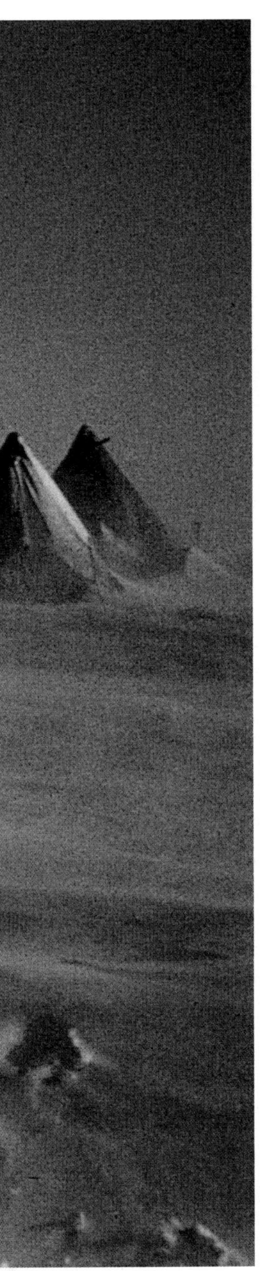

polar mentality that accepts, even welcomes, the long monotonous grind of polar travel, the conservatism that rejects new foods, equipment or ways of doing things in favour of the well-tried ways of tradition. There were aspects of Fuchs' approach that even Lowe found he had to agree with. The question of tent-sharing was one. Rather than leave it to the individual, Fuchs posted on the notice board the list of the six tent pairings with a footnote stressing that they were final and that there would be no swapping during the journey. Lowe wrote:

'At first I thought this was a mistake but looking back I realise that Bunny was right. Over the long journey where the going was mostly a monotonous unchanging ice desert with occasional moments of fear and excitement, there had to be an attitude of hardness and an intelligent determination to quash the inevitable personal differences and be ever-aware that we simply must live cheerfully together. The philosophy took the general line, "You volunteered, so get on with it."'

Above all, whatever reservations Lowe or others might have had about Fuchs' style of leadership, they could not help respecting both his determination and ability. Nobody ever challenged his commands. The morale of the traversing team remained high throughout.

It was a long-drawn-out marathon with its own built-in routine. There was, of course, no night and they could have travelled twenty-four hours a day, around the clock – as indeed Hillary did on quite a few occasions. Fuchs, on the other hand, settled into a steady routine, partly dictated by his own policy of staying out in front the whole time. He could only motor for as long as his own endurance would keep him going. On the whole they worked an eighteen-hour day, with six hours in each twenty-four given over to rest and sleep. At the end of a stint, Fuchs would signal the stop, the vehicles would draw up and the pyramid tents would be taken off the sledges. There was always something of a race to be the first party to erect one's tent and have a brew going. One man would have the outside berth and he would do all the outside jobs, while the one with the inside berth would disappear into the tent the moment it was erected, would accept and place the reindeer-skin mats, sleeping bags, food box and stove and would then get a brew on, trying to have it ready by the time the outside man had finished his chores of staking out the tent and preparing everything for the 'night' outside.

The evening meal was the traditional sledging ration of pemmican hooch, a huge slab of butter plastered over a biscuit and very sweet cocoa. It was monotonous, never varied but somehow in the extreme cold the taste buds seem to be anaesthetised and you can eat almost anything. The key thing was that this sledging ration had sufficient calories to keep them going in the extreme cold. One of the reasons that Scott's party had died was that they were not taking enough calories each day and, as a result, slowly starved to death, losing the strength to withstand the cold and the gruelling labour of hauling their sledges. Hillary had shrugged aside the traditional Arctic ration and, in this perhaps, made a mistake. Fuchs told me:

'Hillary threw out all the sledging rations and put in a lot of tins of sausages and beans and other tinned foods. The Americans said to me when we arrived at the Pole, "We're glad to see that you're in such good shape. Hillary and his party were on their last legs when they got here." That was their comment. It was the food they'd taken with them. They didn't have enough sustenance.'

And then sleep – it was warm enough in the down sleeping bags, though through the journey the bags got progressively more damp from the condensation of sweat as it reached the outer layers which could be -30°C. The jangle of the alarm having woken them, the outside man would reach out, struggle to light the Primus stove and then shove on to it a panful of snow or ice collected the previous night. He would then have a few more precious minutes of warmth, lying dozing to the sound of the Primus. Once it was ready, a big mugful of tea and a biscuit overloaded with butter, perhaps some porridge, preceded the most painful moment of the day – getting out of the warmth of the pit for another gruelling day of travel. Everything was in an automated routine: outside man gets dressed and out first, then the inside man, who passes everything out of the tent, including the ground sheet. His final act is to drop his trousers and relieve himself in the precious shelter and comparative warmth of the now empty tent. Having done this he crawls out and the outside man takes his turn. It is very important to get one's bowels into the correct rhythm to avoid the agony of a frozen bum!

Once the gear was loaded onto the sledge, it was time to start up the vehicles. Every piece of metal was around -30°C, cold enough to give you a frost-burn if you touched it with a bare hand. The gasolene had been specially treated to expel all water or water vapour, since this would inevitably freeze, and little particles of ice would then block the jets of the carburettor. Even so, there could still be some icing. They used hot air guns, sometimes even played a blow torch over the cylinder block and fuel tubes to warm up the engine and get it going. An engine would roar into life, then another; the laggards might be given a tow start, or one of the engineers would come over to give the unfortunate driver the benefit of his expertise until, at last, all the engines were throbbing away.

Fuchs would give a wave from his Sno-cat, *Rock'n Roll*, and away he'd go, his team obediently following. Sometimes it was easy going in smooth, firm snow and the vehicles could cream along at a steady four to five miles per hour. More often the snow was deep with the tracks sinking and thrashing into a slough of snow or, even worse, the ground was heavily crevassed with huge chasms, some of them 1000 feet deep and big enough to house St Paul's Cathedral. It was the covered crevasses that were the problem. A dog team could have crossed many of them, unaware that they even existed, but a big Sno-cat could break through a snow bridge several yards thick. The only way to get through a badly crevassed area was to go out on foot and probe for the holes – slow, tiring work. Even so, it was possible to miss some. Snow would suddenly collapse under the front Sno-cat and it would lunge forwards and downwards, restrained only by the tow rope leading back to the heavily laden sledge. Pontoons swung at crazy angles, the vehicle poised over the dark chasm. It could take anything from five to twenty hours using all five vehicles, either heaving or anchoring, to lift it out smoothly.

There were the occasional cocoa-breaks during the day, when drivers from different vehicles might come over and chat for a few minutes. Hal Lister and George

Lowe held literary lunches in the Weasel cabin; lunch was a buttered biscuit, and their guests would take turns at discussing and describing the books they were each reading at the time.

The only change in the routine came when a day, or part of a day, was devoted to maintenance. This happened all too often, for the tracks had to be greased every few hundred miles. This was a hideous job, for the grease, congealed by the cold, resisted all pressure to pump it into the frozen nipples on the tracks. If you got any grease on your anorak, and it was almost inevitable that you did, the windproof quality of that particular patch was lost for ever; you had to lie in the snow, crawl under the vehicle, bend contorted to reach round awkward corners, all in the bitter cold. For someone like myself who is unmechanical, the very thought is appalling, and yet the crews became fond of their charges, attributing to them an almost human character as they coaxed and struggled with their foibles on the long drive across the Antarctic.

Fuchs, at last, reached South Ice – the depot and advanced base they had established the previous year – on December 21st. Unemotional as ever, he quickly diffused any euphoria amongst his team with the admonishment as they approached the little hut covered in snow, 'Well, there it is. We're going in now. And don't forget – no looting.'

And, as Fuchs addressed his little team, Hillary had actually set out on the last leg of his dash for the Pole. He had fulfilled all his duties in reaching and supervising the stocking by air of Depot 700. By this time the Weasel had come to a grinding halt, but the three farm tractors were still going strong. Even so, some members of Hillary's team were worried about their prospects. Now out of range of aerial support, they were wondering what would happen if their way was barred by soft snow or extensive crevasse systems. George Marsh and Bob Miller wanted to explore the region around Depot 700, but to do this effectively they needed another depot put in by the tractors. Hillary suspected this was a ploy to deflect him from the Pole and felt that it would be just as easy to put in a depot from the air. They spent a day talking round the pros and cons, the one thing remaining fixed in Hillary's mind being the determination to make a push for the Pole, even if it meant taking just one tractor. He felt that he had fulfilled his duties as the leader of a big scientific expedition, with the prime task of supporting Vivian Fuchs' crossing. Now he was the climber, sitting in the top camp, with the summit in sight. He talked the others round to his view and they resolved to go for the Pole.

They set out on December 20th with the three tractors. That evening there was a message from his Committee, forbidding him to go beyond Depot 700. Since he was already beyond it, he chose to ignore the directive, sending a message to Fuchs that he was heading for the Pole, the first time that he had actually declared his intention.

They stormed on through soft snows and heavily crevassed regions, travelling twenty-four hours at a go, taking turns at the stressful job of making the route out in front, swapping the driving between the five men who were now divided between the three tractors. On Christmas Day they paused to listen to a special Christmas broadcast from New Zealand and to eat a Christmas dinner washed down by brandy. It was warm and cosy in the caboose. They were now about 250 miles from the Pole.

Fuchs and his party were still at South Ice, where the entire team managed to cram into the little hut, now buried in snow, for their Christmas dinner. The following day Fuchs sent a message to Hillary, asking him to put in another depot between Depot 700 and the Pole, which would mean abandoning all attempts at going to the Pole. Hillary commented:

'I didn't have to do much figuring. We had just enough fuel to reach either the Pole or back to Depot 700. The only way we could establish a depot was to stop and sit where we were – and hope that Bunny would arrive when our food ran out. It would be a lot easier – and safer – to fly some more fuel into Depot 700. Or get a few drums deposited at the Pole by the Americans. I had the unkind suspicion that this was an excuse to stop us going on to the Pole without actually telling us not to.'

Hillary ignored the edict and kept going. It was savagely cold; the snow was soft and their progress worryingly slow. He abandoned everything that was not absolutely essential, paring down their food and fuel to the bare minimum needed to reach the Pole, and still they pushed on. At last, on January 4th, they sighed a tiny black dot in the distance – then another, and another; it was the line of marker flags leading them to the Pole, where the Americans had an International Geophysical Year base. He had reached his summit, with the minimum of reserves to spare. They were tired and hungry, had only twenty gallons of fuel left, but that did not matter for they had achieved their objective. There was no scientific or geographical purpose in their dash; it was an adventurous self-indulgence that any climber would find irresistible. Hillary wrote:

'What did we achieve by our Southern journey? We had located the crevasse areas and established the route and we had been the first vehicle party to travel overland to the South Pole – that was something, I suppose. But we had produced no scientific data about the ice, and little information about its properties. We showed that if you were enthusiastic enough and had good mechanics you could get a farm tractor to the South Pole – which doesn't sound much to risk your life for. The press had a field day on the pros and cons of our journey, but for me the decision had been reasonably straightforward. I would have despised myself if I hadn't continued – it was as simple as that – I just had to go on.'

How different were Fuchs' motives. A great deal of invaluable scientific work was done both by Fuchs on his side of the continent and also by the large scientific contingent attached to Hillary's support party. But the journey itself was an adventure, similar in concept to sailing round the world or making the traverse of a mountain top. Fuchs claimed that his reasons for crossing Antarctica were those of scientific curiosity but, by making it a single dramatic push from one side to the other, there was undoubtedly a conflict between the needs of a comprehensive scientific programme and the exigencies of a tight schedule. It could be argued that more would have been achieved if the traverse had been spread over several years. As it was, they did manage to make a series of seismic soundings of the depth of the ice cap, but the other scientific work was inevitably of a fairly perfunctory nature. Hal Lister, the glaciologist, admitted rather ruefully that he had to fit his own programme, of examining snow and ice layers immediately below the surface, into periods when the expedition happened to pause for maintenance or some other purpose. I suspect that Fuchs, the scientist and Antarctic explorer, was after all not so very different from Ed Hillary in his motivation.

But Fuchs was still 380 miles from the Pole and the Antarctic autumn was approaching. At the Pole, Hillary was becoming more and more worried by Fuchs' slow progress. He was haunted by the appalling spectre of spending another winter in Antarctica. He had done his job, had achieved his goal, and wanted to go home to his family. Already he had been away for over a year, average by polar standards, but a long time to a mountaineer whose expeditions are unlikely to last for more than six months. Hillary's two mechanics, Murray Ellis and Jim Bates, stated categorically that it was getting too late in the season and that under no circumstances were they prepared to wait for Fuchs to arrive at the Pole. Hillary, therefore, sent Fuchs a message, suggesting that on reaching the South Pole, Fuchs should fly out for the winter, leaving his vehicles behind, and then return the following summer to complete the journey. This, of course, was completely unacceptable to Fuchs, who immediately replied, 'Appreciate your concern but there can be no question of abandoning journey at this stage. Innumerable reasons make it impracticable to remount the expedition after wintering outside Antarctica. Our vehicles can be and have been operated at -60°C but I do not expect such temperatures in March.'

Fuchs called one of his rare expedition meetings and read out both Hillary's message and his own reply. In Lowe's words, 'There was no discussion of either the message or the decision – and we drove on. Nobody in the party had the slightest wish to postpone our crossing of the continent; on that score we were in full accord with our leader.'

It was unfortunate that a copy of Hillary's message was released to the press by his Committee in New Zealand. It had been meant as a helpful suggestion, but the press,

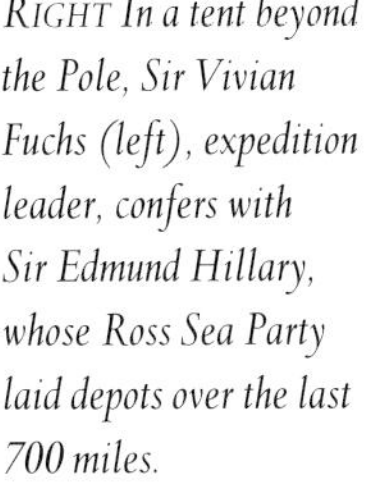

RIGHT In a tent beyond the Pole, Sir Vivian Fuchs (left), expedition leader, confers with Sir Edmund Hillary, whose Ross Sea Party laid depots over the last 700 miles.

who already had had a field day in creating a 'race for the Pole' between Fuchs and Hillary, with the big question of whether Hillary was disobeying orders, now had the sniff of another controversy in the doubts expressed about Fuchs' ability to complete the trip that year. Fuchs, as always, remained aloof. He had stated that he was going to finish the trip that year and, as far as he was concerned, that was enough. Hillary accepted Fuchs' decision and offered his services as guide once Fuchs' reached the Pole. He did not wait there, however, but flew back to Scott Base for a few days' rest.

Fuchs pressed on, now making very much better progress, the going being over reasonably firm snow and free of crevasses. On January 19th, the small convoy of vehicles, bedecked in flags and bunting, reached the Pole at last. In that moment of intense excitement, as the vehicles cruised up to the little collection of huts that marked the South Pole Base, and as Fuchs jumped out of the leading vehicle to be greeted by Ed Hillary and Admiral Dufek, Commander of the Americans in the Antarctic, George Lowe was still baffled, downright exasperated by the enigmatic Fuchs. 'Bunny Fuchs was like the profile of the continent itself – tough, flat, unchanging, dogged; and after three years in his company I could not say I knew him.'

In many ways, Fuchs' own appraisal of himself mirrors Lowe's observations. Fuchs told me in the summer of 1980:

'I don't allow things to unbalance me; I try to keep a steady course. Some people say this is very uninteresting. George, for instance, actually said to me, "Come on. Why is it that you never seem to get enthusiastic about anything?" I said, "You mean you want Caesar to exhort his troops?" And he said, "Well, something like that." I said, "Well, if we get into a state of euphoria we're going to make mistakes just as much as we would if we get into a state of melancholia. As far as I'm concerned we just proceed and things come to pass. No need to get excited about it!"'

And proceed they did. After a few days at the South Pole, sleeping in warm beds, eating gigantic meals in the American mess hall and working on the Sno-cats, they were ready to start once again.

The significance of the Pole was strange. Unlike the top of a mountain, it was merely a geographical point on the Antarctic plateau, barely half-way across in journey terms. The presence of a hutted camp, with many of the comforts of civilisation, made it all the more bizarre. And yet there was a feeling of having reached a top, certainly one that Hillary had felt and one that Fuchs' party could also share. Even though the journey from the Pole to Scott Base had some very difficult and heavy ground to cross, it had the qualities of the down-hill run on known ground, with the tracks of Hillary's vehicles marking the way. Hillary himself flew into Depot 700 to help guide them to the head of the Skelton Glacier and then down it. Even so, this was the most exhausting part of the journey. Racing against the Antarctic winter, they still stopped at regular intervals to make their seismic soundings of the ice cap. They were beginning to get run down and tired, all too ready to end their journey.

At last, on March 2nd, the four Sno-cats, the only vehicles to complete the entire crossing, rolled into Scott Base. They had travelled 2158 miles across the Antarctic continent. Vivian Fuchs had estimated that it would take them a hundred days. He had completed the journey in ninety-one.

FOURTEEN 14

The Longest Polar Journey

Wally Herbert's Team Cross the Arctic Ocean, 1968-69

THE TWO POLES PROVIDE PARALLELS BUT ALSO EXTREME CONTRASTS, as opposite to each other as their seasons, when the perpetual darkness of mid-winter at one Pole is contrasted by the continuous glare of summer sun on the other. In common they have the cold, the wind, the snows and the ice, but that is all. The South Pole is set on an ice cap 9386 feet thick, in the heart of a huge continent. The North Pole is in the midst of an ice-clad ocean, a gigantic jig-saw of shifting ice floes, whose geography is in constant flux, dictated by the surge of the seas beneath and around the ice. floes are split, then subdivided again and again; great floes are swept together, one climbing on to another, a microcosm of the action of the drift of the Earth's tectonic plates. Pressure ridges of ice blocks are hurled up as the floes crash and grind together. From the air the line of a pressure ridge seems little more than a few ripples, but to a man standing on the bucking ice it has all the threat and violence of a severe earthquake.

The interior of Antarctica is the most sterile, empty desert in the world. There is no life, no vegetation, not even lichen, just snow, ice and barren rock. There is, however, life in the Arctic, nurtured by the black seas beneath the ice. fish provide food for the seals, and polar bears stalking the seals have been spotted wandering in the remotest parts of the Arctic Ocean, far from solid land. But this animal life cycle is insufficient to sustain man. As in the Antarctic, he must carry his food and fuel with him as he combats the fierce cold, the glare of the long summer and the dark of winter. In the Antarctic there are the dangers of hidden crevasses, while in the Arctic there is the ever-shifting sea, the threat of your shelter being split in two, of falling into the icy waters, or being engulfed in the gigantic grinder of a shifting pressure ridge.

The heroic age of exploration at both Poles was around the end of the nineteenth century and the beginning of the twentieth, but while the Antarctic has a theme of conventional heroism, of good team-work and good chaps where, even in disaster, they died with a stiff upper lip leaving the right kind of message, in the Arctic there has always been a strain of the contentious that goes back to the earliest efforts to find the fabled North-West Passage. There are tales of mutiny, of cannibalism, of disintegration. In the story of the first men to reach the North Pole there is an ugly dispute that has not been fully resolved even today.

ABOVE Pencil and scalpel self-portrait of Wally Herbert, who conceived the idea of a complete crossing of the Arctic Ocean, via the North Pole.

In many ways, Robert Edwin Peary was of the same mould as Captain Scott or Ernest Shackleton. An officer in the Civil Engineer Corps of the US Navy, he devoted a large part of his adult life to Arctic exploration in Northern Greenland and then to his efforts to reach the North Pole. A gruff, outspoken man, he was weak in both tact and diplomacy, but was almost obsessively thorough and very determined. His attempt in 1909 was carefully planned, using a combination of Eskimo experience of the Arctic and the modern technology of the time. His specially-designed ship, *Roosevelt*, sailed as far north as possible into the ice before the arrival of winter. Early the following spring he set out using a series of trail-breaking parties to force the way for him to a point just 153 miles from the Pole. Then, with his Negro manservant, Henson, and four Eskimos, he cut loose to push through to the Pole in the space of five days' hard sledging. It was only on his way back home he learned that Frederick A. Cook, who had been his doctor on his first polar expedition, had claimed to have reached the Pole a full year before.

Cook's story was certainly remarkable. He claimed to have set out from the north point of Axel Heiberg Island, 520 miles from the Pole, with four Eskimos. Two of them returned after a few days, leaving the threesome to make their push for the Pole. Cook claimed to have reached it on April 21st 1908, but there were many discrepancies in his claim. How could he have carried all the food that the three of them, plus the dogs, would need for the length of time he claimed they took to get there and back? He had lost all the paper-work of his navigational readings, having left his instruments on his way out with a member of Peary's party. Cook claimed that they vanished, while Whitney, the man who had accepted Cook's belongings, denied there had ever been any written records and claimed he had only been given instruments. Two factions quickly formed, each bent on discrediting the other. The problem is that there is no way anyone can prove he has been to the Pole. It is not like a mountain, where, except in the worst weather, photographs can give positive evidence that the climber has reached the top. It all comes down to credibility. In the end Cook's story was dismissed, not just on the evidence or lack of it, but also in the light of earlier claims he had made to have climbed Mount McKinley for the first time – a claim which was also discredited. Peary was given official recognition and his name appears in all atlases today, though even in his case the proof was not conclusive. His average progress rate while breaking trail with support parties had never exceeded twelve miles a day and yet, once he pushed forward with Henson and his four Eskimo companions, he claimed to have averaged twenty-five miles a day, both on the way to the Pole and all the way back to *Roosevelt*. This was remarkable if compared with the progress of others; Nansen, one of the greatest Arctic travellers, had only once managed to travel twenty-five miles in a day on polar pack ice.

It is probable that the North Pole was still untouched until it was invaded by modern technology, when man could reach it not only from the air but also by nuclear submarine, and USS *Nautilus* cruised beneath it on August 3rd 1958, only a few months after Fuchs had completed his crossing of Antarctica. But no-one had reached the North Pole across the surface since Peary made his bid in 1909 and the greatest journey of all – a complete crossing of the Arctic Ocean – was still untried.

It was this concept that captured the imagination of Wally Herbert. A luxuriant beard and a quiet intensity of manner, eyes wrinkled from gazing into the wind and glare of the snows on the British Antarctic Survey, give Herbert the unmistakeable stamp of a polar explorer. Born in 1934, he was the son of an Army officer who had risen up from the ranks.

By the age of fourteen he was dreaming of being an explorer, but there seemed little chance of realising this ambition. His father, with whom he had a strained relationship, partly no doubt because of his long absences, wanted him to go into the

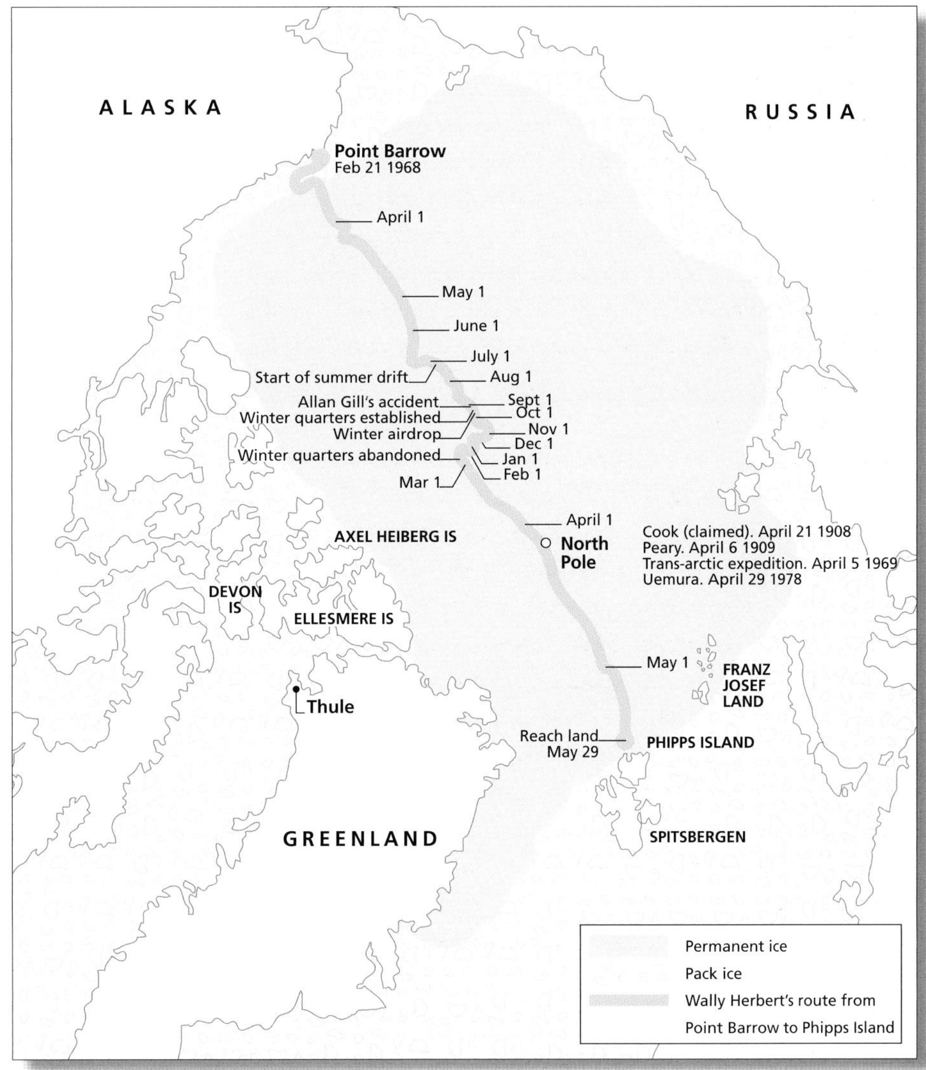

RIGHT The route across the Arctic via the North Pole taken by Wally Herbert.

Army. But Wally felt uncomfortable with what he had already seen of life in the officers' mess. He told me: 'I was given a kind of grooming in officer's behaviour; I would have to play billiards with the captains and talk politely with the CO, dress for dinner and all that sort of thing. It was a deadly, deadly way of spending your holidays as a teenage lad.'

And yet the Army seemed to open up the only road to any kind of adventure, and so he signed on for twenty-two years at the age of seventeen, going into the Engineers to train as a surveyor which he hoped would take him into unexplored lands. Diffident, unsure of himself, he failed to get a commission and, within weeks, bitterly regretted joining the Army. He spent most of the next three years fretting over whether they would let him out at the end of this initial period. Fortunately they did; once again, he showed an adventurous streak, hitch-hiking home from Egypt around the Middle Eastern countries and back to England, where he started looking for a job. He seemed a long way from a life of exploration and adventure in a job at a surveyors' office on the South Coast.

He made few friends; quiet, introverted and very lonely, he seemed trapped in a humdrum life with very little future. As so often happens, it was a coincidence that led him to the life to which he was most suited. Wally told me:

'I was sitting in a bus; my raincoat was soaking wet and there were drips coming off everything, steaming in this horrible smelly bus. The bus lurched and a newspaper fell off the luggage rack smack into my lap. It was open at the public appointments page and two of the things I noticed straight away were one advert for a surveyor in Kenya and another one for team members for an expedition to the Antarctic.'

He had found the answer to his discontent. On reaching the office he didn't dare answer the advertisements during working hours, so slipped into the lavatory, sat on the loo with the top down and wrote off for further details. Interviews followed and he was offered both jobs.

'I had to make a choice, Kenya or the Antarctic. I'd always dreamed of going to Kenya and had never really thought much about the Antarctic at all, but at this point, without really thinking it out, I immediately chose the Antarctic. There was some magic in the word "expedition" which touched the romantic in me. I could easily have gone to Kenya and have spent the rest of my life in the hotter parts of the world.'

At twenty, Wally Herbert joined the Falkland Islands Dependencies Survey, at Hope Bay, Antarctica, and found a contentment he had never known before:

'A monastic life without religious exercise. There, we were a world of men in harmony with our environment – twelve men around a bunkhouse fire, or two men in a drumming tent, or one man in the solitude of summer-warmed hills. We saw a paradise in snowscapes and heard music in the wind, for we were young and on our long exploratory journey we felt, with the pride of youth, that we were making history.'

At the end of his two-and-a-half-year stint, Wally hitch-hiked through South America and the United States before returning home to England. A trip to Spitsbergen, another stint in the Antarctic, this time with a New Zealand expedition operating out of Scott Base, and he had achieved the experience and, perhaps, the spur that led him to undertake his journey across the Arctic. In Antarctica he had conceived an exciting plan of exploring a range of mountains last visited on Scott's expedition and then, at the end of the season, making his own dash to the South Pole to mark the fiftieth anniversary of Scott's ill-fated journey. It meant a tremendous amount to Wally Herbert, but the authorities turned it down. He had too great a respect for authority to ignore the veto, as his name had allowed Hillary to do in 1958. As a consolation, he made his way with his dog teams down the Axel Heiberg Glacier, the route taken by Amundsen in his historic journey to the Pole in 1910. But Herbert's memory of the Antarctic was forever tarnished by his disappointment.

'I didn't ever want to go to the South Pole from that moment on or to ever go back to the Antarctic – I'd worked it completely out of my system because I knew that next year they'd be coming in with aeroplanes to photograph the area and to put their surveyors on our bloody mountain peaks and on our survey claims. They'd make better maps than we'd made ourselves. It seemed like the end of this whole phase of my life – I must go and do something new.'

Back in England, living at his parents' home, he was existing off the small advance for a book about his Antarctic experience and the proceeds of a few lectures. It was at this stage that he started to think of the Arctic and that longest great polar journey, the crossing of the Arctic Ocean. Wally has a very strong sense of history and he is intensely patriotic.

'It was absolutely imperative that it was a British expedition that did it because of the four-hundred-year tradition and heritage and all the blood, sweat and scurvy and folklore that was built into this.

'But at the time it didn't occur to me that it should be me because I hadn't enough experience, I was still too young and I hadn't had an expedition on my own. I'd led expeditions in the field, but I'd never actually organised them or raised the money for them.'

The idea was there, but also the self-doubt. I felt very much the same before I led my first expedition to the South Face of Annapurna. In Wally's case the transition from vague dreams to a dogged determination to get his concept off the ground came through a growing realisation of how feasible the scheme was, given the right mixture of dedication and support. The ice floes of the Arctic Ocean are in constant movement, driven by the ocean currents. Explorers of the past had tried to utilise this movement; Nansen, in *Fram*, allowed himself to be trapped in the ice off the coast of Siberia, hoping to drift over or close to the Pole. In the event, he did not get close enough to make a successful dash over the ice to his objective. But now much more was known about the pattern of drift. The Russians had been establishing scientific stations on the ice and were drifting slowly across towards North Greenland. Since the drift was in a circular direction, swinging round and over the Pole, Wally saw that it would be possible to go in with a small party, using dog teams for fast, light progress when conditions were suitable, but always going on the line of drift, so that even when sitting out the summer period when there were too many open leads of water, or the winter when it was too cold and dark, they would still be sweeping, however slowly, in the right direction. He liked the idea of dog teams, had little sympathy with the encroaching technology of the noisy Snowmobile that he had seen used more and more in the Antarctic. His preference for dogs was both romantic and practical. Quite apart from being a traditional mode of transport, completely in keeping with the spirit of adventure, there was less to go wrong with a dog and, if it should die, at least its fellow-dogs could eat it. A broken-down Skidoo or Snowmobile, if you could not repair it, was just a pile of useless scrap metal.

Even so, Wally realised that he could not be completely independent. There was no way his party could carry enough food for the sixteen months it would take dogs and men to cross the Arctic Ocean on its longest axis from Point Barrow to Spitsbergen. This meant he would have to depend on supplies from the air, which also meant that he would need good radio communications with the outside world. All this was going to cost a lot of money, and the co-operation of government bodies, not just in Britain but in the United States and Canada as well. It was a formidable challenge for a thirty-two-year-old, who was not well-known, had no connections with the establishment or media, and no real qualifications except for some sound experience in the Antarctic. But in spite of his doubts and frequent rebuffs Wally Herbert doggedly pursued his vision.

In 1964 he took the first draft of his plan to Sir Vivian Fuchs who was both interested and encouraging. Wally then managed to get a small grant from the Royal Geographical Society and went off to the States to research his project. He even flew his proposed route in a DC8 but, on his return to England, now heavily in debt, the Royal Geographical Society rejected his 20,000-word submission on the grounds that there was too much adventure and insufficient scientific weight to the scheme.

But Wally struggled on, writing hundreds of letters to everyone who had ever had anything to do with the Arctic. His determination paid off and, slowly, he gathered a body of influential people to support his plans in a Committee of Management, bristling with illustrious names, from Sir Vivian Fuchs to the Sergeant Surgeon to the Queen. With this kind of support, Wally was now able to get the approval of the Royal Geographical Society. It was important to him not merely for the launching of his expedition, but also on a personal level, as a seal of acceptance by the exploratory and scientific establishment of which Wally desperately wanted to be part. This extract from his book *Across the Top of the World* is revealing:

'By the time I left I was almost certain I had, at last, the approval of the Society – an approval confirmed later by the pleasant expressions and, in some cases, even the smiles of the members of the Committee as they walked in threes and fours through the halls to the gentlemen's cloakroom (where I had hung about for almost half an hour, knowing that I would, if I waited long enough, meet them as they came in to collect their bowler hats).'

Wally was now able to go forward at full bore with his plans, but it was still very much a one-man venture. He had chosen his team – all of them old hands from the Antarctic – Roger Tufft, a school teacher living in the Lake District, Allan Gill, whose life has been devoted to the empty spaces of the Antarctic and Arctic, and Fritz Koerner,a glaciologist who was working at an American university. From my own experience of climbing expeditions, I have always found that a level of involvement by all members of the team has helped in both increasing commitment to the venture and in building a sense of unity before setting out. It was perhaps unfortunate that as Wally's team were all so scattered, it was impractical for any of them to help in the actual organisation. This led to even greater pressure on Wally while the others remained almost uninvolved until they actually joined the expedition, though it seems unlikely that Wally would have delegated much responsibility, even given the chance. Allan Gill commented, 'I think Wally has to do the whole lot; he has to do it his way and I would never even suggest taking on a share because I just don't think it would work.' Roger Tufft, who was particularly interested in the design of the sledges and practical details of the training expedition, regretted that he was not consulted and been more involved.

It was now October 1966; Wally was still a long way from getting the £54,000 he thought he was going to need, but he had just enough to carry out the training expedition that he felt was an essential prelude to the main venture. Fritz Koerner was tied up with his job in America, but Allan Gill and Roger Tufft were free to go. They planned to spend the winter near the Eskimo settlement of Qanaq, in North-West Greenland, so that they could try out the little prefabricated hut Wally had ordered for wintering on the main expedition. In the early spring they set out on a long sledge journey across Ellesmere Island and then up the Nansen Sound to the top of Axel Heiberg Island, the place that Cook had claimed to have set out from on his bid for the Pole. They had to prove themselves and their gear capable of a long sledge journey over the broken pack ice of the sounds between the islands to convince potential sponsors that their plans for the polar crossing had at least a chance of success. So Wally was determined, at all costs, to complete the journey.

BELOW Allan Gill, the toughest and most experienced member of the expedition, was also its emotional anchor man.

The project also provided a test in their own relationships. Roger Tufft was the same age as Wally, had joined the Falkland Islands Dependencies Survey at the same time; they had sledged together and had got on well, but that was ten years before. Since then they had seen little of each other. After leaving the Antarctic Roger Tufft had gone with Bill Tilman on two of his long and adventurous sea voyages; he had also been exploring in Lapland and Spitsbergen and manhauling sledges across the Greenland Ice Cap. Welsh by birth, a school teacher with an excellent mind, he was used to taking the initiative and it was, perhaps, inevitable that he and Wally would clash. Allan Gill, on the other hand, was much more easy-going than Roger. Polar regions were his life, with the short periods he spent in civilisation a slightly uncomfortable interlude. Quiet, very modest, lean almost to the degree of emaciation, Allan Gill, then aged thirty-six, was the oldest member of the team. He had learnt as much as possible about polar regions, turning himself into a first-class scientific assistant who could cope with almost any aspect of polar life or research. He did not have the same conflict of loyalties that Roger had between a life and career in civilisation and the expedition they were about to undertake. For Allan, if he were not on the polar crossing, would have joined some other Arctic expedition and, in fact, had already turned down an invitation to lead a very attractive American scientific expedition.

Their journey stretched them and their equipment to the limit. The lightweight sledges disintegrated under the loads and they had to obtain the heavier Eskimo variety. Having thought themselves proficient dog drivers from their experience in the Antarctic, they now found that they were little better than novices when compared with the Eskimos. They ran out of food, reached the last stages of exhaustion, were well behind with their schedule and yet Wally still clung doggedly to his original plan, knowing how vital it was to gaining his sponsors' confidence.

Altogether, they travelled 1200 miles and were only 143 miles short of Resolute Bay, their eventual destination, when Wally realised that they could afford no more time. In only six months he wanted to set out from Point Barrow on their great journey. He therefore radioed for a 'plane to fly in to pick them up.

It was on June 19th, while they waited for the 'plane, that Roger Tufft told Wally he had decided to pull out of the expedition. Roger felt that there was insufficient time to get the main trip organised; their gear had proved inadequate and the radio had not been sufficiently powerful but, most important of all, Roger and Wally had found their personalities no longer seemed compatible. There had been a level of stress throughout their journey, with Roger frequently disagreeing with Wally's decisions.

Wally flew out first with some of the gear and it was six days before the 'plane was able to fly back to pick up Allan Gill and Roger Tufft – six days of agony for Wally for he could not help wondering whether Allan, also, might decide to defect. Wally wrote:

'I knew, and I guess he knew too, that if he joined Roger and backed out, the trans-Arctic expedition would fold up; for it would be impossible for me to convince my Committee, sponsors and many supporters that the plan was still viable and that I, as the leader, was still competent, if two of my chosen companions, after a nine-month trial in the Arctic, had lost confidence in my leadership and in the feasibility of the plan.'

There would be no time for private discussion, for Allan Gill had to fly straight on from Resolute Bay to join a summer scientific camp on Devon Island. As he climbed into the aircraft, he said to Wally, 'I'll see you in London in September.' It was an expression of support and loyalty that Wally would never forget.

The Committee were undoubtedly shaken by Roger Tufft's resignation, insisting that Wally telegram Gill and Koerner to obtain their assurance that they were still part of the expedition. Fritz Koerner, who had not been on the training expedition, had a difficult decision to make. A close friend of Roger Tufft, he had great respect for his judgement. In addition, Fritz's wife, Anna, was due to have their first baby around the time they were going to set out from Point Barrow. He was also concerned about the scientific content of the expedition. He was attracted by the adventurous concept of the crossing of the Arctic Ocean, but only if he was also going to be able to complete some sound glaciological research on the way. Nevertheless, setting aside his doubts, he cabled his acceptance.

Above Ken Hedges, a late replacement from the Royal Army Medical Corps.

But Wally still had to find a replacement for Roger Tufft. His Committee of Management favoured a doctor and, accordingly, made enquiries through the Royal Army Medical Corps for a suitable candidate. This was how Ken Hedges came into the expedition. At thirty-one, he was medical officer for the crack Special Air Service Regiment. He had no polar experience, but did have an impressive set of adventure credentials as a military parachutist and frogman.

While working for the necessary qualifications to get into the Royal Military Academy, Sandhurst, he had had a serious motor bike accident. He was very lucky to survive at all and was in hospital for nine months. He made an almost complete recovery but had lost some mobility in his limbs and this was sufficient to stop him getting through the Army medical tests. The trauma of the accident with the accompanying physical pain, enforced immobility and fears for the future proved an important turning point in his life. He had had a happy childhood with a close-knit family background in which a Christian belief had played an important part; the accident had strengthened his belief, directing it into a positive evangelistic conviction which was to form the main stream of his life. With a strong sense of gratitude for the medical skill that had saved him, he resolved to devote his life to medicine and thought initially in terms of studying to be a male nurse. It was his father who gave him the necessary encouragement and financial backing to get the 'A' levels he needed to gain a place at medical college, become a doctor and eventually join the Royal Army Medical Corps.

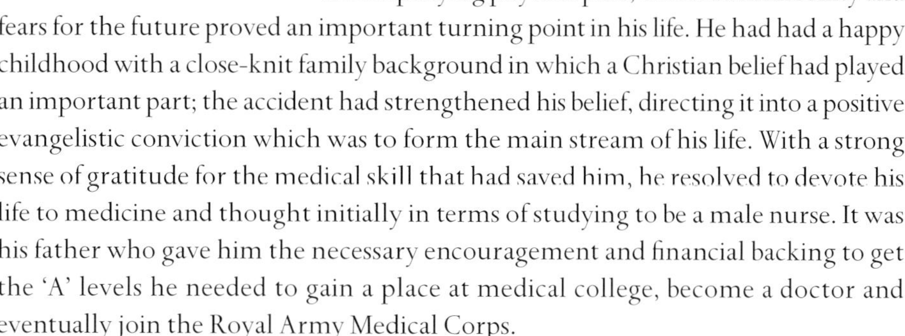

Wally had never seen the need to have a doctor on the expedition. Of the applicants, he favoured a seasoned Antarctic man, who was also a geophysicist, called Geoff Renner. With the same background as the other three, he knew and understood polar life and travel. But Wally was overruled partly, I suspect, because he did not put over his own views strongly enough, always having been in awe of the polar establishment on his Committee. He told me:

'It was easier for Fuchs. He was very much older than I at the time he did his trans-Antarctic crossing, and had a certain authority and charisma through having been the Director of the British Antarctic Survey. He could say, "Right, now look here gentlemen we'll do it this way", and they would listen and go along with it. But I couldn't do that. Possibly it was my training from Dad; I had a kind of awe and respect for age, prestige, position and title. I felt that I had to call them Sir. One or two of them called me Wally occasionally, but it sometimes seemed to stick in their throats. They were absolutely charming and very helpful, but there was this very strange sort of relationship I had with them.'

ABOVE Fritz Koerner, a glaciologist. His baby daughter arrived just in time for him to join the expedition at Point Barrow.

So Wally went along with the Committee's preference for Ken Hedges who, but for his complete lack of polar experience, seemed a tough and pleasant personality. They first met in a London pub. Wally remembers how he spent the entire interview trying to describe to Ken just what polar travel and living was like and, as a result, he hardly asked Ken anything at all, discovering very little about his background and interests.

There was little enough time to balance out the question of team composition anyway. With so many things to do and Wally scurrying between his parents' home in Warwickshire and his office in London, it was still very much a one-man-band. Ken Hedges and Allan Gill were due to fly out by RAF Hercules transport 'plane with the bulk of the gear, first to Thule to collect the dogs, and then on to Point Barrow at the end of December. Wally was going to fly out direct to meet them there in early January 1968. Anna Koerner's baby was due towards the end of January and Fritz was determined to be with her at the birth and make sure everything was all right before leaving her for sixteen months. This didn't suit the Committee and Fritz and Anna were brought over to London to discuss the problem. Fritz remembers the incident vividly.

'The Committee said: "You must leave on the dot." We went on to discuss this and the discussion got down to the birth being induced. I can remember the exact words Old Smiler (that's what we called Sir Miles Clifford) said: "I think it's a good idea. You don't mind having the child induced, do you, Anna?" Anna was just looking at them, amazed, and they were all sitting there, puffing on their pipes.'

Wally flew out of England on January 10th and joined his party at Point Barrow a few days later. Point Barrow is like so many Arctic stations, a collection of huts and hangars jutting out of the empty, snow-covered tundra. Their 70,000 pounds of supplies, sledges, tents, food for men and dogs, were stored in a big warehouse. Ken Hedges had certainly been plunged in at the deep end, having already driven a dog team seventy miles in the pitch dark and cold of mid-winter from Qanaq to the US Air Force Base at Thule. It was the first time he had ever handled dogs or been exposed to such extreme cold. The next weeks were spent in frantic preparation. Dog harnesses were adjusted and restitched by the Eskimo women, sledges and tents were checked, radios tested. The supplies which were going to be air-dropped by the Canadian Air Force had to be sorted out. They made short journeys over the ice to try out the gear and train the dog teams and all the time, out there to the north, was the vast stretch of ice covering the Arctic Ocean – implacable, huge, menacing. They were not yet a complete team, but Fritz Koerner's daughter arrived, by natural birth, on January 31st; Fritz was at Point Barrow by February 8th and, at last, they were ready to set out.

The overall plan was to put in as much sledging progress across the polar pack ice before the summer melt made travel impossible. Then for two months they would camp on a suitably substantial floe which would itself continue creeping on towards the Pole in the circular polar drift. In the autumn they would sledge on again until the four months of winter darkness obliged them to set up camp once more; then with the spring would come the last frantic dash for Spitsbergen before the ice broke up beneath them.

The first and perhaps most difficult problem of the entire journey was to find a way of crossing the eighty-mile belt of fractured young ice between the Point Barrow coast and the relative solidity of the polar pack ice. This was a region of shifting currents, where the great ice floes were ground together against the immovable land mass, an area of piled up, ever moving pressure ridges, of changing leads of open water. Day after day Wally flew over it in a Cessna 180, but what he saw was never encouraging. There was no sign of the ice compressing to form the vital bridge they needed and, as the days slipped by the tension increased. Back in London the media printed stories

BELOW The sledges had been designed so that they could be converted into boats for crossing short stretches of open water.

of gloom and doom, while the worries of the Committee could almost be felt over the radio waves.

At last, on February 22nd, the ice bridge to the polar pack seemed at least feasible, and the four set out with their dog teams and sledges, along the coastline and then out onto the piled rubble of ice that marked the edge of the Arctic Ocean. For the next eighteen months they would be travelling across the constantly shifting ice, which would rarely be more than six or seven feet thick and which could split beneath them at any moment. The dash for the relatively stable pack ice foundered into a laborious crawl almost immediately, their way barred by the first pressure ridge, a twenty-foot-high wall of ice blocks. They scrambled up to get a wider view. What they saw was discouraging.

'As far as the eye could see there was chaos – no way seemed possible except the route by which we had come. It was like a city razed to the ground by a blitz or an act of God, an alabaster city so smashed that no landmarks remained. It was a desolate scene, purified by a covering of snow that had been packed down by the wind; dazzling bright yet horrifying.'

The only way to get through was to cut down the walls of ice, using the debris to build ramps for the sledges to be heaved or pushed across and down into the rut beyond. It was -41°C, but their clothes were soon damp with sweat, a dampness that would turn into a bitter chill as soon as they stopped their exertion. And then, once they had forced the first ridge, there was another, another and yet another. There was mush ice, which was just particles jumbled together, barely fused by the pressure of the floes on either side, only a few inches thick, a quaking bog with thousands of feet of black, sub-zero waters beneath. They skeetered across these sections, the dogs scrambling, yapping frantically, the men shuffling, striding, fearful of the easily-imagined horrors of immersion in the waters below. There was little rest at night with the constant groaning of the ice and the fear of it splitting beneath the tents. And there was the even greater fear of disgrace and ridicule. What if they couldn't break through to the pack ice beyond? They would have to return to face the waiting media, the sceptics who said they had no chance anyway. They were all frightened, but the fear of failure and of ridicule was greater than that of death. It was the same feeling that Heyerdahl had had as *Kon-Tiki* limped painfully from the coast of Peru.

Doggedly they fought their way from floe to floe, edging northwards whenever possible, though they were also at the mercy of the winds and currents which were sweeping the ice they were crossing steadily towards open waters. After sixteen days of struggle, they were only seventeen miles from Point Barrow. At this stage they were travelling light, carrying only a few days' food and relying on being resupplied by the Cessna, whose pilot also tried to advise them on the terrain lying ahead. For most of the time his information was discouraging. They were now 400 miles behind schedule. This was serious, since they needed to be in the right place by the height of summer to find a suitably large ice floe on which to drift through the summer months towards the Pole. If they were forced to stop short of their planned destination, they would be in the wrong region of drift and could be swept away to one side of the Pole. Wally, therefore, resolved to keep sledging well into the summer, even though this would

ABOVE Crossing the polar ice; each man was responsible for his own dog team.

mean more problems with open leads between the ice floes. He had anticipated this and had designed the sledges so that they could be turned into boats for crossing short stretches of open water.

By March 20th they had at last broken through the coastal fracture zone and were on the permanent polar pack ice. There were still pressure ridges to cross, open leads to negotiate, but their progress was now very much faster. They were making sixteen or seventeen miles in a day. But they were now increasingly confronted with another problem. There were seams within the fragile unity of the group, the beginnings of a division into three and one, and Ken Hedges was becoming the odd man out. Wally wrote:

'Ken's problems were social; physically he was in good shape, professionally he was admired and encouraged by his regiment for joining the expedition, but it was inevitable that the difference in training and temperament would set him apart from the three of us.

'Ken was a good officer, a Christian and a gentleman. We were three seasoned polar men. The many years we had lived in isolated polar camps had left their mark on us; we would no doubt be regarded by a genteel society as rough, crude, self-reliant and irreligious. We were obsessed by and in love with the polar setting and the hard physical challenge of polar exploration. We were old friends; Allan and I had made a tough journey together the previous year; Allan and Fritz had made others; the three of us had gone through the same basic polar training at the same Antarctic base – Hope Bay. There was a close bond between us, a mutual trust and respect; we spoke the same language. Only a man with precisely the same background would have fitted instantly into such a society; it was therefore no surprise to us that Ken had felt alien at the start of the journey; but it had been worrying us for some time that he did not appear to be slipping naturally into our way of life.'

In any enclosed community little idiosyncrasies can become a savage irritant, and the way a person scratches his nose, stresses certain syllables or gulps his tea can become a quite irrational focus to externalise much deeper and more serious differences. The most obvious difference between Ken and the others was more than a mere mannerism. It was his religious belief, but this seems to have focused all the other differences of experience and background into something that was easily definable, and indeed mentioned to me by each of the others. Ken was a devout Baptist, the other three either atheist or agnostic. They found Ken difficult to live with. Little things would grate, like the way he would often go off to pray or meditate on top of a nearby pressure ridge – 'humbling' the others called it, because of the characteristic stance he adopted, or the meek yet impenetrable front which they felt he put up between them in all arguments. It was a rift which was only to get wider as the months passed, driving Ken even further in on himself. Wally writes: 'Ken, by his own admission, was unhappy in our society because he felt we were not "bringing him in", and there was little we could do to improve the situation, for as far as we were concerned we had tried to interest him in our way of life and evidently failed.'

Their daily routine did nothing to alleviate Ken's feeling of isolation. For a start, they each had their own dog team and through the day travelled separately, often hundreds of yards apart. The only time they came together was at an obstacle and, even here, Ken must have been forced anew to face the difference between himself and the others as the three polar experts pooled their knowledge and experience to manoeuvre a sledge over a pressure ridge or across an open lead. It was inevitable that Ken remained an onlooker, however willing he may have been to take an active part.

When I went to see him, he did not want to talk about the differences that occurred between himself and the other three; he did observe, however:

'We didn't meet as a team until a week before we set out and so there was no fellowship in that team. There was among the other three because they had all sledged together, but, as a team, in which twenty-five per cent was new, meaning myself, there was not that sense of fellowship. I didn't have this sense of friendship, facing the fifty-fifty chance of dying, which is how I rated our chances. I was carried along by several conceptions; one was of acquitting myself as honourably as circumstances permitted, coming from the SAS and being a commissioned officer; also, there was this vague sense of British history, particularly in its polar sense. There was an absolute dedication and I put my life on the line on this one. I would endeavour to commit myself with honour, come what may and just hope that I wouldn't have to pay the full price. There was a sense of resignation about it all.'

It was also very frightening; Wally Herbert described it for me:

'We were all shit scared in our own desperate sort of ways to come through this period and each of the four men had their own way of handling this situation. We'd been in the Antarctic and Arctic in many dangerous situations; we'd experienced the dark before, but to Ken it was new and he was cold, he was uncomfortable; he was afraid as we all were, but for him it was new and so presumably for him it was very much more frightening.'

And there was also the dog team. This was what Ken found the most difficult. Much of polar living and travel is simple, basic survival, of getting used to putting up a tent in a blizzard, of struggling with a Primus stove, of plodding over mile upon mile of featureless ice, but managing a dog team is a real skill and one that needs years of experience to master fully. The other three had all driven dog teams in the Antarctic and the previous year Wally and Allan had gained further experience, but Ken had to learn from scratch. Essentially a kind man, he found it difficult to discipline his team in the way to which they were accustomed. He told me:

'I wasn't driving my dogs; I was walking out in front of them, whistling to the silly creatures to follow me, which they did. I remember Fritz saying to me, "Come on, Ken, you know you can't walk across the Arctic like this. You'll have to learn sooner or later to drive from behind rather than lead from the front." Eventually I did, though I don't rate myself a masterful sledge driver by any manner of means.'

As spring crept into summer, with its eternal, glaring daylight, the going became harder, with more and more open leads to find their way through. Everything was wet with snow – a watery quagmire, the ice increasingly mushy, their sleeping bags perpetually damp, their rucksacks soaked through, the tents a soggy mess. There was the growing worry of whether they could find a sufficiently large and solid floe on which to drift through the summer into the following autumn when, once again, they would be able to resume their progress. They had sledged 1180 miles over the polar pack ice – further from land than any other polar traveller; at the same time they had managed to carry out some scientific work. Each day Fritz had contrived to measure the floe thickness and snow density. They had seen the tracks of the Arctic fox and polar bear, but they had actually seen only twelve seals, four gulls, a little auk, a flight of duck and two long-tailed jaegers in the five months they had spent in this icy wilderness. Some Arctic explorers had theorised that you could survive by hunting in the Arctic Ocean, but Wally's team would have gone very hungry on what they had observed and certainly could not have fed the dogs!

This was becoming a disturbingly relevant topic, for the little radio – their only link with the outside world – had developed a fault. Without it they would be unable to guide in the supply aircraft, and it was unlikely that they could be found without an exact fix on their location. After two days' nerve-wracking struggle they managed to discover the fault, a broken wire coming in from the power source. A day later they had a glimpse of the sun through the clouds, made a fix and were able to radio their position.

They had now reached their destination for the summer, a large and solid-looking floe that seemed as if it would survive both the long summer melt and any battering the seas might give it. On July 12th a Canadian Air Force Hercules brought their supplies for the summer – food, fuel, replacement clothing, tentage and scientific instruments for Fritz Koerner's research programme. For a few weeks, until the ice hardened up once again, they could relax, relying on the constant drift of the current to carry them towards the Pole. Although relatively warm, with the temperature just above freezing, it was misty, miserable, very humid and they saw the sun through a screen of drizzle. There was always some tension. Would the floe survive through the summer? It had already split once, only three hundred feet from the little village of tents the press had named Meltville. On another day, one of the very few fine, cloudless days they had, their floe was invaded by a polar bear and its two cubs. Alerted by the yapping and snarling of the dogs, they had no choice but to kill the bears before the dogs were killed or scattered. Ken Hedges had grabbed a rifle, but it jammed and it was Wally who shot the bear and cubs. They were all shocked by the incident but Ken particularly so, both because of the failure of his rifle and also by the necessity for killing these magnificent, beautiful yet deadly animals.

They were still behind schedule and Wally wanted to start out again as early as possible to try to make some more progress across the floes before the arrival of winter. When they set out on September 4th, the temperature had dropped to below freezing – but only just. The surface of the slushy snow covering the ice was frozen into a thin crust which broke at almost every step and they sank through to their knees into the icy, soggy mush. At the cost of constant, exhausting effort they were making only two miles or so a day. Everything was wet and their way was forever barred by open leads between the floes. Inevitably, tempers were short and the stress within the group came closer and closer to the surface. After Fritz had a blazing row with Ken over tactics, he and Wally talked over the problem:

It was like a marriage that had failed in spite of efforts on both sides to make a go of it

'Once again, we found ourselves talking about the relationship between Ken and the rest of the party – which was clearly strained. The incompatibility did not manifest itself in dramatic outbursts but in a deep and nagging disapproval of each other's ideas and ideals. It was like a marriage that had failed in spite of efforts on both sides to make a go of it. The big question, not unlike the married couple's, was whether to put an end to the relationship before the winter set in [Ken could be sent out on a light aircraft which would attempt to land about September 25th to bring in some delicate scientific instruments], or whether out of respect for the institution of "the polar expedition" (as with couples who respect the institution of matrimony), we should stick it out to the end. Both Allan and Fritz felt Ken should be sent out. To Ken, a devout man, forgiveness and reconciliation were not only basic principles of his faith but a solution he considered dignified and honourable. While I agreed with Allan and Fritz, I felt bound as leader of the expedition to give Ken the opportunity to see the expedition through to the end for his own sake and for the sake of those whom, in a sense, he represented.'

At least three of them could, on occasion, talk it out among themselves with a sense of unity, but it must have been much more difficult for Ken who inevitably felt totally isolated and must have sensed that the others were talking behind his back.

But the struggle went on; their way was now barred by a strip of mush ice about two hundred feet wide at its narrowest point. It was a jumble of everything from ten-foot blocks to a porridge-like mush, held together only by the pressure of the two big floes on either side. The nightmare thought was of being caught in the middle of the strip when the pressure from the two floes was released. Should they drift apart only a few feet, the larger blocks would capsize and plunge, the mush would dissipate and dogs, sledges and men would be struggling in the heaving, tumbling sea. Wally and Fritz had gone ahead to find a way over the strip, but it was too wide, too chaotic. Discouraged, they returned to be confronted by an even greater crisis.

Allan was sitting, huddled in the snow, beside his sledge, his face contorted in agony. The previous day he had pulled a muscle in his back, but this was something which was obviously very much worse. He was unable to move and in extreme pain. Quickly, they erected a tent and somehow manoeuvred him into it. Ken diagnosed that Allan had either badly slipped a disc or torn a muscle and gave him a morphine injection. Whichever it was, it was essential to get him evacuated as soon as possible, but before that could be done they had to find somewhere safer to camp. They were on a very small floe that was already beginning to break up. Fritz and Wally went back to search for the floe on which they had spent the summer and had left only a few days before. It was only a few miles away and when they returned Ken reported that Allan's condition had not improved. Wally sent out the first news of the accident stating: 'If no miraculous recovery within next few days, will have to ask ARL to fly him out in the Cessna that brings the geophysical equipment. Need with the utmost urgency a replacement ex-Falkland Islands Dependency or ex-British Antarctic Survey geophysicist. Renner first choice.'

After a few days' rest, Allan Gill was fit enough to be moved and they carried him, carefully strapped onto a sledge, back to the big floe on which they had spent the summer. But in these few days, as so often happens after any catastrophe, they were beginning to reassess the situation. Allan was feeling a little bit better. They were not going to be able to move now until after the winter. He could not come to much harm resting in their winter quarters and, if he did recover, he would be able to complete the journey with them after all. Wally and Fritz even concocted some other schemes. They had been trying to hand over their winter quarters, complete, to another research organisation, so that their scientific work could be carried on through the following summer. Should Allan be unfit to travel, he could stay on at the winter hut to run the scientific programme with Ken Hedges to look after him. This would free Wally and Fritz for their dash to Spitsbergen. Plans floated back and forth in their tiny microcosm but they were also linked to the big, outside world, were dependent on it for supplies and the winter hut, and unfortunately had already involved their Committee, 6000 miles away in London, in the decision-making.

Wally now told Ken Hedges that they had decided that Allan would stay for the winter; there was no need for him to be lifted out straight away, but Ken thought differently, pointing out that Allan needed hospital treatment if he were not to risk suffering for years from a weak back. He could even be crippled for life. Ken was not moved by Allan's plea that he was prepared to take the risk and stated that if Wally ignored his advice he would have no other choice but to resign from the expedition, though he would remain with Allan to care for him as long as he was on the ice.

It was a stalemate. It was also another crisis both for the expedition and for Ken. This was the first occasion when his own expertise had been needed, and the other three had rejected it. One can sympathise with and understand both stances. As so often happens, there was no clearly right course to take, but it certainly accentuated the split within the expedition still further. If Ken had felt isolated before, it was very much worse now. Ken gave Wally his medical report on Allan, addressed to the Commandant of the Royal Army Medical Corps, and asked him to send it out. The following day Wally sent out his own assessment of the situation to the Committee, recommending that Allan Gill should be allowed to stay through the winter and be evacuated the following spring, should this still be necessary. A few days went by and then the fatal message arrived: 'While recognising Allan's great wish to winter, we regretfully decided that on medical grounds and to enable earliest possible start next spring, he must, repeat must, be evacuated in Phipps' 'plane. A three-man party is regarded as the minimum acceptable risk, therefore Wally, Ken and Fritz to winter and complete journey.'

Wally was furious. In effect, the Committee, sitting in a cosy London office all those thousands of miles away, were taking over the command of the expedition and making operational decisions over his head. Confronted by the two conflicting opinions on the fitness of a member of the team, the Committee had to act as arbiter and had no real choice but to back the medical opinion, inevitably supported by the Commandant of the RAMC, against the opinion of the expedition leader. Wally described the impact their judgement made on him:

'Ken was with me at the time the message came through. I read it out with difficulty for the words stuck in my throat... Ken went back ahead of me to the tent where Allan and Fritz were having a brew; I walked around for a while trying to get a grip on what I suppose was a mixture of anger and the deepest personal sympathy for my old sledging companion. I crawled through the tent and squatted on a box at the foot of Ken's bed. Allan and Fritz looked up expectantly.

"You've shot your bolt, mate. They want you out."'

It is not surprising that Wally exploded that night over the radio to Squadron-Leader Freddie Church, their communications linkman at Point Barrow. They used to chat for half an hour each day on a seldom-used frequency, and Wally had come to treat it as a direct, private conversation which must have been an important therapeutic release for him. Now, speaking about the Committee's decision, Wally said into the microphone, 'They don't know what the bloody hell they are talking about.' It was the exasperated outburst that any of us might have made to a close friend, knowing that it would go no further. But Peter Dunn, the *Sunday Times* correspondent who was covering the story, had made quite sure that he, also, was in the little radio shack that day. Freddie Church had had no chance to warm Wally of this and Peter Dunn heard the entire outburst. Freddie tried to persuade Peter Dunn that this was confidential, that it could destroy Wally's career if his remarks were publicised, but Dunn, the newsman, was adamant. Someone else could have been listening in to the conversation and to protect himself with his own paper he had to send the story out. He did so, with an embargo that it should not be published without his clearance. The cable arrived in London on the Monday, when the staff of Sunday papers take a rest day. But the duty sub-editor, recognising it was hot news, passed it on to *The Times* – but left out Peter Dunn's embargo. The newsdesk of *The Times* immediately saw it as a headline scoop and had it set up for the following day's paper. It was only just before going to print that editor, William Rees-Mogg, felt he should warn Wally's Committee what he was doing. He 'phoned Sir Miles Clifford first, but he was out of the country. He then 'phoned Sir Vivian Fuchs, the deputy Chairman. Fuchs was appalled that this had been leaked to the press and even threatened *The Times* with an injunction, but Rees-Mogg responded, quoting their right to publish anything they wanted about the expedition – and did so. Up to this moment the rest of the media had taken comparatively little interest in the expedition but now, with a big juicy scandal, they seized upon the story, besieging Fuchs and the other members of the Committee for an explanation. Caught off-balance, anxious to justify their actions, the Committee muttered about Wally Herbert suffering from 'winteritis' – a condition of isolation and stress that can cloud judgement and become a danger to all concerned.

But the expedition had to go on. They were now due to have an air drop of the prefabricated hut and all their supplies for the winter. This came in on time. But Wally was determined to keep Allan with them if he possibly could and luckily for him the smooth, new ice around them was undoubtedly on the thin side for a light 'plane to land. Very soon it would be too dark. So ice and weather conditions collaborated to prevent the 'plane landing and, in the meantime, Allan Gill was showing positive signs of recovery, hobbling around the camp and doing his best to help in the day-to-day work wherever he could. The autumn progress had been negligible. In the eight days they had been moving they had covered only six and a half miles. They were now 240 miles short of the scheduled wintering place, but even so they set to and started to prepare themselves for the winter, assembling the little hut, building primitive furniture and preparing the various scientific programmes they planned

Below A Canadian Air Force 'plane makes a low pass overhead after an airdrop of winter supplies.

to pursue – while the floe on which they were living would, they hoped, drift steadily closer to the North Pole.

They were faced with six months of immobility, much of the time in total darkness, squeezed into a tiny hut whose floor space was about fifteen feet square. Each man had his own little area. Ken built a nook of shelves around his bed, with a blanket to give himself some privacy; he was to disappear behind it, into his own little world, for days on end, coming out only to relieve his bodily functions. Wally built a packing-case desk on which he could work on his reports and the book he would have to produce at the end of the expedition, while Fritz had an area devoted to his scientific work. Allan opted for sleeping throughout the winter outside in one of the tents, where it was bitterly cold, but at least he could get away from the tension of that tiny hut.

There was external stress as well. On November 20th, when they were plunged in perpetual darkness, the floe cracked only 250 feet from the hut, between them and some of the supply dumps they had laid out scattered over the floe. They could hear the cracking and groaning of the ice, interspersed with staccato cracks, as the floes jostled and ground against each other in the black night. Picking their way across their floe by the light of hurricane lanterns, they saw that what had been a substantial island was now reduced to one half a mile long and only 800 feet wide. Wally and Fritz set out with dog teams and found a more substantial home for the rest of the winter about two miles away. The next few days were spent in relaying their twenty-seven tons of food, fuel, other supplies and, finally, the prefabricated hut to the site of their new home, all this in the dark, in temperatures of around -35°C.

And then back to the routine of scientific work for ten hours a day – of cooking and washing up, of reading and sleeping, all in the unchanging dark and cold. Added to the stress of their uneven relationship was the worry of whether they would be able to complete their journey at all; they were so far behind their schedule, so far from the North Pole, let alone from Spitsbergen. Allan Gill exercised quietly, slowly building up his mobility and strengthening his back. He was determined to finish the course if he possibly could. Ken Hedges, isolated and now in a profound depression created by a near-insufferable situation, was still equally determined to complete the expedition.

At this stage Fritz Koerner was probably the least unhappy member, for he was totally involved in a massive scientific programme, too extensive for one man to carry out. He was working flat out throughout the winter, going out in all weathers to check his instruments, exercising at the same time both himself and his dog team, working for hours over his figures and snatching the minimum of sleep.

They had relied on drifting steadily towards the Pole, but their star shots showed that the progress was more of an erratic zigzag. Yet through the winter they did slowly drift closer to their goal. And, as the winter slipped by, they started preparing for their journey the following spring. Wally built a snow house out of blocks in which each one of them worked on his own new sledge which had been dropped in with all the other supplies, strengthening the framework, sewing harnesses and making sure that everything was ready for their dash to Spitsbergen.

ABOVE Wally Herbert in his corner of the expedition's cramped winter quarters made daily contact with Squadron-Leader Freddie Church at Point Barrow.

There were still plans to fly Allan Gill out in the early spring and Geoff Renner had been brought to Point Barrow to replace him. Wally was quietly determined, however, to hang on to Allan if he possibly could. He wanted to set out from his winter quarters on February 25th, still in the dark and cold of winter, to give them the maximum time to make the journey all the way to Spitsbergen. They were almost ready to go, the sledges part-packed on the 24th, when the seas decided for them. Suddenly the ice around them began to erupt in a terrifying icequake, splitting and breaking all around the hut. It was time to get out – fast. They finished packing, scrambled over opening leads to rescue dogs and loads and, still in the dark in temperatures of around -43°C, set out on the last, and by far the longest, leg of their journey. They were carrying not only the food and supplies they were going to need in the next few months but also a huge load of scientific instruments and specimens, the fruits of Fritz Koerner's work from the previous summer and all that winter.

The journey to the Pole was even more fierce than the previous year. It was bitterly cold, with temperatures down to -50°C. Even in the depths of winter the ice was no less active, heaving into rippling pressure ridges, breaking up into leads of black waters – even blacker than the sky above. They froze over in moments, but there was always the fear of the fresh ice breaking. They kept going for eight hours at a time; that was as much as they could manage in the bitter cold. Sometimes they only made a couple of miles, the broken ice was so bad. And it went on day after day, as they slowly clawed their way towards the Pole. They saw little of each other during the day. It was usually

Fritz out in front, with Wally taking up the rear to give Ken, or anyone else, a helping hand. Allan Gill was usually just behind Fritz and would slip into the lead whenever he had a chance, though he was not meant to go out in front. Ken was nearly always in third position, infinitely methodical and careful in the way he packed his sledge, but travelling through the day in what seemed to Fritz a dream.

There were moments of great beauty as well as excitement and danger. Wally wrote: 'On 12th March we saw the sun for the first time since 6th October. It was a blood-red, beautiful sight after five months and seven days – a living, pulsating thing it seemed to be, slowly drifting on a sea stained red with the blood it released.'

A few days later Wally, bringing up the rear, realised that he was being followed by a polar bear. His rifle was not loaded and the few rounds of ammunition he always carried were in the pocket of an anorak stuffed into the front of the sledge out of his reach. The bear was rapidly overtaking the sledge as Wally crawled along the top, screaming at the dogs to keep going, and dug out the anorak. By the time he had loaded his rifle the bear was only 150 feet away; he raised the rifle and pulled the trigger, but it had jammed in the cold. The bear was closing fast. In desperation Wally slapped the bolt with the palm of his hand; the rifle fired, sending a shot up into the air, but it was enough to alarm the bear which ambled away behind some ice blocks. This was just a few miles from the Pole.

Allan was still due to be flown out once a 'plane could land near them; this was still a constant course of irritation within the party and Fritz, who was sharing a tent with Ken Hedges, had some blazing arguments on the subject. Not only was Wally trying to find every possible means of postponing a landing, but Fritz also had a feeling that Weldy Phipps, the pilot who was meant to fly in, was quietly conspiring to help Allan Gill remain with the crossing party by finding various excuses for not coming. And so, as the sun slowly crept up into the sky Allan who was by far the toughest and most attuned to this environment – in Wally's words 'the emotional anchor man of the party' – stayed on with the expedition.

On April 5th Wally calculated that they had, at last, reached the Pole. It looked like any other bit of ice, anywhere in the Arctic Ocean, but this was it – the very top of the world. Immediately Wally sent a message to the Queen to announce their achievement. And then, a few moments later, Allan Gill, who had also been calculating the results, poked his head into the tent to announce that he thought they might be seven miles short. There followed an exhausting hide and seek game in slow motion, as they tried to find this elusive point. It took them another twenty hours of hard sledging before they finally satisfied themselves that they had truly reached it. Wally described the moment:

'It had been an elusive spot to find and fix – the North Pole, where two separate sets of meridians meet and all directions are south. Trying to set foot upon it had been like trying to step on the shadow of a bird that was hovering overhead, for the surface across which we were moving was itself a moving surface on a planet that was spinning about an axis beneath our feet. We were dog tired and hungry. Too tired to celebrate our arrival on the summit of this super-mountain around which the sun circles almost as though stuck in a groove.'

ABOVE The traditional photograph at the North Pole, April 6th 1969, after some frantic sledging to establish the elusive exact spot.

One cannot help wondering if Cook or Peary hadn't fudged their calculations when standing exhausted in this featureless, shifting expanse of sea-borne ice some sixty years before. The Pole had, however, been reached overland the previous year, when Ralph Plaisted and his party drove their Skidoos from the region of Ellesmere Island, but then they had been flown back to the safety of land. That same summer of 1968, Roger Tufft, who had withdrawn from Wally's expedition, had joined up with Hugh and Myrtle Simpson, a husband and wife team who combined science with polar and mountain adventures. They had tried to reach the Pole on skis, hauling their sledges and carrying all their food with them to be independent of air drops. It was a simple, lightweight venture that had appealed to Roger. But the initial rough ice had been too difficult, their gear inadequate, and they had been forced to abandon their attempt.

Wally's team were undoubtedly on the Pole; they had spent twenty-four precious hours making sure. They put the camera on a tripod and took a delayed-action shot of themselves standing, statuesque in their furs, by a laden sledge and an unfurled Union Jack. The picture has a nostalgic, slightly sad quality about it. It could have been taken sixty years before; the furs, the sledge, the bearded frosted figures would have looked just the same.

The journey was by no means over but at least they were now making some fast times, the four sledges stretched out over several miles, following in each other's tracks, heading ever southwards towards Spitsbergen. It became something of a mad gallop. Fritz Koerner remembers:

'You'd make a frantic dash in the morning to get off first because whoever was off first led. It was quite childish really. It was a mad rush to pack. Allan and I would just bundle everything into a couple of tarpaulins, chuck them into the sledges and then go like hell to the other side of the first pressure ridge, where we would pack things a bit better and then tear off again, to make sure that we were first. Wally and Ken were much more methodical. Wally even had a special place for his ice axe, though I think Ken was the most efficient of all.

'Once out in front, you'd stay there all day. Allan wasn't meant to lead, because of his back, but every now and then he'd catch me up and he'd say, "Look, Uncle Ben's out of the way, what if I lead for a bit?" We called Ken Uncle Ben – the very fact that we had a different name for him showed that he was away from us. And I'd say, "Sure." And away he'd go.

'Then Wally would come up at the end of the day and he'd quietly say, "Allan led a bit, didn't he?" And I'd say, "How the bloody hell did you know?" "Oh, I noticed the tracks curling round the other set."'

They were all tired, underfed and stretched to the limit, both physically and mentally. It was a race with the summer melt, for they had to reach solid land before the southern edges of the pack ice began to break and drift off into the Atlantic. There were plenty of crises to test them still further. The tent Allan and Fritz were sharing was burnt down one day, when they left the Primus stove unattended. The tent could be patched up, but Allan's sleeping bag was badly damaged and most of his spare clothes destroyed. Ken Hedges very nearly lost his sledge and dogs when he tried to cross a wide lead. The others came up only just in time to rescue them. There was the constant threat of marauding polar bears, who became more numerous the further south they went. But the ice was very much smoother than it had been on the approach to the Pole and they were making good, fast progress. There were signs of land, an old tree trunk sticking out of an ice floe, sea shells and moss on the surface of the ice, an increase in bird life.

Then, on May 23rd, Wally saw some piled clouds on the distant horizon. They looked like the kind of clouds you would see above a mountain range. That evening he was able to pick out the exposed rocky peaks jutting up into the sky. They were very much at the end of their journey. But the ice floes were now beginning to break up, and there was a real risk of being swept out into the open sea before they could actually make a landfall. The frigate, HMS *Endurance*, had sailed up towards Spitsbergen to meet them and could always rescue them by helicopter, but this just would not have been the same. There now seemed little hope of reaching the shores of Spitsbergen, but there were some small islands just to the north and they decided to go for these.

No longer on the permanent pack ice, they were dodging from the haven of one small floe to the next, at the mercy of currents and wind, heading for Phipps Island, a little pile of barren rocks jutting out of the ice. To reach it they had to cross wide areas of broken mush ice, manoeuvring from ice block to ice block. It was probably the most dangerous moment of the entire journey. Wally described it:

'Our route back to the floe was cut off. The whole floating mass of ice rubble was simmering like some vast cauldron of stew. We rushed from one sledge to another as each in turn jammed in the pressure, or lurched as the ice which was supporting it relaxed or heaved; at one point my sledge turned completely turtle and ran awkwardly over a six-foot drop from one block of ice to another.'

They spent a frightening, uncomfortable part of a night on a tiny floe. They had failed to reach Phipps Island and were being swept to the north, but there was an even smaller island in the path of their drift. On May 29th they were close enough to make a dash across the broken mush ice to the island. Fritz stayed behind on the floe, to keep an eye on the camp, and Wally gestured Allan and Ken to make a dash for the land. Wally wrote: 'It was some moments before the full significance of what Allan and Ken had done got through to me and, when it did, it

BELOW Ken Hedges very nearly lost sledge and dogs in a wide lead.

was through a small chunk of granite Ken pressed into my hand. "Brought you a small bit of the island," he said.'

They had completed their crossing of the Arctic Ocean, without doubt one of the greatest and most exacting journeys ever made. They had been very dependent upon air support, but it is unlikely that they could have attempted the journey without it. In many ways, the stresses within the team and how each man somehow came through makes the achievement even more impressive. In the short period that the four had to wait for the helicopter to pick them up and take them back to that big, wide world, of receptions, press conferences and questions, Wally, as any leader would, desperately sought unity within the team, wanting the story of their achievement to have the weight and majesty it deserved as one of the great polar journeys of all time. There was a long and bitter argument over how much of their differences should be revealed but, finally, they all agreed to present a united front.

The helicopter from *Endurance* came sweeping in and hovered down on to their little ice floe. The captain of *Endurance* jumped out, shook hands with Wally and the rest of the team. The journey was over. The stress, depressions, despair and discomfort of the past fifteen months were now something of the past. In the wardroom of *Endurance* Ken was laughing and joking with the ship's officers, providing a fund of amusing stories from the past months, most of which for him had been a nightmare. Allan Gill was already thinking of his next trip out into the empty wastes of the Arctic, while Fritz was absorbed by the vast mass of work he had in front of him from his scientific observations during the journey.

And Wally – this journey represented six years of hard, grinding effort, of solitary work and responsibility, of endless obstacles, many of which had seemed insuperable at the time. He had overcome them all. He had been successful. But success is so very ephemeral and, for Wally, that success was tainted. Somehow, the achievement did not gain the recognition that he felt and I believe it most certainly did deserve.

In the early part of the century there was a huge, devouring interest in all things polar. The early polar explorers were international heroes whose names really were household words. In 1969, however, Wally Herbert's journey across the top of the earth gained scant attention. It was the time of the moon shots. Apollo XI had gone into orbit round the moon only a few days before Wally made his landfall; Neil Armstrong was the first man to set foot on the moon just a few weeks later. The media and the rest of the world, craning their necks into space and obsessed with fast-moving technology, hadn't time to follow the slow, laborious movement of four men with their dog teams, across the top of their own planet.

It was only in the New Year's Honours List for the new millennium that Wally Herbert's huge achievement has been publicly recognised with a well deserved knighthood. His journey remains the longest polar trek of all time.

FIFTEEN

The Last Great First

Round the World Non-Stop by Balloon

THE RACE WAS ON. It had started just before the first edition of *Quest for Adventure* was published in 1981, with an attempt by Maxie Anderson and Don Ida who set out from Luxor in Egypt and travelled 2800 miles before being forced to land near the village of Murchpur in India, after their canopy had sprung a leak. The circumnavigation was only completed in the spring of 1999, eighteen years later. Arguably this was the last of the great firsts, a challenge on the same scale as the first ascent of Everest or reaching the Poles.

The very concept of ballooning, of trusting one's life to a huge bag of gas or hot air and the vagaries of the winds, has a romance unequalled by any other adventurous activity. True, technology was to play an important part in eventual success, in the design of balloon and capsule, and with the use of satellite met. reports and communications. However, the final arbiter remained the pattern of the winds and the balloonists' ability to read them, and their only steering aid was to gain or lose height to try to catch the wind direction they sought.

The people involved were also interesting in their different ways. It is undoubtedly a rich person's sport – Anderson, Abruzzo, Branson and Fossett all fall into that bracket. But wealth was not an essential, as shown by the team who finally succeeded – Bertrand Piccard, a Swiss psychiatrist, and Brian Jones, an ex-Warrant Officer in the Royal Air Force.

As with all human advances it was an evolutionary process with each group learning from the experience of their predecessors. After *Double Eagle*, flown by Max Anderson, Ben Abruzzo and Larry Newman, made the first balloon crossing of the Atlantic, Abruzzo and Newman began to consider the greater challenge of the Pacific, crossing it with Ron Clark and Rocky Aoki in November 1981. They set out from Japan in a huge helium balloon on November 9th to land, four days later, on a wooded mountainside near Covello, California.

Up to this time all the long record-breaking flights had been made by helium balloons and although hot air balloonists were also stretching their limits they were still a long way behind in terms of performance. In 1980 their record distance was still only 480 miles. It was in 1986 that Per Lindstrand, a balloonist from Sweden, 'phoned Richard Branson, who had just captured the Blue Riband for his speed boat crossing of the Atlantic, to suggest he undertook an even greater challenge, the first crossing

RIGHT Undeterred, Bertrand Piccard launched Breitling Orbiter 3 on March 1st, even though he had no real chance of catching up with the Cable & Wireless balloon.

BREIT
ORBITER

of the Atlantic in a hot air balloon. This would mean flying five times further than anyone had flown a hot air balloon before and staying in the air three times longer.

Lindstrand, who had been a fighter pilot in the Swedish Air Force, had stumbled across ballooning as a result of a ski accident that left him with a leg in plaster and grounded from flying. He bet his fellow officers that, if he couldn't walk in the next month, he'd fly across the airfield. To win the bet he stitched together some surplus parachute canopies, welded a frame and some burners and put together his first hot air balloon, which he duly flew over the airfield. It triggered a career both as a balloonist and balloon manufacturer, based initially in Ireland then moving to Oswestry in England. He was planning to build the biggest hot air balloon ever to carry all the fuel needed for the burners and then to fly at 30,000 feet to use the jet stream to blast them across the Atlantic.

Branson was intrigued, commenting:

'As I studied Per's proposal, I realised with amazement that this vast balloon, a huge ungainly thing which would swallow the Royal Albert Hall without showing a bulge, was actually intended to cross the Atlantic Ocean in far less time than our *Atlantic Challenger* boat with its 4000-horsepower engine. Per reckoned on a flying time of under two days, with an average speed of 90 knots compared with the boat's speed of just under 40 knots. It would be like driving along in the fast lane of the motorway only to be overtaken by the Royal Albert Hall travelling twice as fast.'

Branson invited Per to come and see him, confessed to finding it difficult to understand all the technical details of Per's plan, but asked him whether he had any children. On learning that he did, Branson stood up shook him by the hand and told him, 'I'll come, but I'd better learn how to fly one of these things first.'

It was to be the start of a long partnership. Richard Branson is undoubtedly an adventurer. An entrepreneurial and innovative businessman, happy to take risks with scant regard for convention, he is certainly the most colourful and arguably the most engaging of all the post-war entrepreneurs. He came from a close-knit, loving and reasonably comfortably-off family background but had a difficult schooling because of his dyslexia. His start as a college drop-out selling cut-price tapes led to the founding of his company, Virgin Records. This was followed by his expansion into so many different fields, most famously Virgin Atlantic Airways, that led to his David and Goliath battle with British Airways. He undoubtedly enjoys his high profile, as a showman delighting in the razzmatazz of show business, and is happy to use his wealth to pursue adventurous projects that attract him. These are of the record-breaking kind: winning the Blue Riband on the Atlantic and being first to cross the Atlantic in a hot air balloon. They were also adventures that he could take part in at a low skill level and ones that would offer a positive commercial advantage. What better advertising hoarding could you get than a giant balloon?

On the Atlantic crossing Chay Blyth had been skipper; now Per Lindstrand was in charge. Branson did his best to get fit and learn the basics but this was within the frame of a demanding business life of meetings, deals and financial crises. The miracle was that he had the energy and drive to pursue these external adventures and even get his balloon licence after a week's intensive course in Spain.

All too often there seems to be an element of the unexpected, almost chaos, in everything to do with ballooning. Perhaps, in part, it is the nature of the sport itself, of trusting this canopy of heated air to the whims of the weather. At take off the balloon, still anchored to the ground like a gigantic Gulliver tied down by Lilliputians, is vulnerable to every breath of wind. Every return to earth is a crash landing, once again hostage to the force of the wind.

The take off in Maine, on July 1st 1987, was no exception. The wind was building up as Branson and Lindstrand climbed aboard. Inside the womb-like capsule, they were unaware that in the launch one of the tethering cables had caught round two of their propane fuel tanks and had torn them off as the balloon bucked in the wind. Freed of the weight, the balloon tore even harder at the remaining cables and shot into the sky trailing a couple of cables with bags holding 400 pounds of sand still attached.

Like it or not, their voyage had started. Per had to climb out onto the gondola to cut the bags free as they soared into the sky towards the jet stream. Soon they were being carried along at over 100 miles per hour, towards the dawn. Except for one storm their journey was fast and furious all the way across the Atlantic, reaching speeds of a 160 miles per hour, although in the gondola there was little sensation of movement. They were borne along in the racing mass of air.

It took them just twenty-nine hours to cross the Atlantic to the coast of Northern Ireland. The challenge then was to land safely and the very speed of their crossing posed a problem for they still had three full tanks of fuel. Per wanted to get rid of these before making a landing and therefore turned off the burners in order to descend and find an empty field in which to dump the tanks. Unfortunately, an eddy of wind caught them and drove them down to hit the ground while still travelling at around thirty-five miles per hour. They were dragged bouncing across the field and in the process lost all their fuel canisters and radio antenna. Then, with the loss of weight, they were catapulted back into the sky. They narrowly missed hitting a house and some power lines, had just one small reserve fuel tank left and the gondola was spinning like a top, thus closing down the mouth of the balloon so the burners could no longer heat the air inside. They had lost all their power and were in semi-darkness inside the gondola. It was chaos.

Deprived of the heat from the burners, the balloon was now falling. Branson climbed out of the hatch and with his knife hacked at the cable that had snagged causing the gondola to spin. The balloon was just 300 feet above the ground. It was at last stable but travelling fast because of the wind.

'I'll try to put her down on the shore,' shouted Lindstrand.

But as they dropped through the thick grey cloud they saw with horror that they had already cleared Northern Ireland and were heading out over a storm-wracked Irish Sea. Lindstrand was trying to juggle between bursts of heat from the burners and releasing hot air from the top of the balloon to manage a controlled descent. Branson had put on his life jacket and collected their rubber dinghy which was attached to him by a cord. Per had been too busy trying to control the balloon even to get his life jacket on.

They hit the sea and were being hauled, bouncing over the waves with the capsule on its side. It was time to separate from the balloon. This was a matter of pulling the lever that activated explosive charges in the retaining bolts that would free the gondola from the cables leading up to the balloon. But this was easier said than done as they were being hurled all over the place and couldn't reach the lever. At last Per managed to get there and heaved on the red lever. Nothing happened. The charge had failed.

'Get out, Richard,' Per shouted. 'We've got to get the hell out of this.'

Per was out first, squeezing up through the hatchway, followed by Branson. They were being towed through the bucking black angry waves by the canopy of the balloon acting like a giant chute in the wind. Clinging onto the cables on top of the angled gondola, buffeted by the wind, drenched in spray, it was a terrifying, out-of-control situation. A bigger gust started to lift them.

'We've got to jump,' shouted Per and leapt for the sea. The gondola immediately bucked higher with the loss of his weight. Branson froze as the raging sea dropped away from him. He was quickly too high to jump.

Per was down in the ocean without a life jacket or dinghy and Branson was in the gondola, rocketing up into the sky, with all too little knowledge of how to bring it back down again. In their fast flight across the Atlantic, Per had done most of the flying. Branson describes his predicament:

'I climbed back into the capsule. It was now the right way up and I felt reassured to see the screens and controls the way they had been as we crossed the Atlantic. I ran through the options: I could parachute into the sea, where nobody would be likely to find me and I could drown; or I could sail up into the darkening sky and try a night landing, should I be lucky enough to reach land. I picked up the microphone, but the radio was still dead. I had no contact with the outside world.'

It was worse for Per as he watched the balloon vanish into the cloud. Several miles from shore, his chances of swimming to land were minimal, as were his chances of being spotted by a passing boat or 'plane – a swimmer in rough seas is barely visible from a distance. Fortunately Per was a strong swimmer, since his father had made him swim daily, winter and summer, in the cold lakes of Sweden. He has a fair amount of body fat and, perhaps most important of all, a sanguine resilient nature. This was just one more crisis to come through.

Branson's first reaction was to parachute. He even climbed out of the gondola and prepared to jump, but at the last minute decided against it. The last time he had jumped had been with other sky-divers. He had pulled the wrong release and had jettisoned his main chute. One of the other divers had pulled the reserve chute for him. He was now on his own in the cloud, 8000 feet above the sea. And even if he managed to get down, what then? He could well drown.

He changed his mind and resolved to keep flying. He reckoned he had about thirty minutes of fuel left. Something might happen. Back in the gondola he took off the parachute, joggled the burners on and off to make a smooth descent and peered through the porthole into the opaque cloud. At last he came out of the cloud, saw storm-flecked waves beneath him, but he also picked out a helicopter.

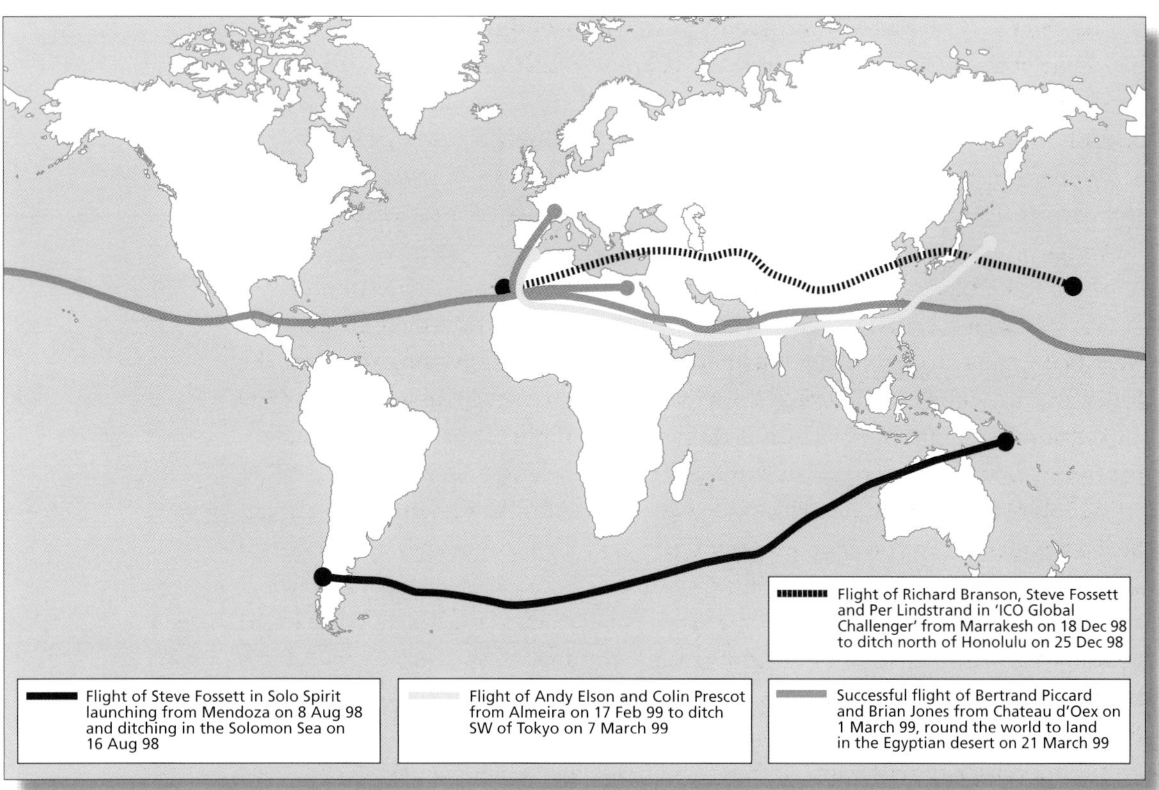

ABOVE Routes of round-the-world balloonists.

He got the balloon down, this time made his jump and a few minutes later was hauled out of the sea. A British frigate, HMS *Argonaut*, just happened to be in the area with a helicopter in the air. But where was Per? He spent altogether two hours in the bitterly cold sea before being picked up by a couple of youngsters in an inflatable, guided in by the helicopter whose lifting winch had jammed. The Atlantic crossing had been a superb achievement but they had both been very very lucky to survive.

But the risk game is addictive. Just two years later, in 1988, they were contemplating the inevitable next challenge – to cross the Pacific by hot air balloon. Once again there were false starts. Their first attempt from Japan in 1989 ended in farce when the balloon fabric, which had been laid out on the ground prior to inflation, delaminated with a night's frost. They returned in 1991 and had an eventful, nail-biting flight. They had a good take off but the winds of the jet stream were so strong they had difficulty in pushing up into it, their huge canopy being snatched by the wind and trailing out in front of them. It was as if they were bumping up against a solid ceiling of moving air. Then, with the balloon accelerating as if hauled by a thousand wild horses ahead of the gondola, which was tilted on its side, suddenly they were part of the jet stream, travelling at the same speed as the racing air, at peace with the elements.

But not for long. It was time to drop their first empty fuel tank. They descended out of the jet stream. Per pushed the button and suddenly the capsule lurched sideways to an angle of about fifteen degrees to the horizon. Could some of the cables have parted? They had a video camera that looked straight down and, re-running it,

Branson saw that instead of just one empty canister falling, there were three. They had jettisoned two full canisters, the result of faulty wiring on the explosive bolts and had lost half their fuel only 1000 miles into their flight.

But they had a more immediate problem. With the sudden loss of weight the balloon was careering out of control upwards. They must stop its climb as it approached 42,000 feet, as this was the ceiling for their pressurised cabin. Higher than that and the windows could burst out, the instant decompression killing them in seconds. They stabilised at 42,500 feet, and edged back down to a safer altitude.

Per, exhausted, cat-napped on the floor, leaving Richard in charge, with the challenging task of keeping the huge balloon in the narrow corridor of the jet stream's aerial travelator.

'Even at this amazing speed, it still takes an hour to fly 200 miles and we had six thousand of them to fly. I tried not to be daunted by the length of the journey ahead, but concentrated on each fifteen minute section. I was desperately trying not to fall asleep. My head kept dropping forward and I pinched myself to keep awake. I suddenly saw an eerie light on the glass dome above us. I looked up and marvelled at it: it was white and orange and flickering. Then I yelled: it was fire. I squinted at it and realised that burning lumps of propane were tumbling all around the glass dome, just missing it.'

Per reacted quickly, telling Richard to gain height so that the combination of extreme cold and lack of oxygen would put out the fire. They took the balloon to 43,000 feet, well above the balloon's safety limit, before the fire died.

He is someone who is quick to criticise. I'd been brought up to look for the best in people

Their situation was still serious. The gondola remained tilted, they were above one of the emptiest stretches of the Pacific, a storm was raging below, there could be no question of ditching and they had lost half their fuel. They also lost radio contact for seven hours with their control centre at San José in California which had the vital information on weather patterns that would help them select the right height at which to fly.

At last, Branson got through. The support team had been getting desperate, envisaging the capsule ditched somewhere in the vast wastes of the world's largest ocean. Bob Rice, the flight director, was able to tell Branson that the jet stream they were riding at that moment was about to swing round to the west to take them back into the centre of the Pacific, but if they lost height to reach 18,000 feet, they should find another jet stream that was sweeping north-east toward the Arctic. This at least would take them to land, though much further north than they had originally planned, amid the cold mountain wilderness that guards the Pacific coast of Canada. Bob also gave them the news that the West was bombing Baghdad. The Gulf War had started.

They lost height, found the new jet stream and were swept with even greater speed towards the coast of America, crossing it after only thirty-six hours of flying time. But they were still not out of trouble. They were heading for a blizzard. They would have to cross the Rockies before they could hope to make a landing. Even when they were over relatively flat ground, it was covered in dense forest. They had to find a frozen lake on which to land. Per opened the hatch and Branson climbed out onto the top of the capsule in the bitter cold. It was snowing hard, but there wasn't a breath of wind as they were travelling with it. He could see the tops of the tall dark pines, like a thousand daggers pointed upwards, racing by beneath them. He took out the retaining pins on the explosive bolts holding the cables attached to the canopy and then remained on top to try and spy an open space on which to land. They were tearing further and further into the Arctic wildness, further away from any kind of help from the ground.

At last he saw a space ahead, a frozen lake. Branson climbed back into the capsule, Per cut the burners and they plummeted down, hitting the ice at around forty miles per hour. This time the explosive bolts worked. The envelope was carried by the wind out of sight over the dark wall of trees and the capsule skidded to a halt. They had crossed the Pacific and miraculously had survived. They even managed to raise Watson Lake Flight Services to tell them that they were sitting waiting to be picked up on a frozen lake in the middle of a forest – only to learn there were 800 lakes in the area.

While they waited for eight hours in a temperature of -60°F, Per was already proposing the next venture – to fly round the world non-stop. After all, they had crossed the Pacific, having lost two fuel tanks, and still had fuel to spare. Branson couldn't help wondering why he had entrusted Per with his life, reflecting on the narrow escapes they had had. They had been through so much together and yet there was a barrier between them:

'I knew that he had pushed the technological boundaries of balloon flying further forward than anyone, but it was sad that we hadn't developed a stronger bond with each other. I get close to most of the people that I spend a long time with. But Per is not a team player. He is a loner. He's often difficult to read. He is someone who is quick to criticise. I'd been brought up to look for the best in people. Per always seemed to find the worst.'

Per felt hurt by these comments, feeling that he had led and organised the team in his first company Thunder & Colt and then Lindstrand Balloons, which had not only built the balloons but had also provided ground control for all the flights that had captured so many records. He felt he was very much the taxi driver, the hired hand, delivering Richard Branson the fame and publicity that Per considered was Branson's principal drive.

I came to know Per in 1989 after the Atlantic crossing and just before that of the Pacific. I had become involved in a venture to fly in a balloon over Everest. It was the brainchild of Hasseeb Zafar, a London-based accountant who wanted to get into the sponsorship business. He examined all the potential adventure records that could be achieved and came up with this idea, the balloon being the perfect advertising hoarding for a company logo. He found a sponsor in Star Micronics, from Japan, the world's second largest computer printer company. He invited Per Lindstrand, as one of the world's most accomplished balloonists, to be the pilot and asked me to take part in the press conference to launch the venture. I was intrigued and couldn't resist the temptation to try to become involved and actually fly over the mountain I had climbed just a few years before.

It was planned for the autumn of 1989. I set aside the time, became involved in the logistic planning and even had a few balloon flights. It was suggested that I should learn to parachute but I have always had an instinctive fear of jumping and decided that jumping out of a balloon over Everest would lead to almost certain death so declined the invitation. Per had a try at climbing on the Bossons Glacier above Chamonix where we went for a publicity balloon flight over Mont Blanc. He discovered that he disliked climbing as much as I did the thought of sky-diving.

I enjoyed Per's company. He has a wry, if at times sharp, sense of humour and I could see that he would always be cool in a crisis, but I felt he was never fully committed to the project. When he insisted on postponing it until the spring of 1990, saying that preparations were not sufficiently far advanced, I decided to pull out. I had already taken on other projects in the spring but, perhaps more to the point, I had serious doubts about trusting myself to the basket of a balloon dangling below a thin envelope of heated air. I began to realise how little I knew about ballooning and, although Per would be doing all the flying, I still found the prospect frightening. I was discovering that I was a climber, not an all-round adventurer. The fact that I suspected, correctly as it turned out, that Per wanted to delay the flight to fit in with his plans to cross the Pacific with Branson also influenced me.

Leo Dickinson, a film-maker and ex-climber, who had taken to the air as a free-fall parachutist and had already been involved in ballooning, crossing the Annapurna range with the Australian, Chris Dewhirst, was delighted to take my place. In the short term my doubts were justified. The spring attempt was hindered by a revolution against the king of Nepal that led to the balloon being stuck in customs while Per waited impatiently at the Everest View Hotel close to their objective. By the time the balloon was at last cleared, he had lost patience and doubted whether the winds would ever be right for the attempt. Leo claims he was keen to have a go, even after Per had left for home, but they lacked a pilot prepared to fly and abandoned the attempt.

Leo, who has never lacked determination, persuaded Ian Smith, the UK managing director of Star Micronics, to stay with the project. He brought in a balloonist and engineer called Andy Elson to act as technician and reserve pilot who succeeded in raising the money in Australia for a second balloon so that the two balloons could film each other. This had always been Leo's scheme. Leo crewed with Chris Dewhirst, while the second balloon was flown by Andy Elson and Eric Jones, a long-time friend of Leo's who was both an outstanding solo climber and free-fall parachutist. This time, with a fully committed team and the benefit of what they had learnt the previous spring, they succeeded, though not without some narrow escapes. Andy Elson's burners went out three times when close to Everest and they started to plunge. They had to relight them each time using the flint strikers but then found that flame was so intense it was melting the fabric of the balloon. He had to coax the burners to give just enough heat to ease the balloon over the top of Everest, clearing it by about 1000 feet.

This all happened in 1991, ten months after the crossing of the Pacific. It is surprising how quickly adventurers forget the sense of fear and the discomforts they have suffered. It was not long before Richard Branson decided to join in the race to

ABOVE Flying over Everest, the balloons had drifted apart. Not wishing to lose the shot, Leo Dickinson montaged two pictures together to capture the moment when the burners in Andy Elson's balloon failed, threatening them with a disastrous crash into the South-West Face of Everest.

be first to fly round the world. There is no way he could have stood aside as the contestants began to line up. He named his balloon *Virgin Global Challenger* and could at least justify the costs as publicity for his Group.

But there was a pause. The world was plunging into recession and no one wanted to invest in ballooning. It wasn't until 1995 that the race got going with Branson being the first at the starting gate. He and Lindstrand decided to add a third pilot, Rory McCarthy, another successful businessman, who was a joint venture partner with the Virgin Group. He was a hang-glider pilot who had set an altitude record for hang gliding in 1984 by being dropped from a height of 36,700 feet from a balloon piloted by Lindstrand.

Branson planned to set off very early in the year from Marrakesh in Morocco, poised to catch the winter jet stream which he hoped would waft them across to Northern India, but the jet stream didn't materialise and they returned home without making a launch.

That same year, 1995, another contender emerged. Steve Fossett is a millionaire businessman, not so much an entrepreneur as a brilliant financier in the options market. In 1999 I met him in Colorado at a party hosted by Tim Cole, his flight director. He was on his way from Washington to Florida to take lessons in aerobatics, flying his own Cessna Citation, at $17,000,000, the fastest non-military jet on the market. Stocky and quiet, there was no side to him, no flamboyance. In a group he listened rather than held court, and yet there was a focused self-confidence.

I interviewed him at 6.00 a.m. the following morning over breakfast, before he took off for Florida. He had changed into a white shirt with captain's bars, symbol of the hours he had spent learning how to fly a sophisticated twin-engined jet and the image he wanted to project.

Fifty-three years old, born of middle-class parents in California and the second of three children, he had a happy and conventional upbringing, being taken back-packing by his father and then becoming a Scout. He was always very competitive, but wasn't attracted to team games. Average at school in academic studies, he just managed to get into Stamford and achieve his degree, before joining IBM as a systems engineer. He couldn't see himself getting to the top of IBM and so moved into the financial industry, joining Merril Lynch. His career then took off and after a few years he went independent, specialising in trading. He made a huge fortune. He told me:

'I was a natural for trading. I was never quite so good at being an employee in a big business organisation. I wasn't very good at pleasing people in office politics but it turns out that in trading I'm very competitive. You know, on the floor of the Exchange, competition is paramount. You try to be the fastest and the most aggressive – you must have seen scenes of people waving their arms aloft – so I could be very competitive but I could also be relaxed, work very, very quietly, very methodically. It's a theoretical business where our speciality is stock options and there are ways of valuing stock options so that you can determine, from your computer model, what you should pay, when they're available too cheap you buy them and when they're too expensive you sell them, and you work out spreading strategies to keep your exposure to market more or less neutral. So it's based on probabilities of success. If you reiterate that enough times it translates into an income. But using sound probability type approaches, that was compatible to me, plus the competitiveness.'

It's all very similar to playing the adventure game and he used the wealth he acquired to pursue individual competitive challenges. Unlike Richard Branson, who bought in the expertise to achieve his records, Fossett wanted to do it for himself. He used his wealth to put in place the necessary hardware and infra-structure and to speed the learning curve in the activity he chose, but this was aimed at achieving personal excellence. His list of achievements is impressive. He has swum the English Channel, taken part in the Iditarod Dogsled Race and the Iron Man Triathlon, skied from Aspen to Vale in a record 59 hours, 53 minutes and 30 seconds and taken part in the Twenty-Four Hours Le Mans Sports Car Race. He also attempted to climb Mount Everest, but had problems with the altitude, found it took too much time and perceived that he could only get to the top by being heavily reliant on others. He didn't repeat the attempt.

In 1990 he made a major decision to give his adventure sports first priority, devoting three-quarters of his time to them and keeping his business just ticking over, once again in contrast to Branson, who continues to expand his businesses and squeezes in his adventures when he can.

At first Fossett concentrated on sailing, breaking eight long-distance sailing records, including the fastest crossing of the Pacific, both with a crew and solo. He also raced, gaining a further eight race records. Fossett was always looking for challenges.

He had followed Dick Rutan's Earth Wind project to be the first man to fly non-stop round the world without refuelling, had thought about ballooning, but it wasn't until 1993 that he focused on it.

'I was in Paris, on my way to Le Mans to do some qualifying rounds when I passed a shop with some scarves in the window; one of them had pictures of the famous aviators of history – Lindbergh, Armstrong, Rutan and so on. So I started thinking about it and said, you know this stuff isn't as inaccessible as you think it is. And whoever makes it round the world first by balloon, they will have earned themselves a place in this pantheon of aviation. So just symbolically I bought this scarf and gave it to my wife.'

He didn't waste time. He bought a Rozier balloon from Cameron Balloons, on the grounds that they had a good track record, and started taking lessons, getting his licence that same summer. Rozier balloons are named after the pilot of the first manned balloon flight, Pilatre de Rozier, who conceived the idea of combining buoyant gases and hot air in hybrid balloons in the 1790s. He was also the first person to die in a balloon while trying to cross the English Channel. Workable designs relying on the de Rozier concept were not possible until recently. The top section of the main gas bag is filled with helium to provide a passive source of lifting power but when helium is cooled at night, it loses its buoyancy and the balloon sinks; when it overheats during the day, the balloon can rise uncontrollably. To provide a dynamic ballast system, a cone-shaped bag is inflated with air heated by burning propane or kerosene. Pilots can control the amount of fuel burned to maintain a steady altitude, or to seek altitudes with advantageous wind directions. Cameron Balloons covered the entire assembly with a lightweight shroud of aluminised film, which reduced the effects of solar heating and slowed nocturnal cooling. The gondola hung below.

Fossett decided to start by flying the Atlantic and invited an established balloonist, Tim Cole, to accompany him. It was a good choice. One of Fossett's secrets of success both in business and adventure has been his choice of colleagues and the way he has kept them with him. The flight went smoothly and immediately Fossett began planning his next venture. He succeeded, in 1995, in making the first solo crossing of the Pacific, flying from South Korea to Mendhem in Saskatchewan in 104 hours. He could have landed earlier but was determined to make sure he had the world distance record – not bad for someone who had been ballooning for just two years.

Part of his secret was to use a fairly low-tech unpressurised cabin and at the same time to have a superb back-up team. Tim Cole became his flight director and he chose the best specialists he could find, following their instructions in coaxing his craft from one weather system to the next on his way across the empty reaches of the Pacific.

By 1996 he felt ready to attempt the circumnavigation of the world. He set out from the Strato Bowl in South Dakota, a natural depression by the banks of a river, giving good protection from the wind. He was using a brand new balloon with a double envelope and solar panels for generating power, and a special tracking device for following the sun. As so often happened with all the contestants the pressure to get the new technology into use meant that there had been very little time for testing. It was a matter of trying it all out on the actual flight.

As Fossett gained altitude after take off, he discovered that Cameron Balloons had miscalculated the amount of inflation of the inner skin and as a result the outer skin was ripping, with splits appearing all over the surface. Nonetheless he kept flying above the biggest storm that had hit Washington that year. At this stage his solar panel tracking device failed which meant his batteries weren't being recharged. He ran out of power about 150 miles out to sea. This meant that he had no communication with his control centre although his GPS with independent batteries was still working.

He weighed up the risks of carrying on blind across the Atlantic with a damaged outer canopy and, not surprisingly, decided to turn back, but even this was not easy for he had to find the right wind to do so. He lost height to get a wind that took him into the Bay of Fundy, between Nova Scotia and New Brunswick. He described what happened.

'I had a hard time. The balloon wasn't performing well because of the shredded skin and at one point I couldn't stop it descending because the burners weren't powerful enough either. I went all the way from 15,000 feet to hit the water. Fortunately it was pretty calm and protected in there. I cut away two tanks to lighten the load and was able to take off to fly back to the coast of New Brunswick. I actually made a nice landing!'

The Virgin team meanwhile moved down to Marrakesh in December 1996 and were ready to fly on January 5th 1997. The night before take off Rory developed pneumonia and he was replaced by Alex Ritchie, who worked for Per Lindstrand. They also had a brand new, much bigger balloon which, as usual, would be test flown on the flight. The final preparations, as always, were fraught, coming to a crescendo as the huge canopy was inflated. The burners roared into action and the balloon, like a huge prehistoric monster straining at its tethers, finally lifted into the skies. They quickly discovered that the safety catches that locked the fuel tanks in place hadn't been removed so they would be unable to drop the tanks once empty. After crossing the Atlas Mountains, Per deliberately lost height in order to go outside and remove the offending safety catches but they were caught in a fierce down draught and could only regain height after throwing out all their ballast, spare food and propane. There was no question of being able to carry on and so they landed in Algeria. It was another abortive attempt but, like Fossett, they learned a great deal from the mistakes that had been made.

Fossett was in the air, once again on his own, just a few days later on January 14th, setting out this time from St Louis, Missouri. He crossed the Atlantic without incident and had intended to take a branch of the jet stream across the British Isles, Northern Europe and Russia, but he missed it and had no choice but to catch the sub-tropical one over Gibraltar, Algeria and Libya, the one that Branson was planning to use. It sounds a little like catching a series of connecting trains and is just about as unreliable! Fossett did not, however, have clearance to fly over China, even though ex-President Carter had tried to get permission for him. This meant skirting the Himalaya to the south and by the time he reached India he realised that he had insufficient fuel and therefore landed at Sultanpur on January 20th.

He had broken his own previous distance record, set over the Pacific, for the longest- ever balloon flight and had learnt a great deal on the way. Flying solo imposes considerable extra strains. He had an auto pilot which fired the burners to maintain a fixed height but it wasn't completely reliable, particularly in coping with sudden down draughts. Because his capsule wasn't pressurised he had to wear his oxygen mask at all times and since he didn't have a heater it became bitterly cold at night. The reason for this abstemious approach was that it reduced weight still further which meant he needed less fuel and consequently could use a smaller and more easily manageable balloon than the huge Virgin one that carried three people and had all the trimmings.

Meanwhile, another contender had come on the scene. Bertrand Piccard from Lausanne in Switzerland is a psychiatrist with a distinguished scientific and adventurous pedigree. His grandfather, Auguste Piccard, pioneered the development of pressurised cabins for high-altitude balloon flights. His work had a considerable influence on future aircraft design and eventually putting man into space. He then turned his attention to deep sea research, designing submersibles that could go deeper than ever before. In his lifetime he establish both height and depth records. His son

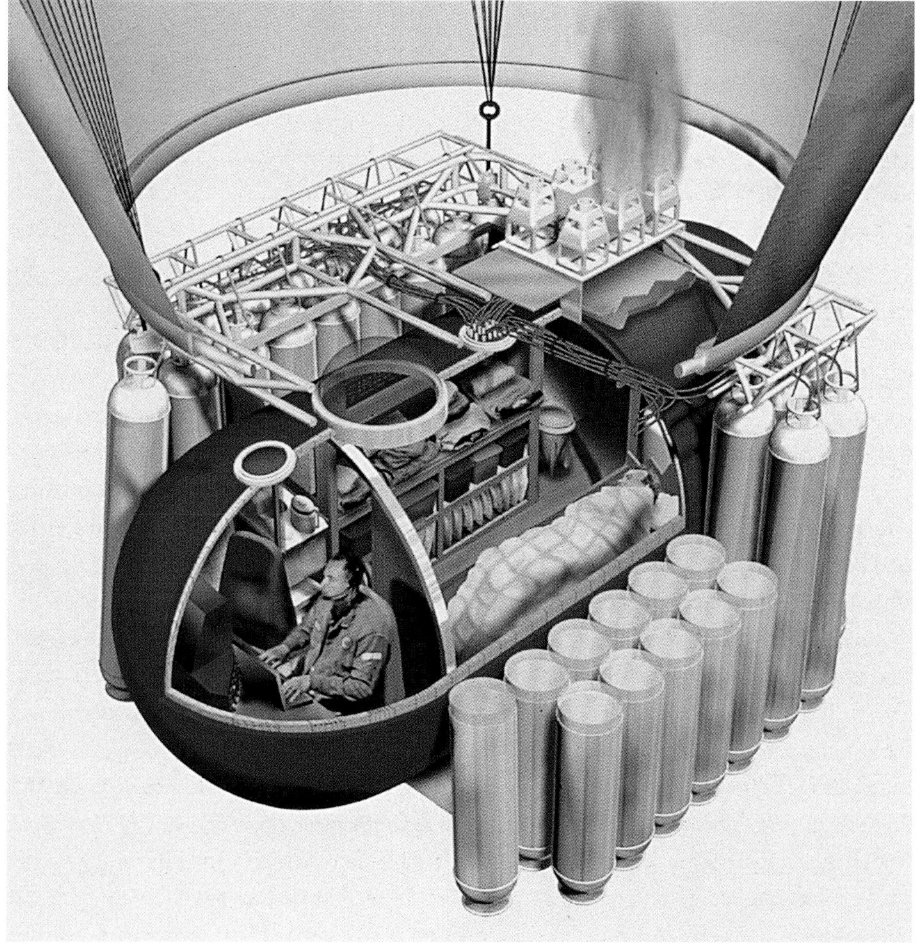

RIGHT Life in the capsule. About the size of a minivan, the 18-foot long Breitling Orbiter 3 capsule was designed to keep two pilots comfortable for four weeks. Jones (left) and Piccard took turns sleeping in one bunk, using the other for storage. The cabin, pressurised to fly as high as 40,000 feet, had an air recycling system that added oxygen and removed excess carbon dioxide with lithium hydroxide filters. Using the fuel controls the pilots could operate the burners, switch tanks, and jettison empty tanks from inside. Keels gave the capsule a flat base and would aid flotation in case of a water landing. Solar panels recharged batteries under the cockpit floor, powering equipment, lights, and a kettle in the kitchen.

Jacques, Bertrand's father, continued the deep sea research, reaching the bottom of the 36,000-foot Mariana Trench.

As a child Bertrand had met scientists and astronauts, particularly when his father had been based in Houston. His own appetite for adventure had taken him into hang gliding while studying at university. He took it to the limit, both in aerobatics and high-altitude flight. It was during this period that he came to know Wim Verstraeten, a Belgian professional balloonist whose balloon he used as a launch pad for his hang glider. It was at a dinner at the great ballooning centre of Chateau d'Oex, near Montreux in Switzerland, that he happened to sit with Verstraeten and some other balloonists and the conversation came round to the Trans-Atlantic Balloon Race that Cameron Balloons were organising. It was light-heartedly suggested that Bertrand, as a psychiatrist, would be an ideal partner for Wim, even though he had never before flown a balloon. The idea took root and Bertrand, still without a balloon licence, won the Trans-Atlantic balloon race in 1992 with Wim Verstraeten, sealing a strong friendship. Bertrand's greatest contribution to their success was to hypnotise Wim to help him sleep during the flight.

Circumnavigating the world by balloon was to someone like Bertrand Piccard an obvious next step and one that would place him in the record books alongside his father and grandfather. Unlike Branson and Fossett, he had no wealth of his own and it was a matter of finding a sponsor. In this he was extremely fortunate. He knew Theodore Schneider, owner and chief executive of Breitling, a Swiss company producing high-quality aviation chronometers. He had helped Bertrand in a small way with the Trans-Atlantic Balloon Race and in return Bertrand had displayed the Breitling logo. It took just one meeting to gain Breitling's sponsorship for the circumnavigation and the company proved to be loyal and immensely supportive over the three attempts.

The ballooning world is a small one and that of long-distance balloonists even smaller. Many of the individuals involved in the circumnavigation of the world became interlinked. This was particularly the case with Andy Elson. Perhaps the most colourful of all the contenders, Andy has an engineering background and ran a small specialist engineering company in Bristol. When he became interested in ballooning, he quickly started taking part in competitions, and he flew with Leo Dickinson to get good publicity pictures of the Star Micronics balloon which was to attempt the crossing of Everest. Leo was impressed, both by Andy's handling of the balloon and his readiness to try anything, and invited him to join the Everest flight.

Andy returned from this first great adventure to be greeted by disaster. His business partner had taken over his company and shortly after that his wife left him. He was faced with a huge debt but he was determined to pay all his creditors, so took tourists on balloon flights over Bath and Bristol, worked for the Bath City Council manufacturing wrought iron gates and did some work for Cameron Balloons on the engineering side. He test flew the burners that Steve Fossett was planning to use for his Pacific flight and happened to be in Korea just before Fossett took off, volunteering to help with the final preparations. As a result Fossett employed him in his back-up team for his first circumnavigation attempt. In addition he became more and more involved in the engineering of the burners and other support systems of the capsule for the Breitling attempt.

Cameron was offering Piccard a complete package, not only of Rozier balloon and capsule, but the control centre and management of the project in flight. Alan Noble, Cameron's marketing manager, was also the project director. Normally the burners are fuelled by propane but Andy saw advantages in using kerosene, which doesn't require pressurised cylinders. The kerosene can be stored in flexible bags. These were tucked away all over the capsule, even under the mattress of the bunk.

Piccard and Verstraeten were ready to fly from Chateau d'Oex in early 1997. Characteristically all the gear for the flight had been hurled in at the last minute, much of it piled onto the bunk, compressing a full fuel bag stowed beneath it, blowing a fuel valve and causing the kerosene to flood the interior of the capsule shortly after take off. They decided to ditch in the Mediterranean without delay.

Andy is arguably one of the most brilliant innovative designers in the balloon business, but he isn't a great organiser, has a quick temper and tends to keep all his plans in his head. In his tourist flight business he had gone into partnership with a quiet and very methodical ex-RAF load master called Brian Jones and he now brought Brian into the Breitling venture as project manager. In Brian's words, 'I was Andy's mother, nursemaid, secretary and general assistant.' They started working on *Breitling Orbiter 2* for the next season.

The season for the jet stream and long-distance ballooning in the northern hemisphere is from December into the spring. The *Virgin Global Challenger* team was back at Marrakesh in December 1997. Richard Branson was in a hurry to get going and, according to Per Lindstrand, insisted on inflating the balloon during the day when there was a greater risk of wind and thermal currents. This was by far the biggest of all the balloons. The wind caught it and away it went, months of work, money and effort with it. However, the team didn't abandon the attempt. They were able to recover the canopy but it was damaged beyond repair. Per's company, Lindstrand Balloons, worked flat out over the Christmas period to manufacture a new one and delivered it to Morocco by January 15th.

Meanwhile the race was hotting up. On December 31st, New Year's Eve, Steve Fossett launched his third attempt from St Louis and some hours later, Kevin Uliassi, an experienced balloonist but a newcomer to the circumnavigation race, lifted off from a 300-foot deep quarry just east of Chicago. Disaster struck Uliassi almost immediately when the device to release the helium failed, causing a build up of pressure that led to the balloon envelope splitting. He showed great skill in landing the damaged balloon. In the meantime Fossett was making good progress, sweeping across the Atlantic and then Europe. His control room's biggest problem was not so much the balloon as getting permissions to overfly the more sensitive countries. He still had no clearance to fly over Libya, and they therefore kept him in a more northerly trajectory, hoping to bring him further south to catch the sub-tropical jet stream once he had permission. But permission came too late. Fossett was too far to the north, flying over Romania in light winds. He continued over the Black Sea but it was becoming increasingly obvious that he would be unable to get further south, the heater in his capsule had failed and he was using up too much fuel. He finally made a landing on January 5th 1998 in the region of Krasnodar to the east of the Black Sea. Once again he had achieved a record distance flight but his end objective had eluded him.

Only a few days after Fossett's landing, Dick Rutan and Dave Melton set out from Albuquerque in New Mexico. Rutan's 1986 achievement in co-piloting the experimental Voyager 'plane round the world without refuelling had been one of the first things to inspire Fossett. Rutan himself now had less luck in his balloon and a similar failure to that of Kevin Uliassi forced him and his co-pilot to parachute out shortly after take off. Dave Melton was severely injured on landing. Back at Marrakesh the Virgin team were hit by tragedy. Alex Ritchie, the third pilot, was fatally injured in a parachuting accident, and they abandoned their bid for that year.

The final serious 1998 attempt was at the end of January when *Breitling Orbiter 2* made its launch from Chateau d'Oex. Andy Elson had been brought into the crew to join Bertrand Piccard and Wim Verstraeten. Apart from anything else, he was the only one who knew how all the new technology worked. The operational manuals were skimpy and all the real information was in his head.

Andy had already been trying to get a circumnavigation attempt of his own off the ground. He had been approached by a man called James Manclark, another millionaire, though not in the same league as Richard Branson or Steve Fossett. Manclark wanted, or needed, to find sponsorship to help cover the cost but hadn't succeeded in doing so. The project had been put on hold therefore and this presented Elson with a wonderful opportunity to make an attempt in a balloon capsule which he had helped to design yet without any financial risk or organisational hassles. His role was to be flight engineer with Piccard and Verstraeten as first and second pilots.

If you refuse to accept what life brings, you suffer, but if you accept your fate, you feel less pain

On their first attempt at launching the capsule was very nearly dropped from the crane lifting it into position after two of the cable terminations parted. Everything had to be checked and re-checked and they finally launched on January 28th 1998. One of the computers was down and Andy had to re-programme it. A fault developed in one of the hatches which meant that Andy had to make a spectacular abseil down the side of the capsule several thousand feet above the Mediterranean to hold it in place while the others re-secured it from the inside. More serious, they somehow managed to lose 1000 litres of fuel, a third of their total supply. Their only chance of success was to jump from jet stream to jet stream and have a fast circumnavigation. So they settled down to flying over Italy, Greece and Iran, wafted by the sub-tropical jet stream.

They still had no permission to overfly China, which meant that, like Fossett before them, they had to skirt round to the south, losing the jet stream. By the time they did get permission, it was too late. They were in the wrong position to pick up the jet stream again and it was obvious they did not have enough fuel to complete the voyage. But they decided to continue anyway, creeping at a low altitude across India's northern plains, getting as far as they could. Bertrand commented:

'I realised how important it is to accept whatever life brings. If we had fought against our situation, we would have suffered a lot: we might even have landed and gone home angry and despairing, blaming the entire world – especially China; but, by making the best of what happened to us, we were choosing not to suffer; if you refuse to accept what life brings, you suffer, but if you accept your fate, you feel less pain.'

A sound, almost Buddhist philosophy. They kept going until over Burma and landed just short of Rangoon. They had achieved an endurance record but hadn't flown as far as Steve Fossett.

Steve was already planning his next attempt. Rather than wait for the northern hemisphere season, he decided to try the southern hemisphere, which meant setting out in August of 1998. It was certainly much riskier, for not only was it mostly over water, but they were very empty waters as well. He set out from Mendoza in the foothills of the Argentinian Andes on August 7th, had problems with his burners over the Atlantic, but kept going. He didn't have much choice. He made the first crossing of the South Atlantic on August 11th, passing 118 miles to the south-east of Cape Town and then on in the jet stream across the huge empty wastes of the Indian Ocean to reach the north-western Australian coast on August 14th. He was carried over northern Australia, had plenty of fuel and it looked as if he had success in his grasp. There was just the Pacific to cross! Thunderstorms were forecast but they were meant to top out at around 29,000 feet and his control centre told him he would be able to fly over them.

They were drinking champagne to celebrate Steve's crossing of Australia when he hit a huge cumulo-nimbus cloud just off the coast of Australia over the Coral Sea. It was now dark. He couldn't avoid it, couldn't climb over it, was sucked into the boiling clouds and caught in a traumatic down draught. His variometer read a descent rate of 2500 feet per minute and he'd been told that you couldn't survive a descent rate on impact of more than 2000 feet per minute. He cut away two oxygen cylinders and two fuel tanks, but the catastrophic descent continued. He lay down on his bunk on the theory that in a horizontal position he'd have a better chance of survival. He watched the barometer. It continued to wind down. He expected to hit the sea at 1300 millibars, but he passed that, the pressure being so low, and it was 1004 millibars when he hit the water. It must have been like hitting concrete and he was knocked out.

When he became conscious, the capsule was upside down, full of acrid smoke, half full of water, tossing up and down with the waves. Something was burning. He had his head torch on so that he could see what he was doing and realised that the burners were incinerating the side of the Kevlar capsule. If he was to survive, he had to get out fast.

He grabbed his dinghy, got the hatch open and crawled out to find that there were flames all round the capsule and that the huge canopy of the balloon had collapsed on top of it. Somehow he had to get from under it before he was drowned or burnt to death. He inflated the dinghy and, lying on his back in it, used his arms and legs to push and pull himself through the water from under the canopy. In the struggle he lost his head torch. Then the only light was the glow of the flames.

At last he got clear of the canopy but a gust of wind took his dinghy away from it. By this time the flames had died down and he couldn't even see where to paddle back to. He was tossing in his tiny rubber dinghy in the middle of the Coral Sea without water, food or light. He assured me later that he had not been too concerned. He had sent out his May Day signal on the way down and was confident that someone would pick him up in due course. An Australian Navy refuelling ship eventually found him after twenty-three hours in the sea. Steve described his feelings both at the time of his catastrophic descent and while he waited to be picked up as one primarily of disappointment. He had seemed so close to success. It would take him several months to replace the balloon. It wasn't so much a matter of cost as time. He regarded the cost as comparatively modest. The southern hemisphere attempt, entirely funded by himself, cost around $400,000. He knew that Branson, Piccard and several others were preparing their next attempts that December when the northern hemisphere season started. It would have been difficult to get a new rig together in time.

ABOVE Fossett, Branson and Lindstrand. The take off was a combination of media razzmatazz and chaotic excitement.

He was still on the Australian Navy vessel when Richard Branson 'phoned him by satellite to commiserate and then propose that Steve joined his team. Fossett's first response was to say, 'Well Richard, it's all very dangerous. I don't know whether we should be doing this. I'll think about it – give me a ring when I'm back home.'

He was back in California a few days later. Richard Branson rang again. 'Have you thought about it?' he asked.

'Not very much,' Steve replied, but then impulsively, 'OK, I'm on.'

He went to visit Lindstrand Balloons to discuss the design of the new balloon with Per, making several suggestions, and coming to the conclusion that, of all the contestants, they had the best chance but even so he didn't rate their chances of success very highly. At least it wasn't going to cost him anything. Richard had invited him along for the ride as co-pilot and Steve felt flattered by the confidence put in him.

This was a new balloon and capsule, much larger and more comfortable than Steve Fossett had been accustomed to. The capsule had two floors, the upper one being the control room which was ten feet in diameter with three pilot stations and comfortable swivel seats arranged round the walls. There were portholes but they were so small that the crew depended on video cameras mounted on the outside of the capsule to see what was going on.

The lower floor had two tiny compartments, one for a single sleeping berth and the other for stores. The only spot in the capsule where anyone could stand upright was in the centre, just below the Perspex dome. The capsule had two compact engines, fuelled by propane, to run the generators, in addition to the burners for heating the air inside the fabric of the balloon. It was the size of a small caravan but the three-man crew were going to be cooped up in it for up to three weeks. They had changed the name of the balloon from *Virgin Global Challenger* to *ICO Global Challenger*. ICO is a satellite communications company and Virgin felt that they were going to get credit for the flight anyway through Branson's high profile, so promoting ICO would cover most of the costs.

They all assembled in Marrakesh in late November but had to wait for the right winds. They were ahead of their competition and had permission to fly over China below the 26th Parallel which meant keeping south of the Himalaya. A weather window came through on December 22nd. The take off was the usual combination of media razzmatazz, the chaotic excitement of any balloon launch and an endearing family involvement that was very much part of all of Branson's adventures. Not only were most of Branson's immediate family there for the send off but also Per's daughter, Jenny, and the children of Alex Ritchie who had died earlier that year from the injuries sustained in his parachute accident.

For once the launch went smoothly, but as they gained height, their rate of ascent stalled. On the previous occasion too much helium had been added and this time the ground crew had over-compensated with too little. Per gave the burners an extra boost to warm the helium, and they shot up at an alarming rate of around 1900 feet a minute, burning some holes in the lower fabric of the balloon. Per got the balloon under control, pressurised the capsule, and they settled down to the regular routine of a long-distance flight. But not for long.

National boundaries and sensitivities play as large a part as storms and technical failure in the hazards of ballooning. Branson was told by ground control that Libya had withdrawn permission to cross its border. They debated what to do. No-one fancied the risk of being shot out of the sky. They could drop very low and try to crawl round to the south of Libya on ground winds but would lose too much time. They therefore decided to lose a bit of height to get out of the faster winds and try to persuade Colonel Qadhafi to change his mind.

Branson had plenty of contacts. He had worked with King Hussein of Jordan to rescue the hostages held by Sadam Hussein at the start of the Gulf War and he also knew Nelson Mandela. The trouble was both would be asleep and he didn't like to disturb them. In the end he dictated a letter himself and had his office in London fax it to Qadhafi. It did the trick and permission was renewed. They hadn't lost too much time, opened up the burners to climb back into the wind and were swept over Libyan air space to the Mediterranean. There were reports of thunder storms over Turkey and Branson was going down with a chest infection and had lost his voice, partly the result of stress, combined with the dry air of the capsule and all the talking on the satellite 'phone. He took an antibiotic and on they swept.

The next challenge was how to get round the aerial exclusion zone over Iraq. The Americans and British had just started bombing and a large balloon might have made a very tempting target for the frustrated and angry Iraqis. Bob Rice, the team's meteorologist, was confident he could steer them on a series of different altitudes through the narrow corridor over Turkey between Iraq and Russia. They were being swept along at a good rate and by the morning of the 21st were over Afghanistan and facing their next crisis. They had permission to fly down a narrow corridor across South China but the jet stream went to the north of the Himalaya across Tibet and they were trying to get permission to take this path. It was 6.30 in the evening and

ABOVE The ICO balloon protagonists, faced with defeat, opted to ditch near Honolulu on Christmas Day.

they were over the northern plains of India. It was crisis time. The jet stream would take them towards Everest and over Tibet. If they dropped height and started trying to crawl round the southern edge of the Himalaya they would lose too much time and, more to the point, too much fuel. Their capsule with its compressor as well as the burners was fuel-hungry.

They discussed what to do. Steve Fossett, newcomer to the crew, was impressed by how well they worked as a team, Branson taking a share of piloting the balloon and the three of them reaching decisions on a consensual basis. They had two choices: to abandon the attempt or go for it without permission. They decided to take the latter course, maintained their height and were carried across the Himalaya and over Tibet. They were playing for high stakes and all felt tense as they talked with their control centre about the reactions of the Chinese.

Branson claimed with some justification that a landing would now be dangerous. It was 9.45 p.m. GMT, they were over mountainous country and it was pitch dark. At ten o'clock the following morning they learnt that at least the Chinese would refrain from shooting them down but they were ordered to land at the first opportunity. The crew claimed that it would be too risky and kept flying through that day on comparatively light winds – they were only travelling at a ground speed of around forty miles per hour. Finally, at three o'clock that afternoon, they were told they could fly over China but that they should clear Chinese air space as soon as possible.

By 5.30 p.m. on the afternoon of December 23rd they were once again over the sea. Their political problems had ended but they still had the Pacific, North America and the Atlantic in front of them. They had been in flight for five days, reckoned they had fuel for a further seven and therefore needed a fast easy run in the jet stream. By Christmas Eve they had crossed Japan, were over the Pacific and at last in the full jet stream, travelling at 30,830 feet at a speed of 146 miles per hour. They might just make it all the way.

But this optimism did not last for long. Bob Rice was already worrying about a trough of low pressure across Hawaii. There seemed no way of avoiding it without leaving the jet stream and going far to the south away from any prospect of a quick rescue. The winds could even have taken them back on their track.

The following morning they were in the midst of the storm system, had lost the jet stream and were faced by defeat. They agonised over what to do. Per Lindstrand told me that he fancied at least trying to make the coast of America, which would have broken Steve Fossett's previous record, but the others, with no prospect of completing the circumnavigation, opted for the safer course of ditching near Honolulu where they could easily be picked up. I can't help wondering if the fact that it was Christmas Day, when thoughts of family are particularly strong, helped to influence the decision.

There were four more competitors waiting to join the race. First off should have been an American outfit called Team RE/MAX, named after the sponsor, one of the United States' biggest real estate companies that already had a large promotional balloon fleet. Dave Liniger of RE/MAX was hoping to fly a huge helium-filled balloon around the southern hemisphere at a height of around 70,000 feet. They planned to set off from Alice Springs in Australia, but the canopy was so huge and fragile they needed an almost totally windless day to launch. It was never sufficiently calm and there is doubt if they were ever really ready. The attempt was abandoned mid-January 1999.

Breitling Orbiter 3 was also ready to go, but after *ICO Global Challenger*'s illicit flight over China, the Chinese government cancelled all permissions. The Breitling management hoped that, being Swiss, they might be able to persuade the Chinese to give them permission, and therefore put the launch on hold while they negotiated. Of all the contestants they were the only ones who had taken the trouble to visit Beijing and they now assured the Chinese that they would not commence their flight before getting permission to overfly China.

In the meantime they had been having some crew problems. Andy Elson had only planned to make the one trip on *Breitling Orbiter 2* since he wanted to get his own show off the ground, initially with James Manclark This fell through and Andy teamed up with another balloonist, Colin Prescot, who ran Flying Pictures, a company specialising in aerial photography and filming from balloons. Prescot had good media contacts and complemented Andy's at times erratic genius with a methodical, more down-to earth approach. He commented on their partnership: '*The Times* called us The Odd Couple, to which Andy replied, "There's nothing odd about us, it's everyone else." We're very different characters. Very different. He's the fiery, brash, blunt, sometimes very rude engineer – boy genius, I always call him – very clever... and I'm not.'

Colin might not have been a brilliant designer, but he was a first-class organiser and also a great diplomat who could appreciate Andy's qualities and cope with his temperament.

Back in the Breitling camp, Piccard had decided to limit his crew to two. Wim Verstraeten's wife had just given birth to twins, and so he was even more preoccupied than usual and had not been able to give the project the time that Piccard felt was essential. He had also observed on the previous flight how out of his depth Wim had been with all the high-tech equipment. Indeed it was surprising how long such a big and physically clumsy man had lasted in the confined space of a balloon capsule. Elson described to me how Wim had once trodden on his laptop without noticing what he had done. So Piccard resolved that, despite their friendship, he would have to make a change. He therefore invited Anthony Brown, a Concorde flight engineer who was also a customer of Cameron Balloons. It wasn't a happy choice, influenced as it was by the PR advantage of the association with the name Concorde and with little reference to how well Piccard and Brown would get on together.

Brown was used to everything being tested and tried with flight manuals and procedures. There just was not the time to do this in the race to prepare *Breitling Orbiter 3* for the next season. It wasn't helped by the fact that Andy Elson was no longer working as their design engineer. He had written down very little of what he had done and Brian Jones, 'his nursemaid', now had to take over the entire project. He told me of the dilemma.

'We showed Tony how the various controls and systems worked but Tony said, "No, I can't follow this. I need to have specifications. I need to have drawings and flow charts." And we said, "We haven't got them. You know that this is a £300,000 budget six-months-to-do-it-in, throw-every-resource-you've-got-and-get-it-out-of-the-door kind of project." He wasn't happy about it.

'Then Bertrand said to him, "Look, Tony, if you can't get your head around this now, how can I trust you when I go to sleep?" Unfortunately, Tony took this as an insult. Bertrand didn't mean that. What he meant was, "How can I have confidence in your abilities?" and not as an insult but as a discussion element, almost. Well that started it really, and it went from bad to worse. There was a discussion with us all over dinner and Tony started off along the lines of, "Well if you can't trust me, Bertrand, I'm not going to fly this thing until I'm ready to fly." And Bertrand said, "Well how long is it going to be?" Tony said, "I don't know but I just have to get my head around all these things." Bertrand said, "But we might have to fly in five days' time." And Tony said, "I'm telling you, I'm not flying."

'And at that moment I thought, I could be flying here! I had an inkling.'

Brian Jones, as well as being project manager, was reserve pilot. An ex-warrant officer in the Air Force, he had spent much of his career as a load master on transport 'planes, something that instilled a steady methodical approach. He had finally left the Air Force to become a salesman in the drug industry. It was while doing this that he had taken up ballooning, eventually going into partnership with Andy Elson's tourist balloon flight project. Brian is quite small of stature, unobtrusive, very modest, easy to get on with and, I suspect, very supportive. He knew more about the project and the technical details of it than anyone, was longing to fly but at that critical discussion felt he could take no part in the argument between Bertrand and Tony. When they tried to involve him, he said, 'Look, don't bring me into this.'

Next morning Tony withdrew from the flight.

This was just three days before their planned launch date. There were posters all over Chateau d'Oex with Tony Brown's picture as co-pilot. Inevitably Breitling were upset and tried to botch up some kind of compromise. But Tony was adamant and Piccard and the entire flight crew were immensely relieved. Brian commented: 'Bertrand said it was as if a big cloud had blown away. The technicians were amazing, because they were my guys. I'd just stepped over the fence; it was quite extraordinary, they went into overdrive.'

But they had a long time to wait while they negotiated with the Chinese authorities and then awaited a suitable global wind pattern. Two American teams, *Spirit of Peace*, commanded by Jacques Soukup, and *J. Rennee*, commanded by Kevin Uliassi from Illinois, gave up but Andy Elson and Colin Prescot decided to set out anyway, even though it would mean a slow and uncertain flight without the help of the jet stream, to avoid Chinese air space. They had obtained permission but this had been revoked after Branson's illicit over-flight.

BELOW Andy Elson and Colin Prescot in the capsule of their balloon before take off.

They knew that they were going to have a long slow journey and that meant taking on more fuel. Andy was still committed to kerosene, convinced that it was lighter because it didn't need pressurised containers and that it burnt better. By accepting a lower altitude ceiling they could increase their pay load considerably with an impressive two and a half tons of extra fuel. This meant devising a piggy-back system for the eighteen barrels hanging over the side and a stronger crown ring and flying wires to attach the capsule to the balloon. Andy had also designed a system that he believed needed less fuel than the balloon designed by Lindstrand. It was the kind of improvisation at which he excelled.

Their *Cable & Wireless* balloon launched from Almeria in Spain on 17th February and swung south towards the coast of Morocco, for they were planning to head far to the south across the desert to keep well away from Chinese air space. Even their own meteorologist, Martin Harris, gave them very little chance of success and most of the other pundits said they were mad even to start and that the only reason they did so was to avoid breaking contract with their sponsor. Andy and Colin, however, while accepting that their chances were slim, still felt they could succeed.

As soon as they had got themselves organised after take off, Andy collapsed onto the bunk and went into a deep sleep. He had been working flat out for days. Colin, on the other hand, was well rested and very happy to take over the controls. They weren't going fast but the voyage was smooth and their equipment was functioning well. The balloon was heading further south than any of their predecessors, crossing miles of empty desert over Mauritania, Burkina Faso and Niger. They even called up the airstrip at Timbuktu to ask if there was any conflicting traffic for a balloon on its way round the world to be told, 'Not today.'

They flew on over Saudi Arabia and the Indian Ocean without incident but not very fast. Their best speed on the voyage was a very brief spell at 59 knots achieved over Saudi Arabia, yet they had plenty of fuel and were in for the long haul. They took the world's endurance record for long-distance balloon flight while over India, beating the record made by *Breitling Orbiter 2* the previous year. Andy was banking on using his skill as a balloonist and the accuracy of the forecasts on weather and wind speed from his control centre to ease the balloon around the south of China.

The risk he was forced to accept in these more tropical climes was that of thunder storms. They hit their first storm system over Thailand. Huge cumulo-nimbus clouds were building up around them. They could hear aircraft asking air traffic control for diversions to avoid the weather. They were right in the middle of it. Andy had gone to bed and Colin was trying to edge the balloon down a narrow canyon between huge cloud walls, his only means of steering the adjustment of altitude by turning the burners off and on.

Suddenly the balloon was engulfed in cloud. There was a deafening roar and it swung violently from side to side. The variometer needle was off the scale at 2000 feet a minute upwards and then, almost as quickly, it indicated 1500 feet a minute down. Andy tumbled out of his dreams and they burned and burned their way out of trouble, Andy taking hold of the emergency propane valves at the top of the capsule while Colin screamed out the instrument readings. There were frightening pauses as the balloon seemed to lurch uncontrollably and then accelerate upwards while the whole envelope flapped and tore above them.

It was difficult to know when to start burning again. But the aim was most definitely to move up. Eventually Colin asked Andy whether they were yet clear of cloud and he confirmed they were. The balloon was at 29,000 feet, only 2000 feet below its ceiling. Timing the shutdown of burners was a fine judgement in itself because to burn through the ceiling would have spilt a lot of gas and sent them downwards again. The balloon levelled out and they sat back in their seats with a cup of lemon and ginger tea (for the first time in the flight they later had a cup of something a little stronger to calm their nerves). It had been a close call. They were now flying at their ceiling of 31,000 feet and at last were above the clouds. but there were more storms ahead over Laos and Vietnam.

Then yet another crisis occurred when they heard from Bangkok air traffic control that Laos and Vietnam refused them permission to enter their air space. They made a hurried satellite 'phone call back to England to wake Lou de Marco, who had recently retired as Head of Flight Operations at the Civil Aviation Authority, and who had organised all their permits for them. An hour passed and they learnt they had, after all, been given clearance. The storm clouds had dissipated and the balloon headed over Vietnam and across the China Sea, neatly by-passing Hainan Island, which belongs to China, by making a series of small adjustment to altitude. They had succeeded in getting around China and were now heading with fair winds parallel to the Chinese coast, north towards Japan. They had been in the air for sixteen days but still had sufficient fuel to complete the circumnavigation, provided they could rejoin the jet streams over Japan.

It had been a remarkable achievement to get round China and still be capable of completing their voyage. Two days later they were over Japan. There were three choices of jets streams, a southerly one that would take them to Hawaii where thunder storms were forecast, a central one which was also heading for storm activity, and a northern one, starting in north Japan, that would give them a clear run across the Pacific towards Vancouver. They headed for this, confident that they could reach it before the next storm system developed. Andy retired to the bunk for a good night's sleep convinced that the next morning they would be on their way across the Pacific.

As dawn broke Colin saw that they were between two layers of cloud with great plumes of snow falling around them. He asked Martin Harris back at Mission Control for instructions and was told to keep edging northwards. They desperately needed some sunlight to recharge the batteries to run the fuel pumps and power their communications system but, even at 18,000 feet, cloud was still above them and they were being blown back to the east. Andy had had so much confidence in his solar panel recharging system he had not brought along any emergency lithium batteries. Had they kept going up to their ceiling of 31,000 feet to get above the clouds and recharge the batteries, their meteorologist warned them that they would have entered the jet stream taking them to Hawaii and cumulo-nimbus clouds rising up to 55,000 feet – something they definitely wanted to avoid.

ABOVE The romance of ballooning where the direction of the wind dictates its course. Breitling Orbiter 3 starting its successful voyage round the world, skimming the Alps as it picks a wind to take it down to the jet stream over Africa.

Colin woke Andy. 'How's the world?' he asked, his familiar start to-the-day remark. 'Not great. Come and have a look,' was the reply.

Their prospects were bleak. They were both all too aware of how near they had been to disaster in the storm over Thailand. There seemed no alternative but to ditch while they could still do so in control, close to land, with the rescue services ready to pick them up. Could they have gone on? Their most serious immediate problem was one of power. They didn't have a generator to charge their batteries. Andy had decided it wouldn't be necessary and wanted to save on fuel. They could manage without the fuel pumps, since they had three days' supply of propane for emergencies, but they would have been helpless without their communication system. They certainly had sufficient fuel to cross the Pacific and, had they had a good run, to cross America and the Atlantic as well. I suspect that the memory of their narrow escape over Thailand had a profound influence on their decision.

They ditched off Japan on March 7th. They had improved their endurance record to eighteen days, but had completed only forty-one per cent of the journey, less than

half way in terms of distance. However, they had lived to tell the tale and they remained good friends.

Meanwhile Piccard had finally received permission to cross Chinese air space and launched *Breitling Orbiter 3* at Chateau d'Oex on March 1st, a week behind *Cable & Wireless* with no real chance of catching them up. He wasn't discouraged, believing that there was a good chance of the competition failing to get round China. At the start of their voyage they were forced to backtrack, heading south-westwards over the Mediterranean to join the southern jet stream over Morocco. Once in it, they were swept along at a good rate over Mali and Algeria by March 3rd, but it was on that day they learnt that Andy Elson and Colin Prescot had rounded China and therefore now had a good chance of completing the circumnavigation.

Piccard told me that he and Brian Jones were not unduly despondent. They got on well together, and were confident in their balloon which had been changed back onto a propane fuel system and, under Brian's meticulous and very methodical supervision, had not had the acute technical problems experienced on the two previous flights. Both teams still had a long way to go. It was a matter of picking the best possible route, guided by their meteorologists and the control centre. Four days later, over the Yemen, they learnt that *Cable & Wireless* had ditched. They were now on their own.

The balloon continued its methodical, relatively slow course across the Arabian Sea, over India and into the air corridor China had allowed them. They had to stay south of the 26th Parallel, and keep south of the Himalaya and Tibet. It was a very narrow corridor and needed all the skill of Pierre Eckert and Luc Trullerman, the two meteorologists, to place them in it. By March 10th they had crossed south China and were over the Pacific heading for Hawaii. This was the most dangerous part of the entire voyage. Their trust in the meteorologists was stretched to the limit when they were re-routed on a course that took them far to the south of the originally planned line to find a promised jet stream that had not yet even formed. Pierre and Luc had run computer projections of the more direct northerly route to find that the same bad weather pattern that had defeated Branson and his crew would overtake them. A radical change of plan, however, is always difficult to take, particularly when it is dictated from a comfortable control room on the other side of the world to two people already fatigued and stressed from eleven days in the confines of a pressurised capsule. They were both afraid, but shared their fear and through this gained the courage and confidence to follow the advice of the meteorologists.

It continued to be frightening, They were heading slowly for one of the most empty parts of the Pacific where, if they had been forced to ditch, rescue would have been a long time arriving. There was even doubt about how much time they would have to abandon the capsule before it sank or capsized. To make matters worse they sighted huge cumulo-nimbus clouds to the south and, as it became dark, they wouldn't be able to spot them until they were actually engulfed. In addition, it was now bitterly cold in the capsule. They were run down, undernourished and unable to exercise. This was the toughest part of the voyage for they were surrounded by uncertainty, but buoyed by the strength of their own relationship. Brian's gentle sense of humour and Bertrand's philosophical strength, combined with their innate trust in the team in their control room back in Geneva, helped them through, although at times Alan Noble, their director, pushed them sorely. He seemed to have frequently adopted an unnecessarily acerbic tone in his instructions to the balloonists.

They were also having problems with the valves of the burners and eventually diagnosed the fault as icing up. The only solution was to lose height to thaw them out so they dropped down to 6000 feet over an empty, still ocean, opened the hatch and climbed out to feel the warmth of the sun and breathe fresh air. They had also been instructed to dump every bit of surplus weight to try to improve their ceiling for the anticipated flight in the high jet stream.

They ascended to altitude once again and began the slow crawl towards their hoped for jet stream. The pressure continued to build with growing friction between the balloonists and Alan Noble reflected in terse faxes and, more worrying, Bertrand began suffering from severe headaches. Brian tried to lighten the atmosphere with limericks faxed back to control. They were still having problems with the burners and therefore decided to make another descent to try and fix them. They dumped even more surplus weight and returned to altitude.

At last, around day fifteen, they began to build on speed and were being blown in the right direction at a height of 34,000 feet towards the coast of Mexico. Their meteorologists had got it right and success seemed possible, though the fuel situation was still critical. They couldn't afford to lose the jet stream. And there were still crises. They tried to drop two of their empty canisters just before reaching the coast, but only one fell and they suspected that the other had somehow jammed. They were afraid it might become dislodged when over land and kill someone on the ground, but they were loath to lose height once again, so tried every device they could think of, including jumping up and down in the capsule, to dislodge the offending canister. By this time they were over Mexico and when it finally worked itself free, they just had to hope it had fallen onto empty ground.

They were now sweeping over Mexico and then they lost the jet stream and began drifting off course towards Venezuela. They were in despair, faced once again by the threat of failure and, even more serious, both Brian and Bertrand became short of breath, gasping for air. There were fears that they were hypoxic, but the oxygen was flowing freely. They wondered if it could be a build up of carbon dioxide and cleaned all the filters but the reading once again showed up as normal.

Medical experts in Switzerland were consulted and one came up with the possibility that they were suffering from pre-oedema of the lungs from breathing exceptionally dry air for days on end. They started wearing oxygen masks which not only increased their supply of oxygen but also trapped and re-circulated the moisture from their breath. A friend of Bertrand, who was a doctor practising hypnotism, called in at the control centre and suggested he talked to Bertrand over the 'phone to help him to relieve his stress.

Bertrand was at the controls and there seemed just one last chance of getting them back on course to find the jet stream – to climb as high as possible. Bertrand opened up the burners regardless of the shortage of fuel, reached a height of 35,000 feet and started to swing onto a track of 82 degrees. They were still only travelling at 42 knots per hour, but it was in the right direction and they were once again in with a chance. He was even able to call his wife Michèle on his mobile 'phone, picking up a signal from one of the Caribbean islands. He experienced a sense of euphoria, flying literally on top of the world, talking to the woman he loved and feeling that success had been snatched from the very jaws of defeat.

They now began to increase speed as they swept over the Atlantic carried by the jet stream. There were still problems, since they were flying through several busy airline routes, but with some persuasion from their own control room they were given a corridor at their required altitude. It was now easier to ignore the bitter cold and the tempo of success was building up with floods of e-mails and requests for interviews from the media. Both Steve Fossett and Richard Branson sent their congratulations with those of thousands of others.

They were swept over the Atlantic reaching speeds of over 100 miles per hour and crossed the coast of Africa at 05.36. But they could see nothing. The coastal desert was uninhabited and not a single light glimmered out of the darkness, though the dawn was superb as the sun crept up above the horizon, casting its long shafts over the desert. They crossed the magic and invisible finishing line of 9.27° West at 10.00 a.m. GMT on March 20th to be the first men to circumnavigate the globe by balloon. In achieving this they had accomplished what is perhaps the last great terrestrial first and, as if to underline their victory, they flew on to Egypt to land in the desert twenty hours later at 6.00 a.m. GMT, on March 21st. They had flown 25,361 miles in twenty-one days, both a world distance and endurance record.

BELOW In Bertrand's words, 'We took off as pilots, flew as friends and landed as brothers.'

It was very much the story of the tortoise and the hare. On paper they were the least experienced participants. But Bertrand Piccard, who did not even have a balloon licence when he won the Trans-Atlantic Race in 1992 as Wim Verstraeten's co-pilot, and Brian Jones, who had never made a long-distance flight before he joined *Breitling Orbiter 3* at the last minute, in fact made an extraordinarily strong team, complementing each other's skills and qualities. Piccard had learnt a great deal from his flights on *Breitling Orbiter 1* and *2*, while Brian Jones, quietly systematic, was a very competent practical balloonist who both liked Piccard and gave him his total support. In Bertrand's words, 'We took off as pilots, flew as friends and landed as brothers.'

They had the benefit of a very high level of support and guidance from their flight control centre with superb wind and weather forecasting but, perhaps most important of all, they also had those lucky breaks with the weather – the key factor in so many great adventures, whether making the first ascent of Mount Everest, sailing round the world single-handed or reaching the Poles.

SIXTEEN 16

Round the World

The First Circumnavigation of the World by Microlight, 1998

Walls of rain swept over foam-flecked waves. He was 200 miles from Greenland with 200 miles to go to the safety of Iceland. Brian Milton was flying a contraption that looked like a yellow motor scooter suspended from a hang glider. He was buffeted by the winds and his ground speed had dropped to 20 miles per hour. His microlight didn't look as if it was meant to fly. It was travelling more slowly than the clapped out second-hand Vespa I owned in the late 'sixties, and yet he was in the middle of the longest ocean leg of his attempt to circumnavigate the world. It was July 15th 1999 and he was on the home leg of a journey in a vehicle, half way between an early flying machine and a hang glider, a journey which only a man of his dogged tenacity would have completed.

Brian Milton, stocky with a broad face that has the quality of a slightly angry bulldog, is neither a rich entrepreneur like Richard Branson, nor a charismatic public figure, but he has always had an adventurous streak. He drifted into BBC radio as a freelance journalist when he was thirty, found he loved the work and eventually became editor of BBC Radio London's breakfast programme. He also got married, had two children, bought a big comfortable house near St Albans and seemed to be settling into a steady BBC career.

He stumbled across hang gliding, which was still in its infancy, in 1974 when he interviewed a man called Brian Wood who had just managed to stay in the air for eight and a half hours – a record at that time. Milton was intrigued and offered to make a thirty-minute programme about hang gliding on condition that Wood taught him to fly.

In those days there were no formal qualifications or procedures. You were simply told what to do and launched by yourself from the top of a hill. Brian Milton's first flight was off the Devil's Dyke in Sussex, and from that moment he was hooked. After buying his first hang glider, he soon started taking part in competitions which in those early days were slalom events with a course of just over a mile round markers placed on the ground. He came second in one of the national competitions and it wasn't long before he became involved in hang gliding politics, creating the British Hang Gliding League, and taking charge of the training of the British team. His influence took the team to the top of international hang gliding, but not without conflict. Indeed Brian Milton's path is strewn with controversy, the product of a single-minded drive and a short fuse. He also became interested in the development of microlights (the concept of putting an engine on a hang glider to give it powered flight), test flying some of the early machines.

In 1978 he very nearly lost his life on one of these early test flights, crashing from 250 feet after his craft went into an uncontrollable dive, which left him with an understandable fear of heights but at the same time quite failed to deter him from planning the first ever microlight flight to Australia. In this enterprise he was forestalled by Eve Jackson who had set out without any publicity and the minimum of cash, in the smallest microlight on the market, to attempt the journey at her leisure, taking fifteen months to complete the flight.

Brian Milton adjusted his Australian sights to the concept of trying to beat the race record made in 1919 by the Australian Ross Smith who flew from London to Australia in a Vickers Vimy bomber with a crew of three in 172 hours of actual flying time. Milton's objective was twofold – to beat Ross Smith's record from London to Sydney and to reach Sydney in time for the 250th anniversary of the Australian Commonwealth.

He was partially successful, taking fifty-nine days, compared with Ross Smith's ninety-six days, but unfortunately arrived three days after the celebrations. It was, however, still a considerable achievement in which all his resolution had been needed. He had crashed when landing on a Greek island, nearly writing off his machine, and had then ditched in the Persian Gulf on Christmas Day while the Iranians were attacking two tankers a few miles to the north. He still had to struggle with the fear of heights, born from his first crash. It was at its worst over India, flying in haze over the dusty plains with nothing to distract him. He was conscious of a djinn standing on the nose of the craft, telling him to jump. It was terrifyingly real. The djinn vanished if he had things with which to occupy his mind, so as a last resort he would imagine making love to any girl he could summon up in his thoughts.

The idea of setting himself another and more ambitious target to race against now obsessed Milton who admits it was fuelled by anger at the lack of notice his Australian flight had received in microlighting circles. This time he would microlight around the world in eighty days, the challenge set in Jules Verne's classic. He began looking for a sponsor to bring his dream to life.

He wrote innumerable letters but was turned down every time, though Richard Branson, heavily involved in his own ballooning venture, at least took the trouble to reply personally. Eventually Brian netted a sponsor, the Liechtenstein Global Trust, a little-known but lucrative fund management company. They were prepared to put up the £300,000 he reckoned he needed in return for the microlight being called *GT Global*.

A friend, Keith Reynolds, a first-class mechanic and experienced hang glider and microlight instructor with whom Brian had often flown, was passionately interested in the project and suggested Milton should use a two-seater weight shift trike with a larger engine than he had used on the Australian flight. Brian had already decided he wanted a companion on a flight of this magnitude and invited Keith to join him as mechanic and alternative pilot. But their relationship was not one of equal footing. Keith Reynolds was put on the payroll, being guaranteed twenty-five weeks work at £800 a week.

The new machine looked like a tricycle motor scooter slung under a hang glider wing. The pilot and pillion passenger sat on scooter seats with no protection from the elements, with the powerful 80 horsepower engine mounted behind the pillion, its propeller facing backwards. The pilot steered with a control bar linked to the wing pivoted above the trike. Pulling it back tilted the wing down to make it go faster, while pushing it away, raised the wing, causing the craft to climb and therefore go more slowly. Swinging the bar to right or left changed direction. There was also a rudder bar for the feet but this was only used while taxiing to change the direction of the front wheel. The only other control was the throttle, which could be manipulated by hand as well as by foot. Brian found it an aesthetically pleasing machine to fly, for it relied so directly on the pilot's weight and muscle. He described it as a cross between riding a cross-country motor bike and a wild horse. Because there were none of the confines of a cockpit, visibility on all sides was superb and there was an accentuated feeling of speed and flight as the air rushed past. In turbulent air it became a real battle with the elements, calling for a gorilla grip on the control bar.

The average cruising speed was around 56 miles per hour though Brian got up to 102 with a following wind when flying through the Rockies. His ceiling was limited to how high he could fly without supplementary oxygen. The highest he reached was when he flew at 12,000 feet over the Greenland Ice Cap. Carrying about 26 gallons of fuel he could manage a maximum of 500 miles in normal conditions without refuelling. With the rush of air and the noise of the engine it was impossible for pilot and pillion rider to hear each other, so communication was by radio fitted inside their helmets, and on the frequent occasions that the radios failed, they had to resort to signals. It was all very basic but robust. The craft could take quite a hammering in the air and even land in a cross wind of 35 miles per hour. It was also relatively easy to service and fix when inevitably things went wrong.

Conflict becomes a recurring theme in the story of Brian Milton's venture. His twenty-four-year-old marriage had ended three years earlier; that of Keith Reynolds ended shortly after Brian invited him to join the project. At least they were now both in the same boat, or in this case, trike. Milton soon fell out with his PR manager, Simon Newlyn. At one stage in December 1997, only a few weeks before the announcement of their sponsorship, GT Global threatened to pull out of the arrangement. Richard Branson reappeared on the scene with first a proposal of sponsorship, then a challenge to make a race of it and finally a suggestion that, if Milton delayed his flight until May, Branson would put up a prize of $1,000,000 for the first to make it round the world. Milton was not prepared to delay his flight, which he wanted to start in March to ensure that he could cross Bangladesh before the arrival of the monsoon, but the threat of the race was to remain with him throughout the flight. His chosen route was a circuitous one following Jules Verne's Phileas Fogg. This meant that, had Branson's sponsored team started racing, taking the shortest possible route and using all Virgin's contacts with civil aviation authorities, Brian would face a serious threat.

ABOVE GT Global was a two-seater, weight shift trike machine with a powerful 80 horsepower engine.

Relations with Newlyn could not have been worse. He threatened to resign on three different occasions and actually did so once but somehow remained the project's media consultant, mainly because the sponsor found it easier dealing with him than directly with Milton.

At last on March 24th 1998 Brian and Keith were ready to fly from Brooklands, the historic motor race track, now an aircraft museum. They had the band of the RAF Regiment to play them off and an escort of thirty microlights to accompany them over the Channel. That day they covered 400 miles, reaching St Dié, just short of the Maritime Alps. This was all quite civilised flying, but their first crisis came on the fourth day, when they were flying over the Adriatic towards Corfu. All their communications died, both between each other and with the outside world.

They had agreed that they would take turns to pilot the craft on alternate days and that day it was Keith's turn. He elected to keep going, managing to reach a Jordanian airliner on the emergency radio frequency so that they could warn Corfu airport that they didn't have proper air to ground communication. So far, the flight had gone well. Even better, Brian found that he had lost the fear that had plagued him on his flight to Australia. He seemed to be getting over his phobia. It was just as well, for they were now heading for trouble. Greece had recently been hit by the worst storm in living memory and was still suffering the aftermath. They were buffeted by fierce winds in the mountain valleys leading to Athens but kept going and then pushed on to Rhodes. Brian was enjoying himself, commenting: 'I remember thinking half a dozen times that day how happy I was to be there. There was nowhere else in the world, even when fighting the horror conditions in the "Valley of Death" near Thisye, that I would rather have been. It was as life should be, on the edge and going somewhere. My usually restless mind was at ease with itself.'

In many ways it was a strange kind of adventure, similar to the experiences of wartime air crew. The risk and danger and wild open spaces of sky and cloud are all there during flight, and in the case of their microlight with its puny engine and its trike, open to the elements, the sense of vulnerability must have been even greater. Yet they were flying from airport to airport, in itself quite frightening as they came in behind the giant airliners with the risk of turbulence. But then, once on the ground, they were back into urbanised living, with hassles over Customs and flight plans, of where to shelter *GT Global*, and finally getting a taxi to the nearest motel,

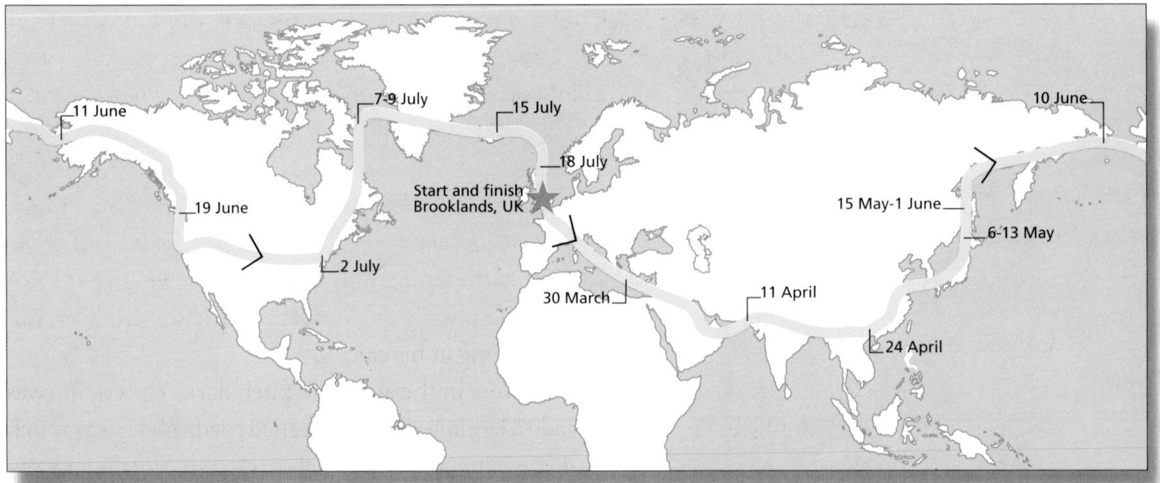

ABOVE The route of Brian Milton's first microlight flight round the world, from March 24th to July 21st 1998, flying 23,130 miles.

where in most cases they could get a bath, steak and chips and a cool beer. In this respect it was very different from the life of the mountaineer or long-distance sailor or even the balloonist who divorces himself from the comforts of the land for the duration of his flight.

Nevertheless the adventures in the air could be all too frightening and varied. They had crossed the Mediterranean from Cyprus, taking off from the British air base at Akrotiri behind an American U2 spy 'plane. They approached the coast of Lebanon and then, as directed by air traffic control, flew into Syria with some apprehension, since a friendly reception was not always guaranteed. They had to fly round Israel to reach Jordan, where Brian had been well entertained by King Hussein on his Australian flight. Once there they would be among friends.

As they flew low over the Syrian desert they were suddenly aware of a MIG-21 banking across their course. *GT Global* was fifteen miles from the Jordanian border. They had no wireless contact with the fighter 'plane. It was a huge dark menacing shape, twisting and banking to either side of their craft and buffeting them in its slipstream. They just kept going, creeping all too slowly towards the safety of the frontier. What did it want, would it fire, had it been authorised to bring them down? It came past them even more slowly and dropped its undercarriage, the universal signal to land. But they could not as the terrain below was too rough. They were now only five miles from the frontier. They kept going and the 'plane just turned away and left them. Had it had any authorisation, or was it just playing its own bullying game with the puny yellow microlight? They had just enough fuel to reach Amman, where they had a warm welcome and were driven to the Hotel Intercontinental as guests of King Hussein.

They were doing well. It was only day nine and they were flying over Saudi Arabia. Brian had hoped to follow the pipe line but was told that there were too many secret installations along its route and therefore he would have to cross the empty desert further to the south. The desert turned out not to be too empty and they were able to follow a long straight road, giving soporific and monotonous flying until the engine began to overheat. One of the advantages of a microlight is that you can land it easily on a road. They waited for a good gap in the traffic and put it down. They couldn't see anything wrong with the engine, but the overflow bottle was full of dark rather oily water, definitely a bad sign. They topped it up with their own spare water supply and begged some from passing motorists, before pulling out into a gap in the traffic and taking off, only to overheat again.

This time they were less lucky. They landed by a large puddle of water, but almost immediately a car carrying an army lance corporal stopped. He asked to see their passports, confiscated them and told them they would have to come with him. Brian eventually persuaded him to allow them to fly to the nearby airfield, with him, still in possession of their passports, following in his car.

It was dusk and, by the time they were in the air, it was pitch dark. The engine was overheating again and so they made a landing on the darkened road, which was much more difficult than during the day. They topped the engine up with more water and took off once again. This time they just made it to Qaysumah airfield. Keith spent the next day trying to isolate the problem in close discussion on the 'phone with the engine manufacturers back in England. He couldn't find a fault and yet whenever he made a test flight the engine overheated. Eventually Keith said, 'We're going to need a new engine.'

Back in England the manufacturer worked through the night to modify the engine for *GTGlobal* and put it on a 'plane to Riyadh next morning. It stuck briefly in Customs but by the following day it was delivered to Qaysumah. Keith fitted it and they were ready to fly with only three days lost. They took off into the hot blue desert sky and the engine temperature soared with exactly the same symptoms as before. Once again they landed on the road, this time near what looked like some kind of garage, and once again, tempers ragged, they grappled with the problem. The coolant was nearly empty. It couldn't be the engine, so it must be the way it was mounted in the trike. They tried to clear anything that could possibly interfere with the flow of air through the radiator, removed the panniers and strapped the contents to different parts of their strange machine, all done in a temperature of 40°C. They took off once again and this time the engine temperature remained constant. They had solved what had turned out to be a simple problem at a huge cost of a replacement engine and a great deal of mounting stress between them.

Their goal of 'Around the World in Eighty Days' was still very attainable

At Dharan Keith was able to make a more long-term modification to the aircraft, tying the radiator to one of the wheel struts. Their machine was looking more and more like an Emmet cartoon construction but the over-heating problem had been solved. If anything, their engine was now operating below its most efficient temperature. They flew on into the Gulf of Oman to reach Muscat. Their goal of 'Around the World in Eighty Days' was still very attainable. The flight over Pakistan and India went smoothly but they were getting into more challenging regions. The mountains of Laos and Vietnam brought greater turbulence and the threat of thunderstorms. It was also becoming more difficult on a bureaucratic level with visas, flight plans and permissions. Grey clouds, forested mountain sides and implacable officials all crowded in. They lost a day at Luang Prabang because of torrential rain and visa problems. On the morning of April 18th, on day twenty-six, it was still cloudy but Brian thought they should give it a try. Keith disagreed. The discussion became heated, Keith accusing Brian of shouting, screaming and bulldozing him into flying.

The weather improved slightly through the morning and Keith, who had at first sat with his face in his hands, began checking the GPS and his maps. Then, without a word, he picked up his flying suit and started preparing *GT Global* for flight. They set out with hardly a word being spoken between them. There were still clouds around but they could pick their way between the layers, flying over the forested mountainous jungle in which the Viet Cong and young American GIs had fought. Gradually Keith relaxed and they began talking again, excited and pleased to have crossed Vietnam and to be descending into Hanoi. They were given a hero's welcome and were told they were the first microlight to reach the capital of Vietnam.

Their elation was short lived. Though they had not been turned down, they still did not have permission to cross China. The authorities continued to prevaricate, despite the valiant efforts of the British Embassy in Beijing, and the days slipped by. Ensconced in their Hanoi hotel bedrooms, Brian and Keith occasionally communicated by 'phone and met for a beer each night. The British Embassy had made them warmly welcome. At the end of one Embassy party they were taken on to a night club called Apocalypse Now, replete with the nose of an American Huey helicopter and Don Maclean's 'American Pie' blaring out from the speakers. The fifth morning saw success at last. Prince Michael of Kent was visiting China and his intercession with the Chinese Vice-Premier had gained their permission. They could fly that day and would be the first microlight ever to cross China.

It was misty and they had a range of 7000-foot mountains between them and Nanning in China but they set out nonetheless. They were now eight days behind schedule. They glimpsed steep forest-clad slopes and narrow serpentine valleys through breaks in the cloud. A forced landing could easily have been fatal. It was nearly dusk when they reached Nanning and were guided down in excellent English by the local air traffic controller. Some of the airport staff, who had been following their flight on the internet, found them a commodious garage in which to put the craft and carried them off to a good hotel and quantities of beer.

Next morning it was stormy, but they set off flying over exquisitely patterned farmland towards a cloud-girt range of mountains. Keith was in the pilot's seat and decided to reach 7000 feet to find a gap in the cloud layers but these soon closed down. They could not see the mountains below, were flying on their instruments and dependent on their hand-held GPS for direction, which Brian called out in as calm a voice as he could possibly manage. That day they flew 342 miles, most of it in cloud, only coming out of it just short of Macau to fly over the flat coastal plain to make their landing.

A short easy flight to Hong Kong and they were back to frightening, stressful flying up the coast of China in heavy cloud. There was no question of sitting out the weather in the comfort of a Hong Kong four star hotel; they had too much time to catch up. Once again they were dependent on their instruments. Brian wrote: 'Blind panic in such situations is dangerous. You are aware that you could spiral out of the

ABOVE The flight was full of contrasts – flying past the man-made peaks of Hong Kong.

sky, so you fall back on technique and suppress your fears. There is only the faintest inkling of how awsomely fearful it is and that provides gallons of adrenaline. We were undersupplied with blind flying instruments, but the turn and bank indicator paid for itself a hundred times over in those minutes of blind descent.'

Eventually they managed to get below the cloud over the sea and they could see the coastline through marching curtains of rain. They were soon soaked and worried about how well their instruments would stand up to the wet. They had been heading for Fuzhou, but headwinds had held them back so they decided to land at a small airfield on the island of Xiamen. They had just sufficient visibility to discern some power cables and made their landing in the gloom. They had a warm welcome which turned a little sour when a giggling girl presented Brian with a landing charge of $850. They were the first private aircraft of any kind that had arrived at Xiamen. Brian laughed at the bill and after some haggling it was reduced to $550. They reached Fouzhou the following morning, managing to haggle the landing charge down from $850 to $100 this time, and continued on their way, flying over chequered farmland and more mountains which were as rugged as those of Vietnam.

They reached Shanghai on April 28th, but their bureaucratic troubles were now increasing. Brian had been unable to get advance permission for the flight from either Japan or Russia, though it was not for want of trying. In Japan, which has 2500 microlight pilots, no microlight is allowed to fly beyond one mile of its home airport. This was going to make it difficult to fly the length of the country.

While their home base wrestled with the Japanese authorities, Brian and Keith flew from Shanghai over the Yellow Sea, in thick cloud as usual, to Cheju, an island off the southern tip of South Korea, hoping to enter Japan. The Japanese relented, but were going to charge them $1200 for every landing. Brian could see his funds draining away. Nonetheless, they were getting plenty of interest, being feted by the press and local microlight pilots in Korea and then in Japan as they flew up to Sapporo and their next crisis.

They were expecting two vital parcels, one containing spare passports with visas for Russia, and the other a replacement GPS for one that had broken down (they had been using their hand-held Garmin to find the way across China and Japan). The visas had been sent to Shanghai, but rather than lose time waiting for them to arrive, Brian had decided to fly on and let them catch up with him and Keith at Sapporo. Neither parcel had arrived. The GPS was stuck in Japanese Customs and, more worrying, the passports with the Russian visas were still in Chinese Customs. They were marooned in Sapporo in an expensive hotel for eight days until at last the GPS and visas arrived but they still did not have clearance to fly through Siberia. They were now forty-nine days into the flight. It was going to be difficult completing it in just thirty days.

Brian wanted to take off anyway and argue their way through once they had reached Yuzhno-Sakhalinsk, while Keith was more cautious, saying that he wasn't prepared to risk his life for the flight. It was a fighter from Yuzhno-Sakhalinsk which had shot down the Korean Boeing 747 that had strayed into Russian air space. Brian was relying on an organisation called the East-West Association to smooth their journey across Siberia and at last on May 13th their representative, Valeri, 'phoned to say permission had been granted. The following morning they set out for the flight over Hokkaido and the thirty-mile leap across La Perouse Strait to Sakhalin Island. As they approached the northern coast of Japan they got in touch with the Yuzhno-Sakhalinsk air traffic control only to be told that they did not have permission to land after all and must return to Sapporo. That day Keith had the controls and Brian sat in the back in a state of rage and misery, thinking out what his next step should be, when the radio from Sapporo came on again to say that they had permission after all. They swung round jubilant, and headed for Russia.

As they landed and taxied in past rusting helicopters and big transport aircraft, Brian could not but notice the contrast with the tidiness and wealth of Japan. But the officials were welcoming, though food at the Sapporo Hotel was expensive with steaks at $18 a time. Both pilots were also impressed by the big blonde girls with long legs and broad smiles who seemed to inhabit the town. They were going to get to know them and the officials all too well before escaping. But that night they were full of hope. It was just a few days flight up Sakhalin and along the coast of the Sea of Okhotsk and they would be poised to cross the Bering Strait and then, whatever the physical challenges, their struggles with bureaucracy would be over.

However, the next morning they were told that the military authorities would not allow them to fly any further into Russia. It was to be a long drawn out war of attrition that eventually destroyed the already shaky partnership between Brian and Keith. They were to be stuck in Yuzhno-Sakhalinsk for more than a fortnight. Brian battled with bureaucracy both on the 'phone to London and Moscow and locally through Valeri, while Keith watched television. Both found some solace with the local girls, Keith proceeding to fall in love with one of them. But the tension between the two men grew with inaction and Brian was faced with ever-mounting bills. Keith was asking for more money once his originally contracted time had run out, and he was also threatening to leave for home if their visas, which were about to expire, were not renewed.

They discussed many options, one of which was for *GT Global* to be escorted across Siberia by a Russian chase 'plane. The cost however could have been around $100,000. With Keith talking of returning to Britain, Brian came up with a cheaper option, trying to persuade a Russian navigator to fly in the spare seat across Siberia. And then their visas were extended, but by this time Brian had decided that taking a Russian navigator was the only option. He told Keith to take a scheduled flight to Alaska and wait for him at Nome on the other side of the Bering Strait.

As if he hadn't troubles enough, he now learnt that Liechtenstein Global Trust, his sponsor, was being taken over and his one good friend and ally in the company was going to be out of a job. At least in Yuzhno-Sakhalinsk he had managed to obtain the services of senior navigator Peter Kusmich Petrov for a mere $245 a day. The next leg of the journey was on.

It was at this point he learnt that Keith had decided to drop out of the flight altogether and was preparing to fly home from Alaska. The plot developed with Brian being told that Keith would consider remaining on the flight provided he could fly the craft solo from Nome to Anchorage, in other words placing Brian in the same position as himself, of having missed out part of the flight and, in the process, invalidating the entire record should they complete the circumnavigation. Brian dismissed the suggestion and Keith flew home to England. It must have been particularly tough for Brian, on his own in Yuzhno-Sakhalinsk with this series of 'phone calls from London and Anchorage from people whom, on the whole, he didn't trust. It says a lot for his single-mindedness of purpose that he didn't give up.

It was June 2nd, day seventy-one, when at last Brian and Peter Kusmich Petrov started flying up Sakhalin Island and then tracking the coast over the frozen Sea of Okhotsk. It was the most desolate, empty yet beautiful country that Brian had ever seen. He felt comfortable with his passenger who even enjoyed taking photographs and operating the wing cameras. Keith's lack of co-operation in this department had always been a source of tension. But it was a serious place to fly, with uninhabited mountains and some big storm clouds building up. They were heading for Magadan on the northern shore of the Sea of Okhotsk. It didn't look as if they could make it to their destination before being caught by the storm so Brian decided to land on one of the roads they could now see below them. It was a rough landing that ended with the craft's front wheel dropping into a hole, breaking the landing lights and then being flipped over on its side by the wind, but there didn't seem any serious structural damage. Peter, however, was not keen to get back in the air before the craft had been checked by experts, though where he was going to find any in the middle of the Siberian steppe was not at all obvious.

BELOW The stress begins to show. Brian, in front, and Peter Petrov riding pillion. In heavy rain, not only they but all their electrical instruments are exposed to the elements.

Brian volunteered to fly *GT Global* on to Magadan by himself. After a shaky take off he was airborne, only to find that the damage was greater than he had anticipated, with the trike pointing in a different direction from the wing. But he was not unduly concerned since he had encountered the same problem on other occasions. His vertigo had vanished, driven away by all the other traumas of the flight. It took Peter a full day to catch up with him in Magadan and then they went on together.

They reached Provideniya, just south of the Bering Strait, on the evening of day seventy-

ABOVE Flying over the Siberian wilderness.

nine. In terms of distance, Brian had covered 12,848 miles and still had 10,054 to go; he had come just over half way round the world in eighty days. But 200 nautical miles to the east was Nome and America. Whatever the challenges that might be ahead, he would at last be among people who spoke his own language and in the familiar western culture. Just 200 miles to go!

He had made sea crossings of similar length before, but there was something about the dark cold sea dotted with ice floes that was particularly threatening – the feeling of flying over the jaws of a trap. The djinn of his earlier travels was just waiting to pounce. About a hundred miles out the cloud began to build up in layers. He decided to try to climb over it, plunging into the featureless white mist and clawing his way up to a height of 5400 feet. Peter suddenly shouted in his ear. 'Ice.' Brian had been concentrating so hard on keeping their craft level and on course with the GPS, he hadn't noticed that they were coated in ice – their clothes, wing, flying wires and his visor, clouding his vision even further. At least they were now in contact with Anchorage air traffic control who promptly declared an emergency. Brian dropped height, weaved his way in and out of the cloud, and at last saw the coast ahead. He had made it to America. A little more flying and he bounced *GT Global* down on the runway at Nome. At last he could relax. 'America was bliss after Russia: toilets with seats, sinks with plugs, taps marked hot water which told the truth, shops and cafés open late in the evening, where food was served cheerfully and not as if a huge favour was being done.'

But he still had a long way to go, and he wasn't even taking the fastest route, for Phileas Fogg had flown via San Francisco. Brian had to think positively. He had by this point lost thirty-three days grounded for bureaucratic reasons but if he could not go round the world in a total of eighty days, he reckoned he could still make the flight in eighty days' flying time. He was short of money, had just enough from the original sponsorship payment to complete the flight and pay off Peter, but not enough to market the venture, which he needed to do to help promote his book sales and the film he had made at his own cost.

And Brian was now on his own, though in many ways this made everything that much simpler. 'I trusted me. My arguments with myself were fair-minded and self-interested.'

There was some challenging flying on his way across Alaska with the engine overheating once again, but he solved the problems, kept the djinn at bay, and continued flying down through Canada and into the States. At San Francisco he learnt that Amvesco, who had bought Liechtenstein Global Trust, had finally decided to withdraw their sponsorship. Brian had a final flirtation with Virgin before deciding to go it alone. With a renewed sense of freedom he flew on along Route 80, beside the railroad followed by Phileas Fogg, past Chicago and New York, pausing to do a photo call by the Statue of Liberty, and then back into the wilderness as he picked his way over the forests of New York State and north-east Canada.

The Atlantic had been crossed by microlight in 1990 by a Dutch pilot named Eppo Newman, travelling from east to west, but he had taken more than a year organising the flight, wrestling with red tape and waiting for the right weather. Brian wanted to complete his flight quickly, and pushed the limits throughout this last leg, flying over pathless mountains and tundra to reach Kuujjuaq on the shores of Ungava Bay, and then across the Hudson Strait to Baffin Island with its jagged granite peaks and sheer rock walls. Brian felt a euphoria:

'As the canyon narrowed I circled close to the mountain walls, surging with joy. Instead of racing in a straight line, I roller-coastered over the sky, diving and climbing and turning, so overcome by the terrific scenery I felt blithe and spiritual. At the same time a small voice kept saying, "Don't take chances now, you are so close."' He was unaware that these granite walls were the playground of extreme climbers or how similar to his were their motivation and feelings.

He landed on Broughton Island for his next sea crossing which was to Greenland. This was his most northerly point, just a few degrees north of the Arctic Circle. There was yet another bureaucratic delay while the Danish flight authorities, with whom he had been negotiating since the previous September, raised some last ditch objections. However, after three days he was at last given the green light and took off over the empty seas of the Davis Strait to reach the west coast of Greenland. The biggest hurdle of all, the Greenland Ice Cap, was ahead. Reaching 9000 feet in height and some 384 miles across on the flight path Brian was planning to take, local pilots doubted it could be crossed without flying to 10,000 feet.

When Brian set out from Sondrestrom the following morning, he had been warned of a front coming in and, as he reached the permanent snows of the ice cap, the white piling clouds were already merging with the white of the snow. Caution prevailed and he turned back while there was still time to find his way to the safety of Sondrestrom. Another day's wait, and on the morning of July 13th with the forecast better, Brian set out once again.

At first it was clear and he reached a height of 8500 feet. It was bitterly cold and then his radio failed. He felt a sense of total isolation. True, he had the emergency radio, but he would have had to take his gloves off to rummage for the back-up system and it was much too cold for that. He flew on, briefly reassured by a sighting of the small unmanned emergency weather station in the middle of the ice cap. He could at least land there in the event of an emergency, but a thin layer of cloud slipped in between him and the featureless white of the ice cap. He decided to keep above it, was forced up to 10,000 feet, then 12,000 feet, higher than he had ever flown before.

The air was getting thin and he was gasping for breath. It was also bitterly cold with ice forming on his visor threatening once more to impede his vision. The cloud below was so thick that he could see nothing of the ice cap. Had the engine failed his chances of survival were minimal. He flew in this white limbo for five hours until at last he became conscious of a change in the far distance from white to blue and slowly the shapes of mountain peaks and deep cut fjords emerged. He had crossed his high hurdle and as he lost height and it became warmer, he was able to dig out his emergency radio and make contact with air traffic control, firstly back at Sondrestrom and then at Kulusuk on a little island off the east coast of Greenland.

He was now faced by his longest ocean crossing, 450 miles to Reykjavik, capital of Iceland, though he had a slightly shorter option of flying into Dagverdhara, an airstrip on a peninsula that jutted out towards Greenland. He couldn't help being apprehensive. It was going to take his fuel capacity to the limit and the prevailing wind tended to be an easterly which would be against him. He had already learnt to his cost how much even a light headwind slowed him down and increased his fuel consumption. That morning there was a westerly at the airstrip, but how long would it last? He decided to set out, thinking he could always turn back.

At first all went well. He had a ground speed, checked out by his GPS, of 50 knots. This would take him to Dagverdhara in six and a half hours, but as he flew over the empty ocean, nursing the engine to keep the revs down, he noticed the speed steadily dropping. The wind had changed direction and he was battling into a head wind. He dropped to 43 knots, but still kept going. It was a similar problem to that of a climber going for the summit of Everest. There is a turn back time to enable you get back safely before dark and a temptation to ignore it as you get closer to the summit. In this instance Brian, who still had a long way to go, swung the craft round and headed back for Kulusuk at a galloping speed of 61 knots, a clear sign of just how strong had been the head wind and how right his decision.

And yet, on getting back to Kulusuk and checking his fuel he was surprised to find how little he had used. Perhaps he could have made it after all? He resolved to go for it, come what may. Next morning the weather forecast was ambiguous but he decided to set out nonetheless. At first it went well with a good fast ground speed of 65 knots. He had a following wind that he hadn't expected which lasted for a couple of hours. Then came a change in the weather that was almost imperceptible, a thin haze that gradually thickened. He was now nearly four hours from the start and had

ABOVE Brian Milton celebrating his safe arrival and the completion of the challenge to fly round the world in a microlight.

crossed the point of no return when the front hit him.

'I came to a wall of heavy rain across my path, and as it approached and I could feel it engulf me, I tried to find anywhere as a refuge. It looked slightly clearer over to the left so I turned and flew that way and found my way round the thickest and most opaque sheets of falling water. This happened time and again. I tried to find the clearest patches and the darker areas of low cloud that showed the bottom limits of where I could fly and still see where I was going. I was thrown up and down, rearing up to 800 feet in the dynamic lift, or falling to 450 feet, constantly wiping the water from my visor, peering at the GPSs to see what they told me. At one time I was making 11 knots and the estimate for getting to Reykjavik had climbed to eighteen hours. Seeing 22 knots was commonplace; it meant I was heading too far north into the teeth of the Atlantic gale. My course was erratic anyway because of the way I was being thrown around.'

He didn't have time to be afraid and was even elated by the struggle, commenting:

'There are moments beyond fear, as I had expected, where life is so fulfilling you cannot believe it and you want to go back and live it again and again. I was carried back constantly into that experience by the frontal gale, but each time I got a little closer to Iceland.'

He fought the winds and turbulence for a further three hours before reaching the lee of Iceland. The wind fell, the sky began to clear and he was able to see the high glacier that marked Dagverdhara, but he elected to push on to Reykjavik, where his film crew were waiting for him and he could truly celebrate his longest and most challenging ocean crossing.

But the flight wasn't over. He was forced to turn back on his first attempt to cross from eastern Iceland to the Faroes and it took him two days to get through the Scottish Highlands, which gave their worst of rain and storm.

At last, on July 21st with an escort of microlights, he flew into Brooklands, 121 days after he had set out on his momentous round-the-world adventure. It was a remarkable achievement. He had flown altogether seventy-one days and had lost thirty-five to bureaucratic hassles. Almost half the journey he had flown by himself and arguably he would have been better off had he been on his own all the way. Certainly his finest moments had been the pure elation of battling alone with the elements over the Greenland Ice Cap and across the storm-wracked seas between Greenland and Iceland.

In all his ventures Brian had a strong sense of history and the romance aviation. As a journalist he approached his circumnavigation as a story that he wanted to tell well, something that Keith could never understand or empathise with. It was an amazing achievement, of dogged bloody-minded tenacity and the taking of some huge risks by a man who was fighting his fear and, at times, just about everyone around him. It was a great adventure.

SEVENTEEN

Dead Man's Handshake

The Linking of Kingsdale Master Cave and Keld Head, 1975-79

THE ONLY SOUND IS THE HISS OF AIR, the 'phutt' of the demand valve closing and the gurgling bubbles of escaped breath, which seem to explode if the roof of the passage is close above. An air cylinder strikes a protruding rock and there is a hollow, reverberating-yet-muffled clang. The diver is in a tiny pool of light, filtered and distorted by the waters around him. His only point of reference is the bed of the passage. He is like the lunar module, skimming the surface of the moon, pebbles and rocks replacing craters, yet there is life in this strange world. A shoal of freshwater shrimps, transparent and colourless, stampede through the beam of light, but the diver is in an environment more alien, more threatening than the cold dark waters of the North Sea, as remote as the emptiness of space, for the waters he penetrates are contained by solid rock. He has swum through long corridors, wriggled through constrictions in a fog of mud, forever fearful of a cylinder jamming against a protruding rock, a hose being caught or torn, mindful his next breath might suck water not air. He does not know where the passage leads, does not know what might be beyond the limits of his beam of light. His only way back, along a maze of waterlogged passages, is the guide line he has laid behind him. Should his equipment fail or should he lose that line, a dark, lonely death will inevitably follow. He must keep cool in a situation which is a scenario for most people's nightmares.

Cave diving is at the extreme end of caving and it allows the cave explorer to venture where otherwise he would have had to admit defeat. The sport of caving has never had as wide a following as more visible and easy to publicise activities. It can boast no obvious Everests, for it can never be known for certain if one cave is indubitably the deepest or the longest in the world. There might always be another just waiting to be found. And yet this is also the fascination of caving, for on a planet that has had its surface thoroughly explored, whose every mountain peak is known and almost all the highest ones climbed by at least one route, and whose every ocean has been crossed, caving still gives vast scope for exploration, not just in distant parts, but beneath the gentle, rolling hills of the Yorkshire Dales, the Mendips and South Wales. Wherever there is limestone there are also caves, sinuous passages, gaping chasms, gigantic chambers, rivers, torrents and lakes, all formed by the slow, pervasive action of water on the calcium carbonate of limestone. Cavers use what artificial aids they can devise to help their exploration; they dig and even blast their way through blocked passages, but the amount of technology that can be used is strictly limited by the nature of the caves themselves. Everything has to be carried, shoved and pulled through narrow passages, down flue-like holes. This in itself defeats most modern technology. Man is still the most effective machine in the close confines of a cave.

In the early 'fifties cavers were intrigued by a system in the Yorkshire Dales between the villages of Dent and Ingleton. Skeletal outcrops of limestone, whitened by weathering, give a hint of what lies beneath; streams vanish into the hillside and then reappear lower down the slopes. One of these streams emerges in a pool at Keld Head in Kingsdale. A large team had drained the pool, hoping to penetrate the passage that led into it, but they were stopped after a few metres by flowing water filling the entire passage. Cave diving was still in its infancy. The Yorkshire cavers were prepared for short sections of waterlogged passage, which they free-dived, relying on coming up for air after only a few metres. It was a very frightening game, for if there was no air pocket, the diver then had to turn round, or if there was insufficient room, back out and return to the surface before he ran out of breath.

Geoff Yeadon

Keld Head was left alone for nearly thirty years, its questions remained unanswered. The pattern of water inlets and caves explored around the high hill mass of Gragareth, extending over the three county boundaries of Cumbria, Lancashire and Yorkshire, showed that all these systems must somehow be linked underground with many kilometres of passages, many of them waterlogged, but, equally, with many of them drained and empty, just waiting for the explorer to find them. A map of the caves already discovered was a little like an early map of Africa, with the spidery routes of European explorers slowly creeping forward into the dark unknown. Keld Head was of special interest to the cave diver for here there were clearly two caving systems, about two kilometres apart, linked by flooded passages.

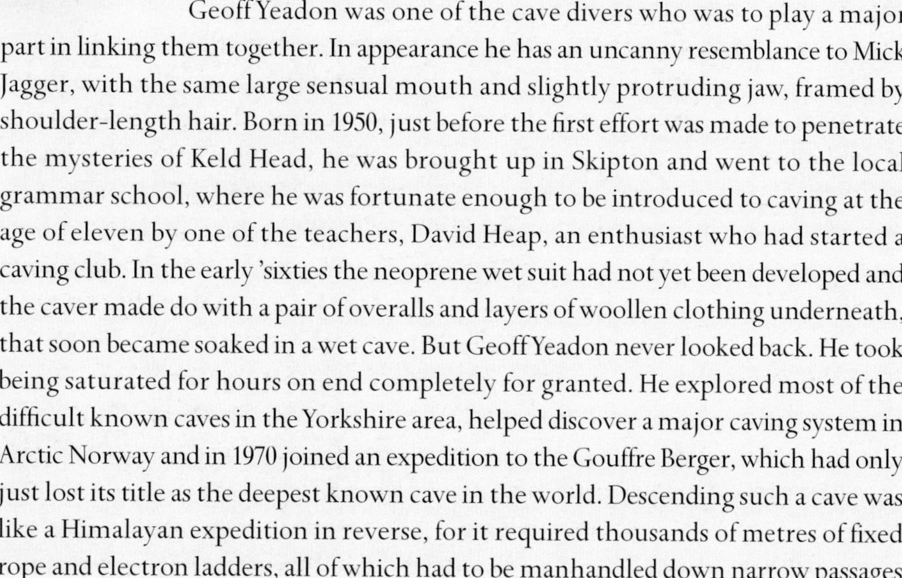

Geoff Yeadon was one of the cave divers who was to play a major part in linking them together. In appearance he has an uncanny resemblance to Mick Jagger, with the same large sensual mouth and slightly protruding jaw, framed by shoulder-length hair. Born in 1950, just before the first effort was made to penetrate the mysteries of Keld Head, he was brought up in Skipton and went to the local grammar school, where he was fortunate enough to be introduced to caving at the age of eleven by one of the teachers, David Heap, an enthusiast who had started a caving club. In the early 'sixties the neoprene wet suit had not yet been developed and the caver made do with a pair of overalls and layers of woollen clothing underneath, that soon became soaked in a wet cave. But Geoff Yeadon never looked back. He took being saturated for hours on end completely for granted. He explored most of the difficult known caves in the Yorkshire area, helped discover a major caving system in Arctic Norway and in 1970 joined an expedition to the Gouffre Berger, which had only just lost its title as the deepest known cave in the world. Descending such a cave was like a Himalayan expedition in reverse, for it required thousands of metres of fixed rope and electron ladders, all of which had to be manhandled down narrow passages and deep shafts. It also meant camping on the way down, since it was too long a system to complete in one push. The main party had reached the second camp, in a huge chamber, and were all asleep, when another member of the team, Oliver Statham (known as 'Bear' because of his size and strength) came plummeting down the rope on his way to attempt the first complete descent and re-ascent in a day. In fact, Statham had come down prematurely, for they had not yet rigged the lower part of the cave. However, Geoff Yeadon decided to accompany him for the final push down, both on grounds of safety and to help carry the ropes. They managed to establish the record and, at the same time, started a partnership that was eventually to lead them from caving to one of the boldest cave dives that has ever been made.

Oliver Statham

Oliver Statham came from a very different background to Geoff Yeadon. Son of an ambassador, he had gone to Sedbergh School in North Yorkshire (now Cumbria) in the midst of superb caving country. He also had started caving while at school. Both of them had gone on to art college and had specialised in pottery. Geoff was now at the Bath Art College and Oliver was working in his own pottery in Skipton.

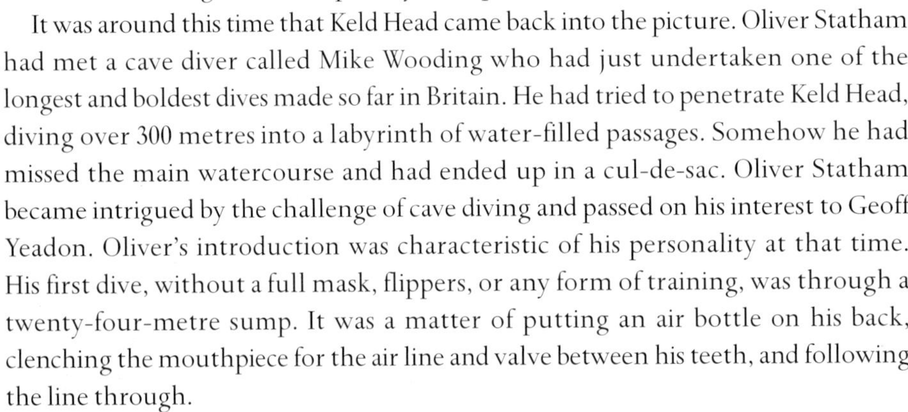

It was around this time that Keld Head came back into the picture. Oliver Statham had met a cave diver called Mike Wooding who had just undertaken one of the longest and boldest dives made so far in Britain. He had tried to penetrate Keld Head, diving over 300 metres into a labyrinth of water-filled passages. Somehow he had missed the main watercourse and had ended up in a cul-de-sac. Oliver Statham became intrigued by the challenge of cave diving and passed on his interest to Geoff Yeadon. Oliver's introduction was characteristic of his personality at that time. His first dive, without a full mask, flippers, or any form of training, was through a twenty-four-metre sump. It was a matter of putting an air bottle on his back, clenching the mouthpiece for the air line and valve between his teeth, and following the line through.

Geoff Yeadon was attracted by the idea but approached it slightly more cautiously and methodically, joining the Cave Diving Group to borrow equipment and going on regular training sessions, starting in the swimming baths of Bristol University. At the end of his period in college, Geoff came back north to do his teacher's training in Leeds. He and Oliver Statham were now able to cave dive together. They could afford to buy their own aqualung equipment and compressed air bottles and chose Boreham Cave in Upper Wharfedale for their first major exploration. Their initial attempt was abortive and very nearly fatal. The first sump, which was forty-six metres long, had already been dived and they knew that it was quite straightforward. Oliver, therefore, did not bother to fit his spare demand valve, but carried it packed away in an ammunition box. He dived first, followed by Geoff. They were very nearly through when Geoff saw Oliver's light coming back towards him. As he came up to Geoff, he made a few frantic gestures towards his valve to indicate that it wasn't working. One emergency procedure is to share a mouthpiece, taking alternate gulps of air from the same apparatus. This, however, needs very cool nerves and a high level of practice and understanding. Oliver, his lungs already bursting, couldn't afford to wait and swept past Geoff in a desperate bid for air, but on the way the tube leading to his mouthpiece caught round Geoff's cylinder, so that Oliver was now towing Geoff. Geoff quickly unhooked his tube from the valve to free himself and Oliver shot off like a torpedo. Geoff followed, hoping that if his friend did lose consciousness before getting back to the surface, he might just be able to tow him to safety and revive him. But Oliver made it and when Geoff followed to the surface, he was already lying on the side of the pool gulping in the air with great, agonised gasps. He had swum over thirty metres under water without the benefit of his air supply.

Nothing daunted, they returned to Boreham Cave a few weeks later. Another cave diver had started through the next sump in the early 'sixties. There were reports of a narrow squeeze, so tight that you had to take off your cylinder and push it through in front of you. This time Geoff set out, leaving Oliver sitting at the side of the underwater stream where it vanished into the rock. The role of support diver is more psychological than anything else, for there is little he can do if anything goes wrong. It is not like being second man on a climb. If his partner does not come back within the prescribed time, he has to plunge into the water and follow the line to find out what has happened. It is just possible that the first diver could have run out of air or experienced a technical fault and has managed to find an air pocket in which to wait for help. But if there has been a serious delay, it is more likely that he has drowned.

BELOW Boreham Cave in Upper Wharfedale. It was the exploration and mapping of cave systems that intrigued Geoff Yeadon as much as breaking records.

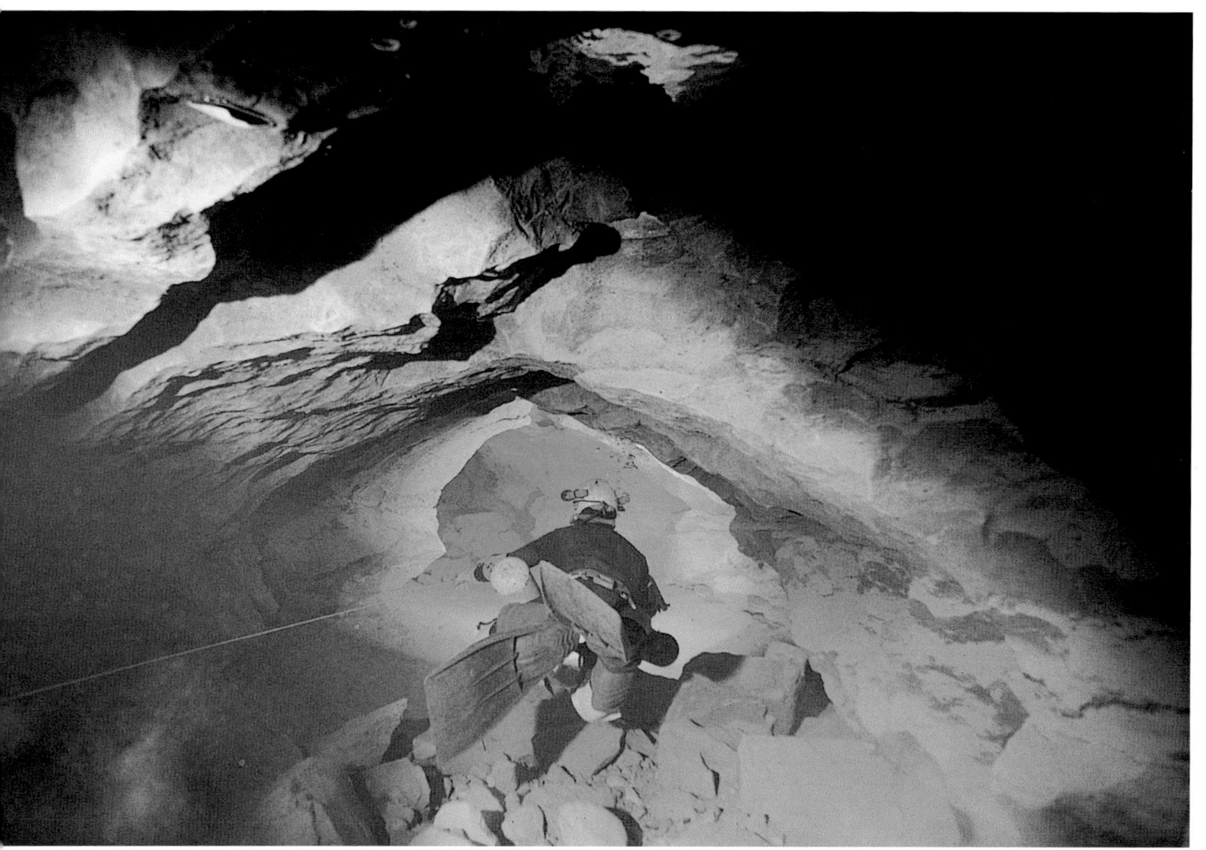

The tension is always less for the leader. Geoff was now engrossed in finding a way through the first squeeze, as the walls converged around him. Getting himself and his bottles at the right angle, he was able to slide through the hole. This was the first time he had been underwater in an unexplored cave.

'I remember being incredibly excited by the size of this huge tunnel, the water all blue, stretching away from me, with no other lines going into it except the one I had in my hand on the line reel. I just finned off into the distance and the tunnel wound round. Occasionally there were lower bits to one side that I aguely noticed, but I was so excited that everything was a bit of a daze. I didn't really take it all in.

'Eventually I popped up into an air space. It was tiny and I had to wriggle along sideways. I really wanted to go back then, but I had no excuse. There was plenty of line on the reel and I still had enough air. I was well within the thirds safety margin used by cave divers. That is, a third of your air to go in, a third to come out and a third for emergency. There was no reason to go back except in my head. My head kept telling me I wanted to go back, but I carried on.'

ABOVE Straw stalactites first discovered by Geoff Yeadon in Boreham Cave, Upper Wharfedale.

He dived back into the water through another hole, came to another air space, slithered down a waterfall into yet another sump, this time twenty-four metres long, with another air space beyond that, and so it went on until at last, 165 metres from the start, he had run out of line and had an excuse to turn back. On the way in, the water had been beautifully clear, but he had disturbed the fine sediment on the bed, so that going back it was like being in a dense fog. His light bounced back on the myriad particles held suspended in the water and he could see little more than a few centimetres in front of his mask. It was a question of following the life line, since he had no sense of direction or scale, but he now found that the roof above him was closing in, pressing him down onto the bed of the cave.

'I remember thinking it definitely wasn't this low. I had my head on one side, grinding over pebbles. I couldn't see a damn thing and, with my head on one side, occasionally I'd get a gulp of water which made me very aware that I was underwater and a long way from home. I had to keep stopping to calm down because my breathing rate kept going up and I knew that if I didn't calm down and slow my breathing rate down, I wasn't going to get out.'

Geoff had made one mistake on the way in which could have cost him his life. He had omitted to anchor the line down on the outside of the corners he had turned and, as a result, it had been pulled tight round the bends in the narrowest part of the bedding plane. He had to keep hold of the line somehow, for, once lost, he would never have found his way back. But by dint of resting, wriggling and easing the line from the tightest edges of the passage, he finally managed to get back to where his partner was waiting by the side of the pool. This was the last time that Oliver Statham went cave diving for a period of six months. Even so, he needed the stimulus of risk in his life and sought it in the sky instead; he took up hang gliding.

Geoff Yeadon's first exploratory dive was considerably bolder than almost any that had been made in Britain at this time and he had learnt a great deal from the experience. He returned to Boreham Cave a few months later, anchored the line to keep it in the wider parts of the passage, and swam into the further recesses of the hole.

'It was like a cresta run, only underwater. It was a beautiful feeling, just flying through this tube without touching the roof or floor, banking over at the corners, with the line reel ticking out. There were beautiful curves, just like a snake with smooth silt banks on either side. I kept glancing behind me and could see this cloud of silt coming up after me. It was a good, safe passage with no nasty nicks in the corners – it was more like an arched tunnel. Then a peculiar phenomenon occurred in front. It was a layer, like a cloud of brown water approaching at roof level and I was in clear water underneath. Then this gradually came down until I was entirely in brown water, and then, unfortunately, the line ran out.'

The only explanation seemed that there must have been an inlet, carrying running water, flowing over the still water through which he had been swimming.

Geoff Yeadon continued his exploration of Boreham Cave, stretching his own limits and developing the techniques that were later going to stand him in good stead in Keld Head. His club bought him a larger air bottle to give him greater range, and to combat the debilitating cold he wore three wet suits, as he embarked on progressively longer dives, finally making one of 762 metres down the outlet that he had sensed was there when he had encountered the ceiling of discoloured water. It was cave exploration at its best and it was this facet that intrigued Geoff as much as the element of making records. He was mapping the cave as he dived, noting compass bearings and distances on a small slate.

It was around this time that Oliver Statham began caving once more. He and Geoff got on well as friends, eventually working together in their pottery, and soon most of their cave diving energies were directed into solving the problems of Keld Head. This was to become a long drawn out siege over a period of years rather than months. In their approach to it they now worked as one, developing techniques and equipment to cater for the sheer scale of a challenge which was at the extreme limit of cave diving expertise.

There was always the problem of funds, for they certainly couldn't afford to purchase the specialised equipment, but here the record nature of the dive became useful. Oliver Statham managed to persuade a diving manufacturer to supply them with specially modified dry suits on reduced terms. Dry suits work on a different principle from wet suits, for they seal the body in a cocoon of air which can be adjusted to allow for different levels of buoyancy by means of an inlet valve from the breathing system, and an escape valve to release excess air. They are not only warmer than wet suits but, perhaps more important, they insulate the diver from the water around him, making him feel that he has the security, however illusory, of being in a submarine. Using these suits, Statham and Yeadon made a series of forays into Keld Head, taking it in turns to run out the full contents of a reel before turning back to allow the other to follow it and then run out another length.

The downstream entrance of Keld Head was a labyrinth of waterlogged passages festooned with the guide lines of previous attempts. One of the first jobs was to clear these out of the way to avoid dangerous confusion. They got some help from fellow cave divers in doing this and it was during the clearing operation that the body of Alan Erith, a novice cave diver who had lost his life about four years earlier, was found. Geoff Yeadon and Oliver Statham helped in the recovery operation before returning to their own exploration. They had already run out 300 metres of line and were obviously in the main passage, which they hoped led to the Kingsdale Master Cave system, about one and a half kilometres away. They were also gaining in confidence.

'We really became more like fish. We'd stop and rest on the bottom, sitting down on a rock, nattering to each other on our slates. We even had drinks of water because we found that after an hour of surveying and swimming you started getting a dry throat from the dryness of the air. You just took your mouthpiece out and had a drink.'

And, weekend by weekend, they pushed the route out; to 450 metres, then 600 metres, then 690. It was a slow, painstaking process. It took a week just to prepare for a dive, to check over all the equipment, clean it, grease it with a silicone spray, get all the bottles filled, and then check each valve again.

At this stage Oliver and Geoff began working from opposite ends of the system. Oliver had hurt his back, so concentrated on the Keld Head end which did not involve any caving prior to the dive, while Geoff started trying to find the way down from the Kingsdale Cave back towards Keld Head. There was a low sloping passage to the first sump, and he worked on this through the summer of 1976, always on his own, relying on casual help from cavers on their way down to help carry his gear to the first sump. This was in a chamber like a gigantic shower, with the water pattering out of the dark above onto the pool into which he was going to dive. The pool led into a maze of winding, water-filled tunnels and blind alleys.

'I got to a five-way junction. It was completely bewildering. I just belayed the line to a rock and sat down (still submerged, of course) and looked at my compass and thought, "Which one's Keld Head?" I picked what I thought was the right way and it

ABOVE A diver encounters a cloud of silt that can appear unexpectedly from an inlet – note the guide cord to the left of the picture.

dropped down a shaft which led into a big river tunnel. The flow increased and the place became enormously wide, but I wasn't quite sure where it was going. I just kept on a bearing, heading in roughly the right direction, until I ran out of line. The next trip it burst out into this incredible blackness with the floor dropping away downward and the roof shooting away up. The water was so clear I thought I might have wandered into another ox-bow but then it narrowed down so much that I would have had to take my cylinders off to squeeze through so I decided that this could not possibly be the way to Keld Head.'

He had made, altogether, six dives from the Kingsdale Master Cave but still seemed nowhere nearer finding the connection with Keld Head. It had been lonely and, at times, frightening work and on one occasion he could very easily have lost his life. He was on his way back, finning quickly through the murky waters, and had just exhaled. When he inhaled, he received a mouthful of water instead of air. He could not see what was wrong because of the murk; it all had to be done by touch, with gloved fingers. He felt his mask and found that all he was left with was the disconnected rubber mouthpiece, the other bits having dropped off. He had to find the other valve, but this also had to be done by touch. The tubes were exactly the same thickness and on his first attempt he followed the wrong tube. His lungs were now bursting – it was like trying to hold your breath for thirty seconds after completing a hundred metres sprint. He was consciously slowing himself down, even though his body was beginning to take over in its desperate need for air, with muscular spasms in his lungs and involuntary twitching in his fingers that made it even harder to follow the tube down to the spare valve. At last he found it, brought it up to the mouthpiece, stuffed it in and pressed the button that would blow out the water flooding the system. He could breathe again. He lay on the bottom of the passage for some minutes to get his panting back under control before finning slowly back to the cave where he had started his dive. 'That was another lesson learnt. Never go that fast again. You've got to move slowly the whole time to keep your breathing rate down so that if anything does go wrong you can hold your breath for a long time.' Because of the difficult access to the start of the dive, Geoff could only wear a wet suit while diving from the Kingsdale Master Cave and carry a limited quantity of bottles. Eventually he felt he could go no further from that end. In February 1977 he made one more attempt from Keld Head, extending the line to 920 metres,which established yet another record for British diving and equalled the European record. They were also getting near to the link-up point from the Kingsdale Cave but, unfortunately, the limits reached by the two explorations were on different levels. The Keld Head passage seemed to be about eighteen metres below the last point that Geoff had reached from the Kingsdale end, and it could be difficult finding the connection between the two levels. In addition, they were now at the limit of the capacity of their bottles.

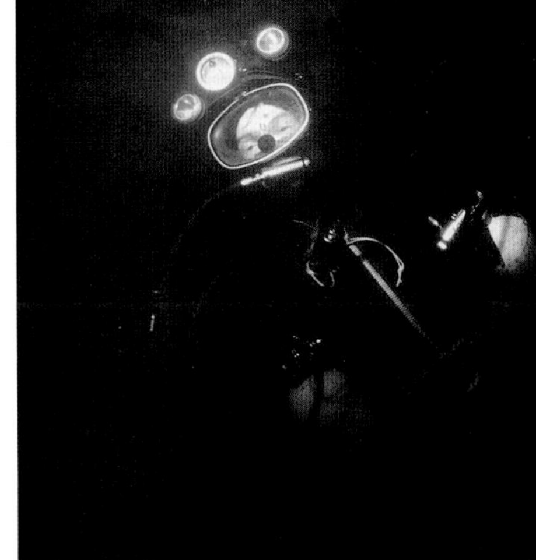

ABOVE Geoff Yeadon in Keld Head.

Meanwhile, Oliver had been writing to cave divers around the world to find out what they were doing. It was such a young activity that communication between different groups was still very poor. One of his correspondents was Jochen Hasenmayer, a very experienced German cave diver. He was intrigued by what he heard about Keld Head and offered to come over to help. Geoff was immediately impressed by Jochen, saying: 'We found that what we thought we'd been pioneering, he'd been doing nineteen years before.'

They were now ready for the big effort to join up with the Kingsdale Master Cave system. They decided to set out at three-quarter-hour intervals with Jochen Hasenmayer, who had larger capacity cylinders, going first, followed by Oliver Statham and then Geoff Yeadon. There had been a lot of rain and, consequently, the visibility was appalling. They could see little more than an arm's length ahead of them.

Jochen swam strongly to the end of the line and then set out, feeling his way along the bed of the cave. Geoff had gone into a cul-de-sac on his previous attempt, but Jochen sensed that there should be a route out to the left. He came upon a narrow fissure only forty-five centimetres wide. Jochen had his big cylinders mounted on his back and this made it particularly difficult and dangerous wriggling through narrow sections, since he was unable to see or even feel anything that might foul the back of the cylinders. Even so, he managed to worm his way through the gap to find that it widened out beyond, but the roof had dropped to a much lower level. He squeezed through, however, and continued running out the reel in a broader channel until it came to an end. Anchoring it in position, he started back, following the line. He had made the same mistake that Geoff Yeadon made on his first long exploratory dive in the Boreham Cave, for he had not anchored the line in places where the route went round corners. So, on his return, he found it had shifted into the side where it was much too shallow for him to squeeze through. Very quickly you lose all sense of direction. He was over 914 metres from the entrance in almost nil visibility. The more he searched and pushed and struggled, the more silt swirled up until he could barely see anything more than a few centimetres from his face.

Oliver Statham had set out three-quarters of an hour behind Jochen and followed the line to the constriction. He had one bottle mounted on his back and one on either side. This meant that his side dimensions were wider than Jochen's, so it was even more difficult, if not impossible, for the big man to wriggle through the narrow gap. He was already very close to using up a third of his air supply and so, desperately worried, he started back down the line, to meet Geoff, who had set out another three-quarters of an hour behind Oliver.

BELOW The sort of constriction cave divers have to negotiate.

Geoff Yeadon told me:

'I met Bear at about 2750 feet, coming back. I immediately felt apprehensive

because, of course, it should have been Jochen who came back first, and then Bear wrote this ghastly note on my slate: "3000, small with back and sides" – which meant the bottles mounted back and side – "No Jochen. Trouble???!!!"

'I replied on the slate: "I will go and look and then turn back."'

ABOVE Cave divers used to communicate under water by writing on slates though now they use electronic means. Oliver Statham's message about Jochen Hasenmayer being overdue and Geoff Yeadon's reply: 'I will look and then turn back.'

Geoff swam on along the line until he reached the constriction. Peering into the gloom he was unable to see any sign of Jochen. He had the same problem as Oliver, for he also had one back-mounted and two side-mounted bottles. He decided to wait until a third of his air had been exhausted before returning. And so he waited in the cold, cloudy water, increasingly worried because Jochen had now been in the cave for more than an hour longer than he and so, even allowing for the greater capacity of his bottles, must be nearing the end of his reserves. There was also the terrible conflict of wanting to do something to help but being helpless to do it and having to face the prospect of abandoning a diving partner to his fate. He had very nearly exhausted his ration of air, and was steeling himself to return, when he felt the rope in his hand twitch. Jochen must be somewhere near. He tugged the rope, just to show Jochen that someone was close by and then somehow wriggled and jammed himself through the narrow gap so that he could at last see the dull, suffused glow of Jochen's head lights only one and half metres away. But between them a sandbank on the base of the passage pushed up to within a few centimetres of the roof. Jochen had not seen Geoff's light and was trying to get through at another point. There was no communication between them. Jochen was not even able to interpret the twitches on the line which he had felt. It could easily have meant that one of the others was stuck as well. And then Jochen's light vanished. He had obviously backed out and then pushed into another passage in his struggle to escape the trap.

There was nothing that Geoff could do, no way that he could catch Jochen's attention. He did not dare go any further through the squeeze, since it would have been almost impossible to retreat with his back and side-mounted cylinders and the guide line now hopelessly out of position. It was hard enough wriggling backwards to get out. Each time he jammed, it could have been for good. Keep calm, slow down the breathing, edge forward a little, wriggle again, very gently, and at last he was out of the squeeze. He looked at his gauges and saw that he was well into his second third of air, but the situation was now very different. Jochen was close at hand and desperately needed his help. The line twitched again. Geoff wriggled once more part way through the squeeze, could see Jochen's light, but Jochen was obviously not looking in his direction. Geoff retreated. His air was being consumed all too quickly, both because of the tension of the situation and because he was eighteen metres below the water surface level, which meant he was using air at three times the rate he would have consumed it just beneath the surface. And then Jochen's light appeared once more, but this time through a hole much too small for anyone to have squeezed through. He had at last seen Geoff's light and swum towards it until they were within touching distance. Geoff reached through and Jochen grasped his hand. Geoff told me:

'I could feel his fingers and his whole arm trembling as he squeezed my hand. I couldn't help wondering what the hell I'd do if he wouldn't let go, but I just tried to keep my hand absolutely still, to show him that I was perfectly all right and in the right place. I was willing him in my mind to go back and have another go at finding the right way out, but there was no way I could communicate that. He just squeezed and squeezed and I'd give a reassuring squeeze back and then, eventually, he let go, patted me on the hand and backed away. I interpreted this either that he was being a Captain Oates, going away and telling me to get out while I could, or that he was going to have another go. I was convinced at the time I was shaking a dead man's hand.'

Geoff was now well into the second third of his air, but he waited by the squeeze, shining his light through it, hoping desperately that Jochen would now find the right way through, and this time he managed it, skirting the sandbank and, still clinging to the line, he manoeuvred himself through the awkward dog-leg leading back to safety. As he came through, Geoff cautiously held back in the roof of the passage. There were tales of divers in both Australia and Florida who had run out of air underwater and had attacked their companions in a desperate effort to take away their air bottles in a fight for survival.

'I didn't know Jochen that well, so decided to keep my distance. I was holding the line so he'd be able to find me but I was in a position to see how nasty he was looking when he came out of the hole.'

In fact Jochen's air just lasted out. One bottle was nearly empty, and there was a little more left in the second. He would not show anyone just how little there was, perhaps to avoid alarming his wife who was waiting at the entrance. Jochen did not want to talk about what had gone through his mind when he was trapped on the other side of what has become known as Dead Man's Handshake. He could only say that it was a nightmare. The fact that he survived at all was due to an extraordinary level of control and, within hours of getting out, they were already planning their return, discussing how they could make the passage safer by anchoring out the guide line, using bigger bottles and changing the way they carried them.

I was convinced at the time I was shaking a dead man's hand

Geoff Yeadon set to work on his gear, making a set of harnesses that had four demand valves and four separate air supplies, all side-mounted. It was so heavy it made his back ache, even underwater. He had also evolved a new strategy to cope with the logistics of such a prolonged dive, planning to drop the two smaller bottles at 213 metres and 427 metres respectively, each of them with two-thirds of their capacity unused. This meant that he would have his reserves in place for the return and would only have to contend with the two large, side-mounted cylinders at the constriction by the Dead Man's Handshake. He went in on April 16th 1977, dropped his bottles as planned, and reached the constriction, which he was now able to negotiate more easily. Mooring the line with lead weights ensured that it would stay in place, guiding them all through the dog-leg at its widest and only feasible point. He went on to the end of Jochen's line and reeled out another thirty metres, but he was now creeping over the third safety factor and he prudently returned. At 1036 metres it was another European record. They were getting very close to his furthest point of exploration in the Kingsdale Master Cave, but they were still some eighteen metres below, and so the junction was as elusive as it had ever been. In addition, their cylinders were still not big enough to carry sufficient air to give them the reserves of safety they needed.

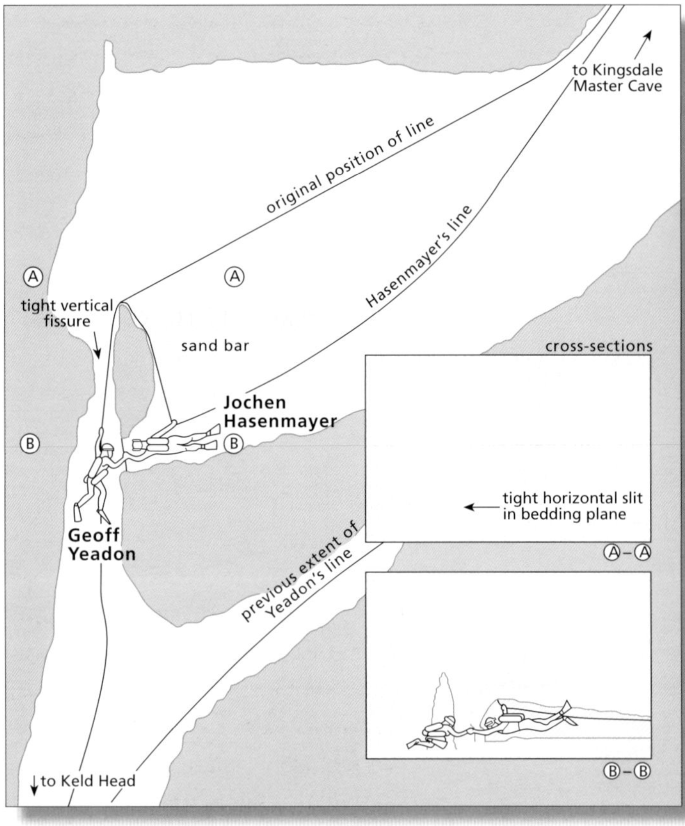

Another summer, autumn and winter went by. Geoff turned his attention once again to the Kingsdale Master Cave, doing another series of dives to try to find the vital link. On June 11th 1978, he organised himself a support team which enabled him to take in a dry suit, packed in a container, and big bottles for a long dive. This time he found the key, 732 metres into the labyrinth. He stumbled onto a passage he had not been down before and came across a hole in the floor. It was black and frightening, an abyss a long way from home.

ABOVE Diagram to show what happened at the Dead Man's Handshake.

On a practical level, a vertical shaft is potentially dangerous, for if it goes too deep and the pressures become too great, there are problems with buoyancy and the danger of getting the bends on coming back up to the surface. There is also the psychological barrier that a hole presents. It is so easy to imagine it going down for ever into the depths of the earth. It's a plunge, perhaps, into our own black subconscious. For Geoff, having a dry suit made all the difference, for he could regulate the pressure inside it and, through this, control his rate of descent. He sank steadily, counting off his descent with the depth gauge strapped to his wrist. It bottomed out at nearly nineteen metres. He was almost level with the Keld Head Cave. The passage swept away in the right direction, wide and inviting. He swam down it for sixty-one metres and, although he could see no sign of their exploration from the lower end, nor of the reel he had left the previous year, he sensed that he must be very nearly there. But he had now reached the vital third capacity and was forced to return.

Their effort had now reached expedition proportions in terms of commitment, time and expense. They therefore began to look for sponsorship, gaining a Royal Geographical Society grant to help buy the big-capacity bottles they so desperately needed. In July that same year, Jochen Hasenmayer came over again, bringing the bottles with him. They were ready to try once more from Keld Head on 6th July. They changed their system yet again, taking in two massive 160 cubic foot bottles at either side and having a single ninety cubic foot bottle mounted on their backs in such a way that they could easily remove it. This was the one they were going to dump on the way in. They also decided to do the dives one at a time, with Oliver going in first then, after his return, Geoff, followed by Jochen.

For Oliver it was the chance to make the vital link, but he didn't find the reel Geoff had left at his far point from the Kingsdale end. He had run out about sixty-one metres, so he should have met up with it; indeed, by their calculation, he should be well beyond it.

Puzzled, Geoff went in, following the route that had now become familiar, sliding carefully through the constriction and reaching the end of the line that Oliver had left. The moment is recorded by Geoff in Martyn Farr's cave diving history, *The Darkness Beckons*:

'Nevertheless, as I came to the end of the line and started to press on into the unknown, I became tensely alert, head jerking from side to side like a night owl. Somehow I found that environment distinctly more alien than, say, that of the Moon. The loneliness gnawed at my nerves as I strained to see the Kingsdale line which I knew must be close at hand. Suddenly an orange line came into view. At first I didn't fully accept its existence but then I realised that I must have been swimming alongside it for some distance... The connection had been made, yet somehow the triumph was tinged with a certain sadness that we hadn't been able to do it together.'

Oliver Statham had been so close, for Geoff's line from Kingsdale had been on the other side of the passage, a few feet away, obscured by the bad visibility.

The joining of Kingsdale and Keld Head was, undoubtedly, the climax to an exploration into the real unknown that is no longer possible on the surface of the earth. But it wasn't over, for a complete traverse still had to be made. Oliver Statham and Geoff Yeadon completed this on January 16th 1979. They had always worked as equals and never was this spirit more obvious than the moment when one of them had to take the lead on this record-breaking attempt. Unable to communicate, they both hung around just inside the entrance, neither wanting to go first. They made the through dive of 1830 metres in two and a half hours and came out together. It was a world record for a continuous through trip between two caves with no available air spaces to use as staging posts. It meant total commitment. There have been longer dives since abroad, but none in anything approaching such appalling conditions of cold, poor visibility and constricted passageways.

There is also an immensely sad postscript to the end of this five-year saga of exploration, for in September 1979 Oliver Statham committed suicide. The huge stress of cave diving, the compelling need to be involved, which brought him back from his lay-off after his narrow escape in Boreham Cave, or maybe that escalator created by fame with the constantly repeated questions, 'What are you going to do next?', possibly, for him, they were too much. One cannot really know. But it was the end of a remarkably complementary partnership which had been essential to solving the problems of Keld Head.

18

Conclusion

IS THERE A COMMON FACTOR BETWEEN the adventures and adventurers described in this book? In basic motivation, spirit, call it what you will, I think there is, even though the adventurers themselves vary enormously in personality and style. In the fifty or so years covered by this book there have been huge social and technological changes which have also affected the way we venture. Yet I believe the fundamentals remain the same.

If we examine the complex mosaic of adventure, patterns emerge; there are differences of proportion but a uniting theme. Every one of the ventures I have described represents a plunge into the unknown to try to satisfy mankind's insatiable curiosity about ourselves, our reactions to stress or danger, to finding the boundaries of our physical capability or that of a craft. In each venture there is some level of risk. Thor Heyerdahl or Vivian Fuchs were not interested in risk for its own sake, considering themselves scientists rather than adventurers, but they were undoubtedly prepared to accept a very high level of risk to achieve their objectives. The climber or cave diver, on the other hand, who is much more directly stimulated by risk, is not trying to do something dangerous dangerously. Rather they each seek out a situation of high risk and gain an intense stimulus, which can reach levels of euphoria, by being in complete command.

Tom Robbins, in his zany novel titled *Even Cowgirls Get the Blues*, defines this: 'The principal difference between an adventurer and a suicide is that the adventurer leaves himself a margin of escape (the narrower the margin, the greater the adventure). A margin whose width and breadth may be determined by unknown factors, but whose successful navigation is determined by the measure of the adventurer's nerve and wits. It is always exhilarating to live by one's nerves or towards the summit of one's wits.'

The margin of escape varies with the individual but arguably gets slimmer as successive generations stretch the limits and refine the techniques. In climbing, the ultimate is undoubtedly going solo, when your life is literally in your own hands and if you fall you are almost certainly going to die. Messner took this concept to the limit on the Diamir Face of Nanga Parbat and then on Everest. The same could be said of long solo ocean voyages or polar treks. Messner and David Lewis use very similar language in describing their need to push themselves to the limit to 'find' themselves,

ABOVE Paragliding high over the Zanskar region in the Indian Himalaya.

though the ingredients of this experience at sea and on a mountain are very different. Solitary sailors need greater reserves of self-sufficiency than mountaineers, the periods that they have to withstand loneliness being measured in hundreds of days. On Nanga Parbat or Everest Messner was alone for a few intense days. The moment-to-moment risk and physical stress were more continuous and unremitting than those of the solitary sailor, who matches them only in concentrated moments of crisis, such as the horror, known to practically every round-the-world yachtsman, of being knocked down in the Southern Ocean.

It is the media who batten on ghoulish statistics after each adventuring fatality. In purely statistical terms cave diving is probably the most dangerous of all adventure activities. But mountaineering, particularly at altitude, must run it close and certainly focuses press attention. One in three climbers who set out from the top camp for the summit of K2 die on the way up or down. Or to put it more personally, Voytek Kurtyka, who climbed the South Face of Changabang with MacIntyre and Porter and is one of the most successful mountaineers in the world, has commented in an

ABOVE Børge Ousland hauling his sledge, which weighed 178 kilograms, across Antarctica.

interview that eighty per cent of the best Polish Himalayan climbers are now dead. Even the survivors, people like myself, Doug Scott, or Kurtyka himself, cannot claim to be alive because we have more cunning, know when to turn back, or are more cautious, for we have all had our narrow escapes when only luck has saved us. Why do we do it if it is so dangerous? The stimulus of risk is undoubtedly a strong lure, combined perhaps with the demonstrably foolish belief that it is never going to happen to me. This stimulus of risk creates a sense of heightened awareness. Doug Scott felt this on the Salathé Wall of El Capitan. He and his climbing partner, Peter Habeler, had already spent one night on the wall; hands were chafed and sore; they were fully committed, for retreat would have been difficult, but Doug was also totally attuned to his surroundings:

'On Broad Ledge a frog leapt on the scene. My surprise changed to wonder as I contemplated that little frog and its place on the vast monolith of El Cap. How many more were there, I wondered. Perhaps enough to fill a ten foot square box. Then he hopped away into the rock, so perfectly camouflaged that I couldn't spot him again. I felt really good up there because of that frog; he seemed to show that we were all in it together – not just the El Cap scene, but the whole business of being alive.

'I looked around with a new intensity and watched a drop of water trickle down the dusty granite, a clear crystal that flashed a brilliant light and was gone, to be burnt up by the sun that had momentarily given it life. I traced his wet path upwards to a crevice and considered its route down through the rock from the melting snow hundreds of feet above.

'I felt completely relaxed.'

It is this sense of heightened awareness and perception of beauty, of being alive, of physical accomplishment, that raises adventure, despite its inevitable periods of grinding effort and agonising discomfort, from being an exercise in masochism to a much broader, richer experience.

The self-imposed hair shirt is present to a greater or lesser degree in every adventure. What would be memorable about the achievement without it? The struggle seems particularly unremitting in polar travel. Wally Herbert's Arctic crossing is still the longest-ever polar journey, but subsequent travellers have refined the challenge. Naomi Uemura from Tokyo was the first to travel alone to the North Pole, but he used dogs and had a supply drop. The first man to reach the Pole unaided, hauling his own sledge, was the Norwegian, Borge Ousland in 1994. Two years later he went on to be the first to cross Antarctica alone and unaided, pulling a sledge weighing 178 kilos and, using a para sail when the wind was in his favour, he covered a distance of to 2845 kilometres in sixty-four days. Polar travel has come a long way since Fuchs' epic crossing in 1957-58.

New materials and improved communication have enabled the modern adventurer to stretch the limits even farther and increase the safety factor. GPS (Global Positioning System) technology gives the sailor or polar traveller an instant fix on their position; satellite 'phones and lightweight radios can aid rescue, as when Ranulph Fiennes was in severe pain from kidney stones on his solo bid to cross Antarctica, or when Messner and his brother nearly drowned in their effort to make a North Pole crossing.

New technology has also created new forms of adventure. The development of the paraglider enabled Jean Marc Boivin to fly from the summit of Everest, while others have undertaken increasingly long flights and journeys. British flyer Bob Drury is exploring the Himalaya by walking to high launch points, then paragliding over peaks and passes as far as he can, attuned to the vagaries of up-draught and wind, until forced to land, then walking on to the next spot from where he can take off once again. He describes its magic:

'I can't believe where I am. The stark clarity of this incredible landscape contrasting against the cold deep blue of the unpolluted high altitude sky leaves me feeling like I should be seeing it all from the safety of a Boeing 747. I've always known that one day I'd get to Zanskar, but never dreamt I might see it while sitting comfortably in a little chair at 6500 metres, suspended under a nylon bag, supported by millimetre thick strings.

'I love the feeling of freedom you get from free flying, you are totally exposed to your environment and the elements on a paraglider. You feel the temperature fall and your heartbeat increase as you rise ever higher and the violent buffeting of the thermals tells you that you're no passenger up here – you, and only you, can keep yourself alive.'

A less attractive, but equally undeniable, element involved in adventuring is the ego factor or, to put a slightly more acceptable face on it, the competitive element. In looking primarily at the innovators in adventure I have found myself concentrating on the record setters in whom this urge to be first plays a strong motivational part. It is a rare adventurer who does not have any of this element in his or her make up. Moitessier belatedly discovered he didn't have it when he was in the position to win the Golden Globe Race and collect the prize and the plaudits, but

BELOW Bill Tilman put an ad in The Times 'Hands wanted for long voyage in small boat; no pay, no prospects, not much pleasure.'

instead he chose to sail on half way round the world again and drop out in Tahiti. Donald Crowhurst had such a desperate urge to succeed he became the victim of his own ego and the publicity machine he had created. Eric Shipton lacked the single-minded ambition to reach the top of Everest but found profound satisfaction in exploring the Patagonian Ice Cap. Exploration was the end in itself. It did not have to prove something or provide an entry for the record books.

Shipton's climbing companion of pre-war years, Bill Tilman, shared the same non-competitive philosophy. Tilman had established himself as one of the world's outstanding high-altitude mountaineers in 1936 when he climbed Nanda Devi (7816 metres), at that time the highest and by far the most technically difficult peak yet climbed in the Himalaya. But he, like Shipton, believed there were more interesting things to do than attaining summits. After the war he turned to adventurous sailing voyages in the Southern and Arctic Oceans. His attitude was summed up by the advertisement he placed in the personal column of *The Times*:

'Hands wanted for long voyage in small boat; no pay, no prospects, not much pleasure.'

Setting aside this extreme viewpoint, the lure of adventure is easy to understand, since I suspect that most of us are attracted by it. With some it gets no further than day-dreaming fantasies or the vicarious excitement of following others in print or on television. For many it is the modest thrill of climbing a local hill on a misty day, not sure of where you are, perhaps a little apprehensive, and then finding the summit, or sailing in coastal waters, or taking a hot air balloon up on a summer's afternoon. Today we can indulge in the more instant thrills of white water rafting, bungee jumping, free fall parachuting or gorge scrambling. Whereas twenty years ago the average walker, sailor or weekend climber was content with what was on their own doorstep, the world has shrunk to such a degree that with better communications, cheap flights and more disposable income, what was once unattainable wilderness now can be reached by package tours, be they to the Poles, the Himalaya or the wilds of Patagonia.

You no longer need to serve an apprenticeship before thinking of walking to the South Pole, sailing round the world or reaching the summit of Everest. A specialist outfit will take you there. While purists decry this development, I see it as an inevitable step in the evolution of adventure and I cannot begrudge the individual who has a dream which is allowed to come true. For the one thing I am certain of is that people in ever-increasing numbers will continue to seek adventure as a foil to a life that is becoming more pressured and dominated by technology, taking us farther and farther from the natural environment.

At the same time there is a danger that the increase in numbers and the commercialisation of adventure could damage the very places in which we seek our release. In this respect we need to find a balance and show some restraint for the sake of future generations. The great superlative challenges, the first ascent of Everest, the first circumnavigation of the world by balloon, the first solo crossing of the Poles may all have been achieved, but there are still unclimbed mountains, unsailed seas and breezes to carry us on our own personal quests for adventure.

Glossary

abeam: at right-angles to the length of a vessel.
abseil: method of descending a rock face by sliding down a rope.
aid climbing: pulling on or standing in slings attached to pitons (q.v.), bolts or hand-inserted wedges or cams.
arête: a sharp rock or snow ridge.

belay: a method of safeguarding a climbing partner from falling by paying out or taking in the rope and anchoring oneself.
bergschrund: the gap or crevasse between the glacier proper and the upper snows of a face (q.v.).
bilge keel: baby keels or projections on the outside of the hull running parallel to the central keel, which enable the boat to sit upright in shallow water.
bivouac: to spend a night in the open on a mountain.
boom: metal or wooden pole extending horizontally from the mast along the bottom of the mainsail.
bouldering: climbing unroped on boulders or very small outcrops.
broach: when the wind blows the boat right over on one side, so much so that the rudder comes out of the water and the boat is uncontrollable.

chimney: a fissure in the rock or ice wide enough to climb up inside.
close hauled: when a boat's sails are pulled in as tight as possible so that the wind strikes them at an acute angle.
col: pass or dip in a ridge, usually between two peaks.
cornice: an overhanging mass of snow projecting over the edge of a ridge, formed by prevailing winds.
couloir: an open gully.
crack line: a crack or series of interlinked cracks in the rock that form a natural line up a rock face (q.v.).
crampons: steel spiked frames which can be fitted to boots to give a grip on ice and firm snow slopes.
crevassse: a crack in a glacier surface, which can be both wide and very deep, made by the movement of the glacier over the irregular shapes in its bed, or by bends in its course.
cwm: a deep, rounded hollow at the head or side of a valley, formed by glacial action.

drogue: improvised contraption pulled along behind a boat to slow it down in heavy weather.

expansion bolt: a bolt driven into a hole drilled in the rock which expands through internal pressure to create a friction grip.

face: a steep aspect of a mountain between two ridges.
fixed ropes: on prolonged climbs up steep ground the lead climber, having run out the full length of rope, ties it to an appropriate anchor. Subsequently all climbers move independently up and down the fixed rope, clipped on to it, using it either as a safety line or, on very steep ground, for direct progress. The rope is left in place for the duration of the climb.
foredeck: area of deck in front of the mast.
free climbing: climbing rock using only natural holds and not pulling on any of the running belays (q.v.).
friend: a camming device placed in a crack used as a running belay or belay (q.v.).
front pointing: climbing straight up steep snow or ice by means of kicking in the front points of crampons (q.v.) and supporting balance with an ice axe or, on steep ground, using the picks of an ice axe and ice hammer in either hand.

gendarme: a rock pinnacle obtruding from a ridge, often surrounded by snow.
genoa sail: large triangular sail in front of mast which is so big that it overlaps the mainsail to some extent and gives the boat greater speed.
GPS: global positioning system – an electronic device that picks up the signal from three or four satellites to give an exact position on the surface of the earth or in the air.

gunwale: (pronounced gunnel) strip of wood or plastic running all the way round the outside of the boat at deck level to protect it from damage by other boats.
gybe: when the mainsail boom crosses from one side of the boat to the other as the wind changes.

halyards: ropes used to raise or lower sails.

jib boom: wooden or metal pole extending out from the front end of a boat to the outer end of which is attached the forward end of the jib sail (q.v.).
jib sail: triangular sail set forward of the mast.
jumar clamps: devices which lock on a fixed rope (q.v.) to support a climber's weight when subject to downward force, but which can be slid up the rope as a method of climbing it.
junk rig: boat with a four-sided sail which is stiffened with horizontal battens and pulled up a single mast like that of a Chinese boat.
jury mast: any temporary mast employed as a replacement after dismasting.

la: pass.
laybacking: the method of climbing a corner by placing the feet on one wall of the corner and using the corner crack for the hands to create an opposing force. Hands and feet are moved alternately upwards.
lead: area of open water between ice floes.
luffing: bringing the boat up into the wind so that the sails flutter and the boat moves more slowly.

moraine: accumulation of stones and debris carried down by a glacier.

off-width crack: a crack that is too wide for hand jamming but too narrow to insert one's body (when it becomes a chimney, q.v.). Climbing these can be very strenuous.

pack ice: large area of floating ice in the polar sea.
pitch: section of climbing between two stances or belay points (q.v.).
pitchpole: when a huge wave comes up behind causing the boat to turn a complete somersault.
piton: a metal peg hammered into a rock crack to support a belay (q.v.).
portage: carrying a boat round an unnavigable stretch or land obstacle to the next navigable reach of water.
pressure ridge: a wall thrown up by the pressure of ice floes grinding against each other.
prusiking: climbing a rope using slings made from two thinner lengths of rope attached to the rope by a prusik knot that tightens and holds the body weight. The knots are pushed up the rope alternately. Purpose-made mechanical devices are also available.

reach: point of sail when wind is at right angles to the sail.
reef: reducing the area of sail exposed to the wind in heavy weather by rolling or tying canvas up round the boom.
rotor: a descending whirlwind caused by air that has flowed over the crest of a mountain peak.

sea anchor: throwing out any old thing on the end of a line in such a way that it will hold the boat's nose into the waves in order to ride out a storm more easily.
self-steering: a wind vane device fitted to the rear of a boat which keeps it facing into the wind on a predetermined heading while the yachtsman works or sleeps.
sérac: pinnacle or tower of ice, which is invariably unstable and dangerous.
sheets: ropes for controlling the trim of the sails.
shroud plate: metal plate on the sides of a boat's hull to which are attached the stainless steel wires giving lateral support to the mast.
sirdar: head Sherpa on an expedition.
standing wave: stationary wave in a river, caused by an underwater obstruction such as a boulder.
stays: stainless steel wire supports for the mast running fore and aft, to the front and back of the boat.
staysail: small triangular sail attached to the front stay.
stopper wave: a stationary wave which is breaking.
storm jib: smallest sail a boat possesses used in front of the mast in very heavy weather to provide basic stability.
sump: a cave passage completely filled with water, leaving no air space, also called a syphon.

traverse: to move horizontally or diagonally across a rock or snow slope. Also the ascent or descent of a mountain by different routes.

yards: horizontal spars two-thirds of the way up the mast which support the rigging.

Select Bibliography

The author and publisher are grateful for permission to quote from the following books:

OCEANS

Thor Heyerdahl, *The Kon-Tiki Expedition*, Allen & Unwin, 1950.
Fatu-Hiva, Allen & Unwin, 1974.
Aku Aku, the Secret of Easter Island, Allen & Unwin, 1958.
American Indians in the Pacific, Allen & Unwin, 1952.
(with E. N. Ferdon) *Report of the Norwegian Archaeological Expedition to Easter Island and the East Pacific*, Allen & Unwin, 1962.
The Ra Expeditions, Allen & Unwin, 1971.

Arnold Jacoby, *Señor Kon-Tiki*, Allen & Unwin, 1968.

Francis Chichester, *Alone Across the Atlantic*, Allen & Unwin, 1961.
The Lonely Sea and the Sky, Hodder & Stoughton, 1964.
Gipsy Moth Circles the World, Hodder & Stoughton, 1967.

Robin Knox-Johnston, *A World of my Own*, Cassell, 1969.

Nicholas Tomalin and Ron Hall, *The Strange Voyage of Donald Crowhurst*, Hodder & Stoughton, 1970.

Nigel Tetley, *Trimaran Solo*, Nautical Publishing Co., 1970.

Chay and Maureen Blyth, *Innocent Aboard*, Nautical Publishing Co., 1970.

Bernard Moitessier, *The Long Way*, Adlard Coles, 1974.

David Lewis, *Ice Bird*, Collins, 1975.

DESERTS

Wilfred Thesiger, *Arabian Sands*, Longman, 1959; Collins, 1980.
Desert, Marsh and Mountain, Collins, 1980.

RIVERS

Richard Snailham, *Blue Nile Revealed*, Chatto & Windus, 1970.

Chris Bonington, *Next Horizon*, Gollancz, 1973.

John Blashford-Snell, *Where the Trails Run Out*, Hutchinson, 1974.

Mike Jones, Blue Nile expedition report, 1972.

MOUNTAINS

Maurice Herzog, *Annapurna*, Cape, 1952.

Lionel Terray, *Conquistadors of the Useless*, Gollancz, 1963.

Eric Shipton, *That Untravelled World*, Hodder & Stoughton, 1969.

John Hunt, *The Ascent of Everest*, Hodder & Stoughton, 1953.
Life is Meeting, Hodder & Stoughton, 1978.

Edmund Hillary, *High Adventure*, Hodder & Stoughton, 1955.
Nothing Venture, Nothing Win, Hodder & Stoughton, 1975.

Wilfrid Noyce, *South Col*, Heinemann, 1954.

George Lowe, *Because It Is There*, Cassell, 1959.

Michael Ward, *In This Short Span*, Gollancz, 1972.

Tenzing Norkay (as told to James Ramsay Ullman), *Man of Everest*, Harrap, 1955.

Walt Unsworth, *Everest*, Allen Lane, 1981. Revised edition, The Mountaineers/ Bâton-Wicks, 2000.

Chris Bonington, *Annapurna, South Face*, Cassell, 1971.

Don Whillans, 'Annapurna, South Face', *Mountain*, issue 12, 1970.

Reinhold Messner, *The Big Walls*, Kaye and Ward, 1978.
The Seventh Grade, Kaye and Ward, 1974.
The Challenge, Kaye and Ward, 1977.
Everest: expedition to the ultimate, Kaye and Ward, 1979.

Solo Nanga Parbat, Kaye and Ward, 1980.

Felix Kuen, 'Der Sieg und die Tragödie' (Triumph and Tragedy), *Der Bergsteiger*, November 1970.

Chris Jones, *Climbing in North America*, University of California Press, 1976.

Steve Roper, *Camp 4: Recollections of a Yosemite Rock Climber*, The Mountaineers, 1994.

Warren 'Batso' Harding, *Downward Bound & A Mad Guide to Rock Climbing*, Prentice Hall, 1975.

'El Capitan', *The American Alpine Journal*, volume XI No. 2, 1959.

Nicholas O'Connell, *Beyond Risk, Conversations with Climbers*, The Mountaineers, 1993.

Pete Kakeda, 'The Milestone', *Climbing*, No. 190, December 1999.

Lynn Hill, 'El Capitan Climbed Free', *The American Alpine Journal*, volume 36, issue 68, 1994.

'First Free Ascent of the Nose', *The American Alpine Journal*, volume 37, issue 69, 1995.

Peter Boardman, *The Shining Mountain*, Hodder & Stoughton, 1978.

Joe Tasker, *Savage Arena*, Methuen, 1982.

Alan Hankinson and expedition members, *Changabang*, Heinemann Educational, 1975.

Andy Fanshawe and Stephen Venables, *Himalaya Alpine Style*, Hodder & Stoughton, 1995.

Mick Fowler, *Vertical Pleasure*, Hodder & Stoughton, 1995.

Mick Fowler, 'A Touch too Much', *The American Alpine Journal*, volume 40, issue 72, 1998.

Andy Cave, 'Changabang: A World Apart', *The Alpine Journal*, volume 103, 1998.

Julie-Ann Clyma, 'Mountain of Dreams, Mountain of Sorrows', *The Alpine Journal*, volume 103, 1998.

Andy Cave, 'Changabang, Storm and Sorrow', *Climber*, September 1997.

THE POLES

Vivian Fuchs and Edmund Hillary, *The Crossing of Antarctica*, Cassell, 1958.

Edmund Hillary, *No Latitude for Error*, Hodder & Stoughton, 1961.

Nothing Venture, Nothing Win, Hodder & Stoughton, 1975.

George Lowe, *Because It Is There*, Cassell, 1959.

Noel Barber, *The White Desert*, Hodder & Stoughton, 1958.

Wally Herbert, *Across the Top of the World*, G. P. Putnam, New York, 1974. (The American edition was expanded from a shorter account published under the same title by Longman, 1969).

AIR

Charles McCarry, *Double Eagle*, W. H. Allen, 1980.

Leo Dickinson, *Ballooning over Everest*, Jonathan Cape, 1993.

Bertrand Piccard and Brian Jones, *The Greatest Adventure*, Headline, 1999.

Bertrand Piccard, *Une Trace dans le Ciel*, Editions Oresol, 1999.

Richard Branson, *Losing my Virginity*, Virgin, 1998.

Brian Milton, *Dalgety Flyer*, Bloomsbury, 1990.

Global Flyer, Mainstream Publishing Company, 1998.

Colin Prescot, *To the Edge of Space*, Boxtree/Macmillan.

BENEATH THE EARTH

Martyn Farr, *The Darkness Beckons: the history and development of cave diving*, Diadem, 1981, Revised edition, Bâton-Wicks, 2000

'*Caving International* interview Geoff Yeadon on cave diving', *Caving International* Magazine, No.5, October 1979.

CONCLUSION

Tom Robbins, *Even Cowgirls Get the Blues*, Bantam, 1991

Doug Scott, 'On the Profundity Trail', *Mountain*, issue 15, May 1971.

J. R. L. Anderson, *The Ulysses Factor*, Hodder & Stoughton, 1970.

Ingrid Cranfield, *The Challengers*, Weidenfeld & Nicolson, 1976.

Wilfrid Noyce, *Springs of Adventure*, John Murray, 1958.

Bob Drury, 'Hamari Kahani', *Cross Country*, edition 62, April/May 1999.

Picture Credits

The author and publisher are grateful to the following who supplied photographs on the pages listed.

Allsport: 301
AP Wide World Photos: 307
Arlene Blum: 132
Chris Bonington Picture Library: 5 (upper), 108, 110, 112, 113, 115, 116, 141 (photo: Keiichi Yamada), 165, 168, 169, 170, 172, 173, 175, 176, 177, 191, 216
Peter Brinkeby: 337
Andy Cave: 218, 225, 226, 229
Julie-Ann Clyma/Roger Payne: 215, 231
Leo Dickinson: 188, 287 (Leo Dickinson and Quantel)
Colin Edwards/Picture Partnership: 315
David Hamilton: 189
Warren Harding collection: 202 (photo: Rich Calderwood), 204, 205
Sir Wally Herbert: 254, 259, 261, 262, 263, 265, 271, 273, 275, 276
© Marcel Ichac/OMI: 128, 129 (both), 138
Mr and Mrs R. L. Jones: 120
Kelvin Kent: 178
The Kon-Tiki Museum, Oslo, Norway: 13, 15, 20, 25
Jean-Claude Lachenal: 136 (photo: Louis Lachenal)
© Dr David Lewis c/o Curtis Brown (Aust) Pty Ltd. Sydney: 81, 84, 88, 89 (Photo: Patrick D. Smith), 92
John McDonald: 209, 211
Reinhold Messner: 195, 196
Brian Milton: 311, 317, 318, 321 (photo: Margie Lindsay)
National Geographic: 1, 246, 251, 279, 291, 304
Gavin Newman: 5 (lower), 325, 326, 329, 331
Børge Ousland: 338
Françoise Pons-Rébuffat: 133 (photo: Gaston Rébuffat)
PPL (Photo Agency) Ltd: 4 (lower), 29, 33, 36, 37, 40, 41, 52
Galen Rowell, Mountain Light Photography: 199, 207
Royal Geographical Society: 142, 143, 147, 149, 151, 154, 155, 158, 159, 161, 162, 233, 237, 245, 419
Doug Scott: 181,
Sir Norman Statham: 330, 332
Steve Sustad: 223, 228
© Sir Wilfred Thesiger. Permission granted by Curtis Brown Group Ltd: 3, 4 (upper), 96, 97, 98, 101, 104.
© The Times: 44 (all), 56, 61, 64, 72, 77, 78
Virgin: 296, 298
Ken Wilson: 182, 183
Yorkshire TV: 323, 324

Index

Author's Note

In bringing Quest for Adventure up to date for the new Millennium, I am indebted to many for their help. First I want to thank my fellow adventurers who have given up their time in talking to me, responding to my questions and affording me a glimpse into their respective worlds.

Maggie Body, editor of practically all my books, including the original *Quest for Adventure*, and Louise Wilson, my secretary all these years, have once again combined superbly to keep me on the editorial track.

On the picture front, Frances Daltrey, who runs my picture library, has proved to be a brilliant picture researcher, locating original pictures and finding new ones. She has been ably aided by her son William and by Margaret Trinder who also helps me in the office. Audrey Salkeld has once again given generously of her wide knowledge of the adventure field and Ken Wilson, old friend and former editor has come up with many useful suggestions.

Susan Haynes, my managing editor has kept us on course and Nigel Soper has done a handsome job in designing the book.

My special thanks and appreciation, as always, goes to my wife Wendy, for her loving support and encouragement.

CB

This edition first published in the United Kingdom in 2000 by Cassell & Co

Some of the text reproduced in this book first appeared in a book of the same title published in 1981.

A CIP catalogue record for this book is available from the British Library
The picture acknowledgements on p. 346 constitute an extension to this copyright page

ISBN 1841881570

Design Director: David Rowley
Editorial Director: Susan Haynes
Designed by Nigel Soper
Edited by Margaret Body and Jinny Johnson
Maps by ML Design
Picture research by Frances Daltrey
Typeset in Spectrum
Printed and bound in Italy

Weidenfeld & Nicolson
Wellington House
125 Strand
London
WC2R 0BB